Faith, Resistance, and the Future

Faith, Resistance, and the Future

Daniel Berrigan's Challenge to Catholic Social Thought

Edited by

James L. Marsh and Anna J. Brown

FORDHAM UNIVERSITY PRESS

New York 2012

Library of Congress Cataloging-in-Publication Data

Faith, resistance, and the future : Daniel Berrigan's
challenge to Catholic social thought / edited by
James L. Marsh and Anna J. Brown. — 1st ed.
p. cm.
Proceedings of a conference held in the fall of 2005
at the University of Notre Dame.
Includes bibliographical references (p.) and index.
ISBN 978-0-8232-3982-5 (cloth : alk. paper)
1. Berrigan, Daniel—Congresses. 2. Christian sociology—
Catholic Church—Congresses. I. Marsh, James L. II.
Brown, Anna J.
BX1753.F255 2012
261.8—dc23   2011037018

Printed in the United States of America
14 13 12   5 4 3 2 1
First edition

To Daniel Berrigan, SJ,
whose writing, life, friendship, and enlightening,
courageous, and persevering witness over the decades
have inspired this work

CONTENTS

vii

ACKNOWLEDGMENTS

We would like to express our appreciation to Rosemary O'Connell for her help in preparing this manuscript for publication. We are grateful to Anna Brown's husband, David I. Orenstein, for his patient guidance and unfailing computer assistance during the copy-editing phase of this book. Finally, we thank Eric Newman and Helen Tartar for their enthusiasm and competence in helping us bring this project to fruition.

FAITH, RESISTANCE, AND THE FUTURE

Introduction

James L. Marsh and Anna J. Brown

This book has its origins in a conference at the University of Notre Dame in the fall of 2005, under the auspices of the American Catholic Philosophical Association. The conference theme, selected by James Marsh, the president of the association for that year, was "Social Justice: Its Theory and Practice." To begin the conference, a special panel session was organized on the influence of Daniel Berrigan, SJ, on Catholic social thought. All of the papers of the panelists are included in this book as well as Marsh's presidential address. To preserve the flavor and excitement of the panel, the editors have preserved most of the essays in their initially shorter form.

Two kinds of questions arose in the panel discussion: What kind of challenge, insight, inspiration, and critique does Daniel Berrigan's life and work offer to Catholic social thought and practice, inside and outside the university? And what can serious academic discussion and critique bring to his thought, that is, how does it test, deepen, and enrich his thought? Almost all of the contributors to this volume have some association with universities in the United States, and slightly fewer with Catholic universities.

To the knowledge of the editors, the discussion in this book is the first of its kind to occur. Berrigan's work has been influential and has been responded to in many extra-academic contexts in the country and the world. But conspicuous in its absence has been any serious academic, scholarly discussion of his work. The editors consider such a discussion long overdue.

We have recruited thinkers and scholars who were already familiar with and known to be interested in Berrigan's work, and those who were less familiar with his thought. The result has been a rich sympathetic and critical treatment of the meaning and impact of his work. What kind of challenge does he present to academic business-as-usual in Catholic universities? How can the work of the individual Catholic academic be transformed if such a person took Berrigan's work seriously, in theory and practice? Do Catholic universities need Berrigan's vision to fulfill more integrally and completely their own mission?

We discerned, therefore, at least two fruitful inside–outside relationships in the book: that between Catholic academe and Berrigan's life and thought, and that between those who are already familiar with Berrigan's work and consciously influenced by it, and those who, up to this point, have not been. Also the book inscribes an arc between the relatively immediate dialogic context of the panel discussion through a series of longer papers, recruited for the book, to the final conversation between Berrigan, Brown, and Marsh.

Berrigan's Life

Dear Friends
I choose to be a jailbird (one species is flourishing)
in a kingdom of fowlers . . .[1]

Daniel Berrigan was born on May 9, 1921, in Virginia, Minnesota, to Frieda Fromhart Berrigan and Thomas Berrigan. He was the fifth of six sons. Of his early years in Minnesota, and later in Syracuse, New York. Berrigan writes: "We were Depression babies, all of us . . . [yet] I remember vividly that we housed and fed a continuing number of homeless men during those dark years of loss."[2] Instilled in Berrigan was the understanding that justice was intrinsic to faith. He reflects, nearly sixty years later, upon what he learned early on in his life:

Despite all, many good people do not give up. Many have a sense, drawn from religious tradition, that they are summoned to a faith that does justice. Together with others drawing on other traditions, they long to create a social fabric woven to the benefit of all, a society marked by compassion and altruism, with special attention paid to the powerless and disenfranchised.[3]

In 1939 Berrigan entered the Jesuits, the Society of Jesus. In a recent interview, he recalls that upon receiving the informational brochures of religious congregations and orders, some sent "nice brochures that showed tennis courts and swimming pools, but the Jesuits sent an unattractive leaflet, no pictures and no come-on language, just a brief description of the training called 'The Making of a Jesuit.'"[4] He studied at the Jesuit seminary, St. Andrew-on-Hudson, in Poughkeepsie, New York, where he received his BA degree in 1946. Prior to his graduation from St. Andrew's, *America*, the Jesuit journal of Catholic thought, accepted his poem, "Storm Song," for publication. In 1947 Berrigan began corresponding with Thomas Merton, thus beginning a friendship that was to last until Merton's death twenty-one years later.

Berrigan's forte was teaching, as he discovered from 1946–49 with the "rough and tough youth"[5] at Saint Peter's Prep in Jersey City, New Jersey. His own education in theology and philosophy continued both at Weston College in Weston, Massachusetts, and Woodstock College, near Baltimore, Maryland. Berrigan was ordained a priest in June 1952. Following the completion of his MA degree at Woodstock in 1953, he went to Europe for further study and lived with a community of French worker priests in Lyons. Thinking back upon his life in Lyons, Berrigan writes: "It was an invitation to become a human being by way of others. . . ."[6] After two months as an auxiliary chaplain at a US army base in West Germany, he returned to the United States and taught philosophy and French from 1954–57 at Brooklyn Preparatory School in Brooklyn, New York.

During his time at Brooklyn Prep, Berrigan accompanied his young charges to Maryhouse, one of New York City's Catholic Worker houses, where they would serve soup to the homeless and join in the Friday night "clarification of thought" meetings. It was there that he met the Worker's cofounders, Dorothy Day and Peter Maurin. Day opened his eyes and heart like few others had. Her gift, aside from accompanying and serving impoverished people, was to make "visible" those who tend to be ignored and to look at war as a primary reason for the impoverishment of so many people. Berrigan points to what moved him so deeply in his essay, "The Long Loneliness of Dorothy Day":

Why, in a sane world, she asked, would a wounded human being lie in a ditch unattended? She began to speak, literally to re-member that body.

The crime, the neglect, were universal, she cried. All over the world, on an "average day," the unemployed and unemployable, the victimized and vacuous, the homeless and feckless, the alcoholics and druggies, the flaky and furious—in great numbers these were struck down, and fell into ditches.

And the world went its amnesiac blank-eyed way, the way named, on the largest signpost of all, lettered in blood—war.

Before the pope spoke up, long before the bishops and priests, Dorothy cried into the contrary wings: *"No more war, war never again! No just wars, no such thing!"*[7]

In 1957 he was awarded the prestigious Lamont Poetry Prize as well as the American Academy of Poetry's James Laughlin Award for his first volume of poems, *Time Without Number*. From 1957 until 1962 he taught New Testament theology at Le Moyne College in Syracuse, New York. During his first year of teaching at Le Moyne, Berrigan wrote a letter to the local bishop in support of Karl Meyer's plan to start a Catholic Worker House in Syracuse. Meyer, a pacifist, had recently been released from jail for war tax resistance. The bishop, furious at Berrigan's efforts to undermine Catholic Just War teachings, "a cornerstone of the Catholic edifice"[8] and for his implication that the Church was not adequately serving the poor, called for Berrigan to be fired from his teaching post. With six Le Moyne Jesuits coming to his defense, Berrigan retained his job. Though he survived his first year of teaching at university, his experience at Le Moyne indicated how Berrigan was to fare in future academic settings: wherever he taught, he spoke out against war, spoke up for the poor, and suffered the disapprobation of the academy—and the Church—for so doing.

From 1963 until 1964 Berrigan traveled throughout Eastern Europe and Africa. There he discovered peace and Christian communities devoting themselves to living the question: "How can we survive as human beings in a world more and more officially given over to violence and death?"[9] Upon his return to the United States, he marched in the Civil Rights Movement in Selma, Alabama, served as an assistant editor of the *Jesuit Missions* magazine, and attended a peacemakers retreat hosted by Merton at the Abbey of Gethsemani in Kentucky. He also tried to answer the question posed by the Eastern European and African Christian communities by saying, as loudly as he could, "no" to war.[10] He incarnated this "no" through an escalation of activism and by cofounding the Catholic Peace Fellowship (1964) and the Clergy and Laity Concerned about

Vietnam (1965).[11] Along with hundreds of students, he was arrested for the first time for an act of civil disobedience at the Pentagon in October 1967.

Berrigan saw the Vatican II era of the 1960s as a new time for both the Catholic Church and his Jesuit order, a time that promised that life beyond the bomb and without war was worthy of being sought and lived. Many in the Church, however, did not agree. One of them, Francis Cardinal Spellman, the archbishop of New York City, ordered Berrigan south of the border for an indefinite period of exile. Spellman's order, publicly announced as a trip that was necessary for Berrigan's work at *Jesuit Missions*, came after Berrigan spoke at a Catholic Worker liturgy for Roger LaPorte, a young man who had immolated himself outside of the United Nations to protest massive suffering inflicted by the Vietnam war. Berrigan, who had been ordered by the Church not to speak on behalf of one who had "committed suicide," opted instead for conscience and compassion, not compliance in this matter. Thus, in November 1965, he took up with the poor in Mexico and in Central and South America.

During an exile of five months he was radicalized even further, particularly when he saw how the misery of the poor was compounded by the massive diversion of monies for war spending. He speaks, for example, of what he witnessed in Brazil, though the same could be said for any of the countries in the Americas that he visited:

> I arrived in Rio [de Janeiro] in January of 1966 in the midst of devastating floods. In the space of a night the rains came down with torrential force, whole towns collapsed, people and shacks fell into a stew of death. I remember the next morning slogging through the mud in the company of a slum dweller who was also a community organizer. He looked at me and said: "My friend, millions for war in Vietnam and this for us."[12]

It was his January 1968 trip to Hanoi, with historian Howard Zinn, that most seared his consciousness and conscience. Upon the invitation of the peace committee in Vietnam, North American peace activists were invited to meet three captured American pilots and accompany them back to the United States. Berrigan, who was teaching at Cornell University at the time, accepted the invitation. In his *Night Flight to Hanoi: War Diary with 11 Poems*, he documents the utter devastation of the land and its people. Being both poetically minded and acutely observant of the concrete facts of life, he dwells on the particulars of daily life in a war-torn country, such as the children he saw when he sought shelter from an air raid in a bunker: "I saw there . . . three beautiful children, like a frieze against the wall in the half darkness, come to life, the children eating in supreme calm their dishes of rice, the oldest girl feeding the smallest child, her brother."[13] He also heard the insights of Dorothy Day and Dr. Martin Luther King Jr. echoed in the comments of the Premier of North Vietnam: "The longer the war continues the worse your domestic problems become. So the question of war is posed with such insistence that you must solve it."[14]

On his return from Hanoi, Berrigan set out to "pose the question of war" to the American people, though in a way that he had not yet dared to imagine. He had come to the realization, as he wrote in *Night Flight to Hanoi*, that whatever the Christian response would be, it would have to be one of nonviolence (and here he is glad to pay tribute to Gandhi) and that such a response would most likely not be welcomed from many quarters of society, the Left included. "To be radical," noted Berrigan, "is *habitually* to do things which society at large despises."[15] His brother Philip, at the time a priest working with impoverished African-Americans in Baltimore and an antiwar resister who had already done time in jail for his political actions, would visit Berrigan, now back at Cornell, and suggest a radically nonviolent way of posing the war question: would Dan be willing to join a few others in the burning of hundreds of draft files in Catonsville, Maryland? Berrigan was willing and on May 17, 1968, cemented a "habitual" pattern of breaking the law and landing underground, in the American jail system.

There are perhaps no better phrases in the Berrigan lexicon that express why he did what he did—and continued to do thereafter—than those contained in the meditation he read prior to his sentencing for the burning of the draft files:

> Our apologies   good friends
> for the fracture of good order   the burning of paper
> instead of children   the angering of the orderlies
> in the front parlor of the charnel house
> We could not   so help us God   do otherwise
> For we are sick at heart   our hearts
> give us no rest for thinking of the Land of Burning
>   Children
> and for thinking of that other Child of whom
> the poet Luke speaks . . .
> And so we stretch out our hands
> to our brothers throughout the world.

We who are priests to our fellow priests.
All of us who act against the law
turn to the poor of the world   to the Vietnamese
to the victims   to the soldiers who kill and die
for the wrong reasons for no reason at all
because they were so ordered by the authorities
of that public order which is in effect
a massive institutionalized disorder.
We say: killing is disorder
life and gentleness and community and unselfishness
is the only order we recognize.
For the sake of that order we risk our liberty   our good name.
The time is past when good men may be silent
when obedience can segregate men from public risk
when the poor can die without defense.
How many indeed must die before our voices are heard
how many must be tortured dislocated
starved maddened?[16]

Though he was released from Danbury federal prison after eighteen months in 1972, Berrigan refused to be "rehabilitated." Throughout the 1970s, he was often arrested outside of the "Blight [White] House" and the Pentagon for protesting US nuclear policies. Reflecting on one experience of jail with his beloved brother Philip during this period, he notes: "We're in deadlock: 24-hour lockup, two in a cell hardly enough for one, sharing space with mice, rats, flies and assorted uninvited fauna. Food shoved in the door, filth, degradation. And I wouldn't choose to be anywhere else on the planet. I think we've landed on turf where the breakthrough occurs. I think it's occurred already."[17] Along with others, he also established communities of resistance, such as Kairos in New York, as well as a larger network of these communities, namely the Atlantic Life Community, whose range includes the whole of the eastern seaboard.

On September 9, 1980, Berrigan, along with Philip and six others, symbolically disarmed the nosecone of a Mark 12A warhead at General Electric's Nuclear Re-entry division in King of Prussia, Pennsylvania. With this action, the Plowshares Movement was born. It was named after the prophet Isaiah's description of a "new" people, a people who will "beat their swords into plowshares and their spears into pruning hooks . . . [and] study war no more."[18] Since that first action, the movement has become worldwide. Its activists, who risk and often serve considerable time in prison, have engaged in over one hundred actions. In his poem,

"My Brother's Battered Bible, Carried into Prison Repeatedly," Berrigan
points to what has sustained him—and his companions in nonviolent resistance—for the past forty years: "That book, livid with thumb underscor-
ings, lashes—I see you carry it into the cave of storms, past the storms. I see
you underscore like the score of music all that travail that furious unex-
plained joy. . . ."[19]

Though his life of activism often fills the pages of books about him,
Berrigan must also be recognized as a major American writer and poet. His
books, *The Kings and Their Gods: The Pathology of Power* (2008) and *Exodus:
Let My People Go* (2008), are two of the most recently published of his over
fifty books, fifteen volumes of poetry as well as hundreds of essays and
articles. Two volumes of his poetry were National Book Award finalists:
Time Without Number (1958) and *False Gods, Real Men* (1970). In 1971, he
was awarded the Melcher Book Award for his *Trial Poems* and *No Bars to
Manhood*. For his play, *The Trial of the Catonsville Nine*, he was awarded the
Melcher as well as an Obie Drama Critics Award and the Los Angeles
Drama Critics Award. During that same year, *The Trial of the Catonsville
Nine* ran for twenty-nine performances on Broadway. In 1972 it won the
Tony award. In 1998 he received the Catholic Book Club's Campion Medal,
an award bestowed upon John Updike a year earlier. Both Cornell
University and DePaul University, among others, house Berrigan archives,
and currently hold a voluminous amount of his books, manuscripts, letters,
articles, retreat notes, talks, and recordings.

Despite a prodigious work ethic, Berrigan has never skimped on being
present to and with others. Any account of his life would have to note the
richness of his friendships with the likes of Merton, Corita Kent, Denise
Levertov, the sick, the destitute, the outcasts, his immediate Jesuit community, and countless others. He also spent numerous hours with the sick
in St. Rose's Cancer Home and the AID's ward of St. Vincent's Hospital,
among other places. He has taught hundreds of courses at US and foreign
universities, and even joined in a strike or two, as he did on behalf of the
maintenance workers at the University of Manitoba in Winnipeg, Canada.
(When he learned that the maintenance staff earned one-fifth of what the
faculty and administrators did, he promptly moved off campus and held his
classes in a downtown apartment the Franciscan priests had offered to
him.)[20] And there is also the daily work of a priest—the celebrating of
Mass, retreats, weddings, baptisms and funerals—faithfully performed for
the past fifty-seven years.

Today, he lives with his New York City Jesuit community, writes
and publishes books, gives talks when his health permits, stewards his

friendships, and continues to pray and act with the Kairos community. In closing, I think here of a few lines from his book, *Ten Commandments for the Long Haul*, which point to the inspiration for a life lived so authentically:

> I never prayed for a miracle. I let the child go. Not knowing what else to do. Not being in command of the universe, or of a single life, including my own . . . To pray for His intervention is to imply my own. I do not know any other way of regarding our impasse, or a possible breakthrough. This is why I am arrested again and again, and will never give up. This is why, as I write this, my friends and family are in jail, or in the courts, or are so arranging their lives as to increase such a likelihood. We believe that every office and charism granted to us over the years—priest, teacher, writer, friend of the dying, spouse, parent—all and each of these verified against our expectation of Christ in the world.[21]

About This Collection

Martin J. De Nys's essay, "Philosophy and the Prophetic Challenge," stresses the fruitful interplay between philosophy and prophecy, and the way in which Berrigan mediates the prophetic tradition to the contemporary scene in a unique and compelling way. Self-appropriation, which starts intellectually and is rooted in the desire to know, must complete itself in commitment, love, and the works of love. Christian philosophers work in a context in which they acknowledge the integrity and critical autonomy of intellectual inquiry, identify philosophical inquiry as a component of a more comprehensive project of self-transcendence and in service to the ends of love, and identify the bases of the works of love as a necessary interrelation between contemplation and engagement. For the Christian philosopher, then, it is important to call on the prophetic tradition as a resource in doing philosophical work, to critique systemic violence, to do philosophy of religion, and to do one's work in a university which may be overly identified with secular culture. She needs to ensure that she subordinates the goals of institutional approval and personal advancement in order to cultivate philosophical integrity.

For Robert Ludwig, Berrigan's major contribution to Catholic social teaching is also his recovery, rehabilitation, and renewal of the prophetic voice and of prophetic action. In his essay, "Daniel Berrigan's Theology: Retrieving the Prophetic and Proclaiming the Resurrection," Ludwig begins with an examination of Berrigan's theological method. He finds, in short, that "Berrigan's method is experiential and historical, heavily dependent upon scripture and orientated toward decision and action." He is particularly appreciative of Berrigan's emphasis on the social dimensions of theology, which serve to temper the "hyper-individualism" of the American cultural ethos.

The prophet's desire is to welcome the "unwelcome truth." Ludwig cites a passage from Berrigan's book, *Ezekiel: Vision in the Dust*, that is as true in our own time as it was in Ezekiel's: "In a place of pure desolation, an entire ecology speaks of the prevailing of death." He is careful, however, to cite two other dimensions of Berrigan's prophetic theology that are just as essential as truth-telling: hopeful listening and hopeful imagination. It is these dimensions that fuel the creative fire of Berrigan's acts of public witness, such as the Catonsville Nine and the Plowshares Eight. Berrigan, according to Ludwig, has been a major force in making nonviolence normative in Catholic social thought. More so, through his efforts to directly challenge the war-making state, Berrigan—and those who have acted with him—have introduced "resistance" as a vital component of Christian nonviolence.

Ludwig's essay ends with a discussion of Berrigan's "Ethics of Resurrection," an ethics that directs its attention to the work of healing, serving, and uplifting the downtrodden. In this cherishing of life and in the daily practices that incarnate the "victory of life over death," Berrigan moves us beyond comfortable mediocrity and into the fresh vitality of what Catholic social thought can be.

Michael Baxter writes in his essay, "The State of Resistance: On the Relevance of Daniel Berrigan's Work to Catholic Social Thought," of being first introduced to Berrigan through his writings, in particular *The Dark Night of Resistance*. He then employs the insights of this book to set the frame for his essay and to provide the essay's final word on Berrigan's contribution to Catholic social thought: *Nada*. Berrigan's unique way of saying "no" is the means by which we are to "enter more dramatically and fully into the truth of things." How and why American Catholic social thought, for the most part, stands on the sidelines of life is the question Baxter sets out to answer in his essay.

Deftly moving through the historical development of Catholic social teaching in America, Baxter points to a concern held in common by Berrigan and leaders of the Church, as well as its theologians and philosophers: how do we move from a disordered political, economic and social life into one that reflects a more "comprehensive peace"? Unlike Berrigan, however, most of the Church's leadership and its intellectuals thought the way to go forward was to move backward through a retrieval and rehabilitation of Thomism and scholasticism. Unrevealed, perhaps even in the minds of these thinkers, was a political agenda that well accommodated itself to the furtherance of American nationalism and, ultimately, empire. Enter Berrigan and his rather dramatic, "No!" For Baxter, the "negative" actions of the Catonsville Nine, for example, serve as a faith-based corrective to the faulty reasoning that anchors much of Catholic social thought.

Corrective measures, of course, are only a first step. Baxter recalls, within the context of a retreat, Berrigan's use of the Acts of the Apostles to demonstrate how Christians may live the "new" life promised by Jesus in the Gospels. Positing Acts as a "kind of family album," from which we learn from Whom we come, Berrigan reminds us that Scripture is not a closed book but an open door. Each of us, in this moment now, is beckoned to walk in, to become literate and to live simply, communally, prayerfully, disobediently, nonviolently, and joyfully. We are invited, in other words, to be fully human.

William L. McBride's "Father Berrigan and the Marxist/Communist 'Menace'" deals with Berrigan's relationship with the Marxist tradition. Does he give this tradition too short shrift in understanding such realities as the Vietnam War? Does Berrigan sense the affinities between Christian and Marxist traditions in trying to overcome relationships between domination and subordination and in their commitment to achieving a nonviolent, peaceful society? Would not Marx's theory of economic exploitation be useful and even essential in understanding why Christian warmongers act that way, and why capitalism and imperialism are incompatible with Christianity? Should not the writings of Marx be seen as complementary to, rather than contradicting, the powerful sacred texts that have served as Berrigan's inspiration?

How are Catholics to respond to a culture of death? Anna J. Brown, in her essay, "The Language of the Incandescent Heart: Etty Hillesum and Daniel Berrigan's Response to a Culture of Death," answers this question by considering the life and thought of Berrigan and Etty Hillesum, a Dutch Jewish woman who died in Auschwitz. This essay first considers the Church's articulation of the culture of death in our contemporary world. It then biographically fleshes out the development of an awakened consciousness and conscience both in Berrigan and Hillesum. The essay concludes with an exploration of their methods of nonviolent resistance and peacemaking: the daily practice of prayer, the constant work of self-knowledge, and a commitment to life in community. Berrigan and Hillesum, by breathing new life into ancient practices, show us what active nonviolent revolutionary love looks like, hence their exceptional challenge to Catholic social thought.

James L. Marsh's essay, "Self-Appropriation and Liberation: Philosophizing in the Light of Catonsville," was his presidential address. The essay argues that self-appropriation from below can be fruitfully complemented by a prophetic Berriganian theology of liberation from above. Marsh's formula to express this relationship is that intellectual, moral, and religious conversion should lead to radical political conversion. To further deepen and enrich the relationship between self-appropriation and liberation, Marxian social theory is used to understand and criticize capitalism, imperialism, and militarism. Marsh further stresses that the events at Catonsville can serve to bring into question an overly comfortable relationship of Catholic universities and Catholic academics to the secular city. In such accommodation, is the academic mission itself compromised? How freely and comprehensively can the desire to know operate when it is constrained by the goals and practices of empire?

William Desmond's essay, "Consecrating Peace: Reflecting on Daniel Berrigan and Witness," discusses the relationship between contemplation and action in Berrigan's work. In the work of peacemaking, there is and must be a contemplative openness to the sacred, a porosity to the sacred that grounds social activism. More primal than the *conatus essendi* is the *passio essendi*; we are first given to be before anything else. We are an original "yes" to being, and an activism grounded in this "yes" tries, with finesse and reverence, to respect the integrity of creation and the human being and is animated by the hope of sanctification of the world. We consecrate peace.

Robert Doran's essay, "Bernard Lonergan and Daniel Berrigan," reflects on Lonergan and Berrigan as the two major influences upon his life, and on the way in which he felt compelled to be faithful to both. Autobiographically, what bound both together in Doran's work was radical resistance to decadence and corruption, and their attempts to provide a positive Christian alternative rooted in the spiritual exercises of Saint Ignatius Loyola. Theoretically, both influences led Doran to work out a notion of psychic conversion: attentiveness to the energic flow of sensation, images, and emotions, to conceive the preferential option of the poor as essential to any fully adequate theology, and to understand and criticize violence as that is rooted in an unjust social order.

In "A Kind of Piety Toward Experience: Hope in Nuclear Times," Patrick Murray and Jeanne Schuler reflect autobiographically on their involvement in the peace movement in the 1960s and '70s, an involvement profoundly shaped by Berrigan, among others. This practical involvement led them, however, into professional philosophy done radically as their chosen way to work for peace and justice. They perceive three seminal themes in Berrigan's thought: a theology of time and history relevant to our contemporary era and pious towards experience, the present age as a "historical rupture" from the past, and a sense in which human thinking has gone awry and become overly instrumentalized. In their view, however, the best way to hold these seminal themes together lies in using the work of Hegel and Marx in understanding and criticizing capitalism, imperialism, and militarism. "We cannot understand the modern world without Marx's concept of 'capital.'" In the light of the Hegelian-Marxist perspective, they raise the question about whether Berrigan's work is too purist and sect-like, and insufficiently pragmatic and concerned with results and history. Does there not need to be a more adequate integration between purity of means, certainly an important aspect of Berrigan's thought, and pragmatic, historical effectiveness and intervention?

In "Berrigan Underground," Thomas Jeannot interrogates Berrigan on his theory and practice of civil disobedience. Using Rawls's theory of civil disobedience in a *Theory of Justice* as a foil, Jeannot argues that Berrigan underground, fleeing the authorities after the trial of the Catonsville Nine, cannot be accommodated to the American narrative after the fashion of Thoreau in *Walden Pond*. We must understand Berrigan along the path of a *via negativa* as defying the best American traditions of civil disobedience and their philosophical justifications. He must disturb us in the way that he disturbed a sober and thoughtful Robert Coles. Hazy evocations of Thoreau or Gandhi or King will not suffice. What is required indeed, if we are to take his great refusal seriously, is a clear grasp of the liberal doctrine he negated, of which the best contemporary version is Rawls. Jeannot asks, "Should we take Berrigan seriously, or shall we write him off as his own kind of merry prankster?" He argues that we need to take Berrigan seriously by understanding his radical reasons for going beyond the liberal doctrine of civil disobedience.

In "Lonergan and Berrigan: Two Radical and Visionary Jesuits," Patrick D. Brown argues that, in their opposition to the inertial thinking characteristic of the conventional mind, and in arguing for a humane, Christian alternative, Berrigan and Lonergan have a basic affinity. Each in his own way is prophetic, visionary, and radical in trying to promote a cognitive and moral breakthrough in human history. Berrigan, of course, in Brown's view is obviously prophetic, visionary, and radical but Lonergan is also in a less obvious way. Brown nails down this thesis by showing how Lonergan's early philosophy of history underpins and informs all of his later work, and how his economic theory attempts to provide a more adequate alternative to both conventional capitalist and conventional state socialist economic alternatives. Lonergan's radical, philosophical, theological, social, and historical theory complements Berrigan's radical prophetic politics and resistance, and vice versa.

The manipulation of fear is a tool of choice, both for state governments and terrorists. In this current time, in which Americans are asked to send their sons and daughters to wage a War on Terror and to sacrifice their civil liberties as well as a substantial amount of public funding to wage that war, Gail M. Presbey's essay, "Government by Fear, and How Activists of Faith Like Daniel Berrigan Resist Fear," could not be more timely. Presbey weaves a synthetic account and makes use of classical and modern Western philosophical thought, Catholic social teaching, contemporary social analyses, and a biographical sketch of Berrigan's life. She then examines the public use of fear, be it in the workplace, in political debate or in warfare, and finally considers Berrigan's own grappling with fear, his courageous, challenging response to fear, and his reaching out in service to those society tends to fear, such as persons living with AIDS.

Berrigan challenges the tepidity of Catholic social thought—or perhaps its conventional rendering and application—in light of devastating social realities, such as the deaths of forty million persons each year from hunger-related causes, the use of napalm which is designed to eat through human flesh, the massive bombing of cities, and so on. He also challenges the Church's refusal to speak about the specifics of particular wars. Berrigan's experience of living under American bombs, as he did in Hanoi in 1968, made speaking in abstractions a moot point. Finally, Berrigan's acts of resistance, often derided as "lunatic" by many, demonstrate the flight of rationality from a public policy that designates nuclear weapons necessary for defense purposes. It is these weapons of mass destruction, with their ability to blow up the entire planet, that are demonic and irrational. Berrigan's ultimate challenge, then, to Catholic social thought is to ask that we remain true to the teachings of Christ, not Caesar.

In "Announcing the Impossible," Christopher Harless asks about the feasibility of continuing, year in and year out, to participate in the kind of public actions of resistance that the Berrigan brothers have become well known for through the years. What good does it do? Do not such actions fall on deaf ears, and has not the American empire just grown stronger since the Vietnam War? Harless's answer to this question lies in seeing civil disobedience not just as a tactic for achieving political goals but as flowing from one's spiritual calling. Rather, the goal of nonviolent direct action has as much to do with the change it brings about in the protester or resister as it does with the change it produces in society. Civil disobedience seeks to be a path towards being human, to "being a man" or "being a woman." This is not to say that protest is primarily aimed at self-improvement, only that people need to make a vision of being human present in their own lives, and through that "making present" to affect the world in the long run. Berrigan's justification for nonviolent action lies in a hope that is grounded in faith and secured by a promise. It goes beyond pragmatism in being a kind of "hope against hope."

G. Simon Harak's essay, "The 'Global War on Terror': Who Wins? Who Loses?" grounds itself in Berrigan's political, economic and moral reading of the American warmongering state, and in the civil disobedience of Berrigan at a Catonsville draft board center. Harak claims that Berrigan's understanding of America's "permanent war economy," one in which anything or anyone may be up for sale or sacrificed, remains fundamentally true. He suggests, however, that there has been a paradigm shift in the ways that America generates and produces its wars since the time of Catonsville. Namely, there has been a movement from wars being a profitable venture to the making of war for the sake of profit. Harak's reading of the "war question," along with his acute sensitivity to the suffering of those ravaged by war, insists that we question the viability of Catholic Just War Theory, just as Berrigan did years earlier.

Using an abundance of empirical data, Harak provides a devastating analysis of how corporations, military contractors, the media, and public relations firms planned, orchestrated and produced the war in Iraq waged under the administration of President George W. Bush. These same actors then invest heavily in the "re-construction" of an Iraq in which *any* of its economic activities may be foreign-owned. For those looking for a substantive change in war making policy under President Barack Obama, Harak's analysis tells the peacemaker to look elsewhere. Like Berrigan, he calls for a nonviolent, peacemaking movement as the only viable alternative to war. Further, both he and Berrigan point to nonviolence as a way of living the truth of the Gospel: love your enemies, put down your sword, and uplift the poor.

Major and Minor Interrelationships

As can be seen from this brief summary of essays, the book is rich in thematic interrelationships. In no less than four of the essays—those of De Nys,

Marsh, Doran, and Patrick Brown—the theme of Lonergan and Berrigan is paramount. One reason for this phenomenon is that Lonergan is or may be one of the most important Catholic speculative philosophers and theologians; and Berrigan is one of the most important Catholic, prophetic liberation theologians. All of the essays see the relationship between these two thinkers as complementary, the contemplative related to the active, the rational to the prophetic, and the intellectual to the liberatory.

A second major thematic interplay is that between Marx and Berrigan. No less than three essays—those of Marsh, McBride, and Murray and Schuler—make that central in their presentations and all insist on complementarity. What is the best way to understand, explain, and criticize the violence, militarism, and imperial expansionism that so concerned Berrigan, and what is the most appropriate practical response to the capitalist social order? All three essays insist that mere reformism is not enough; radical interpretation and critique demand a radical response, and vice versa.

What emerges in the essays of De Nys, Anna Brown, Presbey, Doran, and Murray and Schuler is the importance of autobiography as linked to and giving rise to theory and the centrality of ethical living as grounding theory. We think that this emphasis stems from the fact that Berrigan's significance cannot be reduced to that of his written work; he cannot be made into a safe academic object. Rather his life interacts with his work and calls for reflection on that relationship.

What this means is that Catholic academics are called upon not just to think about their academic work, important as that is, but how their concrete lives as persons are related to that work. How can one be an authentic academic and person in a bourgeois university? The rationality of the Catholic academic needs the prophetic critique of a Berrigan if that academic's life and thought are to be adequately rational. Berrigan's work thus raises the old Socratic question of "the examined life"—is it worth living?—in a contemporary context. To the extent that the Catholic academic does not engage the institutional context in which she is working, theoretically and practically, how adequate is her academic and personal practice?

The essays of De Nys, Ludwig, Baxter, Marsh, Desmond, Doran, and Patrick Brown engage the question of contemplation and action. Again what is insisted upon in all of these essays is complementarity but in a way that challenges the practice of the Catholic academic. These essays argue that mere contemplation is not enough, not just for ethical, political, and religious reasons, but also for reasons endemic to the life of the mind itself. The life of the mind, the intellectual life, has a necessary, practical, critical moment, and Berrigan's critique of the nonengaged or disengaged purely contemplative academic has a point to it. On the other hand, as Desmond among others insists, practice, critique, and action without porosity to being and God are also deficient as activism. Disembodied, disengaged contemplation and mindless activism are the Scylla and Charybdis through which a Berrigan-inspired theory and practice of rationality have to pass.

Several essays, including those of Harak and Harless, raise the question of the relevance of Berrigan's thought for today. Have not the capitalism, imperialism, and militarism, which he criticized in the 1960s expanded and grown more violent today? Instead of Vietnam now, we have Iraq and Afghanistan. Instead of Agent Orange, we have depleted uranium; instead of My Lai and tiger cages we have Abu Ghraib and Guantánamo. It is the conviction of all of these authors that Berrigan's work, as illuminating and important as it was in the 1960s, is even more illuminating and pertinent now.

Many other important thematic interconnections abound in the book: for example, the relationship between Berrigan and Rawls (Jeannot) and the relationship between Berrigan and Hillesum (Anna Brown). Not to detract from the reader's delight, we hope, in personal discovery, we note also minor themes and interrelationships. John Courtney Murray is discussed negatively and critically in Baxter and Marsh's essays but more positively in Murray and Schuler's essay. The Lonergan-Berrigan connection is mentioned briefly in Ludwig's essay, and Howard Zinn is brought up as a foil to both Berrigan and Rawls in Jeannot's essay.

Future Questions

The *whole* of Daniel Berrigan's challenge to the *whole* of Catholic social teaching and its application is beyond the scope of this volume, or any one volume. The essays in this volume locate their considerations and critiques within an academic setting, and mostly that of the Catholic university or college. Its authors are philosophers, theologians, political scientists, and public servants; many among them would also consider themselves to be peace activists. The areas within Catholic social teaching most emphasized in this volume are those of the Church's teachings on war and social justice, with a particular regard to poverty. Father Bernard Haring, CSsR, an advisor to the Second Vatican Council and to its most important document, *Gaudium et Spes*, wrote: "There [is] no more important sign of the times than the violence epidemic—the arms race, the nuclear weapons, ever

increasing terrorism . . . and the ideology behind it all, namely, an all pervasive belief in the efficacy of violence."[22] Our authors, like Berrigan, call
attention to what even the Church believes are most deserving of our
thoughtful consideration and engagement.

Most authors give priority to Berrigan's prophetic reading of Scripture.
Certain authors emphasize the contemplative dimension of Berrigan's life
and thought, while others point more toward his radical political and social
engagement. All authors regard Berrigan as a major Catholic thinker and
a formidable challenge to "life as usual" within the academy. More so, given
the catastrophic nature of our current political, economic, social, and environmental crises, all agree that Berrigan's voice and vision must now be
taken seriously, particularly within institutions of higher learning.

The authors hope that this book will be the first of many books to consider the challenges presented by Berrigan in this thought and life. This
collection of essays introduces a number of questions that, together with
those articulated below, must also be held in fruitful contemplation and
developed in future discussions of Berrigan's work. Before listing these
questions, one may well consider a passage from Kierkegaard's *For Self
Examination* that he used as a preface to his "What Is Yet Lacking?"—an
article that is sharply critical of the Catholic university's uncritical alliance
with the military:

> Indeed, in our age they talk about the importance of presenting
> Christianity simply; not elaborately and grandiloquently. And about
> this subject . . . they write books, it becomes a science, perhaps one may
> even make a living of it and become a professor. But they forget or
> ignore the fact that the truly simple way of presenting any Christianity
> is—to do it.[23]

Taking Berrigan's cue from his use of Kierkegaard and from his own
example, our first set of questions asks why, for the most part, university
and college professors do not take a more activist position—in any of the
multitude forms that may take—on their campuses? Why was there not,
for example, a mass outcry on Catholic campuses during the 2003 US invasion of Iraq, an invasion that was soundly condemned by Pope John Paul II
and Pope Benedict XVI? Why was there minimal protest at Boston College
when former Secretary of State Condoleeza Rice was invited as a commencement speaker and when former Attorney General Michael Mukasey
was invited to give an inaugural address at the Law School? Both Rice and
Mukasey, as part of the inner circle of the Bush administration, gave the
"green light" for our nation's use of torture; yet, torture is defined by the

Church, in *Veritatis Splendor* and *Gaudium et Spes*, as an intrinsic evil and is absolutely prohibited.

The answer most often given to this set of questions is that the role of the faculty is to develop the "life of the mind" in accordance with (the rather narrow) standards set by the academy. Further, it is inappropriate to comment on an area, such as torture and the politics behind it, in which one is not an expert. Berrigan, in *To Dwell in Peace*, views these stances as ill-formulated and as a cop-out. He recognizes, however, that no less than his own Jesuit order adopted this way of thinking and acting:

> Jesuits were teachers and writers and missioners and chaplains of hospitals and prisons and the military. Our work lay in the future, we were told. And for the present, our forte, as well as our tradition, we were told, placed us exclusively in the life of the mind. So we were instructed. And so we came to see ourselves; and so our future took shape, or misshape. It is perhaps unnecessary to suggest, some fifty years later, that there was a grievous imbalance here, or the imbalance that still awaits correction. The works of mercy at odds with the works of justice. The "life of the mind;" which is to say, conscience, quite decanted . . . Jesuit campuses peopled by apolitical refugees of the times, Jesuits and others are a seedbed of reaction and militarization. There the ROTC marches, government research is lusted after; and theology bows in shame.[24]

A second set of questions that emerge was implied by Berrigan in a recent interview conducted by author and journalist Chris Hedges. In "Forty Years After Catonsville," Berrigan laments present political, economic, and social realities: "This is the worst time in my long life. I have never had such meager expectations of the system. I find those expectations verified in paucity and shallowness every day I live." As opposed to academic theologians, Berrigan turns to Thomas Merton and Dorothy Day to provide light in dark times. From Merton, Berrigan's trust in "prayer and the sacramental life" as disciplines needed to "survive America" was reinforced.[25] Day, he goes as far as to say, "taught me more than all the theologians. She awakened me to connections I had not thought of or been instructed in, the equation of human misery, poverty and war making."[26] The questions here are why are the connections made by Day not being made within our colleges and universities? Why would someone as thoughtful and as articulate as Berrigan have to go outside of the academy to see what should be obvious, especially to those who have had the privilege of advanced study? Furthermore, is there a need for "prayer and the sacramental life" to balance the overdevelopment of "life of the mind" within the academy? Finally, in these "worst of times" is thought and discourse within the university substantive or shallow; is it characterized by richness or paucity?

In his meditation on the minor prophets of the Old Testament, *Minor Prophets, Major Themes*, Berrigan himself asks a set of questions that are worthy of our consideration. Working with the text of Hosea, he examines the interrelated themes of the natural ecology, the moral ecology and the economy:

> How are we conducting ourselves in the world? Is greed riding high? Have institutions become idolatrous? Are the poor neglected, and injustices multiplied? The answers to such questions shed all the light we require concerning the prospering of the natural world.[27]

Pope Benedict XVI, in his most recent Encyclical Letter, *Caritas in Veritate*, essentially asks the same questions. Citing the "malfunctions and dramatic problems" of the current global economic crisis, he claims that "human destiny" is now in the balance. More specifically, he calls for an examination of "the technical forces in play, the global interrelations, the damaging effects on the real economy of badly managed and largely speculative financial dealing, large-scale migration of peoples, often provoked by some particular circumstance and then given insufficient attention, [and] the unregulated exploitation of the earth's resources . . . ."[28]

Given all of the intellectual tools and resources of the university, it is quite stunning that there was such little forewarning of this impending economic disaster. Our sense is that Berrigan would point us in the direction of the poor; had we focused our attention rightly, we would have seen that for the poor, the global economy, for the most part, has always been disastrous. It is difficult, however, to pay attention to the poor when there is so much money offered—through government, corporate, and military contracts—to pay attention to the well-off and to the military enforcement that maintains "the scandal of glaring inequalities."[29]

In his book, *Exodus: Let My People Go*, Berrigan claims: "Money has taken on an ominous pseudolife, a new name: *Mammon*. It is as though the imperial face on the coins were speaking aloud, instructing their handlers as to whose pockets they would line."[30] When millions in dollars of contracts are offered, how will the poor fare when war reigns down upon them? How will even the life of the mind fare? Who will dictate the terms of intellectual inquiry?

Our final set of questions pertains to the recognition of Berrigan's life and thought at our Catholic, particularly Jesuit, colleges and universities. Berrigan is an award-winning playwright and poet who has published over fifty books, yet his work is rarely studied in college curriculums. Though he looms large in the history of Jesuit justice and peacemaking, he has not been invited nor has his work been promoted at any of the three *Justice in Jesuit Higher Education Conferences*, which are agenda-setting and which bring together representatives from all twenty-eight of the North American Jesuit colleges and universities. Berrigan, who was probably most read during the time of the Catonsville Nine action in the late 1960s, has been publishing up to the present moment. His acts of public witness have also moved with the times; the Plowshares actions of the 1980s, for example, speak directly to (continuing) the threat of nuclear weapons. Is Berrigan too demanding for most colleges and universities? If so, to whom or to what are colleges and universities beholden? Berrigan has been known to quip: "If you want to be a Christian, you had better look good on wood." Have those teaching at Catholic universities and colleges given up the Cross for the sake of comfort and convention?

Philosophy and the Prophetic Challenge

Martin J. De Nys

In various forms, if only as a quarrel, an association between philosophy and poetry extends throughout the history of philosophy. That sort of association does not exist between philosophy and prophesy. For obvious reasons the earliest philosophers, who were required to define the relation of their task to the activities of poets, had no awareness at all of prophets. As interactions between the philosophical and the biblical tradition developed, the prophetic dimension of the biblical tradition was not prominent in those interactions. For many this need not be a problem. But for Christian philosophers, because we are among the philosophers who live and work in connection with the biblical tradition, it is a matter for concern. The significance of the prophetic writings for Christian self-understanding has become increasingly evident on the contemporary scene. As a consequence, the absence of an association between the oracles of the prophets and philosophical inquiry in the work of Christian philosophers presents itself as a problem that needs to be addressed and remedied.

This problem is the reference point for my comments about the significance of Daniel Berrigan's work for philosophers. Berrigan mediates the prophetic tradition to the contemporary scene in a unique and compelling way.

In part this is because he is a poet, and prophecy is intimately linked to poetry. In part this is also, of course, due to the manner in which he has conducted his life, as well as to those of his writings that explicitly address the texts of biblical prophesy. An indication of some questions a Christian philosopher might ask in responding to this mediation of the prophetic tradition is the goal of my remarks.

I will begin with some comments about features of the context or life-world in which a Christian philosopher works. By this I mean the normative context in which someone who is a Christian and a philosopher does specifically philosophical work. Given this, I do not define this context, for example, with reference to its biblical basis. An effective presence of the biblical tradition should be an ingredient in the lifeworld of all Christians, and thus does not specifically determine the context of a Christian who is doing philosophy. That said, it is still the case that an understanding of this context is important for my purposes, because it is a context that disposes one doing philosophy to be receptive to mediations of the biblical, and in more particular terms the prophetic, tradition. I will associate the features I discuss with two names familiar to many: Bernard Lonergan and Thomas Merton.

It is very clear, as Lonergan's work develops from *Insight* to *Method in Theology* and beyond, that the supreme imperative governing self-transcending subjectivity is, one might say, "be in love."[1] This demand does not come forth, as Hegel might say, "like a shot from a pistol."[2] It concludes a complex account of experience, understanding, reflection, and deliberation that shows the necessity of the transcendental imperatives that belong to each part of that account: be attentive, be intelligent, be reasonable, be responsible.[3] It looks back to a developed cognitional theory and to an identification of what Lonergan calls the intellectual pattern of experience as the setting that self-affirmation, in relation to that theory, requires.[4] It is the outcome of an account of subjectivity in which the root of cognitive activity is found in a pure desire to know[5], and in which a steady attempt is made to identify and counter the many biases that would counter that pure desire.[6] Still, the account of self-transcending subjectivity to which cognitional theory belongs imposes on those who pursue cognitive activity, and specifically on philosophers, the following two requirements.

First, while philosophical work must be governed by the pure desire to know and contextualized in the intellectual pattern of experience, the intellectual self-appropriation that such work needs may not occur in isolation. It must be a component of a process of self-appropriation that addresses the whole series of possibilities that belong to finite self-transcendence.

Second, the fulfillment of those possibilities requires a response of unqualified love to a source that both elicits that response and makes that response possible because of the love with which it has flooded out hearts.[7] In other words, an essentially intellectual self-appropriation, and philosophy which is its completed outcome, operate within their own context in relation to wholly cognitive sources and ends, and within a larger context in which knowledge for knowledge's sake becomes truly its own self by serving the ends of love.

To serve the ends of love calls for works of love. In specific terms those works include indefinitely many possibilities, philosophy being one of them. The basis that secures all of them is the interrelationship of contemplation and moral engagement. Thomas Merton is a witness to the necessity of that interrelationship. It is clear to him that human fulfillment requires us to "escape from the prison of our own false self, and enter by love into union with the Life Who dwells and sings within the essence of every creature and in the core of our own souls."[8] He also knows that one "cannot enter the deepest center of himself and pass through that center into God unless he is able to pass entirely out of himself and give himself to other people in the purity of a selfless love."[9] The fruit of contemplation understood in these senses is the ability, Merton says, "to see things as they really are."[10] But that vision must take the form of specific insights. For Merton, one of these insights is the realization of the "incongruity of praying to the God of peace, the God Who told us to love one another as He had loved us, Who warned us that those who took the sword would perish by it, and at the same time planning to annihilate not thousands but millions of civilians and soldiers, men, women and children without discrimination, even with the almost infallible certainty of inviting the same annihilation for ourselves."[11] When the aspiration to commit myself "to other people in the purity of selfless love" is joined to a realization of this incongruity, engagement and social praxis are, in some form, mandated. The steady vision of things that contemplation makes possible calls for engagement, just as engagement needs the steady vision that contemplation supplies. Thomas Merton shows that, at bottom, contemplation without engagement is empty and engagement without contemplation is blind. Others who have shown this in our time include Dietrich Bonhoeffer, Dorothy Day, and Daniel Berrigan.[12]

I am suggesting, then, that Christian philosophers work in a context in which they acknowledge the integrity and critical autonomy of philosophical inquiry; simultaneously identify philosophical inquiry as a component of a more comprehensive project of self-transcendence and as in the service of the ends of love; and identify the basis of works of love as a necessary interrelation between contemplation and engagement. Throughout these comments I will assume that the norms of the context in which Christian philosophers work call for these characteristics. At the very least, one who does philosophy within this context and also encounters mediations of the prophetic tradition must ask questions about the relation of that tradition to the definition and treatment of issues in philosophy. In his activities and writings, Daniel Berrigan presents the content of the prophetic oracles to us and gives powerful assistance in framing some of those questions. I want to discuss briefly questions of four different sorts. The first has to do with the importance of encountering the prophetic tradition as a resource on which one might draw in doing philosophy. The second has to do with philosophical inquiry in relation to the issue of violence. The third deals with philosophical considerations of religion. The fourth is about our relation to the institutional context in which many of us work.

First, and for me most basically, Berrigan reminds us, "As God's compassionate and clairvoyant and inclusive image, each prophet strives for a divine (which is to say, truly human) breakthrough in the human tribe. Lacerating, intemperate, relentless, the prophets raise the question again and again, in images furious and glorious, poetic and demanding: What is a human being?"[13] Suppose that a truly human breakthrough in the human world could at times become so unfamiliar an event that most of us could not recognize it as such? What then would become of our inquiries into human nature and especially to our ethical inquiries? From a biblical perspective this situation is not at all unlikely. William Stringfellow, for example, says that, "biblically speaking, the singular, straightforward issue of ethics—and the elementary topic of politics—is *how to live humanly during the Fall*."[14] It is entirely appropriate for a Christian philosopher to understand our human condition by referring, among other things, to the symbol of the Fall. It would hardly be surprising if, in this errant situation of estrangement from God, others, the world, and ourselves, it were difficult for us to recognize genuine human breakthroughs. But then attention to them is all the more urgent if one is trying to determine how to live humanly in that situation. Stringfellow adds that "the use of the adverb *humanly* renders the question political: there is, in the biblical witness, no way to act humanly in isolation from the whole of humanity, no possibility for a person to act humanly without becoming implicated with all other human beings."[15] The oracles of the prophets, and the deeds and words of those who mediate them to us, have the capacity to break open our assumptions and radicalize our conceptions about what it means to live humanly and to be implicated with all others. That may be just what our ethical inquiry needs. There follows a first and very basic question for a Christian philosopher. Do we, as philosophers, need something like an encounter with the oracles of the prophets, or with some mediation of the prophetic tradition, in order to know what it is to live humanly?

A second question follows from the identification the prophets make of the evils that prevail in the human world and of their outcome. The evils are idolatry and injustice. They are twins. Jeremiah, as Berrigan points out, knows that "idolatry permeates every misdeed. They are unjust to one another, taking base advantage of widows and orphans, even killing the innocent. Such behavior already implies . . . 'worshiping false gods.' "[16] The outcome is "the normalizing of violence, near and far, as a matter of daily record."[17] Violence becomes pervasive, multiform, systemic, a part of the way things are. At the limit, people build high places and sacrifice their own children.

> We of the failing twentieth century declare in horror: "How far we stand from such abominations." And yet how near in actuality—the actuality of war, of urban violence, of inferior schools, of bad housing, of no medical care, of no future. The children of the affluent are sacrificed as well, in the fires of greed and consumerism. And children are sacrificed massively to gods of war, repeatedly, relentlessly: the Iraqis, the Panamanians, the Guatemalans, the Vietnamese— burning their sons and daughters in the fire.[18]

On this occasion I can do no more than assert my conviction that words like the ones I just quoted are not to be dismissed as rhetoric, and that violence is globally and systemically operative in domestic and international political relations, economic relations, many educational institutions, and countless other areas of human endeavor, public as well as intimate. And I can only assert the claim that, in these matters, not to be part of the solution is very, very truly to be part of the problem. But if we may allow for a moment for these views, we must also sadly recognize that many philosophers, including those working in social philosophy and critique, find that a failure to take account of and respond to this brings about an entirely tolerable and in fact comfortable situation. I believe, in fact, that the professional norms that guide philosophical work today strongly encourage philosophers to ignore multiform and systemic violence. But can that be acceptable for one whose philosophical work is in dialogue with the oracles of prophecy? A constant theme of those oracles is the solemn obligation to shelter those who fall prey to the threats of violence: the orphan, the widow and the stranger. Even a casual encounter with Isaiah suggests that a failure to take account of and respond to the reality of violence in the world is unacceptable and inexcusable. And Jeremiah, for whom Yahweh at a critical point forbids armed resistance, gives no comfort to the indifferent.[19] So this is a second question for Christian philosophers who encounter a mediation of the prophetic tradition like the one that Berrigan presents. Can we suppose that the failure, characteristic in current philosophy, to in some way take account of and respond to systemic violence is in any way excusable? Or better, can we suppose that our failure to do so is in any way excusable?

A third question has to do with philosophical inquiry insofar as it addresses issues related to religion and God. Some of us pursue inquiries of that sort. We do so through phenomenological consideration of the necessities and basic distinctions which an understanding of religion requires, through analyses or hermeneutical construals of religious discourse, to metaphysical considerations of the difference between the world and God, of what can be said of God in the light of that distinction, of how those things are said, and in other ways. One who has encountered the prophetic tradition knows that it stands in thoroughgoing opposition to what Berrigan calls "an acculturated and childish religion," to idols, and to the idea of God as "a Niagara of pablum, spilling his childish comfort upon the morally and humanly neutral, whose faces are raised blankly to partake of that infantile nourishment."[20] One might suppose that addressing these matters is wholly a pastoral or a theological task. But is that entirely so? Suppose one is a philosopher who comments on religion and whose work is affected by the biblical and specifically by the prophetic tradition. Might it not be a part of one's philosophical task, whatever else one is doing, to present an understanding of religion that calls for a free and mature self capable of moral responsibility and genuine self-transcendence, and a concept of God as one who both opens the possibility for these qualities and demands their cultivation? Might inquiry into issues more traditionally associated with philosophy of religion allow for, or perhaps even require, attention to matters like these?

A fourth question deals with the institutional setting in which we do philosophy and our professional understanding of our work. I believe that we need to pay very serious attention to Daniel Berrigan's comment that "the university, as presently constituted, is a function of technological American society. The university does not exist, to analyze, interpret, or gainsay the self-understanding of the culture it serves. It has no prophetic gift or function. It is in no sense 'over against' its culture."[21] It seems credible as well to say that much of the work we do as individuals conforms to this situation. Much of our work involves planning and implementing research agendas that are judged as noncontroversial within the larger profession, agendas whose implementation is safe within the institution, and whose successful implementation receives predictable rewards. Clearly it is always necessary for all of us always to be learning from the profession into which we have entered what the problems are with which our professional work deals and what the nature of that work is. I mean to say nothing that would in any way detract from the truth or the importance of that. But, using Daniel Berrigan's words again, it is possible to do this in a way that entails being "committed, in a sterilized, selfish way, to the life of the intellect:" to do that "is to bring the mind and its proper function very near to ruin."[22] If one's work is ultimately governed by the goals of institutional approval and personal advancement, even what is called critique can be a disguised version of conformity. Suppose the background against which one does philosophy includes a mediation of the prophetic tradition. Especially then, must we not sometimes ask if the times demand that we detach ourselves from the goals just mentioned and stand our ground in determining our philosophical work?

I would like to conclude with four observations. First, I have mentioned some questions that might be asked by a Christian philosopher who allows a mediation of the prophetic tradition to affect his or her work. These are far from the only questions. I mean them to be illustrative, I present them as a possible starting point for a dialogue that would greatly expand their number and revise their content.

Second, these are questions for persons on any point of the spectrum of political and social views. Why couldn't any Christian philosopher, conservative, libertarian, liberal, or radical, ask if our fallen condition is such that we require something like an encounter with prophetic oracles to shake us into a more adequate understanding of what it is to be truly human? Why couldn't any such philosopher ask if there is a normative disposition in our profession that allows us to ignore the systematic violence that plagues the lives of so many people in the world in so many ways, and if that is even possibly excusable? Why couldn't any such philosopher, assuming that one does philosophy of religion, ask about the necessity of presenting an understanding of religion and of God that is mature, responsible, and true to the religious as well as the philosophical sources upon which a philosopher must draw in order to understand religion? Why couldn't any such philosopher ask if the times require us to stand against the goals of institutional approval and personal advancement in order to cultivate our philosophical integrity? I don't think there is any point on the spectrum of social and political opinion that allows a Christian philosopher the comfort of saying, "At least, I don't have to deal with those questions."

Third, I maintain that the sort of thinking that proceeds from questions like these does not undercut the classical philosophical tradition that we inherit. It expands and radicalizes its possibilities. The questions suggest that there are problematic limits that belong to philosophical work in many of its contemporary manifestations. But, I believe, one overcomes those limits not by transgressing the possibilities of traditional philosophy as such, but by reaching into the deepest aspects of those possibilities and realizing them in new ways. In this manner we find new ways to belong to the classical philosophical tradition, and new ways for that tradition to belong to us. I believe that, in the absence of that, the tradition will wither.

Finally, I have had the work of Daniel Berrigan centrally in mind in these comments. But I have also been constantly mindful of the life and work of William Stringfellow. I think of Stringfellow especially when I read words that Berrigan wrote in reflecting on the trial of the Catonsville Nine and on the approach to resistance that the Catonsville Nine adopted. Berrigan says, "We never indulged in the romantic hope that others would come to agree with us. Such a hope, it seemed to me, would have indicated a closure of mind upon our own method as the sole way. God knows, as many methods as good men can discover are required if we are to break out of the present impasse."[23] William Stringfellow was a good man, rooted in the biblical tradition and its prophetic component, who, as a civil lawyer, a canon lawyer, and a theologian, discovered his own authentic and incisive way to contribute to breaking out of the present impasse. I would suggest that a philosopher reflecting on the work of Daniel Berrigan might best be trying to find a way that is authentically his or her own way, as a philosopher and a human being who lives in these times, to do the same.

Daniel Berrigan's Theology: Retrieving the Prophetic and Proclaiming the Resurrection

Robert A. Ludwig

Daniel Berrigan is one of the most remarkable and significant American Catholic theologians of the past century. Like Thomas Merton, Martin Luther King, Jr., William Stringfellow, and others, he has done theology largely outside of the academy, although he has maintained a continual connection to the classroom, teaching undergraduate and graduate students in numerous universities across the country. His list of publications is prolific, including more than fifty books and countless essays and articles.

A Theological Method

For Berrigan, theology is more than faith seeking understanding. Theology is an engaged faith seeking authentic living. Such engagement perceives the social and cultural as integral to the individual's encounter with God, whose Word emerges enfleshed and active amid the noise and the hype of clamoring egos and the patterned strategies of unseen powers. Interpreting this Word involves a hopeful listening, grounded in scripture, prayer, and the discerning community. The end of theology is living this Word—courageously, authentically, with others—allowing this faith to lead us in hope, without excessive speculation about where it might lead.

Clearly not a systematic thinker, Berrigan has nonetheless fashioned his own methodological pattern. Far from theologies grounded in the metaphysics of classical mind, Berrigan's approach is experiential and historical, heavily dependent on scripture, and oriented toward decision and action. Transcending from previous focus on natural law, Berrigan's method is hermeneutical, always interpreting experience—his own, the common experience of our time, and that of the biblical writers. He brings a poet's eye to his interpretive task, frequently seeing what others miss, looking deeply via penetrating metaphors that cut through the surface of things, attempting to lay bare the existential choice between hope and despair, between life and death, between fidelity and the ego's pragmatism of success and results. Interpreting lived experience and the biblical Word, in a broad-based community seeking to affirm life and justice and love, and desiring to enact that interpretation authentically—this is Berrigan's methodological approach, similar in many ways to the theological method of people like Bernard Lonergan[1], who focuses great responsibility on the person before God and others and seeks to penetrate to the truth of our lives via a process that moves from experience to understanding to judgment to decision and action. The process is a movement toward deeper levels of conversion. Berrigan's intuitive methodology (again, he is not a systematic thinker) resonates, too, with the method of David Tracy, whose focus on *meaningfulness* is not totally dissimilar to what I mean when I use the term *authentic* in reference to Berrigan.[2] Like Tracy, Berrigan sees no need to look elsewhere for God, as if God were "out there." Human experience is the realm of God's involvement with humanity, and interpreting experience and scriptural text together lays bare faith's encounter with the divine dynamic within this world and our responsibility.

Earlier I made a passing comment that, for Berrigan, the social and the cultural are integral to the individual's encounter with God. In a time in which hyper-individualism dominates one's self-understanding, this is a critically important insight. Here Berrigan resonates with the Second Vatican Council's *Constitution on the Church in the Modern World*, which called on the Church to examine its relationship with culture and to reflect on the social, economic, and political contexts in which we hear the Word of God and seek to enact it. How can we isolate our encounter with God from these contexts without creating an idolatrous pseudo faith? Can God be found today in the suffering of the poor and the victims of violence? These are recurring Berriganian questions that challenge believers to find themselves in the network of relationships and the web of interconnections that is global society and world culture today.

Berrigan's theological method is not explicitly grounded in philosophical arguments. Indeed, he is much more at home with narrative theology, images, and metaphors drawn from experience and the scriptures, and reflecting upon his own experience than with philosophical abstractions. Nonetheless, the results are quite similar to the methodological patterns developed by contemporary theologians: focusing on this world and human experience, recognizing how deeply we are embedded in contexts, recognizing the Word of God through the work of interpretation, and ultimately moving toward decision and action—living our faith and hope in patterns of relationships and choices and activities that embody justice and love here and now.

Retrieving the Prophetic Character of Christian Faith

In Berrigan's case, theology's interpretive process results in what I see as his most important contribution to Catholic social thought: the retrieval of the prophetic dimension of faith. He has remarked that he is "impressed at how selective Jesus was in his use of his own tradition," which is to say that he sees Jesus and the gospel interpreters focused almost exclusively on the prophets and the prophetic. Berrigan's corpus does not include any commentary of the four canonical gospels, but he does have book-length commentaries on the Minor Prophets,[3] Isaiah,[4] Ezekiel,[5] Jeremiah,[6] Daniel,[7] Job,[8] Wisdom,[9] and Lamentations.[10] He, also, has published commentaries on the Acts of the Apostles[11] and the Book of Revelation.[12] In these commentaries and elsewhere, Berrigan discovers a theme that resonates in his own experience: what Walter Brueggemann has called "the alternative community."[13] Biblical faith calls us to critique "royal consciousness" and to "embrace the pathos" of God in hopeful imagination—a task that clarifies one's allegiance and perspective in terms of faith, not in terms of lesser authorities.

> The prophets stand as correctives against bowdlerizing chaos of
> imperial history, the perversion and suppression of truth, the pretense
> of immortality, the triumphant arches . . . the pyramids and royal
> tombs—the preposterous sham of the superhumans. Come down, come
> down, is the prophetic cry; we shall take your true measure! Judgment

is the pivot, the meaning conferred by the prophet on the otherwise meaningless charade of power. Accountability is demanded.[14]

"The prophet strives for a divine (which is to say, truly human) breakthrough in the human tribe," he writes. "Lacerating, intemperate, relentless, the prophets raise the question again and again, images furious and glorious, poetic and demanding: What is a human being? . . . Through the prophets, Yahweh strives mightily for a breakthrough on the human landscape of history, to bring light to our unenlightened human tribe to speak the truth, unwelcome as it is, of who we are and who we are called to become."[15]

This retrieval of the prophetic is, clearly, the locus of so much controversy surrounding Berrigan's thought and behavior, even among those committed to the Catholic emphases on service and social justice during the past century. One could argue that much of modern Catholic social teaching was, in fact, an attempt to persuade the citizenry and the state regarding public policy. Largely deduced from a natural law approach to Christian anthropology, Catholic social thought sought to modify the economic, social, and political impact of structural abuse within socialism and capitalism by arguing from the dignity of the human person to a set of rights and duties played out in socio-political and economic dynamics. This is not Daniel's approach—although that was, in part, where he began. Rather, his vision of Christian faith and authentic discipleship takes a more radical stance, looking behind not only the privatization of faith with the Enlightenment, but also the marriage of church and state in Constantine. He's focused first on the biblical world, where tension between the prophetic and royal consciousness finds New Testament expression in Jesus's proclamation of the reign of God subverting the sovereignty of the principalities and powers, including especially imperial pretensions. Whether in the prophetic activity of Isaiah, Jeremiah, Ezekiel, and Daniel, or in the prophetic community portrayed in Acts and the Book of Revelation, Berrigan finds biblical faith in hopeful tension with the dominant culture—focused not on correcting the policies of the *polis* so much as on fidelity to God's Word.

Here I'd like to suggest that Berrigan's biblical approach necessarily picks up the eschatological tension present in the faith of Israel and in the Jesus movement. It is a soteriological tension between present suffering and the promised future, between the now and the coming to be, between idolatry and death and God's sovereignty and life. This eschatological tension was morphed into a metaphysical dualism as Christianity moved into the Greco-Roman milieu of classical philosophy—and particularly in the time after Constantine. The soteriological tension became focused between this world and an eternal realm, the promise relegated not to a transformed future but to a heavenly realm. Theology's efforts in the past century have been away from classical dualism and toward faith's invitation to personal and social possibilities in human life. Salvation is the present experience of transcendent faith, hope, and love—the dynamic relationship between God's saving love and our openness to that love. This dynamic relationship is present and active not only in a personal way but in the dynamics of society and culture. Thus, the retrieval of a more biblical eschatology—and with it, a saving tension between today's suffering and God's justice and mercy.

The larger point here is Berrigan's retrieval of the prophetic. Historical scholarship today largely supports Berrigan's bias, as it builds a broad consensus around Jesus in postexilic Galilee and the prophetic tradition. What was John the Baptist, first, and then later, Jesus, doing in Galilee in the twenties? How did Jesus interpret and enflesh God's Word among the destitute poor and social outcasts during a time of imperial commercialization of land and arbitrary rigidity regarding purity regulations? Was the Jesus movement an alternative community in the prophetic mode, as Brueggemann clearly suggests? What were the historical factors that conspired in Jesus's crucifixion? What do we make of his persistent attention to rich metaphors and parabolic speech? And, finally, was faith in Jesus's resurrection over against the forces that sought to silence him? For Daniel Berrigan, Jesus must be seen and interpreted against the backdrop of Jewish prophecy, where the Word of God is assaulted in the name of national ego and public expediency, and where idolatry is preferred to the demands of faith and hope, of love and justice. "Through the prophets the imagination of Jesus is nourished by images both godly and human," writes Berrigan. "These prophets speak the truth to power. They stand for something, in their eyes infinitely more precious than life itself: fidelity, the *hesed* of God, in the betraying world. And they suffer the consequences, more often than not. They go into exile along with their people, and keep the spirit of covenant alight in dark times."[16] Prophetic faith speaks God's truth and suffers the consequences, remaining steadfast, even though it may seem like spitting into the wind, accomplishing little. Prophetic faith, ultimately, cannot be reduced to oracles, but lives and acts—sometimes in symbolic actions, always modeling imaginative alternatives with astonishing energy.

Daniel Berrigan represents a prophetic challenge to American Christians and to people everywhere over the past century. His prophetic witness does

not begin at Catonsville, nor does it end at King of Prussia. It was his ter-
tianship (1953–54) near Lyons in France that first enlivened this prophetic
focus. There, under the direction of Pere Charmot at Paray-le-Monial,
Daniel discovered scripture as the rich source for imagining faith in action.
And there, too, he discovered the worker-priests who had found their ministry side-by-side with underpaid laborers in ordinary life—a model of
priesthood he immediately recognized as authentic and relevant for his
own future. Further, the relationship of faith and public life was an issue
that haunted Europe in the decade immediately following the defeat of
Nazi Germany, the fall of the Vichy government in France, the rise of the
Confessing Church movement, and, of course, the Holocaust destruction
of European Jewry. What is faith if not courageous public witness for justice and peace in threatening times? And, yes, the issue of the day was
France at war in postcolonial Vietnam—something that Daniel would
think deeply about as he studied the Pauline letters and the fourth gospel
and talked with worker-priests about their life and ministry—all of this not
even a decade past America's nuclear annihilation of Hiroshima and
Nagasaki.

Reading the Western landscape in the middle of the twentieth century,
Berrigan conjures up Ezekiel's chapter 37:

> In a place of pure desolation, an entire ecology speaks of the prevailing
> of death. A sere landscape, dry bones. No sign of life. And then—a sign.
> One after another, the bones stand upright, connect one to another,
> grow animate. Skulls speak aloud. And death, lodged in cadavers like a
> parasite, in institutions like a colony of termites—death shall have no
> dominion! Ezekiel (or Yahweh) had cannily chosen the occasion and
> locale: in a place and time when death seemingly had won every
> round, death, in the end, loses. Then and now, an image to confront
> (and confound) a culture of death![17]

The interpretation is stark, but what is striking about Daniel Berrigan is his
ability to see straight and not blink—to look at the dark forces raging all
about and not be overcome but, rather, to see beneath and beyond them in
hope. One of his favorite phrases is "and yet . . . and yet"—his unwillingness
to surrender faith's hope, grounded in a living memory and a summons,
Christ risen! The broader tendency among us is denial, the practice of
seeing only what we want to see, pretending it to be hope. That is why
Berrigan is so frequently seen as only negative and depressing, a critic who
sees only problems. But "denial called hope" closes its eyes to the suffering

world and celebrates a false optimism and refuses responsibility and accountability—a condition he gently refers to as "the rotting of the mind."

Within a decade, Daniel began to focus his attention, first on the war in
Vietnam, then on nuclear arms, and now on the American empire and permanent warfare. It is important in examining his activity and his thinking
around these concerns to remember the larger arc of his theological orientation: interpreting experience biblically, that is prophetically.

Peace, Nonviolence, and Resistance

And so we come to the special relevance of Daniel Berrigan for Catholic
social thought—his attempt to retrieve Christian nonviolence as normative
and his blending of nonviolence and resistance as the pattern of discipleship in our time and place. Drawing from and dependent upon Dorothy
Day, Dr. King, Mohandas Gandhi, Thomas Merton, and many others,
Daniel and his brother Philip made peace their life's work. To get a sense
of how radical the shift that Berrigan introduces to Catholic social thought
is in terms of the Christian commitment to peace and nonviolence, I will
quote Dan's comments as recalled by John Dear in the foreword to a
collection of Dan's writings that appeared last year. The occasion was
a conference organized by the New York province of Jesuits on nuclear
weapons held in New York in the early eighties, featuring several generals,
"just war experts," and Daniel Berrigan. It was during the Reagan presidency at the time the US bishops were preparing their pastoral letter, *The
Challenge of Peace: God's Promise and Our Response*. After generals and just-
war theorists had presented their arguments, Daniel said this:

> The Christian response to imperial death-dealing is in effect a non-
> response. We refuse the terms of the argument. To weigh the value of
> lives would imply that military or paramilitary solutions had been
> grotesquely validated by Christians. There is no cause, however noble,
> which justifies the taking of a single human life, much less millions of
> them. "Witness of the resurrection" was a title of honor, self-conferred
> by the twelve apostles. They were called to take their stand on behalf of
> life, to the point of undergoing death, as well as death's analogies—
> scorn and rejection, floggings and jail. This is our glory. From Peter
> and Paul to Martin King and Oscar Romero, we are witnesses of the
> resurrection. We want to test the resurrection in our bones. To see if
> we might live in hope. We want to taste the resurrection. May I say we
> have not been disappointed.[18]

In the church that I grew up in during the 1950s and early 1960s, Catholic social thought was focused on the just-war theory with its criteria regarding *jus ad bellum* and *jus in bello*. The clarity of Jesus's teaching to love one's enemies, "Blessed are the peacemakers," and the first Christian centuries' norm of pacifism had all been lost to the conversation. In my Catholic high school, during our junior year class in American History, Father Schwarte brought in representatives of the Army, the Air Force, the Navy, and the Marines. When I naively raised a question about the possibility of Catholic conscientious objectors, Father Schwarte's response was quick and direct, "Only if you have a yellow stripe down your back, Ludwig!" Clearly, Catholic academics would have been more nuanced and measured in their thinking at that time than was this diocesan priest; nonetheless, the incompatibility of Christian faith and war was simply not a serious part of the conversation. In recent decades, however, in no small part because of Daniel and Philip Berrigan, Christians everywhere have begun to wonder what happened to "love your enemies and do kind to those who hate you." How did it morph itself toward the facile and unquestioning presence of Christians in the military—and "Christian' policy makers, with the support of "Christian" voters, justifying war and weapons of mass destruction?

The encyclical teachings of Pope John XXIII, particularly in *Pacem in Terris*, and later Vatican II's *Gaudium et Spes*, began to shift papal thinking— the condemnation of nuclear war and the spiraling arms race, the growing awareness that the morality of war needed to be completely reevaluated, and the explosion of Catholic conscientious objectors during the Vietnam era, when some 20,000 of us determined that there was a complete incompatibility between our Christian faith and participation in the military. But from the early sixties on, it has been the Berrigan brothers who carved out a new direction—one that suggested not only no direct participation in military projects, but active resistance to the vast military establishment and governmental policies grounded in military threats and solutions.

"Witnessing to the resurrection" publicly—protesting war and the preparations for war, unmasking the hidden agenda of first-strike nuclear weapons and the idea of a winnable nuclear war, practicing civil disobedience in protest to war and weaponry, refusing to pay taxes, making connections between the opulence of the American lifestyle and governmental policies that "protected our national interests"—linking peace to resistance in the name of Christ became the pattern that expanded from Catonsville to the Plowshares Movement to the School of the Americas Watch to supporting nonviolence among those involved in "the troubles" in Northern

Ireland, the assault on the poor in Central America and the Palestinian people in the Middle East; and continuing protests in the face of the first Iraqi war and the terrible aftermath of 9/11—blazing terror in Afghanistan, "shock and awe" over Baghdad, the permanent pattern of "war on terror." Decade after decade—speaking in churches and schools, leading retreats, working with veterans, nurturing the Catholic Workers, encouraging the young (including a few promising new Jesuits), marching and getting arrested, in courtrooms and prisons—the continuing refrain: open your eyes to the suffering, make connections and take responsibility, bring your conscience and your compassion into public witness, resist the lying seductions and manipulations, don't be afraid, let your bones live!

And what of the "just war"? Berrigan writes this:

> The "just war theory" is in fact a cruel oxymoron. War, no matter its provocation or justification, is of its essence and nature supremely unjust. The injustice of war implies a blasphemous inflation of human authority, that humans are allowed to decree who shall live and who shall die, to dispose of human differences by disposing of humans. We are done with that theory forever.[19]

This unbending dismissal of "just war" is a radical shift from the assumptions of Catholic social thought throughout most of the twentieth century (and for centuries prior—all the way back to the first Christian centuries). To draw a clear line between killing and discipleship, between war and military preparations for war and witnessing to Christ risen, between violence and nonviolent love—this advances Catholic social thought toward fidelity and the prophetic.

Ultimately it urges Christians toward resistance. Berrigan's time in Europe, during the first decade after Germany's Third Reich and World War II, made him acutely aware that silence is too easily assumed to mean assent. Refraining from killing and from direct participation in warfare is not enough. Active resistance to war making, to celebrating and honoring warriors and to a heritage of militarism, standing over against the rhetoric of violence and threats—to the vast network of profit-making weapons industries, political lobbying for new weapon systems, secretive global surveillance, clandestine practices of torture and assassination, speaking truth to power through creative actions of resistance—this is the path of Christian fidelity in today's world. Civil disobedience that leads to public trials and, perhaps, prison is a pattern with Daniel and Philip. But they are clear that the ways of resistance are myriad, and that everyone must listen carefully to the Spirit's lead in determining their own path of witness. The *how* of resistance is open to individual discernment and varied; the urge to resist in some form, however, is integral in this novel approach to Catholic social thought. To follow Christ is to actively resist the culture of violence, threats, and war making.

An Ethic of Resurrection

Throughout all of this, Berrigan's witness to the resurrection blended the work of nurturing community—at Jonah House and the Atlantic Life network, the Jesuits on Thompson Street, the New York–based Kairos community—with teaching at Fordham and many other colleges and universities in visiting professorships, serving as consultant in producing the film on "The Mission," hospice care with victims of cancer and AIDS. And every day the quiet time of prayer and reflection and the work of reading and writing.

Berrigan's contribution to Catholic social thought is more than a retrieval of a Christian norm of pacifism. It goes deeper. War, its preparations and its aftermath, its untold costs in human suffering and wasted resources, its domination of culture and the economy—this is merely the focal point in today's world for the dynamic of sin and grace, death and life, imprisonment and freedom, idolatry and faith's surrender to God in Christ. Berrigan sums it up beautifully in an essay entitled "An Ethic of Resurrection":

> Our ethic is a gift of the God who rolled the stone back, who beat death at its own game. If that be true, something would seem to follow. The death game is not our game. We are called to undergo death, rather than inflict death. And in so acting, to cherish life. And the vocation is no less urgent or valid in our stalled and death-ridden culture. A calling to works of solace and rescue.[20]

This ethic of the resurrection is grounded, as one would assume from what has been said above, in scripture—particularly in his reading of the New Testament narrations of the disciples' postresurrection experiences. His understanding of Jesus's resurrection finds expression in his reflections on Caravaggio's lost rendition of the risen Christ.[21] The painting itself has apparently been destroyed, perhaps purposefully. Far from the triumphalist and glorious artwork found throughout the sixteenth and seventeenth centuries portraying the risen Christ in sublime victory, Caravaggio's painting shows an emaciated and stunned victim of brutal violence barely stumbling from his tomb. The risen Christ is a survivor who has paid a great price and is now alive in the world. Berrigan refers to this lost painting in retreats and lectures, implying that standing with the risen Christ today means walking with the victims, undergoing suffering, staring down the principalities and powers whose only power is death. Freed from fear, we walk with the one who survives and who becomes present in the world through a network of witnesses.

How can we imagine the risen Christ present in the world? Berrigan looks to the Fourth Gospel, which responds to this question through a series of "I am" sayings.[22]

"I am the bread of life" (6:35)
"I am the light of the world" (8:12, 9:5)
"I am the gate for the sheep" (10:7)
"I am the good shepherd" (10:11)
"I am the resurrection and the life" (11:25)
"I am the way, the truth, and the life" (14:6)
"I am the true vine, and my Father is the vinegrower" (15:1)

In each of these images, the risen Christ is tied to his disciples in the world, feeding human hungers, enlightening the darkness, guiding through example, confronting death and bringing life, bearing great fruit. Like Jesus, the disciples have the power to lay down their lives and the power to take up their lives—through courageous witnessing of truth to power, life over death. This, I would argue, is Berrigan's great insight for Catholic social thought, moving us beyond the atrophy of "Christian realism" and the paralysis of natural law—into a fresh new approach that asks first about faith and fidelity and pushes hope beyond measured academic arguments and this or that set of political results. Can we embrace hope and act on our faith, trusting it all to God?

This is not a new sectarianism and cannot be dismissed as fringe—though it may appear so from the vantage point of a church that is deeply wed to cultural conventions, including American economic and political hegemony, "nuclear deterrence," and permanent warfare. The assumptions of Christians amid conventional Western culture today make access to the New Testament resurrection ethic challenging, indeed. Yet, for Berrigan and for the communities he and his brother have inspired, this resurrection ethic is, quite simply, the challenging Word of God inviting us to be open, to arise, to come out, to choose life, to—yes—come follow me!.

The State of Resistance: On the Relevance of Daniel Berrigan's Work to Catholic Social Thought

Michael Baxter

Like many, I initially encountered Daniel Berrigan through his written words; first, in an introduction to a 1969 book edited by David Kirk of the Emmaus Community in Harlem under the title *Quotations from Chairman Jesus*; then, in *The Trial of the Catonsville Nine*, a classic of the Catholic left published a year later; then, in other books that came my way during those years, including *The Dark Night of Resistance*.[1]

As a young, restless, unschooled reader of things radical and religious, I caught the title's allusion to the daunting vision (or antivision) offered by John of the Cross in *The Dark Night*. But I did not grasp its—dare I say it—theological and philosophical significance. The allusion suggests that if you practice the methodical—the relentlessly methodical—program of sensual and spiritual purgation set forth by John of the Cross, you will find yourself living a life that is anything but "American Catholic" in the conventional sense of that unfortunate phrase. That is to say, you will not be living the life of a typical, well assimilated, upwardly mobile, college-educated, late-twentieth or early-twenty-first century Catholic in the United States: going on to business, law, or medical school, getting a lucrative job, getting married, moving to the suburbs, raising kids, and getting enough in your 401(k) for a long and comfortable retirement, all along the way piously asking God to bless your aspirations; or in the case of religious and clergy, going through formation or the seminary, getting trained for ministry, getting an assignment, getting another assignment, pursuing a career in the Church, and then retiring into a routine of morning prayer, Mass, golf, lunch, nap, evening prayer, supper, and a couple of hours watching television before compline. Whether it be embodied by laity or clergy, liberal or conservative, male or female, this kind of conventional American Catholic life, according to Daniel, must be renounced.

Daniel himself has tried to do this in his life. His career—if you can call it that—has been anything but conventional. And he seems not to have grasped the concept of retirement. A clue as to why can be found at the outset of *The Dark Night of Resistance*, where he proposes "the state of resistance as a state of life itself," along with the explanation that, "like it or not, this is the shape of things. We will not again know sweet normalcy in our lifetime."[2] Whatever one's state of life, if lived fully, it will embrace this further state: resistance. By means of the oblique, evocative, prose poetry that has become his hallmark, this is the point Daniel makes in *The Dark Night of Resistance*.

Daniel wrote this book while on the run from the FBI, while "underground," to use a word that calls to mind Dostoevsky's bizarre depiction of a man living beneath the floorboards, writing notes that are reflective of, and created by, the schizophrenia of modern society. Catholic social teaching, it can be said, is the Church's attempt to propose a cure for modernity's schizophrenia. The cure lies, in the words of *Rerum novarum*, in "a return to Christian life and institutions," a return that will bring us back to the original, comprehensive, multifaceted peace for which we were created: peace of soul, of household, of city, of cosmos.[3] But what *is* Christian life? What *are* Christian institutions? Leo XIII had the Christian life and institutions of the thirteenth century in mind, but these are unavailable to us. So what forms of Christian life are available to us in this modern, or postmodern, era? What practices and institutions can sustain them? And how is this to be discerned?

One way is the method of John of the Cross, renouncing what is not God and not of God and acting accordingly, by resisting, and seeing where that takes us. But how do we know what is not God and not of God? By putting into practice the teaching and example, the grace and peace, the life and death of Jesus. This, I think, is the key to what Daniel has been saying and doing all these years. Jesus.

But explaining Daniel's life and work with a single word, even the name *Jesus* does not suffice philosophically. Most philosophers, even Catholic philosophers, are trained to ask, in response to the explanation that one is following Jesus, "Yeah, sure, this is all well and good in *practice*, but how does it play out in *theory*?" So I want to explain the relevance of Daniel's life and work to Catholic social thought by suggesting how it plays out in theory, specifically, by casting it in terms of the relation of faith and reason, theology and philosophy, and thus showing the significance of his jarring "no" to US war making and his consistent remarkable "yes" to making peace.

Against the broad background of Catholic philosophy in the United States, Daniel Berrigan's "no" to war and "yes" to peace is remarkable and exceptional. The collective mission of Catholic philosophers since the post–World War I period has been to show how scholastic thought, and Thomistic thought in particular, provides the United States of America with the intellectual and moral resources needed to fulfill its aims and purposes, properly understood. A key impetus for this self-appointed mission came from *Aeterni Patris*, the encyclical promulgated by Leo XIII in 1879 calling for a revival of the study of philosophy as inaugurated by the great apologists of the patristic era, especially Augustine, and developed by the great intellects of the scholastic era, especially Thomas Aquinas, who, "of all the scholastic doctors . . . stands forth preeminently as prince and master."[4]

As historians William Halsey and Philip Gleason have shown, it is difficult to overestimate the importance of *Aeterni Patris* among Catholic philosophers of the early twentieth century.[5] It established their *raison d'etre*. The fact that worldwide academic acclaim was given to such figures as Desire Mercier, Maurice De Wulf, Etienne Gilson, and Jacques Maritain gave Catholic philosophers the sense that they were returning from an intellectual exile that had been in force since the beginning of the Enlightenment. At first, the scholastic revival, as it was called, was mainly a European affair. It made its way to the United States only gradually, due to the relatively underdeveloped state of Catholic colleges and universities before the World War I. But after the war, as these Catholic institutions were brought up to modern academic standards, the scholastic vision took root and spread. Indeed, the key motivation for modernizing Catholic colleges and universities was to propagate more effectively the Scholastic intellectual vision. For this same reason, dozens of Catholic professional academic societies were founded in the postwar years, including, in 1926, the American Catholic Philosophical Society.[6]

The purpose of the American Catholic Philosophical Society, later renamed the American Catholic Philosophical Association (ACPA), as stated in its constitution, was "to promote study and research in the field of philosophy, with special emphasis on Scholastic philosophy."[7] Accordingly, the early years of the *Proceedings of the ACPA* offered what one would expect them to offer: papers on metaphysics, ontology, epistemology, ethics, all devoted to furthering philosophy in a Thomistic key, and refuting the errors of various opposing philosophical schools: naturalism, materialism, pragmatism, skepticism, agnosticism, and the most pernicious of all, atheism. But these papers were by no means purely academic or theoretical or—to use a word that for many functions as a reproach—"philosophical." They were also, very consciously, practical. Indeed, they were outright political.

In his inaugural address to the ACPA, delivered on January 5, 1926, Father Edward Pace explained why. Referring to the chaos of the war and the challenge of social reconstruction, Pace noted that in recent years "philosophy has been confronted with questions of practical import," and he bemoaned its lack of adequate answers because—and here he referred to the general philosophical scene in the United States—"there is no place for the idea of a Supreme Lawgiver or of any sanction beyond the inevitable process of evolution, cosmic, mental, and societal." And with no respect for a Lawgiver, there is "no respect for law which is the first essential in a true democracy." The solution, Pace declared, is to develop a philosophy of the state, of legislation, not just for those who make the laws but "for the people for whom the laws are made." In other words, "we need a philosophy of citizenship, and the larger part of this should be sane philosophy of education."[8] Pace went on to explain his rationale, which can be summed up as follows: what the nation needs is a philosophical account of the state, civil society, law, citizenship, and morality, all grounded in the existence of God, the Supreme Lawgiver, whose ordinances come to us through the natural law and can be ascertained through the exercise of reason. What the nation needs, in short, is scholastic philosophy.

Question: On what basis could Catholic scholars realistically expect scholastic philosophy, developed in the medieval period, to be embraced in the United States, a nation putatively founded in the modern period on the basis of principles derived from Protestantism, Deism, and Enlightenment rationalism?

The answer to this question can be found in the work of Moorhouse F. X. Millar, a Jesuit philosopher at Fordham University. It goes like this: The nation was actually *not* founded on Protestant, Deist, or Enlightenment principles; it was founded on medieval scholastic principles, by thinkers working, unwittingly, under the sway of Augustine, Aquinas, Bellarmine, Suarez, and the other "schoolman" whose thought was appropriated by the English Whigs, especially Edmund Burke, and through them, by the founders of the United States, Madison, Jefferson, Hamilton, and others.[9] As implausible as Millar's narrative may have seemed to non-Catholics, Catholic scholars believed this to be the true story, as can be seen by perusing Catholic journals founded in this period, such as *The Commonweal* (as it was first called) in 1924, *The Modern Schoolman* in 1925, *Thought* in 1926, and *The New Scholasticism* in 1927. All of them were geared to bringing scholastic philosophy to the nation so as to bring it out of crisis and return it to its true intellectual and moral foundations.[10]

Looking back forty years later, the president of the ACPA, Ernan McMullen, found the intellectual overconfidence and missionary zeal of its early members to be breathtakingly audacious and naïve.[11] While this may have been true, it is also true that this same basic Americanist agenda has shaped Catholic social thought in the United States ever since. It can be detected in the work of Jacques Maritain, Yves Simon, and Heinrich Rommen, all refugees from Europe, who took up the task of articulating the Thomistic foundations of democracy in the United States as the necessary alternative to the fascism that had overtaken their homelands in the thirties and forties. After World War II, a wave of American-born Catholics took up this task as well. The most influential of these was John Courtney Murray, whose articles in the forties and fifties and whose book *We Hold These Truths*, published in 1960, are now commonly credited with articulating a rapprochement between Catholicism and the United States.[12] And the preponderance of Catholic social theorists since Murray have been working within and revising the framework that he established, in the mode of public philosophy or its theoretical surrogate, public theology.[13]

It is important to note here that *public*, in this framework, consists of terms and categories accessible to all parties in this pluralistic society (Protestant, Catholic, Jew, secularist, Mormon, Buddhist, Muslim), regardless of their substantive theological beliefs in, say, the Trinity or the divinity of Christ, and regardless of membership in any specific religious body. This is why Catholic social theorists have been able to claim that their social vision is for everyone, for the nation as a whole. Even with the infusion of religious language into Catholic social thought that came in the wake of Vatican II, the same theoretical paradigm remained in place and thus the same basic agenda: to employ Thomist philosophy, or some equivalent, to bring the nation out of crisis and return it to its original moral and religious foundations. Not surprisingly, therefore, this scenario of national crisis and Catholic rescue lies at the rhetorical core of the work of Moorhouse F. X. Millar in the thirties, of John Courtney Murray in the fifties, and of neoconservatives, such as George Weigel, and liberals, such as David Hollenbach, throughout the eighties and nineties, and into this first decade of the twenty-first century.[14] Thus the discourse of US Catholic social thought for the past eighty years has been generating some version of the so-called Catholic Moment—all the while shaping itself into an ethic designed to meet the aims and purposes of the nation.[15]

In the context of this Americanist agenda, Daniel's contribution to Catholic social thought in the United States has been to challenge it. This contribution, as I have mentioned, has had a negative and a positive aspect to it. The negative aspect consists of uttering a resounding "no" to US war making in word and deed, in theory and in practice, through radical preaching and prophetic action. Taken together, Daniel's writings and his witness at Catonsville and King of Prussia and in so many other "actions" (as they are called in "the resistance") should be taken as a life-long *theological* statement. By this I mean it is a statement of *who* God is—not *that* God is, or *what* God is, but *who* God is—and thus a statement of faith in Jesus Christ as revealed in scripture, in the sacraments, the witness of the martyrs, the lives of the saints, and the life of the Church as it is gifted by the Holy Spirit to bring reconciliation and peace to the nations. But this single, substantive *theological* statement has bearing on *philosophy* inasmuch as it discloses how the philosophical reasoning of Catholic scholasticism in the United States has been corrupted by the aims and purposes of the nation, how it has degenerated into nationalist ideology and thus is at variance with right reason.

To be more specific, the statements and actions Daniel made at Catonsville and King of Prussia, as well as the many others that he instigated, should be seen as a mode of unmasking the faulty reasoning used to maintain, as the US Catholic bishops had maintained, that the Vietnam War is a just war or that nuclear deterrence is morally acceptable under certain conditions.[16] In the light of Daniel's statements and actions, the dark logic of John Courtney Murray or Richard John Neuhaus or the US Catholic bishops is revealed for what it truly is: reason placed at the service of an imperial lust for domination. What we have here in Daniel's life is an instance of enacted faith—the poetic words and dramatic actions of faith—elevating, perfecting, and correcting reason. In response, the task of philosophy is to return to the primary and secondary precepts of the natural law and relearn what the commandments of God ("the Supreme Lawmaker," as Pace would have it) teach: that it is always and everywhere a sin to take intentionally the lives of the innocent, that no mode of utilitarian logic can justify mass murder, that modern states (including the United States) have proven chronically incapable of adhering to the principles of just war, that perhaps in this day and age just wars cannot be waged for the simple reason that just states do not exist.

I do not wish to be misunderstood. This is not fideism. This is faith correcting reason. And this dialectic between faith and reason should bring into greater relief the importance of philosophers whose reasoning is more in line with what we know by faith, philosophers such as Elizabeth Anscombe, John Finnis, and Joseph Boyle, who have consistently decried the pragmatism of nuclear deterrence policy, or Alasdair MacIntyre, whose Marxist critique of the state and market combined with his Thomistic-Aristotelian account of the good challenges the Americanist assumption that the state is the primary mechanism for embodying justice.[17] On this score, the parallel MacIntyre draws between our time and that of the Dark Ages is as pertinent now as it was a quarter century ago: "this time, however, the barbarians are not waiting beyond the frontiers; they have already been governing us for quite some time."[18] What MacIntyre has concluded about the state on the basis of reason, Daniel has been proclaiming on the basis of the more certain avenue to truth: faith.

But lest we remain mired in a moment of negative dialectics, I should like to emphasize the positive aspect of Daniel's contribution to Catholic social thought. Here I am reminded of something that Daniel said in 1987 at a retreat for the community that had grown up around André House, a house of hospitality for the poor and homeless in downtown Phoenix. The retreat was on the Acts of the Apostles.[19] Offering a running commentary on the early chapters, Daniel remarked that the Book of Acts serves as a kind of family album for the family of faith, wherein we learn from where we come, and from whom, and the price of our birth. Moreover, the book (he urged us to see) is not closed, as if holiness and heroism were preempted by our ancestors and has since fled the earth. No, the story is left open, awaiting *our* acts and *our* choices. And then he said, in reference to the description of the Christian community in Acts 2:42–47: "people today are living this way." In saying this, he spoke of what is possible: worship, community, breaking bread, healing the sick, getting hauled into court, selling possessions and distributing them to those in need—a kind of recovery program from the sickness of sin, from social schizophrenia, a way beyond the legacy of the fall into a new way, a new life.

It is not surprising that Daniel would allow his view of human possibility to be defined by scripture stories. After all, he was formed in the Spiritual Exercises of Ignatius, influenced by the *nouvelle theologie* of de Lubac, encouraged by the Council, and inspired by words and work of Dorothy Day.[20] Taken together, these influences pointed Daniel beyond a mode of piety that locks spirituality into an interior sphere of private devotion; beyond, as well, the standard, mid-twentieth century scholastic notions of civil society, the state, the law and what is politically prudent; into a new philosophy—or, as Peter Maurin said, "a philosophy so old that it looks like new."[21] In this ancient yet ever new philosophy, the stories of Jesus and the first generation of apostles provide the set, the scene, and the script for enacting the dramatic struggle between good and evil, life and death, true and false peace, genuine community and its many counterfeits. It is a struggle that might get you arrested, taken to court, thrown into prison, or motivate you to take flight from the authorities. It might even send you underground, there to discover that your life "above board" has really been a schizophrenic existence underneath the floorboards. In any case, if you persevere in the struggle, you will find yourself in a dark night, discerning what is not God and not of God, and resisting accordingly, making your way in the manner of John of the Cross, from negation to negation: not this phony piety, not that ideology, not this esteemed career, not that prestigious ministry, not this false peace, not that fabricated idol, not this law, not that imperial authority.

The way of the dark night is a way of ceaseless renunciation, *nada* after *nada* after *nada*, but through it all, one loses, quite literally, nothing. As Daniel writes, "to cut free from the things people ordinarily give their hearts to, is not to lose the world, or the hearts of others, or the moral complicity with the fate of others which is all our longing and very nearly all our fate. No, it is to regain these things in a new way. It is to enter more dramatically and fully into the truth of things."[22]

This captures well the contribution of Daniel's life and work to Catholic social thought: it has helped us to enter more dramatically and fully into the truth of things.

Father Berrigan and the Marxist-Communist "Menace"

William L. McBride

Father Berrigan seldom refers to Karl Marx in his writings. His training as a Jesuit, and indeed a Jesuit with considerable interest in theology and philosophy, has given him a deep acquaintance with the Church Fathers and the Scholastic tradition—the tradition of what used to be called, and which some still call, *philosophia perennis*. Above all, of course the texts from which he has drawn his greatest inspiration are the Judeo-Christian Scriptures themselves. So what point is there in reflecting on his relationship, actual or potential, to the Marxist tradition?

Well, for one thing, there is Vietnam. Father Berrigan's name is intimately connected with that country, against which—or at least against the more dynamic part of which—the government of the country in which he was born and has spent most of his life, hurled manpower and weaponry on a vast scale. Indeed, as is well known, Father Berrigan experienced US military bombing on the occasion (in 1968) of his own mission to Hanoi. The Marxist connection here is that the Hanoi-based regime claimed to represent a certain version of communism, ultimately inspired by Marx. To this day, in fact, it still does. So Father Berrigan, in opposing the war draft and the US government's prosecution of the war itself, was supporting the claims to self-defense of a self-styled Marxist state. As were so many of us, but almost none with his degree of commitment.

There were many in the Catholic hierarchy and laity who regarded "Godless Communism" as the great foe to be defeated at all cost, including the cost of waging war if and when (seemingly) feasible. Francis Cardinal Spellman of New York, to whom Father Berrigan refers in his autobiography and in some of his essays, was archetypical in this respect. During World War II, when the immediate enemy was Nazism, he decreed that the most militaristic stanza ("Then conquer we must / When our cause it is just" and so on) of the *Star-Spangled Banner* be sung at the conclusion of Sunday Masses in his churches. This practice ended after the Allied victory, but Cardinal Spellman then moved to the fore as the anticommunist Cold War warrior *par excellence*. During the Vietnam War he made regular Christmas visits to the American troops there, wearing a military uniform. He epitomized, as it were, the other soul of the American Catholic Church, the establishment soul, which Father Berrigan's admirers regarded, and continue to regard, with a certain amount of horror.

Which of the two souls—the war-oriented or the peace-oriented—represented a more authentic Christianity? For those whom Father Berrigan's courage and commitment have inspired, the answer is obvious. But it is an interesting fact—interesting anthropologically, philosophically, and theologically—that the supposedly monolithic creed which is Catholic Christianity could be embodied in two such drastically different world-views even within a single country. If we look back across different countries and continents and nineteen hundred years of what claims to be a continuous tradition, however, we encounter such a bewildering variety of outlooks as to make the Berrigan/Spellman divergence appear comparatively slight. Just imagine the two of them, individually or together, for example, in dialogue with someone like Origen!

It is small wonder, then, that similar remarks can be made concerning divergences of worldviews among those who have called themselves communists in the Marxian tradition, even though that tradition is of such comparatively recent origin. Ho-Chi Minh, whose regime the US government tried so hard to defeat, claimed to have taken inspiration not only from Marx but also from some of the best-known historical American political figures. In the Vietnam of today, great new prosperity has come to some while the old ideals of community and even of family, which were generally maintained during the Ho-Chi Minh era, now seem increasingly quaint and irrelevant. (Contemporary Vietnam has a very high divorce rate, for example.) What is left of Marxism other than a name and some shared, though slowly fading, historical memories?

Now that, in most other parts of the world as well, Marxism apparently exerts so little practical influence—whereas it seemed to exert so much just forty to fifty years ago—it may be interesting, in retrospect, to try to identify some essence of it, some trait that all the self-styled Marxist regimes and parties of the past shared, or at least purported to share. Perhaps we can best locate it in one underlying commitment—a commitment often honored more in the breach than in the observance in actual communist practice, to be sure: a commitment to overcome social relations of dominance and subordination. As the opening words of the *Internationale* express it, *"Debout, les damnés de la terre!"* This was certainly the goal of the Vietnamese Communists in their struggle, first, to prevent French colonialism from regaining control of the country after World War II, and then, in the aftermath of the battle of Dienbienphu, to prevent the US government from taking on the mantle of the French in the southern half of the country.

But can it not also be said that this goal of overcoming dominance and subordination relationships is, in significant respects, a not inexact description of the essence of Christianity (with due apologies to Ludwig Feuerbach) as well? Of course, Christianity has the all-important otherworldly dimension that Marxism lacks, but within the present world its founding ideals have been the uplifting of the poor and wretched, and the repudiation of cruelty.

During the era of US war against Vietnam, domination—as epitomized in the bizarre and ultimately stupid metaphor of preventing dominoes from tumbling—and cruelty—as embodied in such forms as Agent Orange and napalm—became the *leitmotifs* of many of the leaders of "Christian" America. How was this possible, given the message of peace that Father Berrigan and other like-minded Christians discern so clearly in their scriptures? How does it continue to be possible that self-styled Christians—at least some of whom we must, I think, imagine to be acting somewhat in good faith rather than purely hypocritically—advocate policies of global dominance and the use of all available weaponry against perceived enemies? This is hardly a new question to raise, of course. The waging of self-righteous (so-called "just") wars,[1] often in the names of various religions including certainly the Christian religion, has been one of the most salient phenomena in the history of the human race—and yet, given the very clear Scriptural message that it would be difficult to deny, the question still remains, at least as it seems to me, a puzzling one.

From my early years at college I remember hearing the story of someone I knew, a candidate for a Rhodes Scholarship, appearing before the selection committee and answering, quite simply, a question concerning the cause or causes of World War I by saying "Original sin." Well, yes, if you accept conventional Christian theology, that would be a correct answer—but not exactly an adequate one. (The college, incidentally, was Georgetown, a milieu familiar to Father Berrigan.) Even granting that we are all the equally tainted heirs of Adam and Eve, this doctrine hardly accounts for the difference between warmongering Christians (and others) and peace-loving Christians (and others); if anything, it makes it harder than ever to understand.

It seems to me that Father Berrigan, in most of his essays and sermons and poems, does not devote much time to the effort to achieve such an understanding. He is a witness, a prophet, and an ultimate optimist despite the incredibly high degree of exposure that he has had to the worst of the warmongers—at least the worst of those in his own country; but he does not appear, first and foremost, to be interested in attempting to explain their Scripture-contemning behavior. I, on the other hand, as a professional philosopher, would like to try better to understand such people (although I have not been very successful). Philosophers have always tried to understand the world, in various ways, whereas for Father Berrigan that is not really the point: the point is to *change* it: in Father Berrigan's favorite metaphor, swords into ploughshares.

Of course it was Marx who coined the aphorism about changing the world instead of seeking endlessly to understand it; this aphorism even appears on his tombstone. Nevertheless, Marx does have an explanatory system—a rather elaborate one at that. It has to do, essentially, with the fundamental role of economic structures and practices, which vary from one major historical epoch to another. Now, if we were to take literally two famous, isolated sentences in Volume I of Marx's *Capital*—"Force is the midwife of every old society pregnant with a new one. It is itself an economic power."[2]—it might be inferred that Marx regards violence as an ineluctable aspect of human interaction across time, as ineluctable as is the taint of original sin for the Christian theologian. But there are several considerations that tend to mitigate this inference. First, in the penultimate chapter of the volume, in which Marx more or less forecasts the coming to power of the mass of workers by a process of "expropriating the expropriators' (that is, the owners of capital)—he says that this process will be incomparably less protracted and less violent than the one that he has just been describing in the immediately preceding chapters, whereby capitalism achieved the ascendancy over the old order. Second, Marx appears to assume, in the comparatively few remarks that he makes about the post-capitalist "society of associated producers," that whatever the details of its structure (which he does not think it appropriate to try to predict), it will be a peaceable, nonviolent one. Finally, and most importantly for my purposes here, what Marx does have to say about the rise to power of the capitalist order, particularly in the chapter on the "Genesis of the Industrial Capitalist" from which I have taken the citation about force, contains such utterly horrible details concerning the historical spread of colonialism throughout the world—including some details about the treatment of Native Americans—as to rival or surpass accounts of atrocities in Vietnam with which Father Berrigan became all too familiar a century later. The implication of this Marxian account, as of many of the other empirical facts documented in *Capital*—for example, reports of British Parliamentary committee inquiries into the harsh exploitation of child labor—is that there is something peculiarly violent about the capitalist system that is not necessarily the case, at least not to the same extent, for "every old society pregnant with a new one."

This Marxian point is one that Father Berrigan might well have exploited—*sit verbo venia*—but that he has not, or very little. In an interesting sense, of course, he himself represents one of the principal institutions of the old, precapitalist society, namely the Church. At the same time, elements of this Church—those very elements for some of whom Father Berrigan has had considerable sympathy, such as the French worker-priests, the Latin American movement of Liberation Theology, and other progressive clergy and laity with similar priorities—have been in the ranks of those who, from a *future*-oriented perspective, regard capitalism as today's "old society," thus giving some plausibility to the idea that the Church is, in a sense, an eternal institution. But Father Berrigan has been more reticent than many other Catholic progressives about identifying capitalism itself as a key to understanding why so many self-styled Christians are nevertheless raging warmongers.

There is, quite clearly, a capitalist *ur*-ethic: it is centered on personal profit maximization as the highest value. Acting in strict conformity with this ethic is simply incompatible with being a Christian as that is understood by Father Berrigan and others like him, since, to put it mildly, Christianity ranks other behaviors and values much higher than personal profit maximization. To be sure, would-be Christian capitalists compromise by not *always* conforming strictly to the capitalist ethic. However, it seems to me that to acknowledge unequivocally the radical incompatibility between the two ethics, a very basic and obvious point, while at the same time recognizing that the compromisers are simply refusing to admit the obvious, is to take a few steps on the road to understanding the "Christian" war mentality.

Dorothy Day, an individual for whom Father Berrigan has great admiration, was certainly aware that capitalism was one name for what she called, in a phrase of hers that he likes to cite, the "filthy rotten system," which of course was meant to include the economic system; after all, her newspaper was called *The Catholic Worker*. War and poverty were for her the two archenemies, and she saw them as intertwined. As Father Berrigan puts it, summarizing her basic outlook, "What was required was a renewal of the imagination, stalemated by two centuries of business as usual, war as usual, poverty as usual."[3] Like him, her orientation was above all an activism based on the Christian message, but not the sort of activism that results, or could result, in a mass movement. To cite Father Berrigan again: "She would offer no political or academic alternative, as such were commonly understood, to things as they were. She had an impetuous dislike for 'alternatives' that accepted things as they were as a given, a point of departure for political action—and so never ventured far from things as they were."[4] So she did not join any political party, including, of course, the Communist Party, which was quite prominent in New York City during the Great Depression of the 1930s when her life's mission began to take clear shape. In addition to the newspaper, as is well known, the Catholic Worker movement developed in the direction of giving shelter and a home to people who were poor and homeless, rather than in some politically revolutionary direction of the Communist Party type. But if we look back at that early Catholic Worker period, when Father Berrigan was still a child growing up in Minnesota, from our distance of some three-quarters of a century, we can see just how many concerns were common between the Communists and Dorothy Day's followers. Once again, of course, with the supremely important exception of their respective attitudes toward religion.

Two other important apparent exceptions are their respective attitudes toward the imagination and toward pacifism. Despite its sloganizing about the bright future of mankind, "official" communism, especially in its Soviet version, had become quite unimaginative by the 1930s, contrary to what Father Berrigan characterizes as Dorothy Day's call for a renewal of the imagination. But as I have already pointed out, Marx himself did not feel justified in trying to draw up detailed blueprints for the future, precisely because of his confidence in the accretion of imaginative new human powers once capitalist structures had been superseded; and there is no doubt that much of the attraction of communism among American radicals in the 1930s stemmed from the sense of excitement and of a radical departure from the existing order that it seemed to exude. As for pacifism, certainly neither Marx nor most of his followers subscribed to it, at least as a viable stance for the present time (Engels, a former military person, would have called it "utopian"), but during the thirties the most bellicose and aggressive foreign movements attracting attention in the United States were Fascist—Nazi Germany, Mussolini's Italy, and then Franco in Spain— and so pacifists and communists could make common cause in opposing them. (Actually, Dorothy Day maintained neutrality with respect to favoring sides in the Spanish Civil War, despite strong pressures from elements in the Catholic Church Establishment to support Franco.)

Later, especially during the sixties and seventies, there was an ongoing so-called "Marxist-Christian dialogue"—or, more accurately, there were several of them—but neither Dorothy Day nor Father Berrigan was especially active in that enterprise (unless we were to count the latter's mission to Hanoi in that category, which would probably be a mistake). One of the best-known and most colorful of the "dialoguers," Roger Garaudy, was a French Communist Party official for many years (before being finally expelled from the Party), whose commitment to this dialogue even resulted in a lecture tour of the United States, with the Jesuit St. Louis University as his first stop. Contrary to the stereotype of the committed Communist as intransigently antireligious, he had always retained many positive attitudes toward religion, and he ended up, later in life, as a very forceful peace advocate and eventually, in a move that he did not regard as contradictory to this, a convert to Islam.[5] There was vociferous opposition to his appearances in St. Louis and elsewhere from the "Red Menace" crowd, but the dialogue was allowed to go forward nevertheless.

It is from *petits faits* such as these that the future historian of the period in question, the best-known period of Father Berrigan's antiwar activism, may come to realize that the underlying realities were in fact much more complex and subtle than the "two camps" mentality encouraged by both the Stalinists and the prowar Christian Establishment has misled many to believe. The movement identified with Father Berrigan and his brother was one of the most salient, the least *petits*, of these "deviant" phenomena.

Nevertheless, I have been suggesting, for him to have paid greater attention than he has done to the Marxian analysis of the nature of capitalism might have contributed at least an additional dimension to the understanding of why so many self-styled Christians, including leading members of the Catholic hierarchy, could have been such advocates of the war against

Vietnam and other wars past and future. In his writings, Father Berrigan certainly hints at the connection between this attitude and a procapitalist mentality, but he does not press the point very much, at least in what I have read by him. Today—although, as I have already observed, there are no longer many self-styled Communist regimes, and even most of those that preserve that label have in reality adopted practices strongly inspired by global capitalism and far removed from the spirit of Marx—I believe that the latter still haunts us; it still offers many clues to better understand the bellicose, imperialist posture which, despite some recent setbacks, continues to characterize the government and many citizens of Father Berrigan's homeland just as it did in the Vietnam War era. When adapted critically and with an understanding of their historical and theoretical limitations, the writings of Marx can be seen as complementary to, rather than in profound contradiction with, those powerful sacred writings which, for all of his extensive reading and experiences, have continued to serve as Father Berrigan's central source of inspiration—despite the incredible abuse and degradation to which they have been subjected by so many of his "conquer we must" coreligionists.

The Language of the Incandescent Heart: Daniel Berrigan's and Etty Hillesum's Responses to a Culture of Death

Anna J. Brown

Daniel Berrigan and Etty Hillesum opened themselves fully to a world ravaged by war and learned to accept, with gratitude and praise, all that this world gave in return. Their acceptance of this world was costly. For Berrigan, it meant numerous arrests and a number of years in jail; for Hillesum, it meant internment in Westerbork and death at the age of twenty-nine in Auschwitz. How did their efforts to resist the dark tides of their time not turn toward hatred and resentment? How were they able to keep to a discipline of nonviolence when much of the world, or so it seemed, opted for violence? How did they remain steadfastly committed to life in the face of so much death?

Though I had happened upon Hillesum's *Letters from Westerbork* in a Canadian bookstore one summer, it was Berrigan who focused my attention upon how she had lived her life. Often, in our Kairos[1] meetings in New York, he would dwell upon the title of her posthumously published letters and journal entries, *An Interrupted Life*. A Jewish woman of remarkable intelligence and insight, she had to put on hold the plans for her own promising young life by refusing the opportunity to delay her entry into Westerbork, the Nazi camp in the northeastern Netherlands, so that she might attend to the suffering of those being rounded up, interned, and sent to an early death by the Nazis. "Would we in Kairos allow our lives to be interrupted?" Berrigan asked.

Berrigan's question, as well as the example he and Hillesum set, get to the question most worth asking: "How we are to live our lives?"[2] For those of us who turn toward Catholic social teaching for guidance in answering this question, Berrigan's and Hillesum's challenge may simply be that we actually live these teachings, both with urgency and with grace. In *Evangelium vitae*, Pope John Paul II describes the "culture of death" as one that "denies solidarity" and is more concerned with economic efficiency than it is with the affirmation of life, in which the strong crush the weak, and in which wars, genocide, capital punishment, euthanasia, abortion, poverty, starvation, or ecological destruction occur "on an alarmingly vast scale."[3] The ability of Berrigan and Hillesum to resist nonviolently the "culture of death" particular to his/her own time, and to do so in a manner that is/was radiantly life-affirming is an all-consuming matter for me. The trajectory of this essay will be to first consider the Church's articulation of the culture of death in our contemporary world; to then dwell upon the development of an awakened consciousness and conscience in Berrigan and Hillesum; and, finally, to consider the means by which Berrigan and Hillesum practiced nonviolent resistance and peacemaking.

Catholic Social Teaching on the Culture of Death

In his encyclical *Evangelium vitae*, Pope John Paul II asserts, "The Gospel of life is at the heart of Jesus' message."[4] He recognizes, through the extraordinarily high levels of violence within the world, that many have turned away from this message. Thus he retrieves the story of Cain and Abel from the Book of Genesis for our consideration:

> The Lord's question: "What have you done?", which Cain cannot escape, is addressed also to people of today, to make them realize the extent and gravity of the attacks directed against life which continue to mark human history; to make them discover what causes these attacks and feeds them; and to make them ponder seriously the consequences which derive from these attacks for the existence of individuals and people . . . And how can we fail to consider the violence against life done to millions of human beings, especially children, who are forced into poverty, malnutrition and hunger because of an unjust distribution of resources between peoples and between social classes? And what of

the violence inherent not only in wars as such but in the scandalous arms trade, which spawns the many armed conflicts which stain our world with blood? What of the spread of death caused by reckless tampering with the world's ecological balance, by the criminal spread of drugs, or by the promotion of certain kinds of sexual activity which, besides being morally unacceptable, also involve grave risks to life? It is impossible to catalogue completely the vast array of threats to human life, so many are the forms, whether explicit or hidden, in which they appear today![5]

The Pope, in an effort to answer the question posed to Cain, "What have you done?" seeks to understand why violence—to the point of barbarism—has become normalized in our world today. While his answer is multifaceted, I have chosen an excerpt that speaks to what he means by a "culture of death":

we are confronted by a larger reality [than just moral uncertainty], which can be described as a veritable structure of sin. This reality is characterized by the emergence of a culture which denies solidarity and in many cases takes the form of a veritable "culture of death." This culture is actively fostered by powerful cultural, economic and political currents which encourage an idea of society excessively concerned with efficiency. Looking at the situation from this point of view, it is possible to speak in a certain sense of a war of the powerful against the weak: a life which would require greater acceptance, love and care is considered useless, or held to be an intolerable burden, and is therefore rejected in one way or another. A person who, because of illness, handicap or, more simply, just by existing, compromises the well-being or life-style of those who are more favored tends to be looked upon as an enemy to be resisted or eliminated.[6]

How we might respond to the "culture of death" has been addressed, among others, by Pope Benedict XVI. In his 2007 Easter Address, the Pope speaks of the Beatitudes as a "manifesto" in which Jesus gives his disciples a "radical model for their lives."[7] More specifically, he speaks to Jesus's claim that we must "love our enemies" and asks how we would live this command today.[8] Though recognizing how difficult it is to love in this way, the Pope says that "Christ's proposal is realistic, because it takes into account that in the world there is too much violence, too much injustice, and that this situation cannot be overcome without positing more love, more kindness."[9] He concludes by noting that "nonviolence, for Christians, is not mere tactical behavior but a person's way of being . . . Loving the enemy is the nucleus of the 'Christian revolution,' a revolution not based on strategies of economic, political or media power."[10] The "Christian revolutionary," for Pope Benedict, must also speak truthfully. In an address given on World Peace Day, he noted that "the obstacles to peace originate in lying . . . how can we fail to be seriously concerned about lies in our own time, lies which are the scenarios of death in many parts of the world?"[11]

One recent scenario of death propelled, in large part, by the telling of lies is the "War on Terrorism" waged primarily by the United States in Iraq[12] and Afghanistan. Since October 7, 2001, this "war" has laid claim to over one million (mostly) civilian lives, created millions of refugees, triggered environmental disasters, justified the use of torture and the shredding of civil liberties, and has cost over three trillion dollars.[13] In this devastating nightmare of war, we are in need of truth tellers. Sadly, those who have the courage to speak the truth about the "War on Terrorism" are, as Berrigan realized during the Vietnam War, "hard to find." His description of the political and social climate of the Vietnam era is one that also well describes the current time:

> Hard to find: America
> now if America is doing well you may expect Vietnamese
> do well if power is virtuous the powerless will not be
> marked for death if the heart of man is flourishing so will
> plants and wild animals (But alas alas so also vice versa)
> Hard to find. Good bread is hard to find. Of course. The hands
> are wielding swords The wild animals fade out like Alice's cat's
> smile Americans are hard to find The defenseless fade away like
> hundred year pensioners The sour faced gorgons remain . . .[14]

Berrigan, who has staked his life on the belief that "the Gospel of life is at the heart of Jesus's message," does not allow the "sour faced gorgons" to have the final say. In the same poem he also writes:

> But listen brothers and sisters this disk floats downward a flying saucer
> in the macadam back yard where one paradise tree a hardy weed sends
> up its signal flare (spring!)
> fly it! turn it on! become
> hard to find become be born
> out of the sea Atlantis out in the wilds America
> This disk like manna miraculous loaves and fishes
> exists to be multiplied savored shared
> play it! learn it! have it by heart![15]

Active Love Is Brought Forth only by Labor and Perseverance

Berrigan and Hillesum have "played it, learned it and have it by heart." What is "it"? How did they come to see "it" and "live it" so beautifully? In Dostoevsky's *The Brothers Karamozov*, the elder Zossima points to "it" and "how to live it" when he speaks with "a lady of little faith."[16] Although faith in God can never be "proved," the way to be "convinced" in faith is by "the experience of active love."[17] Zossima presses the matter further by cautioning that in our love of the other, we must avoid lies, particularly the lie of seeking praise for one's good works.[18] To attain an active and selfless love[19] of the other is, according to Zossima, a "harsh and dreadful thing compared with love in dreams."[20] Active love requires "labor and perseverance" and does not look to see "who is watching or praising our efforts."[21]

Neither Berrigan nor Hillesum shunned the "harsh and dreadful" reality of "active love;" instead, they moved more deeply into it throughout the course of their lives. In *The Dark Night of Resistance*[22]—written while he was "underground" just after being sentenced for the Catonsville Nine action[23]—Berrigan gives an account of the difficult yet life-affirming path walked by the peacemaker (fully cognizant, of course, of the brutal and barbaric qualities of the path tread by those ravaged by warfare):

> There's a war on; can you smell death? Do you know what peacemaking is costing us? Where are all the good things you purportedly hold in escrow and never share with us? Have you ever attended one of our political trials, seen us dragged off, read the cheap price put on our lives and death by the frosty eye of power? I have a dream: I dream of every resisting commune with a guru (Christian, Jewish, Hindu, Zen) in roving residences; sharing that thing, whatever its risks and follies; leading men and women into their unexplored inner spaces; making room for love, for hope, where there seemed no room because there was no light.[24]

In his poem, "Etty Hillesum," Berrigan likens Hillesum to the Biblical "woman at the well."[25] Hillesum set for herself the task of being the "thinking heart of the barrack [Westerbork],"[26] a place "where there seemed no room because there was no light." In this dark place Hillesum shone radiantly. Might we, too, learn how to "make room for love" and to shine radiantly with an inner light? The doing of this kind of work is, finally, our own. We may be encouraged in this work by first learning about it through the biographical stories of Berrigan and Hillesum. What were their first steps in the development of a life of active love for each of them? How did they remain faithful to what they had started? How did they remain standing within the furnace of warfare?

OF DEEPER ORIGINS

In the first entry of *The Dark Night of Resistance*, written in April 1970, Berrigan sees his life in a different light: "the state of resistance [will be] the state of life itself."[27] Further, he writes: "No . . . Everything begins with that no, spoken with the heart's full energies, a suffering and prophetic word, a word issuing from the nature and direction of things."[28] Two years prior to writing *The Dark Night of Resistance*, Berrigan penned a poem he called "My Name." In it, we get a sense of his internal musings and thoughts about his life as a citizen of the United States during the time of the Vietnam War:

> . . . an American name in the world
> where men perish
> in our two murderous hands
> Alas, Berrigan
> you must open those hands
> and see, stigmatized in their palms,
> the broken faces you yearn toward
> you cannot offer
> being powerless as a woman
> under the rain of fire—
> life, the cover of your body
> Only the innocent die.
> Take up, take up
> the bloody map of the century.
> The long trek homeward begins
> into the land of unknowing.[29]

Berrigan spent the next forty-one years of his life "taking up the bloody map of the country," choosing to dwell within the "land of unknowing" and living "the original blessing of Genesis [which] was abundance . . . ."[30] In choosing to resist the destructive ways of the US government, its military and its corporations, he found himself crouching down in the bomb shelters of Vietnam; exiled to South America; burning draft cards in Catonsville and then spending eighteen months in a federal prison for doing so; and, birthing the Plowshares Movement and, once again (and again and again) returning to prison. At the same time, he "made room for love" by writing his poems and prose; by marrying husbands and wives, baptizing their children and burying their parents; by opening young minds at university and joining his students in strikes and protests; by abiding with the sick, the poor, the addicted and the so-called useless; and, by deepening his friendship with countless others in the celebration of Mass.

In "By Night I Went Out by the Back Window While the FBI Was Fumbling at the Front Door," the second chapter of *The Dark Night of Resistance*, Berrigan comments:

> A man is of no use to the future unless the full force of the present world has turned him inside out, like a pocket before a mugger and his knife. Stripped clean!
> Stripped clean I wish to say, so that a man joins, at one liberating stroke, the masses who have also been stripped clean by the mugger, the exploiter, the respectable thief. And being so violated, and understanding the simultaneous and systematic violation of their brothers throughout the world, have passed into new ways of thought, new ways of living, have seen themselves in a totally new way, neither that of the victim (to which the theft aimed at reducing them) nor that of the accomplice or thief.[31]

The biography of Berrigan, as it wends its way from the dank holes of prison cells, to bomb shelters, and to squatter's shacks, brings its readers— even if only vicariously—face to face with the "force of the present world." He also presents his American readers with a challenge. In the movement from being "stripped clean," applying this experience universally, and finding a new way of being in the world, he had to become "un-American." How so? In *The Dark Night of Resistance*, Berrigan has the following to say about the American way of life:

> The American family is a perfect nest of sitting ducks for the American Enterprise, that death-ridden domestic and universal plan of non-values and specious control. Produce, in isolation and selfishness, the children who will, as the only available option for human beings, have bought the bag. Teach the young to grab, to want, to consume, as the first native human gesture. Self-improvement, self-help, consumerism— war: the dregs of the American Dream . . . Keep the "majority" from their earliest years narcotized with illusions of the good life, security, conventional morality . . .[32]

Berrigan's continual *kenotic* work keeps him from being trapped within the political, social, and economic aspects of what he would call the American nightmare; it has also kept him from being caught within an American religious "culture of infancy,"[33] which takes "an Infant Jesus to its religious heart, changing His Underpants on major feast days . . . [and is] a religion for infants."[34] His insight into this form of American religious culture came to him while he was in Hanoi in January 1968. Along with historian Howard Zinn, he went there to accompany three American soldiers who were being sent back to the United States. While waiting to meet with the soldiers, he was able to see firsthand the effects of the American-waged war upon the people and land of Vietnam.[35] He also saw many images of the Buddha, which prompted him to write:

> The many faces of the Buddha were the many faces of man; under
> perpetual fire, nearly extinguished, stubborn as the soil, drawing
> his skills and methods from the rhythms of wind, rain and sun . . .
> The changeful face of the Buddha, his thousand arms touching the
> extremities of the spiritual universe; embracing all, including all . . .
> The face of the Buddha is the face of man tortured, stricken, inward,
> ecstatic . . . man who has swallowed fire, and lives.[36]

Berrigan, who entered the Jesuits in 1939 and remains a Jesuit to this day, had yet again been "stripped clean." Viewing the Buddha amidst the bombs had awakened him, had allowed him to rise from "the Long Sleep" of American "bad policy, refusals of life, Western fanaticism, religious frenzies and [a] murderous anti-humanism."[37] Of course, and consistent with Berrigan's movement from being "stripped clean" to being able to see that other human beings exist and suffer to understanding the social and religious forces that cause unnecessary suffering and to "making room for love," he does not allow what is antihuman to have the last say. After meditating upon the many faces of the Buddha, Berrigan recommits himself and joins with others to "save the earth and those who dwell upon the earth . . . in order to make poetry, in order to make love, in order to make sense."[38] In order to do this work, however, he finds that he must "interrupt" the order of the day. He must go, he believes, " . . . underground . . . to resign from America, in order to join the heart of man."[39]

A LIFE LIVED FULLY

In September 1943 Etty Hillesum, along with her father, mother, and brother, were herded onto a train, whose final destination was Auschwitz.

While en route to Auschwitz, Hillesum flung a postcard to her friend, Christine van Nooten, from the train. It landed on the ground near the town of Nieuweschans where it was picked up by a Dutch farmer and mailed to van Nooten. Despite her sense that death was near, both for her and her family, Hillesum did not write with a despairing hand. Instead she wrote that her family left the Westerbork camp singing and that her first act on the train was to open the Bible. She also wrote of her gratitude for all who had supported her, as well as her family, during their time in Westerbork. The lines written on the postcard are simply luminous. They speak of a heart and mind so open that they were able to hold both a love of life and firsthand knowledge of Nazi terror at the same time.

Two years prior to her death in Auschwitz in November 1943, Hillesum began the work and practice of opening her heart. Berrigan, in his poem, "Etty Hillesum," points to the astonishing result of her efforts:

"Here goes then," wrote this woman I never heard of.
And, "I don't want to be safe, I want to be there."
Wrote this woman.
She is like a God I never heard of.
She is like the bride I never married.
She is like a child I never conceived.
Like death? Death she heard of.
Death she walked toward, a child lost
in the glowering camps.
After years and years—recognition!
I heard a cry: "My child!"
The ineffaceable likeness, Death.
Her child, her semblance.
Wrote "In such a world I must kneel. Kneel down.
But before no human." In the furnace
lust and its cleansing, birth and its outcome.
To kneel where the fire burns me, bears me.
Eros, God, Auschwitz.
She wrote: "To live fully
outwardly, inwardly, my desire. But to renounce
reality for reality's sake, inner for outer life—
quite a mistake."
Wrote to her lover: "Dear spoiled man
Now I shall put on my splendid dressing gown
and read the Bible with you."

O singer of songs, O magnificat Mary
O woman at the well of life![40]

The woman at the well, according to the Gospel of John, asked that Jesus allow her to drink the water of life just once so that she would not have to return to the well again. In August 1943 Hillesum, writing to a friend while in Westerbork, related a conversation that took place within the camp: "When I went into the hospital barracks, some of the women called out, 'Have you got some good news? You look cheerful.'"[41] In the language of the camp, "good news" meant that one's call to be transported was postponed, that one was to be released soon from the camp, or that the war was soon to end. For Hillesum, however, the reason for her good cheer in the hospital barracks had simply been her sighting of a rainbow earlier that morning.[42] That her sighting of the rainbow could spark a blazing "inner light" speaks to her diligent practice of self-reflection and prayer commenced just over a year before her entrance into Westerbork. Like the woman of John's Gospel, Hillesum no longer needed to return to the well. She knew that within her—and each of us—flow the living waters of life.

Jan Gaarlandt, in his introduction to Hillesum's *An Interrupted Life* and *Letters from Westerbork*, notes that when Hillesum wrote her journal entries from 1941–42, "those were the very years when the scenario of extermination was being played out all over Europe. Etty Hillesum was Jewish and she wrote a counter scenario."[43] Hillesum's writing of a counter scenario was an act of responsibility and resistance. She discovered, however, that the process of writing and of self-clarification was difficult. It wasn't inertia that bogged her down but more feelings of shame, a lack of self-acceptance, and a lack of confidence. Further, she was beginning her study of self at a time when the world around her was drowning in a tide of death. In the summer of 1941, she wondered if the work of self-exploration was a selfish waste of time:

> So many of our most promising, vigorous men are dying day and night. I don't know how to take it. With all the suffering there is, you begin to feel ashamed of taking yourself and your moods so seriously. But you must continue to take yourself seriously, you must remain your own witness, marking well everything that happens in this world, never shutting your eyes to reality.[44]

In her book, *Enduring Lives: Portraits of Women of Faith and Action*, Carol Flinders suggests that Hillesum's practice of "marking everything well" became the basis of her spiritual practice, which was "not so much a systematic method of meditation [as it was] an assiduously cultivated moment-to-moment vigilance . . ."[45] In order to bear witness, Hillesum believed that she needed first to see and then surmount certain defensive postures, such as vanity. To surmount vanity simply means coming to terms with the "ordinariness" of one's life. Put another way, Hillesum wrote: "Life itself must be our fountainhead, never something or someone else."[46] Or, as Hillesum scholar Alexandra Pleshoyano writes, Hillesum "drew upon [even her understanding of God] her own distinctive way . . . 'You must learn to trust your own experiences, observations, and intuitions . . . rather than believe that you have to get everything out of a book.' "[47]

Hillesum, who held a law degree from the University of Amsterdam, who was pursuing a degree in Slavic languages from the Universities of Amsterdam and Leiden by 1941, and who planned to also study psychology was not adverse to learning from books. In addition to her studies of law and language, she passionately loved poetry and literature, particularly the poems of Rilke and the novels of Dostoevsky. It was, at least in part, the suffering she endured at the hands of the Nazis and those who supported their policies that propelled the development of her "own" voice. Hillesum formulated her development this way: "I will think through all so that I can see clearly in the 'workshop' of my head, but I will also feel and suffer all in the 'fiery furnace' of my heart.' "[48] Her constant and courageous effort to look "at everything that happens in this world" had begun to bear fruit; she had begun to open her heart.

Hillesum, as she chronicles in her journals, saw that "most people carry stereotyped ideas about life in their heads."[49] Her antidote to this malady was to "rid . . . all preconceptions, slogans, sense of security [and] find the courage to let go of everything, every standard, every conventional bulwark. Only then will life become infinitely rich and overflowing, even in the suffering it deals out to us."[50] Though she was only in her mid-twenties, her ability to "let go of everything" would most likely astonish the most seasoned of Zen masters. Reading her journals is like seeing a Zen *koan* come to life. I think here of the *koan* in which an esteemed professor, expressing an interest in learning about Zen, visits with Master Nan-in. Instead of answering questions about Zen, Nan-in pours the professor a cup of tea, and keeps pouring even though the tea has now overflowed the cup. Startled by this action, the professor asks Nan-in to stop pouring the tea. Nan-in does as the professor requests and then congratulates him on his insight: No one can learn Zen with a mind already full of "opinions and speculations."[51] For Hillesum, a blister on her foot was "her overflowing cup of tea." It awakened her to the fact that "intellectual powers alone do not get one very far when things get serious. The walk to and from the tax office taught me that."[52]

In a letter that she wrote in the spring of 1943, Hillesum asked a friend, "What does 'wise' mean to you?"[53] Looking to go beyond the typical response of "self-preservation at all costs," she continued to write: "All this talk of egoism is getting boring. Since people have been telling each other for centuries that man is basically an egoist, one actually begins to believe it and actually becomes egoistic. There are so many sides to a human being that it would be nice to try something else, just for a change."[54] Berrigan, while serving time in Danbury prison for the Catonsville Nine action, was also thinking along the lines of "doing something else," particularly when it comes to state matters: "Our sin is to parrot the state by our murderous treatment of one another, or to cherish like a death wish, a cancer in the bowels, our return to the 'normalcy' of the state—which is to say, the society in which murder is the daily round of activity."[55] The gift presented to the peacemaker in the biographies of Berrigan and Hillesum is the example of two people who made a steadfast and courageous effort to "break though the net," to make a clean break from the "stupefying effect of habit, inheritance and routine. To be the occasion of a fresh start for man, because he has made it for himself."[56] In addition, get a clear sense of what it means to actively love those who are suffering and to be in solidarity with them. Hillesum wrote of that kind of love and solidarity this way: "I believe that we can extract something positive from life under any circumstances. But we have the right to say that only if we do nothing to escape, even from the worst conditions. I often think we should shoulder our rucksacks, join others and go on transport with them."[57]

Methods of Nonviolent Resistance and Peacemaking

In this section of the essay, I focus upon three practices of nonviolent and peacemaking employed by Berrigan and Hillesum: a daily practice of prayer; the constant work of self-knowledge; and the nurturing of friendships and community life. I have chosen to focus upon these particular practices because, quite simply, they work and because these "quiet" but necessary practices are sometimes overlooked both by academics and activists. For Berrigan and Hillesum, however, nonviolent resistance and peacemaking are rooted in these practices. Further, they can be practiced at any moment, not just during an action of civil disobedience. Hillesum realized this early on in her young life. While experiencing a moment of self-pity after a day of mind-numbing typing and filing in Westerbork, she regained her equilibrium by reminding herself of the "real work" at hand: each of us must provide an alternative [e.g., to hatred, to killing, and so on], a dazzling and dynamic alternative with which to start afresh . . ."[58]

PRAYER, MEDITATION, AND STATE RELIGION

While serving time in Danbury prison for the Catonsville Nine action, Berrigan found the rigors of prison life to be mentally, emotionally and physically traumatizing. As he chronicles in his prison journal, *Lights On in the House of the Dead*, it seemed to him as if the "sky was falling in," for there were few of the external crutches around that we often use to keep ourselves going. Just about six years later, as he sat in jail with his brother Philip after being arrested for digging graves on federal property, Berrigan experiences a similar trauma but writes, "We're in deadlock: 24-hour lockup, two in a cell hardly large enough for one, sharing space with mice, rats, flies and assorted uninvited fauna. Food shoved in the door, filth, degradation. *And I wouldn't choose to be anywhere else on the planet. I think we've landed on turf where the breakthrough occurs.* I think it's occurred already"[59].

Though Berrigan chose to place himself in a position for a breakthrough to occur, would he be ready to receive the insights and the grace afforded by it? In every moment of our lives, "breakthroughs" are possible. These moments, which do not repeat themselves in exactly the same way, are often missed, be it in days crowded with activities and in minds crowded with thoughts. Is there a practice, then, that encourages the insight (or insights) afforded by the breakthrough to grow and develop within us? For Berrigan, the discipline of prayer is that practice. In *Lights on in the House of the Dead*, however, he wrote of prayer as "dead yeast."[60] If the God to whom you pray remains silent, wherein lays his hope? Berrigan, who went to prison because he would rather have "his hands manacled by the state as opposed to [allowing his] hands to pray over weapons of the state,"[61] found out that the world would have him silenced. In all of the silence of God and of the world, where are we to turn?

Berrigan refused to turn away from the present moment, even if that moment included suffering. He stayed put, "without fretfulness or complaint, or (above all) without constructing a future which is a cop-out from reality."[62] There is concreteness to a prayer life that has been chastened by suffering and steeped within the present moment; there are typically no flights of fancy, pious pap or lifeless abstractions. There is concreteness to Philip Berrigan's quip—often stated by Berrigan before an act of civil disobedience: "Hope is where your ass is." It turns out that to remain present, to not look for a way out, is the way to let others into our lives. For the Christian peacemaker, who is charged with the command to "love your enemies," there is no "outside" of the purview of the Good News.

In a poem and brief meditation on the seventy-sixth Psalm, Berrigan reminds us of the promises heralded by the Gospels: the poor will be assisted, the captive and the prisoner are to be set free, the hungry will receive sustenance, the blind will be able to see, and so on. He then asks whether we see Jesus taking sides against the wealthy, the jailers, the warmongers, and so on. His response, shaped by years of peacemaking, Biblical study, and prayer:

> We have to trust—in a century ridden with division, hatred, distrust—
> that in so acting, Jesus and God, His Father, were doing something
> more profitable to us, more significant, than merely taking sides.
> (What an abstract notion that is, after all, stale, fraught with jealousy,
> ego. Can we not offer something better to our times, to the people
> of the mid-70's, castaways, and survivors?)[63]

Hillesum often pointed out how much easier it was to hate; yet, she was determined to love. Berrigan says much the same. The peace activist takes stands, for example, "against war," not sides "against the wealthy," because essentially all are on the same side, the side called *life*. Death does not have the final say; the "dead man," Jesus, walked once again.[64] This is the Christian hope against all hope, and how Berrigan grounds a life of peacemaking in prayer.

This kind of hope is hard won. In his poem, "Come to Think of It, Hospital Is Another Working Metaphor for this Place," Berrigan first describes a visit he made to a dying woman as a young Jesuit and then the visits he made to the inmates of the Danbury prison hospital. In both instances, he is forced to reckon with prayer as "dry yeast":

> . . . wearily, half submerged in that icy pall,
> "The stitches broke in the night, I am dying."
> Factual: a weather report from the ravaged land and sea of her life
> A young priest unused
> to the uses of silence, close to tears,
> what could I summon? God's mercy?

A weak gesture, her moan
waved Him (and me) aside,
a malodorous fly in that foul place: "Don't speak to me of that;
the pain, the pain!"
Every morning I mount
twenty unbroken metallic steps to the prison hospital.
Twice a day, morning and night
The sick call lines up, 30 prisoners or so
pass muster under the eye
of the beefy ox administrator . . .
He tosses them right and left—
to relief, oblivion
Oblivion: "Say there where's yer copout?"
Relief: a high, a pill
A wide-screen pneumatic empty-brained
Grade C drive-in flick
Transfiguring transubstantiating
to visual spurts, spurious bliss—
prison, hospital
A piss stained rotting tenement wall
Indelibly daubed
"abandon hope."[65]

When Berrigan writes about prayer while in prison, he often writes of silence. As in the example of the dying woman, prayers of petition, for example, are waved away when one is awash in pain and consumed by suffering. Silence is the prayer of those who suffer, and the witness to such suffering learns how to be simply present. In a different sense, the "priceless gift of silence,"[66] was often lost amidst the raucous racket of the prison ward. The groans and screams of those who were "consigned to oblivion," who were seeking relief from the misery of the prison miasma often shattered the silence of the cells.[67] In Hillesum's journal, readers are privileged to witness one who learns how to kneel; in Berrigan's journals, we are witnesses to one who is "just beginning to learn to believe."[68] In the face of a silent God, he learns to keep going, in faith and with gratitude. Even though his acts of civil disobedience and time in prison may have "no noble outcome in the world,"[69] still Berrigan learns to "praise Him because He is silent, although He is silent. To serve His honor in a darkening world, which honors only death."[70] The prison cell, with its cacophony of neighboring yells, groans, and vulgarities, is his monastery; here he learns to appreciate the "encompassing power of a silence in which God is free (He must be free) to bring the future into being."[71]

In *Lights On in the House of the Dead*, Berrigan reflects upon the life and prayer of his friend and soul mate, Thomas Merton. In one of these reflections, he refers to Merton as the "very emperor of illogic, a Zen man who waited on God, who in the manner of a godlike man refused to interfere with the patient workings of the great Absent One."[72] To study Merton's life and practice of prayer may be of great benefit to the peacemaker. His way of seeing and praying is a way that Berrigan himself has learned from and mastered. The "Zen person" has the ability to see through the hustle and bustle of life: "He realized, I think, how little all the gigantic sums of talk, logic, effort, sweat, striving, machinations, reasonableness, prudence make . . ."[73] this, of course, may well be appreciated by the peacemaker for whom, when the weight of the world's oppression and suffering bears down, gives into the temptation to work at a frenzied and frantic pace. The "third eye" of Zen sees that, essentially, there is nothing going on, which is an insight that is entirely freeing and liberating once realized and integrated into one's being.

Of course, the silence of Zen is as loud as the roar of the lion—can you hear it? For Merton and Berrigan, and for Hillesum as well, the deep well of life is not diminished even in the most difficult of circumstances. This, for Berrigan, is what makes the example of Merton so compelling: "He put his ear to the ground and heard, as from a gigantic shell, the humming inwardness of the universe."[74] The energies of the peacemaker must be centripetal in nature, says Berrigan. Our ability to trespass on the state's land and being arrested rather than to worship the mighty weapons of the state must flow from this center, must register life's vitality. It is essential for the peacemaker to see this, for to break the "iron logic of Mars"[75] is to invoke the wrath of the State, the modern incarnation of this god. It may well be that the peacemaker, if she chooses this path, will be "broken, discredited and punished—so that the war itself may proceed on its bloody and tragic course."[76] Will we have the fortitude to remain praying and to remain standing? Will we have the strength to see through the logic of the state and break free from the grip of its religion, a religion that sanctions war?

When Dr. Martin Luther King Jr. offered his appraisal of mainstream American Christianity during times of war, he said:

> In a world gone mad with arms buildups, chauvinistic passions
> and imperialistic exploitation, the church has either endorsed these

activities or remained appallingly silent . . . national churches even functioned as lackeys of the state, sprinkling holy water upon battleships and joining mighty armies in singing: "Praise the Lord and pass the ammunition."[77]

Berrigan, in his writings, agrees with King's assessment. Each of these men paid the price for unwillingness to go along with a church aligned with a war-making state; King paid with his life, Berrigan with a number of years in prison. In *Lights On in the House of the Dead*, he writes a rather moving reflection on the reasons why it is necessary for the peace activist to pay up. He starts by working through his own reading of Plato's *Apology* and puts forth his thoughts in the manner of a Socratic dialogue: "Can the just man survive the state? Socrates: He ought not to care. What can the just man do when falsely accused? Answer as best he can. What can the just man do? Pay the price. What about his wife and family? Think of justice first."[78]

In a letter that Berrigan wrote to the Weathermen, a student activist community who opted to use violence as a means of protest during the Vietnam War, he makes clear that "no principle is worth the sacrifice of a single human being."[79] When Berrigan claims that the "just person" will turn away from family and friends, he is not saying that we are to live in "splendid" isolation. In fact, a good part of his letter to the Weathermen—as well as in much of his other writings—constantly emphasizes the importance of being deeply connected with other human beings. When, for the sake of justice, we turn away from family and friends, we do so because we refuse "to place one's well-being, good time, expectations of shortened imprisonment ahead of the iron course of injustice toward others. The gods of the state are, after all, the inflated ego of power, technology, money in the rake's progress, dragging all before the abyss."[80] In his essay, "To Limbo and Back: A Latin American Exile," he suggests that a life of faith and prayer teaches us how to be human and nothing else. Hope is found, in large part, in the life of the community we build with one another, something that both Berrigan and Hillesum saw clearly and took seriously.

The Hard Work of Self-Knowledge

In "An Ethic of Resurrection," Berrigan points to the Gospel's clarity for a Christian way of being in the world: "Blessed are the peacemakers; Love your enemies, do good to those who do ill to you; Peter, put up your sword . . ."[81] He also notes that these commands are often the "first casualty of war."[82] They are also the first casualties in our daily living with one another, even in living with "ourselves". Hillesum thought as much, and considered the possibility that war stemmed from our inability to see and work through an interior confusion. In a March 1942 journal entry, she wrote: "All disasters stem from us. Why is there war? Perhaps because now and then I might be inclined to snap at my neighbor. Because I and my neighbor and everyone else do not have enough love . . . ."[83]

At the time that Hillesum describes the flaring up of anger toward one's neighbor, she was well aware that "the whole of Europe [was] gradually becoming one great prison camp"[84] and that the Nazis wanted nothing less than the "complete destruction"[85] of the Jewish people. In the close to seven hundred pages of her journal entries and letters, however, there are no hate-filled diatribes against the Nazis and the German people. In fact, she was determined to "take the field against hatred."[86] There are certainly expressions of moral indignation, anguish, despair, and stretches of depression, but what more often fills the pages of her journals is evidence of the effort to pay attention to what is going on "inside" of herself. The more Hillesum paid attention to herself, the more capacious that self became, so much so that she writes, near the end of her life, "we should be willing to act as a balm for all wounds."[87] It must be evident, of course, that when Hillesum writes of "paying attention," she is not speaking of a narcissistic self-absorption. She, like Gandhi, is engaged in a rigorous and self-tested "experiment in truth."

One of Hillesum's gifts to contemporary peacemakers is the written record of her practice of paying attention and an interior transformation. By reading through her almost daily journal entries, we are able to trace the transformation of one who, at first, is often overwhelmed by an inner feeling of being "tightly bound" to one who, while looking at rain-ruined jasmine blossoms one year later, says "somewhere inside of me the jasmine continues to blossom undisturbed, just as profusely and delicately as it ever did. And it spreads its scent round the House in which You dwell, oh God."[88] Though her later journal entries still record moments of doubt, despair, and fatigue, she describes her pervasive inner feelings as those of tranquility, radiance, receptivity, and simplicity. "We must forget all our big words," she writes, "begin with God and end with Death, and we must become as simple as spring water."[89]

However tempting it is to be carried aloft by the sheer beauty and poetry of the "jasmine passage," one would have to skip over the internal ground that Hillesum plowed in order for such beauty to blossom forth. A few entries prior to that one finds her writing about the ease with which she navigates life's bigger questions but the difficulty she still finds handling petty concerns. Three days after writing about the "jasmine within," she wrote that the crux of suffering for most people was a "lack of inner preparation,"[90] and then added, "before they even step foot in camp."[91] It is her second point that may catch one up short: How could Hillesum speak to a "lack of inner preparation" when the cause of the Jewish suffering was the political, social, and military actions of the Nazis?

Her emphasis upon the work of inner preparation does not ignore external realities. Hillesum's point is that we pay inordinate attention to the external at the expense of what's going on internally.[92] When this imbalance occurs, there is a consequent tendency to separate ourselves from life and from one another. In February 1942 Hillesum wrote of a conversation between her and her friend, Jan Bool. Bool asked rhetorically, "What is it in human beings that makes them want to destroy others?"[93] Her response was to remind Bool that he, too, was a human being and that the only answer to such a question was to "turn inward and root out all rottenness."[94] Hillesum, like Dostoevsky's Zossima, was acutely sensitive to self-deception and actively worked on "not lying to herself." She understood just how high the stakes were in this kind of work: "Nazi barbarism evokes the same kind of barbarism in ourselves, one that involves the same methods if we could do what we wanted right here and now."[95]

Another dimension of inner preparation is that of acceptance. In Hilesum's case, it was the acceptance of suffering and of an early death. She began this work by learning how to listen. Rather poignantly, she referred to the practice of listening as one of *hineinhorchen*.[96] Though she did not translate the German *hineinhorchen*, she described it as the act of "listen[ing] very intently, with my whole being . . . at the end of the day I feel like a patient farmer who has once again ploughed an infinitely small piece of the great field of the spirit."[97]

Through the practice of *hineinhorchen*, she built enough of a base to begin working on "the art of suffering," which she believed many in the West were unable to do. Most saw suffering beneath their ken or had turned away from the reality of death. They had given up their lives "to a thousand fears instead."[98] For Hillesum, the acceptance of suffering and death was the only way we would be able to live fully. How is this to be done? Simply by seeing beyond the narrowness of the ego and into the vastness of life itself:

> I am in Poland every day on the battlefield . . . I often see visions of
> poisonous green smoke. I am with the hungry and the ill treated, and
> the dying every day, but I am also with the jasmine and with the piece

of sky beyond my window; there is room enough for everything in a single life. For belief in God and for a miserable end.[99]

Community Life

When Hillesum wrote that we must "pray for all suffering people," she included the German people among them. In one of the last entries in *Lights On in the House of the Dead*, Berrigan, in accord with Matthew's Gospel, casts a critical glance toward the "absolute primacy of the bloodline."[100] For the Gospel writer and for Berrigan, God's will is first and all else flows from that; we simply learn to "move with one another in the movement of life."[101] Right relationships with other human beings were refined and mastered in community and often beyond our immediate circle of family and friends. While they both write of solid, loving, and numerous ties with family and friends, they also write of a communal embrace of the stranger and of the enemy. I do not wish to be sentimental here.[102] The ties that bound them to family, friends, strangers, and enemies were often forged through struggle. At times, the rightness of the relationship broke down. What remains constant, however, is a commitment to stand with other human beings.

In this section on life in community, I focus upon Hillesum's effort to put her dictum, "We must be a balm for all wounds," into practice. In some instances, this meant nothing more than serving lukewarm coffee to her fellow Jews in Westerbork. Her being fully present in the act of serving others, however, made it seem as if she were handing out gold coins instead of coffee. I also draw attention to Berrigan's commitment to the formation and forging of nonviolent communities of resistance. According to Philip Berrigan, such communities were a means of answering the question, "How does one maintain fidelity to God and to sisters and brothers when the overwhelming weight of culture, institutional religion, and official Statecraft locks one into unbelief and alienation?"[103] In my nearly twenty-year involvement with the Kairos community, I have found that to engage in civil disobedience, to risk arrest, and to sustain a prayerful life of peacemaking is just about impossible outside of community life.

In an early journal entry, we find Hillesum working to build community amongst the Jews, Christians, Germans, Dutch friends, students, and widower with whom she lived. She worked not only to build community but also worked to make sure that it flourished. This task, even her small and local community, was difficult at times:

Ours was and is a bustling little world, so threatened by politics from the outside as to be disturbed within. But it seems a worthy task to keep this small community together as a refutation of all of those desperate and false theories of race, nation, and so on. As proof that life cannot be set into pre-set molds.[104]

Hillesum's worthy yet modest task of community building well served those she later came to meet in Westerbork. It seems a modest effort, I suppose, to work on building community when a war of extermination is being waged. However, in the midst of the Nazi storm, Hillesum was able to hold her ground, to keep doing what she had always been doing: "When a hungry child [in Westerbork] started crying, I would go over to them, stand beside them protectively, arms folded across my chest [and] force a smile from those huddled, shattered scraps of humanity . . . And all I did was just stand there, for what else could one do?"[105] In "just standing there," Hillesum stood on the side of humanity and on the side of life. In her refusal to hate and to kill, I once again hear Berrigan's poetic cry of praise, "O, woman at the well of life!"

After a few months in Westerbork, Hillesum had every reason to shut down. Aside from the horrifying conditions within the camp, she was often physically sick, many of her friends were dead or were soon to be sent to Auschwitz, and her parents and brother were now interned with her. It was precisely at this moment, however, that she chose to widen the community of those she loved. She did so by setting for herself the work of being the "thinking heart of these barracks" and then, "the thinking heart of a whole concentration camp."[106] When she first started writing in her journal, she noted that she often found that she had little time for the daily tasks of life and for others. She came to realize, however, that the feeling of "not having any time" was not so much literally true as it was more an indication of her chaotic and fragmented inner state. Now, in the final months of her life, she found that she had "all the time in the world"[107] to talk with others, to be present with them. Hillesum well put to use her practices of interior knowledge and transformation and community building beyond the scope that she had ever imagined was possible—no one and no place was excluded. In the midst of the worst at Westerbork, Hillesum was able to say: "I feel at home. I have learned so much about it here. We are 'at home.'"[108]

After the Catonsville Nine action, Berrigan reports that he often felt most "at home" in communities of resistance. He goes as far as to say that "the more I move around, the more I realized that whatever I do should be judged in relationship to these communities."[109] In *The Raft Is Not the Shore*, a series of conversations between Berrigan and the Buddhist master and peace activist, Thich Nhat Hahn, he best articulates what he means by a "community of resistance." Such communities, many of which were not opposed to the use of violence, germinated in the protest and social movements of the 1960s. The roots of nonviolent communities of resistance, Berrigan suggests, were found primarily, though not exclusively, in religious and faith-based communities.[110] Post-Catonsville, activists realized that one person acting alone or that one action alone was not enough to seriously disrupt institutional and systemic oppression and violence. The very act of preparing for the Catonsville trial, for example, where needs of housing, support for families of the defendants, and so on, had to be met, provided the impetus to found communities dedicated to resistance as a way of life.[111]

A communal life of resistance loosens the grip of the "demonic" on us, says Berrigan. His reading of the Gospel's "possession stories" speak to him of people and institutions who are enthralled, perhaps unconsciously so, by worldly powers, which includes everything from the inflated ego to the bomb-wielding nuclear state. Resistance is one means of dispossession. Though we tend to view exorcisms as the subject of horror films these days, Berrigan suggests that there is something to be learned from Biblical stories of "being possessed" and "the act of dispossessing." What we are dealing with is nothing less than "invasion, loss of the soul, loss of self-understanding on the part of many modern people. In the form of almost madness, one is invaded by the demonic values of this world and runs with them."[112] Community building is an act of liberation and an act of love.

Communities of resistance respond modestly to a world gone mad. Modesty must not be understood to mean a half-hearted or less-than-inspired response. It means that one responds to the world neither as "super-human" nor "sub-human" but as human. It means that one does not need either fame or fortune to keep going. It means that a life of prayer, interior reflection and action are enough to sustain you for the long haul of resistance and peace making. It means that when you have found "good bread," you share it with others and in service to them. As Berrigan puts it so beautifully: "The bread is good bread, and precisely for that reason, it is meant to be broken, shared abroad. And this is not a matter of grudging diminution. Good bread declares in odor, and taste, and texture, I am for you. Take and eat."[113]

Conclusion

"To live fully,"[114] a phrase often repeated by Hillesum and also cited by Berrigan in his poem about her life, requires, paradoxically, that we learn to accept suffering and death. It is this acceptance that curbs the human propensity to inflict upon others what we refuse to accept ourselves. After reading through John Paul II's *Evangelium vitae*, it would not be possible to deny the great magnitude of suffering in the world. More so, it is impossible to deny that much of this suffering we inflict upon one another, whether it be through warfare, economic, political, and environmental exploitation, or social alienation. Pope Benedict's *Easter Address* points to the revolutionary move we must make: speak truthfully about the culture of death, love your enemies and begin the work of nonviolence. Berrigan and Hillesum, in an inordinate way, show us what active, nonviolent, revolutionary love looks like. They disarmed themselves, and then made it their work to disarm the world. They have shown us how to breathe new live into the ancient practices of inner clarity, prayer and meditation, and community life. In so doing, they have shown us how to be Christian and how to be human. For this, we may be deeply grateful. Now the work of active love and nonviolence is up to each of us; may we all benefit from the incandescence of their example.

Self-Appropriation and Liberation:
Philosophizing in the Light of Catonsville

James L. Marsh

> Our apologies   good friends for the fracture
> of good order   the burning of paper
> instead of children   the angering of the orderlies
> in the front parlor of the charnel house
> We could not   so help us God   do otherwise
> For we are sick at heart   our hearts
> give us no rest for thinking of the Land of Burning Children
> and for thinking of that other Child of whom
> the poet Luke speaks.[1]

These words, of course, are from *The Trial of the Catonsville Nine*, written by Daniel Berrigan. The words are uttered by the character Daniel Berrigan in the trial of himself and eight others, who entered the draft board in Catonsville, Maryland, removed hundreds of draft files, poured blood on them, and burned them with homemade napalm. It was an act of nonviolent, civil disobedience that called into question not only the Vietnam War but also the growing identification of the Catholic, Christian religious consciousness with the secular, war-making state and economy. The Catholic Church in the 1960s moved from being a marginalized, ghetto church to being mainstream American, fully part of the secular city. And there was much joy and celebration and self-congratulation among American Catholics about this phenomenon. Is it not great to be part of and to participate in the American Dream in the greatest, most powerful nation in the world? And Catholic universities followed suit in the great celebration.

For many thousands of Catholics, Christians, and other religious people, and I include myself here, Catonsville made all of this problematic. A big question mark emerged about the celebration. What if the American

Dream is in fact, to a significant extent, a nightmare? What if the price of human affluence is more and more men and women coming home in body bags? What kind of unhappiness lurks behind the superficial happiness promised by Madison Avenue, and what kind of ugliness lurks behind the pleasing, commodified images of Hollywood? Is there a danger of Catholics and Christians, even those who are liberal, being too uncritically pro-American in a way that implicitly or explicitly violates their moral and religious consciences? Summing up all of these questions into one, the main question that emerges from the play for me is this: "How do we live as human beings, citizens, philosophers, and Christians of conscience in the midst of the most virulent empire in history?" And to add a few evidential indicators on that point, we might note the more than twenty million people a year who die in the Third World due to structurally induced starvation, the three billion out of six billion on the planet who are forced to live on less than two dollars a day, the 1.2 billion who live on less than 1 dollar a day, and the virtually worldwide extent of the American empire under President Bush.[2] What previous imperialists like Alexander, Caesar, Napoleon, or Hitler could only dream about is within our reach. Many in the United States celebrate this state of affairs enthusiastically, but we as philosophers by our very calling should keep our distance and be more critical. Is this situation something to be celebrated or mourned, praised or condemned, supported or resisted? Is this global domination compatible with our philosophical, Christian consciences or incompatible?

Berrigan, from a prophetic, religious, and biblical perspective, argues incompatibility, and that is his challenge to us. His play is prophetic in a couple of ways: first, about the injustice of the Vietnam war, and second, about the kind of country the United States was more and more turning into—more militaristic, more consumerist, exploitative, and imperialistic. And how can we deny that, almost forty years later, we have become, or are several further steps along the way to becoming, precisely the kind of nation he was warning us against? Two wars in the Golf, the self-contradictory terroristic war against terrorism in Afghanistan, and the problematic intervention in Kosovo are indications of this point. The United States and the US-led empire have within their grasp worldwide domination, hegemony, and exploitation.

Berrigan's play from above, from a prophetic religious viewpoint, challenges us as human beings, philosophers, and Christians to philosophize in its light. What would it be like to philosophize in the light of Catonsville? If, as he says, Christianity in its full prophetic reach is incompatible with capitalism and imperialism, then what would a consistent Catholic philosophy look like? And by *Catholic* I mean the state of philosophy at Catholic universities and colleges and, more specifically, a tradition of *philosophia perennis* that has developed from Plato to Aristotle to Augustine to Aquinas to Maritain and Lonergan. My recommendation in my 2002 Plenary Session Address, "Justice, Difference, and the Possibility of Metaphysics: Toward a North American Philosophy of Liberation," was that a new step has to be taken to respond to the destructiveness of the New World Disorder.[3] Philosophical reason has to become formally practical and transformative as well as contemplative and speculative, and the most adequate content for such a practical reason is radical, not liberal or conservative. This rationality linked to radicalism is threefold: a self-appropriation leading horizontally to an ethical-social critique of capitalism, and vertically to a metaphysics, philosophy of religion, and liberation theology grounding a critique and overcoming of neo-imperialism. This triple rationality and radicalism is based on and flows from self-appropriation. As I state in one of my earlier books, *Radical Fragments*, "To think and to think radically—the phrase is redundant."[4]

Already some indications are emerging for you of how I think philosophy needs to respond to the Berriganian challenge. As I began to work out my own perspective, especially in the trilogy *Post-Cartesian Meditations, Critique, Action, and Liberation*, and *Process, Praxis, and Transcendence* when I came to Fordham in 1985 and began to meet and get to know Berrigan, the man, and his students, disciples, and colleagues, I experienced a strange shock of recognition as I began to sense that Berrigan and his witness were at least part of what my work was leading up to and pointing to philosophically, social theoretically, metaphysically, and religiously. Even though my own work is in my own voice, if I were to describe it in terms of persons and thinkers who have deeply influenced me, the trajectory would be from Lonergan as the father of self-appropriation to Berrigan as the author of *The Trial of the Catonsville Nine*. And perhaps, in between the two, Marx as the father of critical social theory. From Lonergan through Marx to Berrigan—two Jesuits and an atheist.

When I arrived at Fordham in 1985, I felt that I needed to confront the great speculative, contemplative Jesuits there like Gerald McCool and Norris Clarke, giants both, learning from them but also challenging them and myself to come up with a more adequate conception of philosophy linking theory to praxis, contemplation to action, celebratory wondering articulation of the world to relentless critique of the world. One of these great Jesuits, John Courtney Murray, who had passed away by the time I arrived, already practiced and embodied this unity of theory and praxis in works like *The Problem of God* and *We Hold These Truths*. But my sense was and is that now we need something like *We Hold These Radical Truths* and that the "we" is not and should not be liberal-conservative Catholics happily at one with the secular city but a radical community on the way to liberation. And the mediating links between theory and praxis need to be worked out more than Murray has done. Perhaps, I thought, what troubles Catholic universities in the theory and practice of justice is a one-sided contemplative conception at the heart of the academic enterprise itself, such that the theory and praxis of justice seemed relatively external to and marginal to serious academic work. And maybe as a philosopher I could do something about that.

As I also wrote in 2002, this triple rationality and its link with radicalism does not deny the legitimacy of any subdiscipline in philosophy, and all or most are present in my three books. But a necessary, legitimate, contemplative element in philosophy has to be complemented by a practical, critical, transformative element. This link between contemplation and action is also affirmed by Berrigan on a religious prophetic level.[5] I argue, for example, for a legitimate, necessary, contemplative openness to the mystery of the natural, human, marginalized, ontological, and religious other, but also that the contemplative articulation has to be complemented by a critique of the socio-economic system that tends to do in that otherness, exploit it, marginalize it, deny it, kill it. And do we reflect practically upon the fate of the natural, poor, dispossessed, and marginalized other in the First World and in the Third World? We can do so only if we are open to the other contemplatively and practically and commit ourselves to a theoretical-practical praxis of liberation from capitalism and empire and militarism, the major enemies of otherness in our time.

What I am going to do in this essay is to respond to Berrigan's challenge from above by formulating a philosophical, social-theoretical response from below attempting to do justice to his questions and his insights. This effort will have three aspects. First, I will undertake a Socratic, existential questioning of our particular national and international situation since 2001, moving from the war and occupation of Iraq to the legal and moral reasons for the wrongness of that effort and finally to the structure of empire that underlies it and that has been with us for many decades. This effort contrasts with my more abstract account of 2002 and presumes that as premise and context. Second, along the way, as the essay proceeds, my thought will interact with Berrigan's in a way that, I hope, is mutually fructifying and beneficial. Finally, at the very end of my paper, my thought joins his and comes together with it. A liberatory philosophy and social theory from below meets a liberatory, prophetic theology from above, and what emerges is a philosophy and theology of liberation of and from the *imperial center*, not the periphery, like Dussel's.

Just as such a philosophy-theology includes but goes beyond previous spiritual and speculative theologies as a more adequate response to our present situation, so my effort criticizes a liberal and conservative ethical-political stance and goes beyond them. While liberalism and conservatism have valid aspects to them, they are judged inadequate because they do not move to a critique of capitalist, militaristic imperialism in principle and thus end up supporting it and tolerating it: and they, liberalism and conservatism, are deficient as social theories because they do not theorize empire in all of its complex rationality and irrationality. By liberalism and conservatism, I mean simply thinkers who support an interventionist welfare state versus those who do not—think Rawls and Nozick. An example of a liberal social theorist, enormously insightful but also deficient in the above sense, is Jürgen Habermas, and an example of a conservative social theorist is Milton Friedman.

I find it important at the beginning of this paper to stress the singular, the individual, and the existential. My attention is on the role of the philosopher rather than philosophy or "philosophy as such." Where do I, Jim Marsh, as this unique philosopher situated in this time and place, stand? Do I stand somewhere, do I pay up for my beliefs, do I speak out, to use a few phrases from Daniel Berrigan, or do I remain quiet, apolitical, aloof, getting on with professional business as usual? "Don't rock the boat." There is a link in his thought between the existential individual and social critique and action that parallels and inspires my own. In my work, this individual aspect is linked always to universal aspects. Self-appropriation is not an act performed by any anonymous subject, by any Tom, Dick, or Harry, but by me, Jim Marsh, as I discover and affirm and choose to know, and be faithful to the exigencies of the pure desire to know. And transcendental method is the explicit experiencing, understanding, judging, and choosing of myself as an experiencing, understanding, judging, and choosing subject in relation to being.[6]

A merely speculative, contemplative philosophy is incomplete even as philosophy. When crisis takes the form of war, as it does now, then, because truth is the first casualty of war, speaking the truth in my own voice becomes an especially important task. And, as I will argue, correlated to the fallible, self-appropriated, self-knowing individual is the dispossessed, marginalized, alienated, exploited other, especially the Third World other. Self-appropriation leads to solidarity with this other and to nonsolidarity with the capitalistic, imperialistic system that exploits and marginalizes this other. Within contemporary academe, the former point is more readily and easily acknowledged than the latter.

Drawing on Lonergan's four transcendental precepts—be attentive, be intelligent, be reasonable, and be responsible—which correspond to the fundamental levels of experience, understanding, judgment, and decision, we could specify and amplify the fourth precept by saying, "speak up," "stand somewhere," "speak truth to and about power," or, more colloquially, "raise hell." And part of that speaking up is questioning false claims and equations such as the equation of the terror directed against us on 9/11 with terror as such. This, as Chomsky points out, is mere retail terror directed by the oppressed against the oppressor, the pirate against the emperor. The more destructive kind of terror is wholesale terror, the terror of the emperor and the oppressor, against the Third World. And one crucial task of the philosopher at all times, but especially in times of crisis, is to make such distinctions.[7] Speaking the truth, then, should be our own task as philosophers in all times, but especially in bad times, because truth is a scarce commodity in such times. Is it any surprise that this speaking of truth is also the task of Christians as Berrigan conceives them: "Unsealing, unmasking, revealing, these are affairs of the truth, of God. Need one add, of ourselves? . . . The unmasking of the Big Lie is a characteristic of Christian activity in bad times: or ought to be."[8] And if such unmasking is necessarily prophetic, is not that claim true of philosophers also, especially of Christian, Catholic philosophers? To our work of contemplatively and theoretically disclosing the truth *positively*, do we not all need to denounce critically and prophetically violations of that truth *negatively*? And if we are passionate lovers of the truth, if our hearts have not grown cold, should not such violations make us angry, make us mourn, make us weep? Berrigan's religious, prophetic critique, then, reminds us of and recalls us philosophers to our own proper work, the rigorous, relentless, no-holds-barred critique of everything that exists.

There is little doubt that we are a nation and world in crisis. The United States, the most powerful state in history, has proclaimed loud and clear that it intends to rule the world by force, a dimension in which it reigns supreme. This kind of behavior puts us in very uncomfortable moral and political territory, a territory shared with the great tyrants and dictators of history such as Alexander, Caesar, Napoleon or Hitler. Unlike these past leaders, we have imperial world domination within our grasp. What they could only dream about we are in the process of realizing. For my part, I am struck by the horror of what the United States has been doing to itself and the world the last four years since 9/11. Just think of these names, places, and dates: Abu Ghraib, Guantánamo, Fallujah, Baghdad, "Shock and Awe," the Patriot Act, the Homeland Security Act, Karl Rove and what he did to Valerie Plame, November and December in Florida in 2000, the Downing Street Memo. Berrigan's works express a prophetic outrage over what was being done in our name and voice in the 1960s. What would it take for us as philosophers to feel a similar prophetic outrage over what is being done now? If you are not angry, you are not paying attention.

Such a situation is readily applauded by many who glory in such expansion, but we as philosophers need to think about this issue ethically and politically. If such expansion is unjust for many different reasons, as I will show, then critique is appropriate, not approval; mourning, not celebration; and resistance, not collaboration and support. And it is the task of the radical philosopher, as I have defined it for myself, who goes all the way with reason in that he allows reason to be fully radical, to question and remove his own blinders and those of others and to be publicly critical of such injustice, relentlessly, in season and out of season.

Has the United States ever been at a lower point morally and ethically and politically? Empire, of course, is not a new reality in our nation since we have been pursuing empire for a few hundred years, but it has never been pursued with such brazen arrogance, with such open contempt for national and international law, with such disregard for the opinion of allies, with such manifest aggressiveness, and with so little justification for anything resembling a just, defensive war.

The war in Iraq was, first of all, an illegal war, in violation of our own constitution, because Congress did not declare war; and in violation of the UN Charter, which forbids wars of aggression and requires the Security Council to approve any intervention. This is just the most recent instance of the United States functioning as a "rogue state" outside the limits of law, much more than states like Iraq that we have condemned in the past and present for functioning that way. Consider our mining of the harbor in Nicaragua in the 1980s, which was condemned by the World Court and which we ignored, and the wars in Afghanistan and Yugoslavia undertaken without UN approval.

In a way that should displease liberals, the war and occupation are also unjust in many different ways. And while I am sympathetic to the pacifist point that a war cannot be just because of the destructiveness of modern weapons, it is instructive to consider the ways in which this war is unjust. The real purpose of the war, that of aggressive, imperial expansion and control of oil, into which I will go later, is an unjust purpose and thus violates the just end principle. As Germany and France insisted, violence was not being used here as a last resort; inspections in Iraq looking for nuclear weapons were working. Why not give them more time? There was no proportionality between legitimate positive effects and negative effects such as damage to environment through use of depleted uranium, civilian infrastructure, water systems, electrical systems, and so on. Reports indicate there was no serious attempt to respect the distinction between combatants and noncombatants, no declaration by legitimate authority, and no morally legitimate means, because the weapons are so destructive. Because the end of the war was unjust, all of its intended effects were unjust, and the first innocent civilian killed made the war illegitimately disproportional. In my opinion, then, the war violates all of the criteria of just war theory. It does not even come close. And because the war was unjust, the occupation is also.

The most comprehensive account of the irrationality and wrongness of the war is that it was an imperial war. Its illegality and its injustice were aspects and effects of the imperial intent of the war. As one person said about the 1990–91 Gulf War, the real story about the war is how our oil came to be under their ground. Such imperial expansion violates a prima facie moral intuition that the raw material, labor, resources, and economic, social, and political institutions of a country should be under the control of the people of that country and redound to their benefit. When some "unreasonable" people like Castro of Cuba or Allende of Chile or Ortega of Nicaragua begin to insist on the legitimacy of that intuition, then they have to be demonized. Political, economic, and social pressure is brought to bear on the government, and when all else fails, we send in the marines. That scenario has been enacted literally hundreds of times by the United States in the last two hundred years.[9] When the Third World other ceases to function as a means to First World well-being and begins to question and resist such a state of affairs, then that other has to be put down, demonized, attacked, and, if necessary, murdered.

What is imperialism? Imperialism or neo-imperialism is simply capitalism transplanted abroad in search of markets, raw materials, cheap or cheaper labor, indulgent, supportive governments, and lower taxes. The New World Order (NWO) is a neo-imperial system with linked, internally related aspects: multinational corporations, US military might as an enforcer of last resort to insure that what we say goes, international organizations like the International Monetary Fund (IMF) and World Bank functioning to keep the Third World in thrall to First World capital, corrupt local monarchies and oligarchies like those currently running Guatemala and

Colombia kept in power by the United States and supportive of US aims against the interests of their own people, rich, landowning capitalist classes in the Third World that exploit and oppress the poor, and police and military officers trained by the United States in the latest technologies of repression, terror, and torture in places like Fort Benning, Georgia's School of the Americas, nicknamed by its victims in Central and Latin America "the School of Assassins." Many of the officers participating in the 1991 Haiti coup and subsequent repressive rule, the assassination of Romero in El Salvador, and the El Mozote massacre in El Salvador are star pupils and graduates of this school.

The basic point or goal of this imperial structure, we could say, using and drawing on Chomsky, is the Fifth Freedom: the right of US, Japanese, and European corporations to rob, kill, repress, and exploit indigenous peoples with impunity. Other freedoms—as our sponsoring of intervention after intervention against democratic governments in Guatemala (1954), the Dominican Republic (1966), Chile (1973), Nicaragua (1980s), and Haiti (1991) indicates—we are quite ready to jettison when they do not serve or when they endanger the Fifth Freedom. Indeed Chomsky and Herman in another work have shown an empirical correlation between increasing terror and denial of democracy in Third World countries and increasing US aid. As terror in Colombia rapidly increased in the last few years, US aid shot up dramatically.[10]

Dussel, using Marx, states that the goal of the NWO is the international transfer from South to North of surplus value, that is, labor time for which labor is not paid. The goal of capitalism in general as private ownership and control of the means of production is to produce and extract such surplus value. Hundreds of billions of dollars per year are transferred from Third World to First World countries, while the poor majorities in those countries starve. Such transfers occur through such mechanisms as debt payments to US banks, the World Bank, and the IMF.[11]

Surplus value is the basis of capitalist profit. Value is the average, socially necessary amount of labor time required to produce a product, and is the basis for exchange of equivalents in circulation. Surplus value cannot arise in circulation because, as a rule, equivalents are exchanged. Therefore, surplus value can only arise in the productive sphere either from means of production or labor. But means of production, which includes instruments and materials of production, can only transfer to the product value what they already contain and cannot be the source of surplus value. Consequently surplus value can only arise from labor working more time than the time for which it is actually paid. Because surplus value as the basis for capitalist profit is inherent in capitalism itself, capitalism is inherently exploitative, unjust. Liberal or conservative reformism can mitigate the amount or degree of this exploitation, but cannot remove it entirely.[12] And while capitalism has achieved some good things such as increased productivity and, as linked to political and social institutions, increased awareness of the dignity of the individual, human rights, and democracy, these achievements are always in tension with and overwhelmed by the bad things such as alienation, domination, and exploitation. And even the good things are so badly distributed that most people do not adequately benefit. Thus the "rich, many-sided individual" that Marx sees capitalism as creating the conditions for is prevented from emerging, for the most part, by the social structure of capitalism itself.

What about, someone might object, the supposed "economic miracles" that have occurred in Central and Latin America in the last fifteen to twenty years? Have the people in those countries not benefited? The general answer to this objection is that the top one or two percent of the wealthy in these countries benefit, but that the fortunes of the poor majorities in those countries have not only not been helped but have worsened. During the 1980s US investments in Latin America were heavy; the result was 230 billion dollars transferred to the United States through debt service, dividends, and profits. The results for most Latin Americans have been disastrous. Over half the population, 222 million people, now live in poverty, 70 million more than in 1980.[13]

My own account argues for an internal link between capitalistic imperialism and militarism. Such a link is also asserted by Berrigan:

> If everything has a price, and everyone, it follows, that the price is—everyone and everything. The market subsumes creation, seizes on all reality: values, religion, fruit of the earth, humans themselves. And to protect, secure, and enlarge this empery, this mad Croesus, war is necessary, inevitable.
>
> At this point, property possesses its possessors; it has become simply idolatrous. And by the same token the human is devalued to the point of absolute contempt. Property and war: Those who wage war in defense of property also dispose of great numbers of noncombatants, the aged, women, children. These have become expendable. They are known to the sycophants of Mars as nothing more than "collateral damage."[14]

These words of Berrigan express, confirm, and develop much of what I have been trying to say here and in my 2002 essay: the internal link between capitalism and war, empire and war; the tendency on the part of empire to subordinate and sacrifice everything to the pursuit of wealth and profit; the tendency of the capitalistic empire to fetishize itself, becoming an object of worship, on which altar millions of victims are sacrificed every year; the tendency of property to alienate us from our own humanity and to possess its possessor, tempting us to confuse being with having; the inevitable tendency of the capitalist empire to marginalize unjustly the poor, colored people, women, working people, and the destitute. To take these words seriously is to see how inadequate liberal or conservative efforts are to reform such an inhumane system. It makes as much sense to talk about reforming slavery—a kinder, gentler slavery—or reforming fascism or reforming apartheid.

In a way similar to Marx, Berrigan asks us to think about the "universal prostitution" of everything human under the reign of capital, commodity fetishism in which a relationship between human beings takes the form of a relationship between things. "I am what I make." But in a way very different from Marx, Berrigan invites us to think religiously and biblically about other noneconomic realities as similarly fetishized and divinized, for example, "Lord Nuke."

> I sought the name of the genius who ran the press and composed its
> message. I came up with the name: Lord Nuke. And in naming him,
> I came on a biblical secret. Naming the beast, breaking the code, was
> also the prelude to any turnabout, any hope: to whatever good news
> one could create. Once the beast was named, one noted with relief how
> the mind was cleansed of false names, those by which the beast deceived
> all. The masks came down: normalcy, security, national interest, family
> values, legitimate defense, just war, flag, mother, democracy, leadership,
> religion. The beast stood there. He was naked and known. More: once
> named, he was also in chains.[15]

What, then, are the real reasons for this war and occupation? We should note here that capitalist empires, like all empires, lie, especially in times of war. We can generally assume that the reasons given for the war are not the real reasons but are ideological and propagandistic, expressed for public consumption and legitimization to a population still decent enough not to buy the real imperialistic reasons. Consequently we can easily dismiss the justification of removing weapons of mass destruction, because none were found; the link between Saddam Hussein and al-Qaeda and Osama bin Laden was not shown; and that Saddam Hussein was an evil dictator is true but such a claim overlooks the fact that we supported him in the 1980s against Iran and that we currently support regimes that are as bad or worse such as Turkey or Colombia.

What are the real reasons? These are imperial and as such unjustified and unjust, and number, by my accounting, at least eight. The first and most important reason is oil, not only because the control and profits from oil fall into the hands of the United States, but such control puts the US government in a position to effect the price of oil by determining how much of it is put on the market at any one time and enables us to secure the role of the dollar as the currency of choice in purchase of oil by other countries. The other reasons are:

To secure the water supplies with which Iraq is very much blessed and upon which all other countries are dependent.

To establish American military and political power in the heart of a major Arab country for an indefinite period to help insure the existence of friendly governments and market economies throughout the region, and to use as leverage against Europe, Russia, and China.

To expand the military budget, and with it the profits of the arms industry, which also includes and relates to the oil industry.

To help Americans to forget that we failed to achieve our objectives in Afghanistan, which was not to remove the Taliban, but to destroy al-Qaeda and capture Osama bin Laden.

To upstage the media attention given to failures of the government's economic policies (unemployment up 35 percent, stock market down 34 percent, and so on since President Bush took office).

President Bush's policies created an atmosphere of permanent crisis with effects of fear and patriotism helping the GOP to push through the rest of the ultra-conservative political agenda and win the 2004 election.

The war and occupation contribute to securing Israel's national interests in several ways: providing Israel with some relief from a growing sentiment among the American public that the United States should cut off or reduce significantly military and economic aid to Israel until it vacates all Arab lands giving some cover to Sharon for dealing as he wishes with the Palestinians, perhaps expelling them into surrounding countries: destroying what is left of Iraq's military power neutralizes Israel's most important rival in the region, establishing a permanent American presence in the area in such a way as to allow US troops to police the whole area for Israel if that is necessary, and controlling Iraqi oil and water resources in such a way as to allow

Israel, our best friend in the Middle East, to have a significant share of both.

We have here a multicausal, multilevel account, stressing economic, cultural, and political factors. Our support for Israel, for example, puts us in the position of favoring it over Muslim and Arab religious and ethnic groups when they conflict with Israel's policies. Thus there is some basis for seeing a religious motive for 9/11, rooted in a fanatical, one-sided form of nationalism and one-sided interpretation of the Muslim religion, but this factor has to be seen in relation to political-economic factors, because, if I am correct, the United States and Israel are enforcing an unjust form of domination and exploitation over the whole region.

Berrigan also challenges us to think about the relationship between religion and empire. One distinction that emerges from all of his works is that between an authentic religious belief that refuses to align itself with empire and criticizes it prophetically, and an inauthentic religious belief that tolerates, supports, and legitimizes imperial violence and exploitation. Reflecting on these last four years, who can hesitate to condemn President Bush's right-wing use of Christianity to legitimate empire? Such a use of Christianity betrays Christianity.

The problem, of course, is not just President Bush; he is too easy a target. The US Catholic Bishops met in the fall of 2001, after 9/11, in Washington, D.C. They presided over a mass for peace, during which an admiral from the Pentagon was invited to read from the Scriptures. The then outgoing president of the Bishops Conference read from the Sermon on the Mount—an urgent plea from Jesus that his disciples love their enemies and react with hatred toward no one. After the admiral's reading, the bishops made clear their support for the war in Afghanistan, and the next day the newly elected president also made his approval of the war clear. Berrigan's response to this sorry state of affairs deserves to be quoted in full.

> If the American Catholic bishops were consistent and honorable, they would publicly burn the Gospels. Then they would contrive a liturgy of a different sort, forming a procession, entering a church, holding aloft the Marine Handbook of War. The Antigospel would be placed on the high alter and incensed.[16]

And again, a little earlier in the same text:

> Church and State, it shortly became clear, stood foursquare, in close collusion. A Crusade: The bishops, demoralized by scandal,

evangelically illiterate, walked *peri passu* with the warmaking
state.
   A warmaking Church, an oxymoron.
   The twin towers fell to rubble. The twin powers turned to war.[17]

We cannot but admire the honesty and truth and truthfulness of these
sentences, which challenge us, challenge me to live up to our vocation as
philosophers to speak the truth. But how often do we do that, and how
often do we temporize and compromise on that task, saying, "Well, on the
one hand," and "then, on the other hand?" How much and how often do
we speak the truth to and about unjust imperial power and how often do we
rule that kind of question out as "not being real philosophy?" Thus empire
rolls on scorching the earth and devastating the people of the earth with
our implicit or explicit cooperation, all quite professionally expressed, of
course.
   It is not just right-wing religion that is the problem, but people inside
and outside the Church, in Christian, Catholic institutions of high learning, for instance, who should know better. In any event, by Berrigan's criteria and my own, any religious belief that does not resist or that tolerates
or supports empire betrays itself, sells itself short as religious belief, as does
all so-called Catholic philosophy that plays the same game. The religious
alternative to this is the "law of the Cross," Lonergan's name for the nonviolent, suffering love of Jesus and his disciples as the answer to the problem of personal and social imperial evil by returning good for evil, love for
hate, in a process of mercy and forgiveness and nonviolent resistance to
our violent and unjust policies and structures. And Berrigan's commitment
to this kind of nonviolent, suffering love in discipleship with Jesus is also
well-known and is exemplified by Catonsville.[18]
   Such nonviolent, suffering love brings into question our system of imperial militarism and violence and links up to and completes the nonviolent
communicative praxis and self-appropriated knowers and lovers in community that I defend in my work. Such violence may be as American as
apple pie, as the old bromide goes, but, if so, America is profoundly anti-
Christian in any full, profound, and complete sense of Christianity. Imperial
violence and militarism are both antiphilosophical and anti-Christian.
   One objection that can be made and has been made is that such nonviolence is merely symbolic and not determinate enough and programmatic
enough to lead to or achieve real change. This objection misses the point
that sometimes such action is quite determinate and programmatic, for
example, in trying to end the Vietnam War, close down the School of the

Americas, or ending the occupation of Iraq. Second, such an objection misses the morally and contemplatively rooted nature of right action, done to achieve results at least in the long run, but also because it is the right thing to do and valid, therefore, independently of results. Third, such an objection misses that such protest and action represents a religious contribution to discussions in the so-called public sphere endorsed by Habermas and others, in which the immediate point is to change and raise consciousness and not directly to change social structures. Berrigan's life and work thus challenge us to expand our notions of what legitimate protest and action are, including not just action oriented to determinate results but also symbolic action oriented to raising consciousness.

Finally, we come to the theme of liberation. Liberation as I understand it is the good that corresponds to the right of justice, the happiness, personal and collective, that corresponds to the duty of striving for justice. Aristotle and Kant come together, which I articulated more fully in my 2002 address and in other works, as I articulated a threefold ethic moving from right to morality to justice. Liberation, then, is the good and happiness of being free negatively from capitalist, imperialist injustice, in its different aspects of racism, sexism, heterosexism, classism, environmental devastation, exploitation, marginalization of the poor, militarism, and so on; and positively liberation is full individual and social self-realization. Elsewhere I have laid out seventeen or eighteen aspects of imperial injustice, but its roots lie in the exploitative process and structure oriented to extracting surplus value from labor.[19]

Liberation, then, is simply the good and happiness that results from doing the work of justice on all levels of collective life, local, national, and international. Negatively, it is overcoming capitalist imperialism in all of its aspects. Positively, it is the self-appropriated community claiming for itself the means of economic, cultural and political self-development and flourishing hitherto cut off from and separated from it in alienating capitalist control and ownership of these means. I have argued elsewhere that the content of such liberation is full economic, political, and social democracy, a minimal welfare state, local, regional, and national planning commissions to give economic and political aid based on need and merit, and a market socialism allowing free exchange of goods and commodities but forbidding exchange between capital and labor, because that distinction is abolished in principle. The structure of empire abroad is to be abolished, as we bring home all our troops from hundreds of bases around the world and dismantle our multinational corporations. We steer a middle ground between a one-sidedly individualistic liberal capitalism and a one-sidedly collectivistic state socialism.[20]

Berrigan's challenge to us, however, is to go further and to come closer to home. For he motivates us to think about a theory and praxis in the imperial center as linked to and in solidarity with liberation in the imperial periphery in the Third World, as articulated in the work of Dussel. Center is to periphery as rich is to poor, powerful to weak, dominator to dominated, exploiter to exploited, First World to Third World. Although such a theory and praxis of liberation in the center is linked to and in solidarity with liberation in the periphery and has the same enemy and same goal, each project is also distinct and has different challenges and opportunities. In the center the ideology mills grind long and hard, twenty-four hours a day, and so much affluence obtains that the temptation to be bought off, distracted, or narcotized is pretty high. On the other hand, there is still in most countries in the imperial center a large space for speaking out, acting out, and demonstrating nonviolently, such that Berrigan's recommended praxis of nonviolence is not only ethically preferable but politically feasible. In the periphery, on the other hand, the oppression, poverty, and exploitation is much more visible and its cause more easy to see, but the political space for dissent is much less. Putting the matter differently, we might say alienation and exploitation in the center come bearing gifts, whereas injustice in the periphery stalks its victims with a gun.[21]

Because of these differences between center and periphery, secular and religious activists in the center have begun a practice of "downward mobility" that opposes the upward mobility of those who wish to serve the empire and benefit from such service. Drawing on disciplines of prayer, contemplation, literacy, and reading to supplement more secular forms of analysis, critique, and motivation, people have begun to free themselves from the narcotizing addiction of consumerism and advertising. Motivated by a "preferential option for the poor," people have begun a "downward mobility," identified with Christ in his downward mobility, opting out of the reckless pursuit of money, pleasure, power, and success, and opting for justice, happiness, community, and genuine social liberation. Juliet Schor in a book written several years ago, *The Overspent American*, has identified in rigorous empirical research a growing community of "downshifters," 20 percent of all adult Americans, who have opted for a simpler lifestyle, more leisure, more time for family and children, more meaningful but perhaps less remunerative work. Put simply, such a lifestyle is more rewarding and enriching, in our words, more liberating.[22] Such people and others in their way of living, their simple lifestyles, their economic sharing, their decisions to live in poor or poorer neighborhoods and to work with and to serve people in those neighborhoods, and their regular practice and support of nonviolent activism and civil disobedience begin to foreshadow and anticipate and create a more just, liberated society, as well as to work for institutional, structural social change. The nonviolent love of God and Christ is translated into a nonviolent love of the neighbor and praxis of liberation.[23]

Conclusion

To summarize my main points: The basic starting point is radical self-knowledge and self-affirmation leading to radical self-choice, radical political conversion, speaking out and acting out against injustice and for justice on behalf of the marginalized and oppressed racial, sexual, heterosexual, and poor others, in the matter before us, the poor majorities of Iraq, Palestine, and the Middle East. If I began the search for truth rooted in the desire to know, then that leads to a choice and love of and speaking up for the truth, and this witness occurs in season and out of season, independently of results. I may hope for and aim for results, but my basic motivation is the rightness of what the situation calls for. What is historically dominant is, as Kierkegaard warns us, a poor guide to what is philosophically or ethically or politically or religiously right and this is especially true today as we see the dominance of "The New Barbarism" and "The Bush Reich."

Paradoxically, full self-knowledge and self-appropriation does not lead to ignoring or being closed off from the marginalized, dispossessed other, but to a response to that other, what we might even call a conversion to that other. But such a conversion is mediated by a transcendental-existential account of the self, a normative ethic, and a meta-narratival hermeneutical account of capitalism and empire. Being faithful to the desire to know truth leads me to a radical choice of myself as human being and philosopher in solidarity with the poor and oppressed of the world. There is a preferential option for the poor that can be argued for philosophically as well as religiously, and this option puts me into theoretical and lived opposition to the socio-economic system that oppresses and exploits and marginalizes the poor, a theoretical and practical *either-or* if you like. Here is another aspect of that link between rationality and radicalism that was described earlier. And this link is different from, and in my opinion, superior to postmodern accounts, in that the dichotomy between self and other is overcome, an account is given of what oppresses the other, and an account is given of why the oppression is wrong.

A phrase of my own that indicates the philosophical link with Berrigan's perspective is that "intellectual, moral, and religious conversion lead to radical political conversion." Intellectual conversion is the movement out of the capitalist and state socialist cave into the sunlight of intelligibility, the world mediated by meaning. Moral conversion is my coming alive to the sphere of moral values on the fourth level of freedom, and religious conversion is simply falling in love with God. Intellectual conversion is an aspect of self-appropriation as I conceive it, and moral and religious conversion flow from it as fruit and gift. Thus the movement of my essay is from self-appropriation articulated philosophically through intellectual, moral, and religious conversion, to radical political conversion, in which the philosophical and prophetic, rational and religious, and philosophical and theological are linked together and flow into one another.[24]

At this point, I am tempted to put matters in more simple terms. Basically the issue is a fundamentally indecent, inhumane society at odds with us as human beings, philosophers, and Christians. And what philosophy and theology counsel is fundamental change in all the basic institutions of society including the groves of *academe*. A fundamental either-or emerges that is at once existential and cognitive, to do that work of criticism and theorizing about fundamental change, or to cop out on that, to temporize, to say like Prufrock, "That is not what I meant, not what I meant at all."

To make these points, however, is not to say or imply that we will do what is required. Philosophers, even Catholic philosophers, are not immune from human weakness and temptation; like everyone else, we can be bought off or intimidated or coerced or bribed to go along in order to get along and thus to betray our calling as human, philosophical, and religious. We can go along in a great communal celebration of empire, setting off rockets on the fourth of July, as Bush tightens the neofascist noose around our necks and we sing "America the Beautiful" at baseball games and the like. Or we can begin, tentatively at first and then more forcefully and confidently, to loosen the noose. We can, to change the metaphor, cheerfully and smugly go down in the self-destructive imperial Titanic, singing the Star-Spangled Banner as the waves wash over our heads, or we can save ourselves by getting off the ship. *Non Serviam.* In fact, that might not be a bad description of liberating philosophy, social theory, and theology in these bad times—to save ourselves and others and as much of the world as possible from the imperial Titanic. We save ourselves and students and colleagues from "America" in this destructive sense; we cease being lost in America.

I end with another quotation from *The Trial of the Catonsville Nine* that is more hopeful in looking forward to a liberated future.

Redeem the times
The times are inexplicably evil
Christians pay conscious   indeed religious tribute
to Caesar and Mars
by the approval of overkill tactics   by brinkmanship
by nuclear liturgies   by racism   by support of genocide
They embrace their society with all their heart
and abandon the cross
They pay lip service to Christ
and military service to the powers of death
And yet   and yet   the times are inexhaustibly good
solaced by the courage and hope of many
The truth rules   Christ is not forsaken
In a time of death some
the resisters   those who work hardily for social change
those who preach and embrace the truth
such overcome death
their lives are bathed in the light of the resurrection
the truth has set them free
In the jaws of death
they proclaim their love of brothers and sisters
We think of such men and women
in the world   in our nation   in the churches
and the stone in our breast is dissolved
we take heart once more.[25]

All of us—students, faculty, and administrators—can be or become such men and women. What would happen, I ask myself, if the thousands of those graduating from our colleges and universities every year learned not to live with late capitalism and love it in a kind of personal and professional upward mobility but to become agents of resistance and social transformation? What would happen if we and our students ceased to be happy campers in the great American dreamland and wasteland, and became creatively unhappy, happy enough with our own humanity to end up challenging a fundamentally inhumane, unjust system that regularly, day in and day out, violates that humanity? What would happen if we and our students in our personal, social, and professional lives became, each in our own way, "bathed in the light of the resurrection"? Now that would truly be a fate devoutly to be wished. That would be to be truly, fully rational and radical, prophetic and liberatory, human and Christian. That would truly be the faith that does justice.

Consecrating Peace: Reflecting on Daniel Berrigan and Witness

William Desmond

The day Nixon left the White House for good I arrived in America for the first time. If I had come looking for America, I had first encountered something unexpected and for the most part nameless. More than thirty years later, I finally read Daniel Berrigan's *America Is Hard to Find*, and it does not so much allay perplexities as arouse new ones. The departure of Nixon punctuated an extended period of political and social turbulence occasioned mainly by the Vietnam War, though the upheavals in social mores—extending to the questioning, even overturning of traditional morality—had been in train for quite a while. The abolition of the draft had taken quite a bit of the sting out of the antiwar protest—certainly as far as middle-class students were concerned. When I came looking for America I found myself in an ethos of moral uncertainty, even disorientation. Some of my contemporaries might preach morality but one worried about a base note of middle-class narcissism in much of it. Perhaps we have been dealing for decades now with an ambiguous mixture of middle-class decency and self-concern. Reading *America Is Hard to Find*, *Prison Poems*, as well as his autobiography, *To Dwell in Peace*, gave me, decades later, a picture of and feel for much of what was nameless to me on first arriving in America.[1] To read those books from an earlier time is also to hear a resonance across time of recurrent alarms of war and terror and death, casual or organized. And faced with new wars, new longings for peace, and new scoundrels in high places the goal of peace seems as distant as ever.

I arrived in America to pursue a PhD in philosophy at Penn State. I remember my first night in New York City, and the sound of police car sirens, and in the morning stepping out into the street and seeing for the first time a policeman packing a gun. The sight sent an unwilled shock through me. Police in Ireland did not carry guns, and the shock had something to do with the immediate insinuation, felt in the flesh itself, of power and violence, and of responses to violence that meet the violator with the violence of opposing power. Did the nameless shock communicate a passage through a barrier in which another world existed: America?

I have come to know an America that is more than the one insinuated by the gun. All things considered, America is a country full of decency and welcoming to outsiders; a country where people can openly protest against war, even if sometimes the proper dismay is initially slow in emerging; a country where genuine merit can be recognized and even rewarded. More than in any other country I have known, among academics (not always greatly loved by Berrigan), I have witnessed genuine generosity by older scholars towards the generation succeeding them, generosity not driven by a mentality of scarcity, secreting in the elders' wariness and defensiveness against the rising generation that will in the course of time displace them.

This earlier period of which Berrigan then wrote was a snarling time. The tangle of the time was also bound up with the relation of religion and politics, so central to all of Berrigan's life and work. My sense is that in the 1960s certain effects of a particular kind of secularization were more in evidence, while now a reaction to that (among other things) has brought about a situation where the promiscuity of politics and religion has assumed newly striking forms. I would like to say something about the difference of politics and religion and their inseparability, and the risks to both politics and religion of a wrong promiscuity. Berrigan has been a teacher on this crucial issue, though the teaching is not a theoretical doctrine but the effort to live as a sign of peace.

An enduring aspect of life in America appears to be how "being American" often functions as a kind of religion, with America itself as a kind of god. I found this strange on coming to American first. There are different pieties, of course: religious piety, political and familial pieties, as well as certain pieties of place. All speak of special bonds of loyalty: to the divine, to one's own family, to one's people or place. That all are bonds of deep loyalty makes them interconnected, though there are crucial differences to be respected. The interconnections can sometimes lead to a loss of differentiation, such that one thinks one is witnessing to God but in fact one is expressing one's loyalty to one's country or tribe. The political piety of the latter is invested with the more universal reference of the former piety (assuming that this is monotheistic); the will to power of a people becomes melded with the will of the ultimate power.

The interconnection of the two pieties of state and religion in America is a point at issue for Berrigan. I illustrate from my own early experience. On first going to a Catholic church in America I was very surprised to see the flag of America on the altar, coupled with the papal flag. I had come from Ireland where no Irish flag was to be found on the altars. Provincial "Irish Catholic" that I was, I assumed *Catholic* is a universal denomination, not an Irish or American one. I see Berrigan seeking to speak for the politics of justice with a religious piety that belongs to no nation—even though his life has been to witness in America. His clash with the piety of the nation as political indicates the difference of the two pieties, albeit often all but inseparable in the mixed condition of concrete life.

Here and there Berrigan mentions a Jesuit whose pride of place softened, if not eradicated, the tension of the two.[2] He was wedged in that difference and rubbed raw by the inconvenient lack of fit between the two sides. The piety of America can lead to the confusion of the powers. Religion as the intimate universal becomes intimate to the American, and everything outside becomes the "beyond," and an American rule is to run elsewhere, perhaps everywhere. In catholic religion there is the intimate universal—each of us in our inmost singularity are called into community with the divine. All the others are called into this intimate universal. We have to partake of their suffering and vulnerability, as we all do of each other. The intimate universal as universal is not a project of political power at all. The kingdom of God is not of this world. This does not mean there is no witness in the world to the intimate universal, but true witness cannot collapse the intimate universal into any project of political will to power, no matter how extensive its immanent imperium. Even if it ruled the world, whether in communist form, or capitalist, this imperium would not be, could never be the same as the intimate universal.

Berrigan is part of a generation older than mine, but my friendship with James Marsh has directed me toward his work.[3] His work is not simply a matter of his books, many though they are, but his engagements in life— religious, ethical, and political. As I imply, particularly of importance is the differentiation and relation of powers: the power of Caesar, the power of Christ. "A Roman Caesar with the soul of Christ" Nietzsche proclaimed as a higher desideratum of will to power and it sounds intriguing.⁴ But in the end, with Nietzsche, it is Caesar who qualifies the soul of Christ and defines its inclusion in a higher will to power. I take Berrigan, as I take Jesus, to witness to something other, in another dimension to the will to power of Caesar—and yet not other as a dualistic opposite is other, but other as caring for the immanent excellence of power, and its governance in accord with proper justice. Nietzsche's striking phrase captures what comes more naturally to us, even Christians—namely to include religious porosity in political power, and hence to put the religious porosity to a use that clogs the porosity with something other than its openness to God. I know Nietzsche intended his phrase as the summary of a higher excellence, higher than the normal Caesar and the (to him) servile Christian, higher than sovereignty and servility. In fact, the soul of Christ risks being mutilated when it is beguiled or forced into the embrace of the putatively higher sovereign. Something like this lesson comes to me when I read Berrigan putting the point very well in *To Dwell in Peace*: "What we are asking of one another is that Mars be transformed into Christ."⁵

Dwelling in Peace as Consecrating Peace

The title of Berrigan's autobiography is well chosen: *To Dwell in Peace.* Reading it, one is impelled to ask: what is it to dwell in peace? Where is the house of peace? Is there no house, only a hole in the ground where the foxes are at home? Or is there something about peace that has no place to lay its head? Is there to be no peace then for the peacemakers? Or is it that one cannot dwell in peace, for there is nothing there that one could claim as one's home, since to be at peace is to be at home everywhere and hence nowhere? Or is peace itself the home, everywhere and nowhere, and is it the place in which no one is to dwell? Seeking to dwell in it, building after building crumbles, for we have taken up residence in houses of stone, idols of possession, no icons of the heart.

Berrigan is an activist, but also a contemplative, and it is this combination that makes his work all the more complex, challenging, and rich. The activist wants to build a house, the contemplative wants to become at home in a house not built by human hands alone. The second home challenges the building of houses of justice, but there is more to it than anything that our activisms can accomplish. There is a doing justice that is intimate to contemplation.⁶ To dwell in peace is to be accepted into a dwelling which is peace. We cannot barge in there, for there is no "there" in there, and any barging disturbs the peace on which it tries to make a claim. To come home here means to do nothing and yet to do everything that makes ready the dwelling of peace itself. Ready for peace itself, ready to receive peace, ready with the right action, when that is called for. What is the right action of readiness? The question sometimes robs us of peace, even in the love of peace.

Blessed are the peacemakers, one of the beatitudes tells us. What are the beatitudes? In one way, they seem to exhort us to what is to be; in another way, they seem just to tell us elementally of what is. This doubleness places the beatitudes in a position of priority, before the *is* and the *ought*. This doubleness is not to be forgotten, for it says something about our finite nature as called to be more than itself. It also says something about that *more* which already, enigmatically, is with us, wording something of our core endowment.

There is also doubleness in the word peacemaker: To make is to make something out of something; but how make peace, out of what elements? Elements not at peace originally? But then peacemaking would be the arranging or rearranging of elements at war; and if those warlike elements have the prior word, surely also they will have the last? Or out of elements that already are irreducibly a being at peace? If the latter, we can only make peace out of peace; our peacemaking presupposes a peace that we do not make, but in which we participate and share. Is it that the first peace is a provisional interim between two wars? Or is it that the peace we make is between a more original peace and a more ultimate one? This may mean that our peace in the middle is always mixed, mixed even with war, but this does not mean that the intermediate peace is the rearrangement or warlike elements. It is the sign of the original peace and the last peace: the peace of original creation and the peace of redeemed creation.

If peacemaking is said to be blessed, we might ask: What is blessing? What is cursing? Do we find ourselves in between these extremities? Do we find ourselves at an extremity in this between? What is it to bless, to be blessed? Can we bless ourselves, determine ourselves to be blessed? Or must there be the receiving of blessing from a source of beneficence other than ourselves? A source that blesses us before we can even attempt to bless ourselves? If we try to bless ourselves alone, and through ourselves alone, do we end up cursed? We can curse ourselves, through ourselves alone. Perhaps just the will to absolute aloneness is indeed nothing but to curse— to turn away from all beneficent sources other than oneself. There seems an asymmetry between blessing and curse: blessing cannot be without the beneficence of the other; curse comes to be in the will to avoid or negate such beneficence.

If peacemaking is blessed, one might also say there is something about it that is *consecrating*. This word might arouse shudders in thinkers who want to extirpate every trace of the sacred in the languages of advanced intellectual commentary. The language of the sacred is the more true. Even those who want entirely to secularize ethics, often find themselves falling into a language of evaluation in which, in the end, something is said to be sacred (the human being, and certain of its rights, for instance). But what right has one to such language if the sacred is just what ought not to be there? No right. And yet, it seems, we cannot entirely avoid the sacred. With peace the consecrating power continues to come back to life again and again. Peace keeps being resurrected in its blessing power, even after the death inflicted on it be all deconsecrations, indeed desecrations. Indeed is not war often a word for events of desecration that try to hide from us their secret source in hidden deconsecrations?

I am interested here in consecrating peace: peace which consecrates us, peace to which we might consecrate ourselves, peace that finally cannot be understood through ourselves alone but calls on, as it is called forth by, a consecrating power that continues to bless being, even when all hell has broken loose in war.

Berrigan came to be consecrated to peace in the midst of war. Who or what is the consecrating power? The story of his life, especially his later life, has a high incidence of strife in it. Peace is struggled for in conditions hostile to it. Again the relation of religion and politics and their tension is of interest. There is here both the heterogeneity and complication of different powers. If there is something consecrating about peace, calling for our consecration, then the redeeming power of the religious is the most important. But how remain true to that power when one lives in war, lives among the warlike, lives oneself as a combatant in life, even though claiming to be a combatant against war. Everything seems to tell against the possibility of peace and living in it.

If political power is the first and last master, as it has been for the great political ideologies of our time, there seems no final dwelling in peace, except the provisional interim in which the balance of political powers condescend to a pause between war and war. In this view, war is primordial, continuing, and ultimate. Where then is the dwelling of peace that is the ultimate blessing, ultimate because the first blessedness? Many of those seekers of peace against the injustices of politics are tempted themselves to become new sovereigns of a counteracting violence. This can do no more

than produce new war, not bless us with original peace. This tends to
happen when politics is invested with the ultimacy that is proper to religion. It is understandable why this is a perennial temptation—especially in
the face of the impotence of seemingly being unable to do anything. But if
we collapse the religious into the political we produce a politics that is
idolatrously religious. A new idol is born from the peacemaker's war on the
belligerent idols of politics.

Berrigan is a witness who stood between these extremes: a religion that
quarantines itself from engagement with injustice, in the name of purity; a
politics that in the name of justice confuses religion and politics and risks
confounding both. Has this been a recurrent worry with the Jesuits? One
goes forth in the bright morning to convert the king, trusting that the
people will follow; one goes among the powerful, hoping the kingdom of
God will infiltrate the kingdom of the world. Alas, the kingdom of the
world seeks to exercise the first sovereignty and the last judgment. The god
to whose greater glory we sing a *Te Deum* is a god who is not God—a counterfeit double. Berrigan's politics are not monarchical, of course. But the
structure of the temptation can be the same, even if the preferential option
for the poor replaces the preferential option for the rich. This is the temptation of the Grand Inquisitor. The question comes: Why did not Christ
accede to the Grand Inquisitor? Such a question, or its like, came to haunt
Berrigan in his endeavors to witness to the Society of Jesus. Indeed, the
question, as it were, seemed to break him in two, making him wonder if
the world and the cross could "ever meet otherwise than in conflict—a
bloody cross-road, a crisis and cross-purpose of soul, of community, of history itself?"[7]

Peacemaking as Agapeic Service

There are revealing passages in Berrigan's autobiography where he worries
about being untrue to what he is called to be. He speaks of the need to
find a soul, a center. He has striking things to say about war as the taking
of life, peace as the giving of life.[8] I would connect the giving of life
with the agapeics of being, and with the ethics of agapeic service: generosity accepted from surplus goodness, generosity passed on from surplus
goodness.

Receiving and passing on: obviously the governance of power here too
engages Berrigan in different spheres. One sees something of it in the presentation of his own family. In some presentations we find the image of

the father as sovereign over all sovereignty, warts and all. Sometimes one worries about the recess of compassion, and yet there is a moving tenderness in the redeeming touch passing between the son and the father, as the father passes away.[9] There are also telling lines from his poem from prison:

> I sit in Danbury prison for illegal
> acts contrary to war.
> Father
> I close my eyes, conjure up
> like a deaf-mote mimic
> your ironic ghost. How convey
> my gratitude, my sense
> of the delicious rightness of things?
> Whatever you denied us, you
> gave us this, which enemies name
> distemper, madness; our friends,
> half in despair, arrogance.
> Which I name, denying both—the best of
> your juice and brawn, unified
> tension to good purpose.[10]

Berrigan is also concerned with receiving from the Church and passing on its gifts, but he also presents an image of the governance of power. In the Church he also finds many sovereigns. These are, or were, the princes of the Church and often they gave him a hard time. This comes to the fore in his life with the question of war. He tells us how ingeniously supple the religious sovereigns proved to be in justifying the status quo—in the name of Christ. Returning to Nietzsche's "Caesar with the soul of Christ," here Caesar can count on those who claim to witness for the soul of Christ. In all fairness, this is not the only image of the official Church he offers. He himself lived another image, and experienced religious community beyond both sovereignty and servility. It is important to keep faith in the face of something that can smack of dubious equivocity in the "official" Church. The power priest can be too given to smooching with the powers that be. Yet there is something more that always is drawn back, that asks us to draw back from corrupting identifications with power. Between these poles— the power of Caesar, perplexed by Christ and the soul of Christ, not seduced by Caesar—religious existence in the world and in all its equivocity is lived. It requires finesse, both spiritual and political, to deem what is fitting in such an equivocal condition. It is not always, indeed rarely, a univocal matter of imposing abstract principles on an unambiguous situation. Judgment of the fitting is not always an easy matter. It was not easy for Berrigan in situations where everything of his life was somehow at risk. One has to recognize the considered mindfulness and prayer that went into some of his decisions—even when an element of ambiguity always remained concerning the most fitting in this or that singular occasion.

Mindfulness of the fitting, being faithful to the soul of Christ, in the face of the sometimes overwhelming power of Caesar, was and is extremely important in his mission of nonviolence. Confrontation with the political sovereigns themselves and their agents can occur even in a war of symbols. Flags fly the loyalty, the political piety of a people, and even their love and hatred: love of their own, hatred of the others, whether an external enemy or a seditious insider. Equally the burning of paper, the draft files, with homemade napalm, is no neutral combustion of indifferent matter. Burn draft files and you burn America. Burning a flag is not an act of neutral free speech; it announces love or hate—or what we take to be lovable and hateful—even as the flag that flies announces love and loyalty—and perhaps sometimes hate and treachery.

All of this is mostly below the level of rational self-consciousness. The rupture to the symbol brings it out of its intimate recesses. And there are loyalties that run deep, just as family loyalties run deep. Did Berrigan always reckon enough with (did he anticipate?) the depths of those love and hate relationships? Could anyone anticipate the vehemence of their hold on us? At one level, it is not difficult rightly to call attention to the discordance between the practice and the ideal of being, say, a Christian, or an American (if America implicates a certain ideal of freedom). But the depths of hatred are dark, as also are the depths of love. To intrude upon those depths is to risk waking monsters, as much as welcoming angels. His experience at one time was of waking the monstrous, waking to the monstrous. Though again, in all fairness, he and his companions did not simply do this, since the monstrous was already abroad and running amuck in that snarling time. His work makes us ask today to what extent we have fallen asleep to the monstrous. 9/11 woke people to the spectacle of a monstrous evil, but the monstrous is not the prerogative of the outsiders alone. The monstrous sleeps in the recesses of accumulated will to power that knows no measure above itself, no measure greater than itself. In the military might now accumulated in the world, the monstrous is surely sleeping. Whether we are the measure of its excess is surely to be wondered. We would be assuring ourselves far too easily, if we were to deem ourselves sure masters of such power.

The piety of politics sometimes provides the monstrance of the gods of the political nation. Berrigan burnt these gods in the name of a higher God. But one is not godless, the other godly. It may well be a matter of an idol usurping the name of God, and surely this is a recurrent temptation of every great political power. The work of Berrigan is a repeated warning against that temptation.[11] Caesar is never to take hold of the soul of Christ, for that soul could never become the possession of any nation. Attempted possession would only take that soul prisoner. Those who witness to that soul may find themselves taken prisoner. Since that soul cannot be taken prisoner, the pretence will be propagated that a changeling is the real thing. (Think here of Kierkegaard's protest against Christendom as counterfeiting Christianity.) Caesar, too, can generate a counterfeit of Christ—in the name of political power, and with the connivance of those occupying the official places of religious sanction. Our happiness in living comfortably in a world of changelings will be shadowed by hostility to irritants who point that something is missing, though everything seems quite in order.

Lest this seems too one-sided, it is important to remember how the soul of Caesar could also take possession within the antiwar movement. I am thinking of Berrigan's relation to and remarks about the Weathermen.[12] He speaks of his time at Cornell, and his dealing with young people who came from good secular background. But he adds that there was nothing of sacramental moments in their lives. All reference to sacred sources and religious inspirations left them cold. But at a certain limit, the end result was the taking up of arms to defeat the taking up of arms: going to war to defeat the agents of war. There is a certain agapeic abdication of enforcing power in the soul of Christ in the face of the self-insistent logic that this is justified—namely, that warlike power alone can defeat warring power. The turn in this direction Berrigan found in Cornell after 1968, when he notes interestingly the heroes were notably people like Che Guevara, Ho Chi Min, Bakunin, Marx and Lenin.[13] One has to think that the left, if that is the right word, also produces its own political theology, as counterfeit as the political theology of the reigning Caesar's. The ruling ideas of an epoch are the ideas of the ruling class, so said Marx. If we change the ruling class to the previously disenfranchised, the same logic of ruling power is not necessarily overcome. We exchange one set of political masters for another. William Butler Yeats had it right in one of his last poems, "The Great Day":

Hurrah for revolution and more cannon-shot!
A beggar on horseback lashes a beggar up on foot.

Hurrah for revolution and cannon come again!
The beggars have changed places, but the lash goes on.[14]

The lash goes on, though global power has learned new counterfeit caresses to mask or mitigate its smart. The fact that Berrigan was aware of the issue places him finally in an entirely different space of spirit to those who succumb to the temptation to overcome war with war in such a way that they only renew war differently. If I am not mistaken, something of a balance was struck in his time in prison. Without the soul of Christ, there was not even survival, to say nothing of betterment. We do not posses that soul and cannot possess it. It is beyond possession and asks a poverty of spirit at the opposite to all grasping of will to power.

Peacemaking as Rooted in the Patience of Being

Peace and poverty are included among the beatitudes, but weeping is also said to be blessed. Will those who would be peacemakers have to weep? Weep in being witnesses whose lives will be attacked, witnesses compassionate for the promise of sojourning humanity they see betrayed, knowing repentantly their own secret proclivities to war. The sources of war are in power first seeking to assuage its own lack, then in seeking to expand itself beyond limits. One can see the connection of poverty and peace.[15] There is a poverty of spirit that is not a lack, and that is peaceful because it grasps at nothing. We live in a time in which we are glutted with ourselves. While we seem to lack less and less, our being glutted with ourselves tells us of a lack in a different dimension; first lack of ourselves, then lack of wakefulness for what transcends us in the dimension of the superior. Consumer capitalism promises to slake all desires, and indeed even to wake new ones, and then in giving us everything, it enacts only the waiting solution—true happiness will come the next time.

One thinks of Plato in the *Republic*: the desire for *more* generates the need for security; hence armies spring up like dragon's teeth, to protect what one now possesses, to annex what others have. There is certain limitlessness to *pleonexia*, this desire for more. This limitlessness is a quantitative infinity. Its *more* is not in the dimension of the qualitative. It does not witness to the infinitude of the human spirit, except in so far as this is indirectly reflected in the spirit of acquisitiveness itself, and its will to appropriate all things other as its own. Other animals are not acquisitive, even in this dimension of the quantitative "more" Our limitless acquisitiveness is sourced in a more positive infinitude of openness to what is beyond us, which we deflect back to ourselves, as we take all things other to ourselves. In thus loving things we do not love things. In this self-love we do not even treat ourselves with the love of true generosity. We have known wars of ideology, but at an elemental level the struggle perennially recurs to hold one's own against others or to take what is other as one's own. Beneath the class war of communism this elemental struggle is there. It is not recessive in the seductive war of consumer possessiveness. Even if we say life craves competition, healthy struggle must respect measure; otherwise war will strive again to be king of all.

The peacemakers try to say: enough. *Polemos* is not the father of all things, as Heraclitus said, with other philosophers concurring. Of course, our efforts to word the audacious thought of *enough* keeps being overtaken by our loquacious economic vocabulary of more and more. Measure goes with consent to *enough*. War is the destruction of measure. When it gets going, there is no limit, there is always more. This means there is always less. For this *more* is death-bound, not life augmenting. Berrigan has a telling discussion of "Lord Nuke" in *To Dwell in Peace*.[16] Compared to a short few decades ago, we are now relatively asleep to the momentousness of the nuclear threat. But the power of destruction accumulated thus, more and more, still carries the extreme danger that has not gone away, though we keep quiet about it. The accumulation of military and economic power is necessarily fraught with danger. There is power surplus to us, though we have brought about the accumulation of power. We wonder what to do with it. Sometimes desire just desires more power, sometimes the only way this can be achieved is by war on the resisting or recalcitrant other; sometimes the unconstrained explosion of this power occurs because Cleopatra's nose is too big—or too small. And all this, to the horrified surprise of the secular rationalizers, outdoing Job's comforters in worldly justifications. Making peace is inseparable from the recovery of measure. This means retrieving a certain destitution of the human soul in which we know our own nothingness.

The poverty of peacemaking is not nihilism, which itself is nothing but will to power with no measure beyond itself. There is something here that is both the easiest and the hardest to acknowledge: Easiest because we all know our ontological vulnerability. Hardest because we find it least easy to grant this and what follows from it. What we intimately know, we expressly refuse to grant. There is an ontological vulnerability prior to definition by our pride of place. Pride of place, our anxiety to secure ourselves, and our place in the sun, even the good governance of power in a decent community, are themselves responses to this prior vulnerability. We make ourselves secure only because we live out of an intimate ontological vulner-ability. Those who fight or simply climb their way to the top embody configurations of power that want to recess everything about our being defined by receiving—receiving that calls for a deeper patience towards what is more than ourselves along. In accession to power, we are tempted, again and again, with the apotheosis of invulnerability. Again and again we succumb.

The peacemaker comes to know that we need to grant a patience of being that is prior to any endeavor to be, a receiving of being before any acting of being. The patience and receiving make the endeavor and the acting possible. I put it thus: More primal than the *conatus essendi* is the *passio essendi*. Spinoza describes the *essence* of a being as its *conatus*—and this is defined by its power to affirm itself and its range, a range potentially unlimited, in the absence of external countervailing beings. An external other, on this view, presents itself as potentially hostile to my self-affirm-ing. The other, so seen, is alien to my self-affirmation. On this view, our relation to the other always harbors implicit hostility. One sees the seeds of war in this. The continuation of the *conatus essendi* must disarm the threat of the other, or arm itself against it. On such a view being patient to some-thing places us in a position of subordination. To receive is to be servile, while to endeavor and to act is to be sovereign. This orientation is what I call *erotic sovereignty*.

This cannot be the last word, or the first, if there is a more primal *passio essendi*. This suggests that we are first given to be, before anything else. Theologically, this has a relation to the idea of creation: we are creatures of a divine source that gives us *to be* and gives us *to be as good*. There is an oth-erness more original than our own self-definition. Being patient, or being in the patience of being, signals our already being in a certain peace of being, before all struggle to be, or striving to become this or that. There is a given peace in the gift of creation, and the promise of a community of peace, a promise that we can help redeem, as well as betray. We can affirm being because we are already affirmed in being. To be at all is to be recipi-ent of this more primal affirmation: the "yes" of life that creates us as what we are, and which, in the first instance, we do not create but receive and enjoy. It is our being to affirm itself—and indeed to affirm itself as good—it is good to be. Yet there is something more that relativizes self-affirmation purely as such—something more that gives us to be at all, and makes us porous relative to something other than ourselves, and not just as a servile passivity. Spontaneously we live this affirmation of the "to be" as good—we do not have a choice—it is what we are. We find ourselves in this affirmation as self-affirming; hence there is a patience to this primal self-affirmation. There is something received in our being given to be, something not constructed through our own powers alone.

I think it is relative to this enigmatic original affirmation that we must think through the meaning of peace more primal than the outcome of striving powers or warring elements. We are an original "yes" to being, but we find ourselves as already given to be in an original "yes" to being that is received and not produced through ourselves alone. (Often it is the love of the mother who woos us into words of "yes" with reminders of the more original "yes." I think Berrigan would agree.[17] Our incarnate being communicates this original "yes." It is true that for us to be genuine peacemakers we have to say "yes" to this original "yes" to being, and develop our powers diversely in a manner that does not go to war. Our endeavor *to be*, whether peaceful or warlike, follows from fidelity to or betrayal of the first given "yes." As true peacemakers we live a second "yes" which tries to respect the integrity of creation and the human being, with finesse and reverence, with indeed the hope of a sort of sanctification. This is part of the meaning of consecrating peace. First consecrated to be by the gift of a primal peace, we can consecrate ourselves in fidelity to its promise. None of this is possible without the more primal patience. The agendas of political ideologists often embody amnesia of this patience, even an active hatred of it, for in and through it we meet the incontrovertible sign of the fact that we are not the masters of being, not even of our own being. The gift that endows our being at all is hated. In thus seeming to be at war with what is other, we are in fact at war with ourselves. What looks like our sovereignty in life is our being in love with death.

Agapeic Service Versus Erotic Sovereignty

The peacemaker is neither sovereign nor servile but seeks a space of released freedom beyond sovereignty and servility. This space has something to do with the community of agapeic service.[18] Agapeic service is not the servility that erotic sovereignty claims to transcend or stand above. The difference of erotic sovereignty and agapeic service is bound up with the difference of Caesar and Christ. To speak, with Nietzsche, of Caesar with the soul of Christ is to misunderstand this difference, as if the released freedom of the second could be reconfigured in terms of the sovereignty of the first. The religious community, as witness to agapeic service, can never be identified with, or folded back into the political community of erotic sovereignty. At its best, the politics of erotic sovereignty embodies the just governance of worldly power; at its worst, it gives form to a tyrannical will to power, refusing any ethical or spiritual measure above itself. Religious communities can become infected with the latter will to power. The wars that were started in the name of Christianity put religion to shame, and make some persons think only something entirely other than religion could prevent war.

Over the course of modernity, one response to such war was a secularization of public and political life, with a privatization of religion. I take the witness of Berrigan to deny the utter privatization of religion, and yet something radically intimate to our being is at issue with religion. There is a "privatization" reflecting capitalism: religion is private property, not a public service—it is something one owns, and which must compete or be traded on the market. By contrast, there is also a communism that expropriates private property and brings religion into public ownership. Capitalist privacy and communist expropriation either distort or deprive religion of the intimacy of its sacred character. Capitalist privacy reconfigures sacred intimacy such that there is no universal community. Communist politics when marked by an agenda of atheism, might claim to be the agent of the social universal, but produces a counterfeit of universal community without reverence for the intimacy of the sacred. (Do Marxist-inspired liberation theologies, granting they speak in the name of social justice, differentiate enough between the communities of erotic sovereignty and agapeic service?)

Though there is something deeply intimate about religion, religion extends to the whole—think of the meaning of *catholic* as *kath' holou*—in relation to the whole or the universal. It is very difficult to confine religion to one domain among others. It is not that religion must exert hegemony over the whole—a kind of totalitarian monism of the sacred whole. If to be religious is to witness to the community of agapeic service, its spirit is a generosity that places itself at the ready for the whole. It is not available just for this here or that there, but potentially is available for all, if need be without any precondition, especially in circumstances where the poor and the needy, in material terms, in spiritual terms, ask our aid.

Even secular ideologies hostile to religion can help the religious community to see that its own concern is not worldly will to power, and the dominion of erotic sovereignty. Religion is not politics, though it has implications for politics, precisely by standing at an angle that is vertical to the immanent economy of political power itself. Religion requires its purgatory of all recessed forms of secret will to power. And this, not as a prelude to the regaining of worldly power, but as enabling the clearer real-ization within religion that there is something more ultimate beyond the community of erotic sovereignty.

Of course, this differentiation might be exploited to marginalize or par-alyze religion in society denying it any competence to speak out on matters of public concern.[19] One might see the differentiation more positively. Erotic sovereignty deals with the governance of immanent power and, when it is just, the ethical excellence going with the right uses of worldly power. Agapeic service is concerned with transcendent good, not simply in a "beyond" but with the faithful enactment of what it asks of us here and now. The religious community as one of agapeic service is not just a moral community. It has to do with the holy. It cannot subordinate itself to the state in the sense of accepting this as the last judgment. There is a divine measure above. This goes against the denial of any "above" or "beyond" in modernity generally. Religion is eviscerated without some sense of this.

The enabling differentiation of the political and religious communities necessarily means a worldly involvement for the religious community, but the modality of the involvement is all-important. It cannot be a secret will to power masked as agapeic generosity—this would be a perversion. It con-cerns bearing witness to the availability of the divine for the human. Most often this communication has again a certain *incognito* aspect—it does not insist on drawing attention to itself, it does not insist on itself. It is impos-sible to confine agapeic service to any one space or sphere—though it is more than happy to act *incognito*. This does not mean capitulation to evil, for the call to witness can find itself placed in danger. In certain situations something is beyond negotiation. Were there to be negotiations, then the inner truth of the religious community would be corrupted. There are "separations," in the sense of enabling differences, that can be the basis of a work of relation and renewed community. The truth of communication comes in bearing witness. A witness is one who stands there before the others, standing for something, not just standing there as himself or her-self, but for something beyond himself or herself. The work of witnessing in that sense must always be in the middle—in the between where separa-tion allows communication with what is other than oneself, in the between where beyond separation community can come to be. In certain situations, the witness draws fire upon himself or herself. There can be a witness to the limit of martyrdom, witness even unto death.

Witness and the *incognito* of the divine: In prison the Berrigan broth-ers were not allowed to say mass, as this was the "job" of a priest, and prisoners were forbidden to practice their job. Instead the brothers become "teachers"[20]. In one of his prison poems Daniel Berrigan offers a lovely image of the brothers celebrating the Eucharist in a clandestine way—the clandestine life of Christ even in prison:

> . . . Silence. Philip whispering over the bread
> (a con, a magian), over the "mt.dew" tin can.
> we broke and passed the loaf, the furtive hands
> of endangered animals.
> my body given for you. my blood outpoured.
> indictable action! as in the first instance
> of vagrant Jesus, in whose flesh rumors and truth
> collided; usual penalty, rigorously applied.[21]

Though the brothers are imprisoned, this clandestine celebration of consecration is outside—freeing the prisoners into a radical outside and a radical intimacy. Agapeic service: the gift that consecrates the intimate universal. This consecration is outside the space of politics also. There is the idleness of communion, even in the manifest elements of the world.

Consecrating Peace as a Form of Witness

In his life, Berrigan tried to bear witness, living in the tension of this double condition between the immanent will to power of political sovereignty and the transcending fidelity to the agapeic servant. He speaks of being drawn into something like this double condition when he discovers himself an outlaw in his own country, "exiles-at-home"[22]; or in choosing to go underground, a reality for him, not a metaphor, of being someone and yet being no one, of being on the boundary while yet in fact being in the midst of life. One thinks here of the underground of Plato's cave that projects the human condition, though the people underground mostly have no sense of being cut off from light. One thinks of Dostoevsky's underground man, though he is spiteful and sick, and full of rancor to all of life, in being placed outside or on the boundary. Dostoevsky makes one think of life in prison, both in his *House of the Dead*, as well as his claim that the measure of a society can be gleaned from the quality of its prisons.[23] Dostoevsky experienced something of a resurrection through his own sojourn in prison. One senses that something of this was also granted to Berrigan.[24] Being in prison shows the double condition of being inside and outside, a double condition that mirrors something of the religious life. One is never simply at home with things, and yet neither is one in rage against things. To be the first would be to sleepwalk through the world; to be the second would be to be an incendiary against the good things life doubtless also gives us. There is a discontent that has the touch of the divine about it, and in that touch something passes to one of a more fundamental being at home, beyond all rage. One thinks of the double condition of the kingdom of God: already with us, and yet not of this world. Or of the double condition of the follower of Christ: in the world but not of it. This doubleness has been mocked as a dualism, or as a contradiction treasonous to immanence. In fact, as a sign of contradiction, it is to be between immanence and transcendence: in the midst of what is given, and yet witness to something above. Patiently to dwell in peace within the opening of this double condition is to await the words of consecration, and to hear them wording the presencing of healing.

I come back to consecrating peace. We cannot consecrate through ourselves alone. Consecrating is not a project of individual autonomy, though it may be deeply intimate to the singular soul. Nor is it one of social determination, though it is a matter of being in a community.[25] There is about it a porosity to receiving from beyond oneself. Becoming more than one's solitary self, one is born to one's singular soul, though this is itself a porosity to receiving from the community of beneficence from which one is what one is. Of course, one can consecrate oneself to something in the sense of dedicate oneself to it. But one cannot consecrate in the sense of determining the sacredness of the event or commitment through oneself alone. When the singular soul is born to itself, it finds itself given to be in relation to what is other to it. Consecrating is an event of receiving and being received into a sacred space. We are consecrated—there is a being consecrated. There is both mission and commission. There is witness to being received into a community of the sacred—of the spirit.

One recalls here of the nature of a consecrated vow. Marriage has been so understood.[26] Entry into marriage is not a contract, which is conditional and provisional. The relation is consecrated in a vow whereby it puts itself under the solicitation and challenge of a higher promise. In making a vow we are called and calling ourselves to *live up* to the vow. There is a dimension of height to it. We do not live up to a contract in that sense. In a contract, there is nothing above us, beyond the horizontal commitment to this or that conditional situation. And if we fulfill the terms of the contract, the terms are always conditional. The vow has something unconditional about it. It is a promise we make, but it is not only what we make. A vow, lived in fidelity, makes us. A vow takes us into a promise to which we are asked to live up. It is not only that we promise, but we are carried into the space of the promise. The space of the promise is the space of a future to be redeemed. It is also the sign of the endowing source that enables the promise in the first place, an endowing source that is not just of the future but passes between past, present and future, being none of these, because above each of these. If something like this holds for a marriage vow, something like it holds for all the religious vows. A vow by its nature refers beyond mere conditions—something unconditional asked of us in conditional circumstances. Can peace really be understood without the endowing of consecration? I take the witness of Berrigan to indicate the answer as no—and of this as something he more and more deeply understood and tried to live. There is his own consecration to peace; there is also, now and then, his being touched by a peace that itself consecrates him. This consecrating peace is not the balance of powers that comes with the suspension of war. This peace—before war, beyond war—is participation in the intimate universal.

Bernard Lonergan and Daniel Berrigan

Robert M. Doran, SJ

Asking what Bernard Lonergan has to do with Daniel Berrigan probably seems to some a transposition to personalities of the age-old question: What does Athens have to do with Jerusalem? Or, in an equally personal transposition, what does Aristotle have to do with Jeremiah? Whether either would approve of what I am about to do in this paper, I do not know. Whether Lonergan approves I will not know until I see him again in the kingdom of God, which I fervently hope will happen and which, I confess, I imagine happening every day. But I may learn earlier whether Berrigan approves or not, and so I proceed in some fear and trembling.

Both were key figures for me during the major transitional period in my life, which occurred between 1969 and 1984, or between my thirtieth and my forty-fifth birthdays, and so I begin this tribute with some autobiographical reflections.

Autobiographical Reflections

The years just mentioned followed something of a classic pattern of transition from what Carl Jung called the first half of life to the second (where, of course, the word "half" is used loosely). Many of the events that Jung speaks about as marking such passages occurred for me during these fifteen years: major archetypal dreams (in some of which both Lonergan and Berrigan were prominent, though never together), significant challenges to both a radical appropriation and an equally radical rejection of elements in my national, cultural, and religious heritage, periods of darkness in which I could not find the way, and an emerging clarity about what I was to do with the remainder of the time God gives me. Never in that period was there a question of being asked to choose between what Lonergan represents and what Berrigan demands, despite the fact that the subsequent course of my life has certainly seemed to be a following more of Lonergan's path than of Berrigan's, a following that did not allow me the time to participate in social movements as much as I may have wanted to do so at times. Only in the fact that Dan and I both spent a great deal of time and energy with persons living with, and dying from, the effects of HIV infection and AIDS did our work have much in common, and even then we were doing this work in different cities—he in New York, I in Toronto—and we were not working together in this ministry.[1] But from the time of the major turning point in my life to the present both Lonergan and Berrigan have been *figurae*, as it were, of something that I had to integrate as best I could into my personal religious stance if I was to have any hope of living peaceably with myself. Never did I experience a dialectical conflict between what one stood for and what another claimed of me. As I look back on my life now, I realize that at every point, most of the time, without adverting explicitly to either of these Jesuit brothers as such, every step that I took had to satisfy what each of them represented to me or there would be something wrong with my choice. Whether I succeeded in such a delicate integration or not is ultimately God's judgment to make, and I will not know for sure until that judgment is in.

What bound these *figurae* together almost from the beginning of my attraction to them? The expression that comes to mind is "their radical resistance to decadence and corruption." In Berrigan's case we are clear about both the resistance and what has been resisted. In Lonergan's case the issue is perhaps not as clearly defined. But I once heard the great work *Insight* (in my view the principal philosophical work of the twentieth century) referred to as a work of resistance against the sterility of some very influential neo-Thomist appropriations of Aquinas, and immediately I recognized in that comment my own appreciation of Lonergan's significance. Interestingly enough, for Eric Voegelin, one of the great commentators on the meaning of "Athens," of Greek philosophy, but also on Israelite prophecy, resistance to corruption is also what Plato and Aristotle, on the one hand, and the great prophets, on the other, had in common.[2]

But I must add that in the instances of Lonergan and Berrigan, as in Israel and Greece, resistance alone is not a sufficient explanation of a life's deeds. The resistance was in each case driven by a vocation to promote an alternative, and I have no doubt that with Lonergan and Berrigan the vocation was from the God to whom each had given his life as a result of experiences rooted in the *Spiritual Exercises* of St. Ignatius Loyola.

At any rate, the personal journey of which I speak began with the Vietnam War. While I was a doctoral student at Marquette University in 1969, I was asked by the university to take a two-year break from my studies in order to become the first director of a new program in Campus Ministry. While the office of Campus Ministry did not open until August 1970, those of us who were hired to staff that office became engaged with student protests that followed the murders at Kent State University in the spring of that year. It quickly became obvious to us that we had our work cut out for us, since some of the protests and protesters were on the verge of becoming violent, and we believed that our efforts had to model and encourage a different way to taking issue with what we believed was a national tragedy. It was an entirely new challenge for me, one that I was probably not quite ready to assume, and undoubtedly one at which, in the last analysis, I failed. During these years I often reflected on Fr Pedro Arrupe's reported comments to some young Jesuits who were working on the edge with issues of poverty and justice: "Be ready to accept failure, while still acknowledging that what you are doing is God's work. For you *will* fail."

My efforts in my two years as director of Campus Ministry included advocacy on peace issues, draft counseling, and antiwar activities, and this part of our service to the university met with greater resistance than did the more sacramental dimensions of our work (except when these incorporated the advocacy, which they often did). While in my studies I was already a thoroughly committed student of Lonergan, throughout this period it was the figure of Daniel Berrigan that was more prominent in my thoughts and in my psyche. Berrigan was quoted more than anyone else in the homilies that I gave on a regular basis during these years. He was present in my dreams on a number of occasions, beginning during these two years but also for several years afterward, always as a friendly figure but also always standing precisely for what we all know he represents. I took away from these experiences, and especially from Berrigan's presence in these dreams, a deep-seated affective consolidation of his message as something that had to remain with me no matter what else I might do in the future. Again, the extent to which I have actually allowed this to happen is God's judgment to make.

On my return to doctoral studies in 1972, I addressed in study and writing a number of the issues that had already engaged my attention in the years of active social involvement. By this time in his own development, Lonergan had made the theme of conversion central in his work, so central that today people who know little else about Lonergan know that conversion is at the heart of his work. He had also returned to the study of economics, driven by deep concerns for the transformation of economic systems so that they could deliver justice.

My own reflection on what conversion entailed, however, took me in directions that were not yet explicit in Lonergan's work, directions that had been opened up, however, by my recent experiences and struggles. While Lonergan was eventually to approve these directions, the initial steps had to be taken alone and, like Lonergan's work in *Insight*, were conceived in my mind as entailing resistance to an intellectual neglect: this time a neglect of the energic flow of sensations, memories, images, emotions, conations, bodily movements, spontaneous responses to persons and situations, associations. In a homily marking the beginning of the Campus Ministry program at Marquette I quoted something that Berrigan had written in an open letter to the Jesuits, published, I believe, in *National Catholic Reporter*, to the effect that, until the individual changes, *nothing* changes.[3] And while I had always recognized that this emphasis was entirely congruent with Lonergan's notion of conversion, I now was beginning to understand that the change demanded could assume dimensions beyond those that are explicit in Lonergan's writings. For what is it that drives and impels the forces of death against which Berrigan has set all his might and energy? From a theological point of view, it is the sin of the world, what good Scholastic theology would have called *peccatum originale originatum* (originated original sin), but precisely as this sin of the world is objectified in the social machinery, including military technology, characteristic of the imperial society into which American children are born, and in which they are raised, socialized, acculturated, educated. So much of this distortion, this creation of a false "second reality," takes place at an elemental psychic level without the children having anything to do with the reception of a grossly deviated set, indeed scale, of values. Surely the turning about, the repudiation of what has been, that is part of any genuine conversion process must include tapping into this psychic reservoir and allowing it to be transformed by God's grace.

And so I developed the notion of a psychic dimension to conversion, to complement and accompany the intellectual, moral, and religious dimensions that Lonergan had highlighted. The psychic conversion that I was talking about was closely aligned to the social concerns that Berrigan represented, for it is in the energic flow of psychic responses that our values first come to be set for us, before we have had any say in the matter, and in the case of Americans (as of course for everyone else) this means universally a mixture of good and evil and often a preponderance of the latter. The conversion demanded of this country in particular cuts very deep, much deeper than we are prepared to admit, as Berrigan has never ceased to remind us. It is the conversion of an entire scale of values from an imperialistic distortion to the fostering of genuine community on a global scale.

I pursued in my doctoral dissertation the connection of the psychic conversion that I was promoting with Lonergan's intellectual, moral, and religious conversion, and, to my great delight and joy, found that Lonergan was heartily supportive of what I was attempting to do. He expressed his enthusiasm to me personally in the fall of 1973, and I can say that in many ways my life has never been the same since then. The path was set, the vocation within a vocation was determined, and that path and vocation were to be intellectual and academic. That much was clear by the time I completed doctoral studies in 1975, though it was further consolidated shortly after I arrived in Toronto in 1979, when Lonergan called me from Boston and asked me to be one of the executors of his literary estate. That request has led me eventually to assuming responsibility, for the publication of his collected works, for the first twenty years of the project together with Frederick E. Crowe: something that, shortly before he died in 1984, I promised him I would do.[4] That promise and the responsibility it demands to secure Lonergan's legacy as best I can have determined the course of my life ever since and will continue to do so until I can work no more.

At the time of Lonergan's death Fred Crowe and I had already succeeded in getting the University of Toronto Press interested in publishing Lonergan's collected works, and we were busy planning for the establishment of the Lonergan Research Institute in Toronto, partly for the sake of seeing to the production of the Collected Works. While the latter institutional venture did not fulfill the hopes that Fred and I had for it, the work that the Institute began—preserving, promoting, developing, and implementing Lonergan's work—continues in other venues and under other auspices. If Daniel Berrigan has experienced that a prophet is not without honor except among his own people, Lonergan knew the same fate, and unfortunately it has continued after his death.

I wish to emphasize that through all of these transformative and determinative events it remained clear to me that I had to take with me on that path the Berrigan influence that had touched my inner life just as deeply as had Lonergan's writings, or else the very pursuit of the path that Lonergan offered to me, in fact gave to me, would not be genuine.

Next, I will discuss the two ways in which I hope Berrigan accompanied Lonergan in my own life as that life moved forward from the point just narrated. These two ways had to do with justice for the poor and nonviolent resistance to evil. I would like to articulate how these commitments have informed my work over the past thirty-plus years, and offer that in tribute to Daniel Berrigan, poor token though it may be of my appreciation for his courage, strength, and inspiration.

The Option for the Poor

How are we to speak today about what Jesus proclaimed as the kingdom or reign of God in human society and history? That was the issue that preoccupied me in the 1980s when I spent a good decade writing what became *Theology and the Dialectics of History*.[5] I took with me into this decade the commitments and orientations that both Lonergan and Berrigan stood for, and a quite central obligation that I put on myself in writing this book was to make sure that each of these orientations was acknowledged in it.

Theology and the Dialectics of History, a book that I admit is too long, is an effort to provide at least some of the basic categories that might be useful in our time to speak about the reality that Jesus proclaimed in his own Jewish context. The book is structured around a vast and complicated development of a very simple schema of a scale of values that Lonergan presents in *Method in Theology*.[6] And the book emphasizes that it is the role of the Church, as the community of the servant of God, to evoke the integral functioning of that normative scale.[7]

The scale itself is a function of Lonergan's complication of his own earlier schema of the so-called "levels" of intentional consciousness: presentations, understanding, judgment, and decisions. For to each of these dimensions of intentional consciousness there corresponds an isomorphic component of the human good: vital values to presentations, the social good of order to understanding, culture to judgment, and personal authenticity to decision. And as the structure of intentional consciousness is not a closed structure but one that is open to the fulfillment that only God's love poured out in our hearts by the Holy Spirit who is given us (Romans 5.5) can provide, so the socio-historical unfolding of the normative scale of values is open to and receptive of the communication of God's grace and God's message. Thus a scale of values is established that proceeds "from below" from vital to social to cultural to personal to religious values, and "from above" from the gift of God's grace to personal authenticity, from personal authenticity to cultural transformation, from cultural transformation to the justice of the social order, and from social justice to the equitable distribution of vital goods to the entire community. While the scale enables us to develop a notion of collective responsibility (something that Lonergan himself called for[8]), I call attention here to the role of the conversion of the individual, the level of personal value. Just as Berrigan once stressed in writing to his Jesuit brothers that until the individual changes, nothing changes, so Lonergan emphasizes that personal conversion is at the heart of social and historical transformation. But I call attention as well to the obvious fact that for each of them personal conversion is not an end in itself but the result perhaps of a series of withdrawals for the sake of a return to caring for the integrity of cultural meanings, the justice of the social order, and the equitable availability of vital goods.

There is a schematic neatness to the scale that probably has led some people to think of it as little more than a model, but that criticism would be justified only if the base from which the scale is constructed is itself nothing more than a model. There is, of course, basically nothing wrong with models. As Lonergan stresses, they may be very helpful in the task of actually describing or explaining reality.[9] But they are not themselves such descriptions or explanations. But if the base of the scheme lies in the invariant structure of conscious intentionality as it moves from presentations to understanding, from understanding to judgment, and from judgment to decision, or in the other direction from falling in love with God to a transvaluation of values, from that change to a new cognitive appreciation of the world, and from that eye of love to action on behalf of justice, then we are talking about more than a model. And such is indeed the base of the normative scale of values.

This is probably not the appropriate place to venture into the further complications of the scale that are due to the dialectical structure of personal, cultural, and social values, except, of course, to stress that these dialectical structures are distorted by the same sin of the world, the same "originated original sin," that, writ large (very large indeed), constitutes by default the social and military monstrosities which so much of Daniel Berrigan's life has committed to calling by its true names: idolatry, lust for power. Thus, the book constructs and amplifies the notion of the scale of values in direct antithesis to the distortions wrought by imperialistic and totalitarian ambitions.

The individual aspects are, of course, not neglected. The scale is a function of the affective component of each of the levels of intentional consciousness, of feeling's response to possible values. The criterion of the scale is the degree of self-transcendence to which we are carried in our responses. And the deviation of that affective self-transcendence is a function of the wounded psychic structures—wounded by forces beyond the individual's control at the time of the wounding—that my notion of psychic conversion was meant to tease out as the individual takes on the task of what Lonergan calls self-appropriation.

But despite these emphases on the healing and conversion of the individual, I argue in *Theology and the Dialectics of History* that a full-scale presentation of the scale of values might constitute something of a transcendental argument for the liberation emphases on the preferential option for the poor, emphases which, however begrudgingly at times, official church teaching has acknowledged. For problems in the equitable distribution of vital goods can be resolved in justice only by transformations in social structures, in technologies, economies, polities, and spontaneous interrelatedness; and these transformations demand changes in the meanings and values by which people live, which changes in turn are a function of the conversion of the person to authentic self-transcendence—until the individual changes, nothing changes. But that personal transformation itself depends on the gift of God's grace, which is required for consistent self-transcendent performance affectively, intellectually, morally, and politically. Conversely, then, God's gift of love effects personal transformation; such conversion shows itself in the transformation of the meanings and values constitutive of a culture; this transformation alone guarantees the justice of the social order, which itself is required for the equitable distribution of the earth's vital goods. The so-called transcendental structure of presentations, understanding, judging, and deciding has been complicated to yield a scale of values that itself provides the church with a firm validation of the liberation insights into the preferential option for the poor. Perhaps it also provides a framework within which contemporary theology can speak of the reign of God, with some hope of continuity with what Jesus meant when he called for a radical conversion in his own context. Explicit consideration is given to the distortions of the scale found in Western imperialism and in what at the time I wrote the book was Soviet totalitarianism. Joseph Schumpter's definition of imperialism as "the objectless disposition on the part of a state to unlimited forcible expansion"[10] was developed in the context of the distortion that such a disposition causes in the entire scale of values.

Violence and Religion

I turn now to considerations that emerges from a closer inspection of the structure and dynamics of genuine religion. "Religious values" as they function within the scale of values will upset and distort the entire scale in the direction of deviation if in fact they really are religious aberrations. And religious aberration is manifest in the involvement of religion with the structures and mechanisms of violence. There is no going back, I both hope and fear at the same time, on René Girard's emphasis on the violent nature of most religion (including a great deal of historical Christianity). We can only move forward, to face the delicate and difficult questions regarding what these insights will mean for the church and its institutions in the twenty-first century, and especially regarding its relations with the other religions of humankind.

In my understanding of a quite complex set of conceptual relations, Girard's work connects with Lonergan's precisely through the notion of psychic conversion, while the latter notion gains from Girard a greater precision than I was able to give it previously. In my previous efforts, I contrasted with other psychological efforts, most notably those of C. G. Jung, the depth-psychological system that emerges when one understands the human psyche—at the empirical level, the flow of sensations, images, emotions, conations, associations, conscious bodily movements, spontaneous intersubjective responses—in light of Lonergan's analysis of intentional consciousness. While it is true that this contrast already sets the stage for a reorientation of depth-psychological thinking and practice on the basis of foundations that ultimately are theological—religious, moral, and intellectual conversion—still, there is a greater precision to be gained by understanding the psyche in Girard's terms. Let me explain.

In his mammoth work on the systematics of the Trinity, Lonergan makes a distinction that I have found helpful not only in explaining what I mean by psychic conversion and how I understand its relation to Lonergan's work but also in introducing within a Lonergan-inspired framework the dimensions that Girard brings to the fore. He writes:

> we are conscious in two ways: in one way, through our sensibility, we undergo rather passively what we sense and imagine, our desires and fears, our delights and sorrows, our joys and sadness; in another way,

through our intellectuality, we are more active when we consciously inquire in order to understand, understand in order to utter a word, weigh evidence in order to judge, deliberate in order to choose, and exercise our will in order to act.[11]

My previous efforts at integrating depth-psychological with intentionality analysis and at reorienting the former in the light of the latter stayed within the kind of framework that this quotation establishes: a framework that, despite the social motivation instrumental in the original development of the notion of psychic conversion, is still highly individual in character. What Girard helped me to recognize more clearly is that the first "way of being conscious" that Lonergan specifies here is precisely *not* at first and for the most part exclusively individual but, in Girard's term, *interdividual*, a function of the priority of the social over the individual. Girard's notion of the interdividual gives us a purchase on the theology of original sin that may prove to be epochal. Lonergan speaks of bias and is quick to acknowledge, especially in what he says about dramatic and group bias, the presence of a psychic component that distorts and derails the quest for meaning and truth and goodness. But for Girard, the dramatic or emotional or psychic component of bias is a function of the mimetic character of human desire. For Girard, what occurs at the level of the passive undergoing of our desires and fears, our delights and sorrows, our joys and sadness, is mimetic. Many, perhaps most, of our desires are not autonomous or innate, but copied from others. "If I desire a particular object, I do not covet it on its own merits but because I 'mimic,' or imitate, the desire of someone I have chosen as a model. That person—whether real or imaginary, legendary or historical—becomes the mediator of my desire, and the relationship in which I am involved is essentially 'triangular.'"[12]

Now what Girard calls the "object" can be located at or related to any of the levels of value in the scale of values. There is mimetic rivalry in the academy and the Church, just as there is in the wider society. Mimesis in itself (or in the abstract) is neutral. But *acquisitive* or *appropriative* mimesis leads to violence, whether overt or covert. Acquisitive mimesis is focused on the object because of the model or mediator, but eventually the object all but drops out of sight, and the subject becomes obsessed—and it is indeed an obsession—almost exclusively with the model or mediator. Mimesis then becomes conflictual. Conflictual memesis is contagious. It can infect a community, an institution, a governing body, a religious establishment, and it can endanger the welfare and even the survival of the groups if affects, at least until the focus turns on one individual or group, namely, the scapegoat, whose immolation, exclusion, or expulsion brings a precarious peace. The victimization mechanism is the origin of a deviated transcendence that characterizes a great deal of human religion.

Such is the basic schema that governs much of Girard's thinking. According to Girard, however, there is a progressive revelation in the biblical texts of this set of mimetic mechanisms, which finally become unveiled for all to see—and so lose their power—in the crucifixion of Jesus. [13] This liberation is one element of the salvation that the cross and redemption of Jesus effect. Perhaps through Girard's help we will come to see it as a central element in soteriology, and perhaps also we will see mimetic violence as the basic element in the sin of the world. The original temptation is represented in the Book of Genesis as awakening a desire to be like God (or like gods). The first murder recorded in the bible is prompted by mimetic rivalry. The Gospels of Mark and Matthew tell us that Pilate knew that the reason the chief priests had handed Jesus over was out of jealousy (Mark 15:10, Matthew 27:18) Lonergan was on the same track, I believe, without having studied Girard's work, and I think this is reflected especially in his recognition of the importance of Max Scheler's book *Ressentiment*.[14] And if the biblical writings reflect a progressive revelation of the mimetic mechanism and of the deviated transcendence, the false religion, that it inspires, perhaps it is also true to say that history since then manifests a terribly slow appropriation of this revelation. Are we poised finally to make it our own in our time? Girard hopes so. The origin of the hope is the resurrection of Jesus: "The Resurrection is not only a miracle, a prodigious transgression of natural laws. It is the spectacular sign of the entrance into the world of a power superior to violent contagion. By contrast to the latter it is a power not at all hallucinatory or deceptive. Far from deceiving the disciples, it enables them to recognize what they had not recognized before and to reproach themselves for their pathetic flight in the preceding days. They acknowledge the guilt of their participation in the violent contagion that murdered their master."[15]

But Girard's hope is grounded also in the other divine mission, that of the Spirit.

> What is this power that triumphs over mimetic violence? The Gospels respond that it is the Spirit of God, the third person of the Trinity, the Holy Spirit . . . In the Gospel of John the name given to this Spirit admirably describes the power that tears the disciples away from this all-powerful contagion: the Paraclete . . . The principal meaning of *parakletos* is "lawyer for the defense," "defender of the accused" . . .

The Spirit enlightens the persecutors concerning their acts of
persecution. The Spirit discloses to individuals the literal truth of what
Jesus said during his crucifixion: "They don't know what they are
doing" . . . The birth of Christianity is a victory of the Paraclete over
his opposite, Satan, whose name originally means "accuser before a
tribunal," that is, the one responsible for proving the guilt of the
defendants.[16]

Because of the gift of the Spirit, there is another kind of mimesis. It is
found in Jesus's announcement of the reign of God, where it becomes an
imitation of the Father that Jesus commands when he says, "You must
therefore be perfect as your heavenly Father is perfect" (Matthew 5:48).
What he means was explained several verses earlier: "Love your enemies
and pray for those who persecute you; in this way you will be children of
your Father in heaven, for he causes his sun to rise on the bad as well as
the good, and his rain to fall on honest and dishonest alike" (Matthew
5:44–45).

The imitation of God that Jesus means when he says, "You must therefore be perfect as your heavenly Father is perfect" (Matthew 5:48),
Lonergan anticipates when he refers to sanctifying grace and charity as
created imitations, respectively, of the divine relations of active and passive
spiration.[17] Active spiration is the Father and the Son as together they
"breathe" the Holy Spirit. Passive spiration is the Holy Spirit thus breathed.
In Lonergan's theological anthropology, being in love without restrictions,
qualifications, conditions, reservations (which, he insists, is the meaning of
the more metaphysical term 'sanctifying grace') is a created participation in
active spiration, while the acts of loving that flow from this entitative elevation coalesce into a habit of charity that is the created participation in passive spiration. But a created participation in active spiration is precisely an
imitation of the Father and the Son, and if imitating the Father means what
Jesus says it means, it is set directly over against the deviated transcendence
that is rooted in acquisitive and conflictual mimesis. God creates in grace
the imitation, the mimesis, that is truly life-giving, and that imitation, that
mimesis, is an imitation of, in fact even a created participation in, the divine
relations themselves. Grace, too, is radically interdividual, and the founding subjects of the relations that it establishes are those divine subjects that
themselves are eternal relations of self-transcendent love.

I am currently writing a volume in systematic theology entitled *The
Trinity in History*. In its present draft form there appears the following:

> "The Trinity in History" would presumably have a great deal to do and
> say about the problems of violence, and the collusion of religion in

violence, that are at the heart of Girard's work. Relating the four-point hypothesis [Lonergan's hypothesis about created imitations of the divine relations] to Girard's mimetic theory from the outset of our endeavors is crucial for unpacking on the level of our time the meaning of the reign of God, and only such unpacking will keep our systematic theology in some sort of continuity with the mission of the incarnate Word in history.

The upshot of the present essay is that Bernard Lonergan and Daniel Berrigan have both spoken something of the truth about this God who manifested Godself incarnate in Jesus of Nazareth and who continues to break the power of violence through the gift of the Holy Spirit? They had different vocations within the same religious order, which itself serves God in the universal Church, but to the extent that they both spoke a true word about the God whom they have served, and especially to the extent that speaking that true word was an act of resistance against the forgetfulness that leads us to not know what we are doing, their vocations cannot be in dialectical conflict.[18] I can only hope that stating this conviction as best I can in the present context is something of small tribute to Daniel Berrigan and that he will accept it in the spirit in which it is offered.

A Kind of Piety Toward Experience:
Hope in Nuclear Times

Patrick Murray and Jeanne Schuler

Personal Musings

I don't have to look far to find the influence of Father Daniel Berrigan, SJ, in my life. Taped to my office door is a bumper sticker for Nebraskans for Peace, a statewide peace and justice organization that came together in 1968 with a small grant from Clergy and Laity Concerned, a national organization uniting religious opponents to the war in Vietnam that Berrigan cofounded with Rabbi Abraham Heschel and Reverend Richard Neuhaus.[1] Opening the door and looking to my right, I see a poster in red, white, and blue depicting a quote attributed to A. J. Muste, "There is no way to peace, peace is the way." The poster originated as a fundraiser for the Marquette University Peace Fellowship, a campus affiliate of the Catholic Peace Fellowship, a national peace group that also was cofounded by Berrigan.[2] Paul Schwartz, Jim Derks, and Terry McDonald, three members of the university-sponsored 14th Street Commune, where I lived during my junior year (1968–69), inaugurated the Marquette chapter. I became the head of the group the following year, when we brought "coconspirator" David Dellinger to give a talk during the trial of the

Chicago Seven. Judge Julius Hoffman banned Dellinger from public speaking after that address to an overflow crowd in Brooks Memorial Union. Paul Schwartz, one of the few Catholics to have registered as a conscientious objector at age 18, boldly wrote Sr. Corita Kent, IHM, a friend of Berrigan's, asking her to donate a poster design.[3] She was too busy to take on the project, but she passed it along to her associate Donald Mekelburg, who provided us with a beautiful Corita-inspired silk-screened poster. At home, looking up in our dining room I ponder a bronze death mask of the crucified Christ, entitled "Our Hope" by its sculptor, Bill Farmer. This work of art epitomizes the testimony of Daniel Berrigan: the crucified and resurrected Jesus is our hope, our only hope.[4]

That I have an office in the Philosophy Department at Creighton University and a home in Omaha, Nebraska, is in part a consequence of my attraction to, and certain reservations toward, Daniel Berrigan during my four tumultuous years at Marquette University (1966–70). Physics had been my passion in high school, and I went to Marquette planning to become a research physicist. Though I did graduate with majors in physics and mathematics, my experiences during those Vietnam War years impelled me to jump the track and go to graduate school in philosophy instead.

I arrived in Milwaukee in the fall of 1966 during the open housing campaign led by Father James Groppi and the NAACP Youth Commandos. Open housing was the last major piece of the 1960s civil rights agenda to be adopted by the federal government (1968); the marches of the Youth Commandos that Father Groppi was leading into white neighborhoods of South Milwaukee created a national stir. My mother, aware that my antiracist and antiwar political consciousness had begun to develop through my participation in the Young Christian Students group at Brother Rice High School in Chicago, warned me not to get involved. I didn't, but I did help organize a fall dance as an alternative to the fall prom held at the racially discriminatory Eagles Club on Wisconsin Avenue. While we danced at the War Memorial to Milwaukee's top rock band, The Messengers, Father Groppi and the Youth Commandos picketed the prom.

Father Groppi was hardly the only Catholic prominent in social activism living in Milwaukee during those years. A group of Marquette students, including several Jesuit seminarians (Mike Williams, Bob Graf, Gus McCarthy, Dick Zipfel), lay graduate students (Jack Cummings, Bill Taylor, Mary Alice Peckham), and undergraduate students (Paul Schwartz, Donna Boyle, myself, and sometimes Art Heitzer) came together during my sophomore year around a weekday afternoon mass in Johnson Hall celebrated by Father Harry Zerner, SJ. Responding to a letter by the Jesuit Superior

General, Father Pedro Arrupe, calling on the Jesuit colleges and universities of North America to combat racism, including institutional racism (a concept new to me) at their schools, our group led a nonviolent campaign that saw the arrest of six students in the administration building, the occupation of the student union by hundreds of students, the (temporary, as it proved) resignation of the black players on the men's basketball team (including future All-American Dean Memminger), and the ultimate acceptance of many of our movement's demands.

An Irish-born family man named Michael Cullen decided to leave his steady insurance job and the comforts of suburban Milwaukee and, with his wife Nettie and several children, to open up an inner-city Catholic Worker hospitality house, Casa Maria. Michael became an impassioned antiwar speaker and activist, and Casa Maria started publishing a newspaper, *The Catholic Radical*. Michael, an infectious believer who reached many of us Marquette students, was one reason why the leader of the Catholic Worker Movement, Dorothy Day, made several visits to town; another reason was the arrival of historian William Miller to Marquette University. Miller wrote the biography of Day, *A Harsh and Dreadful Love*, and I believe that he was the reason why she chose to house her archives at Marquette. I had the privilege of introducing Dorothy Day at one of her talks at Marquette, and, in the summer of 1969, I got to spend more time with her at an antiwar conference held at the Catholic Worker Farm in New York.

The spring of 1968 was a loaded time for me as for many. Our antiracist campaign peaked then; we had conducted a 40-day Lenten bread and water fast prior to the events leading up to the occupation of the Brooks Memorial Union and the resignation of most of the current black students at Marquette from the university. On April 4, a shock wave went out from the assassination of Dr. Martin Luther King Jr. and the urban riots it precipitated. I recall that the weekend following the assassination, Paul Schwartz and I made a retreat directed by Daniel Berrigan at the ICA house in Evanston, Illinois. As a speaker, few if any others pierced me as he did. That spring I was elected to be student government legislative vice-president, while my friend and the former Students for a Democratic Society (SDS) leader, Art Heitzer, was easily elected president. That summer Art and I attended the National Student Association's annual conference at Kansas State University, which overlapped with the Democratic National Convention in Chicago and the Soviet invasion of Czechoslovakia, making it perhaps the most intense week of my life. There I saw the film *The Battle of Algiers*; its juxtaposition of terror in the cause of national liberation with

French colonial torture hit me like a brick. One of the many speakers we heard there was Chicago comedian and civil rights and antiwar activist Dick Gregory, whom Art resolved to bring to Marquette that fall.

A month after Dan Berrigan led that retreat in Evanston, he, his brother Phillip, and seven others entered the draft board in Catonsville, Maryland, hauled all the A-1 files out to the parking lot, poured homemade napalm on them, burned them, and awaited arrest. This action of the Catonsville Nine raised the stakes of the nonviolent opposition to the war in Vietnam and soon changed my life. The following September, 1968, Michael Cullen and the thirteen other members of the Milwaukee 14 entered a Milwaukee draft board, took out its files, and burned them. As I later learned, their action was timed to precede Dick Gregory's talk at Marquette, after which he led a candlelight march from campus to the downtown jail, where the Milwaukee 14 were imprisoned. That was the year I was living in the 14th-Street Commune. Next door to us was another community of students that included a couple members of the Milwaukee 14 (Bob Graf and Gerry Gardner). That year and the next, antiwar sentiments and activities intensified. One of my housemates was among several students who burned their draft cards at a mass celebrated by Father Groppi at his home parish that fall (1968). (Oddly, when FBI agents would come to question him, he was never home.) That year (1968–69) there was a major campaign challenging the presence of ROTC on Marquette's campus. As chair of the student senate (ASMU), I had appointed a special committee, headed by my housemate Thomas Ferguson, to investigate the issue. Its controversial report (prefaced by a section of the charter of the University of Paris banning weapons on campus) led to demonstrations against (naval) ROTC at which six students were summarily suspended from Marquette, including my housemate Michael Coffman, who was then head of Marquette's chapter of SDS. Another anti-ROTC demonstration culminated in the occupation of St. Joan of Arc Chapel, which the occupiers, some sixty of whom were arrested overnight when they refused to evacuate for an alleged bomb threat, renamed Camilo Torres Chapel in honor of the Colombian priest who became an armed revolutionary.[5] Among the mementos to bygone days displayed on the walls of the basement bistro of the student union at Marquette is a photo from the 1969 Marquette yearbook of me (in sport coat and tie) marching in an anti-ROTC protest on the old tennis courts.

Violence was increasingly in the air at home as the war in Vietnam wore on and on. The summer of 1969 saw the breakup of SDS, the leading radical student group, and the emergence of the Weathermen, who organized the "Days of Rage" in Chicago that fall. Factions of the antiwar movement at Marquette, as around the nation, began to think in terms of violent opposition to the war, some to train for it, and some to enact it. This shift toward violence was aggravated by the climate of heavy surveillance (a photographer for the Milwaukee "Red Squad" regularly parked on our block of 14th Street), the government's use of spies and agent provocateurs, and President Nixon's decision in the spring of 1970 to invade Cambodia.[6] That invasion touched off an unprecedented wave of protests and student strikes around the country; four students were killed at Kent State and two more at Jackson State during this wave of campus unrest. A strike at Marquette led to the canceling of final exams, as happened at many campuses around the nation. Late in the course of the protests, a firebomb was thrown at Marquette's College of Journalism building, doing little damage.

During this period it was dawning on some student activists that the causes of racism and the war ran much deeper than many of us had first imagined. I remember a flyer, put out by the antiwar group the Committee of Returned Volunteers, that encapsulated the emerging point of view; it read: "Vietnam is a stake, not a mistake." The social disorders that the Movement strove against were coming to be seen as deeply entrenched, not the sort of thing that a series of spring demonstrations on or off campus would clear up. Increasingly, talk turned to institutional racism, structural violence, and structural analysis. Terms like *capitalism*, *ruling class*, and *imperialism* found their way onto the tongues and typewriters of student radicals. Marxist ideas, which had been largely suppressed for a generation by McCarthyism—Joseph McCarthy was a Senator from Wisconsin and a graduate of Marquette's School of Law—began to circulate, usually, and not surprisingly under the circumstances, in crude form. In the year prior to the break up of SDS, which had grown out of the anti-Communist Left, its journal, *New Left Notes*, increasingly gravitated toward Marxism, anti-imperialism, and sympathy for violent resistance. These too were the days of the decline of the Southern Christian Leadership Conferences, Stokely Carmichael's call to Black Power with the reminder "Violence is as American as cherry pie," and the rise of the Black Panther Party. With these developments, and others, such as the emergence of the Maoist group Progressive Labor, the Weathermen, and soon a rash of neo-Stalinist groups, Dan Berrigan's Christian nonviolence, which propelled him and his brother Phillip to the cover of *Time* magazine (January 25, 1971), came to be seen by many student radicals as irrelevant or worse. I rubbed shoulders with such students but was not one of them.

President Nixon began the lottery system for the military draft in the fall of 1969, and I drew a low number, which meant that I would face induction after graduation in the spring of 1970. As I thought about my options, I was forming my stance on participation in war. I knew then that I would not fight in the Vietnam War, but was I opposed to all war? I concluded, on religious grounds, that I did oppose all war, and I filed for conscientious objector status. (Eventually, and mysteriously, I was granted CO status while in graduate school, and, by a quirk of timing, I never had to do alternative service.) The witness of Jesus, Gandhi, the Reverend Martin Luther King Jr. and Catholics such as my friend Paul Schwartz, Franz Jaegerstaetter, Gordon Zahn, Dorothy Day, Michael Cullen, Jim Forest (another member of the Milwaukee 14 and a leader of the pacifist Catholic Peace Fellowship), along with Father Daniel Berrigan, played a formative role in my decision. So did books such as Jim Douglass's *The Non-Violent Cross*, Thomas Merton's *Faith and Violence* and his collection *Gandhi on Non-Violence*, Tolstoy's writings on nonviolence, and Pope John XXIII's encyclical *Pacem in Terris*. My senior year I had become an enthusiast for the writings of Jacques Ellul, in part because he represented for me a Christian Left alternative to the vulgar Marxism of the time. (Ellul cited the Bible and Marx's *Capital* as the two most formative books for him.)[7] Reading his defense of nonviolence on Christian grounds (at the time I was under the misimpression that Ellul was Catholic) in his book *Violence* gave me a further, persuasive reason to commit myself to Christian nonviolence.

Redirected by the turmoil of the late 1960s, Patrick began graduate philosophy studies at St. Louis University in the fall of 1970 still eager to change the world but conscious of how far he was from understanding it.[8] Jeanne, who was already an activist before entering St. Louis University in the fall of 1969, and Patrick met after mass just before Thanksgiving 1970, and our friendship soon included a network of students for whom being Catholic and ending the Vietnam War were intertwined. "What should we do?" was the recurring question during the teach-ins and protests. How do we root action in a way of living? Passages from scripture captivated us. In spring of 1970 conversations began that led to the formation of two communities inspired by Jesuit ideals and passages from scripture where Jesus's followers shared all they had. Community nurtured countercultural desires into a deeper reality. With a sense of belonging to a larger movement of resistance and faith, we listened to Daniel Berrigan read poems in our living room one evening. The work and joys of learning to live together did not overwhelm this group of friends. Over thirty-five years have passed and amazingly the community continues. The study of philosophy took us away from St. Louis but not from the realization that our being and happiness depends on being known and loved. Philosophy that turns away from the world and from the ultimate truth of shared personal life is lost.

Though we sided with Berrigan and the Catholic Workers in embracing Christian nonviolence, life in community, prayer and participation in the sacramental faith life of the Church—and we shared a good deal of their wariness regarding the versions of Marxism then in circulation (for their reductionism, determinism, endorsement of violence, and pelagianism)— full identification with Berrigan and the Catholic Worker met with some resistance. Theology classes had taught us about the "remnant," a powerful Biblical image planted also in Patrick's father's beloved book *Mr. Blue.*[9] Nevertheless, we were put off by what we perceived as an embrace of marginal status, a purist's indifference to the effectiveness of political action, an affirmation of anarchism, and a stripe of anti-intellectualism. In Berrigan and the Catholic Worker, we had already found the take-home message of Marx's eleventh thesis on Feuerbach, "The philosophers have only interpreted the world; the point is to change it." No doubt, but, as our later studies taught us, Marx was criticizing the philosophers not only for lack of nerve, a failure to "pay up," as Dan Berrigan might put it, but also for merely "interpreting" the world as opposed to understanding it. Marx's admonition was no mindless call to the barricades.

Three Seminal Themes in Berrigan's Thought

Written and rewritten around the Second Vatican Council (or Vatican II), *They Call Us Dead Men: Reflections on Life and Conscience* takes readers into the mind of Daniel Berrigan in the years leading up to the movement against the war in Vietnam that put him into the national limelight.[10] Up to Vatican II, the Roman Catholic Church had been wary of the modern world when not outright hostile to it, as, for example, in Pope Pius IX's "Syllabus of Errors" (1864). The great modern thinkers were placed off-limits to the faithful. In the years prior to the council, James Collins, later our teacher at St. Louis University (and Patrick's dissertation director), would get permission from the archdiocese for his Catholic students to read the classics of modern philosophy, since most of them were on the Index. That Teihard DeChardin's writings on evolution and God were published only after his death signals the Church's refusal to engage the issues of its time. All that changed with Vatican II; as priests turned to face the faithful and speak in the vernacular, the Church entered the open waters of the modern world. The new appreciation of the Church as thrown into the world and history—one important document of the council was entitled "Pastoral Constitution on the Church in the Modern World" (*Gaudium et Spes*)[11]—comes through in Berrigan's poetic prose: "The Body of Christ, of which the Apostle writes with such passion, is a reality of human history. It is subject to time and to human use. It is available before mankind. It wears the clothing of life. It knows what we might call the innocence and pain of a given moment when its own judgments are still as unfinished as a child's. This Body of Christ has a kind of piety toward experience."[12]

Berrigan discovers a theology of time and history in St. Paul, who already "brought to the faith an instinctive piety toward experience."[13] Paul "was marked by a respect for things as they are, for man's history and thought and sensibility . . . . Paul knew that man is not subject to the cycles of nature in the way that the subhuman world is. Man's dignity is precisely that he can create history by acts of intelligence and love."[14] History opens the space where the drama of humans recognizing, asserting, and living in accord with their dignity plays out. Time's clearing is sacred and a summons, "Paul spoke of the essentially moral and sacred structure of time. Time was task; it was the envelope of decision and new direction; it was to be redeemed . . . as Paul sensed, the Christian was called to be a shaper of history."[15] Another Paul, Pope Paul VI, emphasized this urgency when, in his 1967 encyclical *On the Development of Peoples* (*Populorum Progressio*), he urged Catholics to "read the signs of the times."[16] Daniel Berrigan is frequently, and with reason, called a prophet for how early, honestly, and fearlessly he reads the signs of our times.

Our times cannot be ignored; they make claims upon us. Berrigan sees here a challenge to intellectuals:

The difficulty is not that they are men of ideas. Men of ideas are rare enough and badly needed at any time. But it is also clear that in every life a reductive process must begin somewhere, or the ideas that began by inducing life end by inducing death. When ideas remain too long unexercised, a man who begins as an intellectual, his mind in good trim, ends shapeless and useless in mind. His ideas grow sour or stale; they lead nowhere.

In the long run, such a man may know a great deal and understand a great deal. But one fault spoils everything. And the fault is simply that a man may deny any claim on him from his own times. The fault is that he may glory in the history of man or the history of the Church as great ideas, but of his own times he may know nothing. The fault is that a man may not think his own times worth the price of knowing.[17]

To "hear the voice of the living" puts demands on us; it calls us not only to think but also to act. Here lies the source of Berrigan's lifelong impatience with the "weightless scholarship" of intellectuals who turn a deaf ear to the voice of the living.[18]

This exacting theology of time and history is one of three themes of *Dead Men* that we wish to highlight. A second is that of historical *rupture*: "Contemporary life offers evidence that mankind is entering a new age. The evidence in sum indicates a break with many aspects of man's past—a rupture so unprecedented and abrupt that men are generally at a loss to give it a name, much less to achieve a synthesis of its features."[19] For Berrigan, the rupture of the period after the world wars is complex, but the most telling mutation can be dated to August 1945, when the United States dropped atom bombs on the Japanese cities of Hiroshima and Nagasaki. Berrigan gravely observes, "There never was a time, that is, when men could announce the simple power to end time, to end man, to end history, to bring down the world."[20] The possibility of human beings putting an end to their own history is a prospect that Berrigan considers likely given humanity's track record. "Everything in our history points to one dolorous conclusion: the eventual or prompt discharge of nuclear weapons,"[21] This may account in part for the present heightened awareness of our historical character. In the years after the World War II, the build-up of nuclear weapons resulted not in a nuclear holocaust, thankfully, but rather in a costly, nerve-wracking Cold War that spurred a runaway peacetime war economy and spun off a succession of hot wars fought with nonnuclear weapons. The age following World War II has been one of struggles against colonialism, white supremacy, and patriarchy. Countries around the globe (though not the United States) signed the UN's 1948 *Universal Declaration on Human Rights*. Population boomed around the world, while in the United States and a number of other advanced industrial nations an "affluent society" emerged during an economic "golden age" that lasted until around 1973. Finally, the rupture, as Berrigan saw it, was profoundly, and ominously, religious: "The West, cut free from its Christian past, is involved in a frightful inner struggle, a kind of death agony of the spirit."[22]

A third major theme of *Dead Men* was that Western thinking had gone awry and badly needed rejuvenation if it was to be able to serve its purpose of providing the right sort of hope and guidance in the task of shaping history. "But the majority of men, sobered by a sense of history, are certain that the hope as stated is groundless, or nearly so, without a profound change in the structure of the thought of modern man."[23] One hope-blocking feature of modern thought Berrigan called its "appalling moral vacuum."[24] Renewing a point as old as Plato, Berrigan wrote of the reduction of reason to an instrumentality:

> the absence of a moral sense inevitably makes of man's intelligence the enemy of man. He is ignorant even of its central importance to his makeup . . . Deprived of moral enlightenment, modern man cannot answer with any measure of certainty the questions life itself has always asked. Who is man? What is his destiny? And what is the meaning of the forces which modern life is precipitating and which are shaking the ground beneath his feet?[25]

Berrigan echoes the judgment of Elizabeth Anscombe in her renowned 1960 article, "Modern Moral Philosophy," which was reminted and circulated more widely in *After Virtue* by Alasdair McIntyre: "The moral attitudes of the West are, in fact, growing progressively less reasoned, less commonly assumed, and more sentimental . . . . It grows almost impossible for us to show an inner coherence and consistency in our actions."[26]

To Dwell in Peace, his 1987 autobiography, can give the impression that Berrigan's Jesuit studies embittered him toward philosophy. But *They Call Us Dead Men* reveals a mind attuned to some of the most promising intellectual developments of the day (Catholic and otherwise) and provides a nontechnical but philosophically acute diagnosis of the times. Of his stay in France after ordination in June 1952, Berrigan recalls, "A number of us, appalled by the doldrums of backbroken domestic theology, had heard other voices reverberating in our bones. By one means or another, we had gained possession of the works of the European scholars, mainly Jesuits and Dominicans, who were even then preparing the ground for the Second Vatican Council."[27] These voices come alive in *They Call Us Dead Men*.

From Peguy's Personalism to Marx's Historical Materialism

We share Berrigan's regard for these three great themes of *Dead Men*: the call to a piety toward experience, inflected as a piety toward the historical character of human beings; the sense of historical rupture, felt especially in the wake of the two world wars; and an appreciation of the need for a "profound change in the structure of the thought of modern man," especially where human self-understanding and morality are concerned.²⁸ To hold these seminal themes together is the task facing philosophy. In *Dead Men* Berrigan quotes the Personalist Charles Peguy as follows: "If the mission of Christianity in its Catholic form was to be carried out, the first requirement was a clear view of the times, of the modern world, and an analysis of the future of Christianity."²⁹ We agree. But for that clear view of the modern world, we turn to Hegel and Marx. The pathway for Catholics seeking to come intelligently to terms with the modern world leads, we believe, from Peguy and Personalism to Hegel and Marx.

In the writings of these two great nineteenth-century German thinkers, we find the most profound resources for grasping the historical character of human existence, conceiving of the rupture of modernity (and postmodernity, if you like), and answering Berrigan's call for a profound change in the way we think. A well-informed "piety toward experience" leads to Hegel and Marx.

With the concept of spirit (*Geist*) that he pioneered in his *Phenomenology of Spirit*, Hegel established as fundamental the social, historical, and cultural nature of human existence. What Berrigan writes of St. Paul, namely, that he "was marked by a respect for things as they are, for man's history and thought and sensibility," fits Hegel like a glove. Hegel recognized in the Enlightenment and the rise of modern commercial societies a historical rupture with which he came to make his peace, even while he detected an internal connection between Enlightenment thinking and a reign of terror and multiple problems endemic to modern commercial societies.³⁰ In the *Phenomenology* and other writings, Hegel offered a thorough criticism of the received modern philosophy, especially that of Immanuel Kant. The special target of Hegel's criticism was a way of thinking that he referred to as understanding (*Verstand*), as opposed to reason (*Vernunft*). In Hegel's diagnosis, *Verstand* thinking adopted a set of dichotomies—for example, subjective versus objective, intention versus action, concept versus object, immediate versus mediated—without first undertaking a proper phenomenological investigation. Though we may sensibly use such contrasting terms for analytical purposes, *Verstand* thinking treats each of the paired terms as *separable* in reality. These dichotomies fail the test of experience.

To our knowledge Hegel's thought has not made much of an impression on Berrigan. (Of course, the same must be said of most professional philosophers in the United States.) The place of Marx and Marxism in Berrigan's life and thought is more complicated. Though observers may associate Berrigan with Marxism due to his sharp criticisms of American imperialism and affluence, along with his support for workers' efforts to organize themselves or improve their wages and working conditions, Berrigan is rather cool toward Marxism.[31] In *Ten Commandments*, he acknowledges being dismissed by Latin American liberation theologians and their North American followers. Berrigan offers this assessment of the dissonance:

> There were, meantime, two difficulties that prevented the liberation theologians and their American enthusiasts from taking us seriously. We were, first of all, nonviolent in principle and tactic, and secondly, we were not particularly interested in a Marxist analysis of current society. These were sins against the Liberation Code. They were not to be tolerated, and we were written off without a hearing.[32]

Berrigan's experience with a Christian-Marxist study group in Detroit was likewise a bust.[33] Berrigan raises theological and sociological objections to Marxism beyond his rejection of any resort to violence against persons. Berrigan wonders, "Do we not have here a taint of ancient pelagianism; the human act that preempts God with assertive human virtue? I would think so. In such a view, the saving gesture of Christ is lost in systems of worldly virtues."[34] Visiting a seminary class on liberation theology, Berrigan further observes, "It seemed to me that a Marxist analysis was old hat, that the West was as post-Marxist as it was post-capitalist."[35] While we are in sympathy with this theological reservation and regard much in Marxism to be retrogressive, we nonetheless find in Marx a telling perspective on history and the deepest available critical analysis of the capitalist mode of production and its implications for society. We cannot understand the modern world without Marx's concept of capital: "The exact development of the concept of capital [is] necessary, since it [is] the fundamental concept of modern economics, just as capital itself . . . [is] the foundation of bourgeois society."[36] Moral ideals and human possibilities unfold within a context of global capitalism. The criticism of the modern world remains incomplete without inquiring about capital.

Yet we seldom ask: What is capital?[37] When the question does arise, it is usually answered with: capital is any resource that is used in the production of new goods or services. Since no human society can do without productive resources, capital, so defined, is common to all societies. The discussion ends there. A generally applicable concept sheds no light on the distinctiveness of modern society. Marx, by contrast, conceives of capital as a social form of wealth specific to capitalist societies: capital is value that is self-valorizing. Put more prosaically, capital is money making more money—endlessly. The drive to make more money transforms communities and global relations. Placing this in the context of Berrigan's second key theme in *Dead Men*, we can say that Marx names capital as the rupture that is modernity. Indeed, because of its inherently dynamic nature, capital is the rupture that keeps rupturing. As Marx and Engels write in the *Communist Manifesto*: "all that is solid melts into air; all that is holy is profaned." This drive to accumulate capital creates an imposing and unstable global order where unseen forces leave individuals and their communities vulnerable.[38] In capital we face a peculiar, asocial way of organizing society that shapes our lives and diminishes our hopes for change.

In his mature critique of political economy, *Capital*, Marx develops the concept of capital dialectically, beginning with the commodity form of wealth and the sphere of simple commodity circulation (the market). Marx directly links liberal conceptions of property, human rights, freedom, equality, and justice to the sphere of simple commodity circulation. Thus, in his penultimate paragraph on the market, he writes:

> The sphere of circulation or commodity exchange, within whose
> boundaries the sale and purchase of labor-power goes on, is in fact a
> very Eden of the innate rights of man. It is the exclusive realm of
> Freedom, Equality, Property and Bentham. Freedom, because
> both buyer and seller of a commodity, let us say of labor-power, are
> determined only by their own free will. They contract as free persons,
> who are equal before the law. Their contract is the final result in which
> their joint will finds a common legal expression. Equality, because
> each enters into relation with the other, as with a simple owner of
> commodities, and they exchange equivalent for equivalent. Property,
> because each disposes only of what is his own. And Bentham, because
> each looks only to his own advantage.[39]

Without an adequate concept of capital, the guiding norms of modern society are skeletal figures. We may observe the emptiness of liberty, the atomism of individualism, the sham of utility, and the incongruity between moral equality and the vast inequalities of material life. But by connecting these defective norms to the relations and ideology of the marketplace, Marx grounds critical consciousness in the world. We begin to see how conceptually, sociologically, and morally rich is Marx's concept of capital when we realize that it presupposes all of this—and more.

Some of the "and more" is already mentioned in the above passage; it is the relationship between the wage laborer (employee) and the capitalist (employer). That relationship begins in the marketplace, specifically, the *labor market*, but it moves on from there to the point of production, where the relationship takes a savage twist:

> When we leave this sphere of simple circulation or the exchange of commodities, which provides the "free-trader *vulgaris*" with his views, his concepts and the standard by which he judges the society of capital and wage-labor, a certain change takes place, or so it appears, in the physiognomy of our *dramatis personae*. He who was previously the money-owner now strides out in front as a capitalist; the possessor of labor-power follows as his worker. The one smirks self-importantly and is intent on business; the other is timid and holds back, like someone who has brought his own hide to market and now has nothing else to expect but—a hiding.[40]

This movement out of circulation into production is a necessary one. Marx's dialectic in *Capital* proceeds by way of mutual presupposition, and one of his most important double conclusions is that capital presupposes the simple circulation of commodities in the market, while simple circulation presupposes capital. The market, then, is a necessary form of appearance of the deeper and profoundly different phenomenon of the production and accumulation of capital.

Modern ideals of fairness and liberty are embedded in a social structure that extracts surplus value from workers in a variety of ways. The contexts in which we understand justice presuppose modes of exploitation. What can be recognized as just is inherently constrained by the money-making treadmill. The latter conclusion has a number of weighty consequences with which liberal social theory and Catholic social teachings have not yet come to grips. Three consequences of the mutual presupposition of the market and capital stand out, as follows.

1. Liberalism argues that a market society is just precisely because it has no compulsory collective goal. On the contrary. Since a market society is a capitalist one, it has a compulsory collective good—the endless accumulation of capital. This repetitive process of capital is what assumes the place traditionally held in noncapitalist societies by shared understandings of the good. The compulsion that pervades institutions and consciousness in both subtle and forceful ways goes unaddressed. We nod in the direction of our historical horizon as a topic that leads nowhere. The question deflected by the liberal conception of a market society asks whether the endless accumulation of capital is the most satisfactory collective goal around which human life can be organized. This is no easy question to answer, given both the experiences with communist states and the crises when capital's

accumulation process goes awry. In *Economic Justice for All*, the US Catholic Bishops set out principles of the common good without sounding out the troubling context of capitalism within which our aspirations take shape.[41]

2. By the same token, the prevalent notion of instrumental reason, which loomed large in Berrigan's *Dead Men*, is undermined. That notion restricts reason to ascertaining means and improving efficiency. Supposedly, reason is unable to evaluate goals or determine human ends, goals freely chosen apart from reason. Reason is a stripped-down tool that solves problems but is unable to figure out existential concerns.[42] The shibboleth of instrumental reason shares liberalism's premise that a commercial society has no authoritative collective goods and is indifferent toward its ends. If a market society is a capitalist one, then (unlike societies with common understandings of what is good for human beings) it may be indifferent toward the particular goods and services it provides, but it cannot be indifferent to the progress of capital accumulation that is achieved through the sale of whatever goods and services are produced.[43] The supposition that reason is instrumental disguises this horizon and cuts off criticism from the start. How can there be criticism of capital if all ends lie outside the realm of reflection?

3. Commutative justice (equal value for equal value) is the gold standard of fairness and equality native to the market. Equality is achieved when all get what they deserve in the ongoing exchanges of a free society. Coercion and cheating are eliminated. This standard is undercut by the complex theory of exploitation that comes with Marx's account of capitalist relations, in particular, the capital-wage labor relation. Basic tenets of the modern (bourgeois) theory of right are undercut once we recognize that the whole system of equivalence in exchange is predicated on the capitalist class's extraction of unpaid, surplus labor from the class of wage laborers, and that the products of wage laborers belong not to them but to their capitalist employers, who need not labor at all (thus flying in the face of the spirit of Locke's labor theory of property, though not the letter of it). Emphasizing his dialectical conclusion that the sphere of simple circulation depends upon the deeper, more complex and morally troubling phenomenon of capital, Marx remarks on this topsy-turvy world:

> [E]xchange value or, more precisely, the money system is in fact the system of equality and freedom, and . . . the disturbances which they encounter in the further development of the system are disturbances inherent in it, are merely the realization of *equality and freedom*, which

prove to be inequality and unfreedom. It is just as pious as it is stupid to wish that exchange value would not develop into capital, nor labor which produces exchange value into wage labor."[44]

These relationships result in two indigestible conclusions for liberal theory and Catholic social teachings alike: the question "What is a just wage?" is turned back with the observation that the very form of wage labor is predicated on the exchange between capitalists and wage laborers, which can endure only as long as the capitalist class can extract unpaid surplus labor from wage workers. In other words, a full grasp of wage labor as a specific social form reveals it to be bound up in a system of exploitation. By the same token, Marx's dialectical theory, according to which value and surplus value (roughly, profit) are mutually presupposing, underscores the irony that the very society for which the principle of commutative justice makes sense, namely a commercial society, is a capitalist one. And a capitalist society can endure only on the basis of the exploitation of the class of wage laborers. In other words, if Marx is right that the market and the (endless) accumulation of capital presuppose one another and that the latter is possible only insofar as the capitalist class succeeds in extracting unpaid surplus labor, then the very concepts of commutative justice and the just wage (which is a special case of commutative justice) mask underlying oppression. Capitalism unfolds in the contradiction between fair exchange and exploitation. Though reform and exploitation are inseparable, the push for a living wage represents progress within a restricted understanding of justice. The tension between the contexts of critique and action is real and honest. Surely Peguy did not anticipate that his call to Catholics to achieve "a clear view of the times, of the modern world," would lead to such outcomes, but what if that can't be helped?

But this is not the direction that Berrigan's thinking took in the years following *Dead Men.*

Spurning the World's Counsel

After *Dead Men,* Berrigan seems to have leaned away from crucial insights of that early book toward a less historically sympathetic stance that emphasizes Biblical and moral purity in the face of history. Evidence of such leanings may be found in Berrigan's meditation—in the introduction to his 1987 autobiography, *To Dwell in Peace*—on a painting of St. Francis embracing a wolf. Berrigan describes this picture as emblematic of the believer's engagement with the historical world. He comments:

> I have no evidence that holiness conquers the wolves of the world. I see no magical outcomes today; evil crushes the lives of countless humans; there are few to intervene, let alone call a halt.
>
> Still there is hope. Goodness, holiness, inventive imagination, in the painting as in life, intervene. Sublimely indifferent to the counsel of the world (complicity, numbness), here and there a Francis places himself in the breach.
>
> What happens then is in even better hands than those of Francis. It is the act that entrances, not the outcome.[45]

We agree with Berrigan that there are no "magical outcomes," yet only miracles would answer hopes such as these. Berrigan's reflection on Francis is profoundly skeptical.[46] We know that the wolf does not lie down with the lamb. Only a miraculous alteration of the wolf's nature could make it otherwise. Humans may act in wolfish—or worse—ways toward other humans; there is wisdom in the saying *homo lupus homini*. Nonetheless, humans are not wolves; humans are self-reflective historical creatures, where wolves are not. For Berrigan, hope remains, but this Pascalian hope is of a different nature than the historical hope of *Dead Men*. Reasonable expectation of successful transformation of the world is now sized up as faithless hubris, "Would the wolf devour one or would the wolf transmogrify into a very lamb? One did not know. More in the nature of truth, the nature of faith, one could not know. To hanker after knowing, to lust after foreknowledge, to clutch at past victories—this was the forbidden quest that brought not joy but all our woe."[47]

With his call for sublime indifference to the "counsel of the world," listening to which is now identified with "complicity, numbness," Berrigan appears to adopt the sort of otherworldly standpoint that Hegel criticizes in various sections of *Phenomenology of Spirit*, employing phrases such as "the unhappy consciousness," "the law of the heart and the frenzy of self-conceit," "virtue and the way of the world," and the "beautiful soul" of conscience.[48] The self can be isolated by its ideals. For Hegel, bringing the good into existence presupposes that we recognize the good that already exists. Without possibilities rooted in the world, what happens to our obligation to read the proverbial signs of the times? All signs are equally bleak. Berrigan's contrast between the "moral beauty" of Francis's embrace and the "brute force" of the wolf's nature—"The heart of the matter was brute force and moral beauty in contention"—evokes just the sort of opposition that Hegel called into question.⁴⁹ Berrigan insists, "It is the act that entrances, not the outcome." But action belongs to the world, and the bifurcation of action and outcome is one of the false moves that Hegel exposes.⁵⁰ Consider the Plowshares movement's action of taking hammers to missile cones. For a reasonable person, the foreseeable outcome of this action is not particularly mysterious: the action is symbolic; it will not accomplish the goal of turning missiles into plowshares. Rather, the action will quickly be halted by the authorities, who will hale the hammerers into court and later into jail. Still, symbolic actions have an honored place in human life. They move us to face issues that we are tempted to ignore. We are challenged and encouraged by the witness of others. Further organizing and resistance often ensues. The various ways that symbolic action influences society in the context of a social movement for disarmament are questions for historically informed practical judgment, not Pascal's flip of the coin.⁵¹

But doesn't Berrigan say of Francis's embrace of the wolf that the outcome is "in even better hands than those of Francis," surely meaning God's hands? This reminder cannot but bring a person of faith up short; all the same, we must ask ourselves how God works in the world and whether or not God works through our intelligently self-reflective action in nature and history. We cannot wash our hands of responsibility for the outcomes of our actions—or inactions. A profound skepticism drives thinking into sharp reversals. The flip-flop of Berrigan's handover of responsibility for the outcome of our actions to God is his assertion that the outcomes are irrelevant to begin with: "The good was to be done because it was good. For no other reason, however plausible or weighty. The good was not subject to efficiency or worthiness or benefit or merit, in meager or ample measure."⁵² But to disjoin action from consequence evokes an unworldly, stoic conception of the good that does not match up well with the Christian theology of creation and incarnation.

Another approach to the point we are making involves a distinction raised by Father John F. Kavanaugh, SJ, a professor of philosophy at St. Louis University. In his book *Following Christ in a Consumer Society*, Kavanaugh distinguishes between the church as a "natural institution" and the church as a "sect." He observes:

> If Christianity is conceived as a natural institution, immersed in world and culture, its visibility and power in communicating Christ's message are enhanced; but there is the danger that in becoming "natural," acculturated, or secular, the actual message is itself distorted. In the

sect model, the Christian community is not seen as a natural institution, and the purity of Christ's revelation is insisted upon; however, the sect has less social power, less influence in communication, and it is easily ignored or lost in the huge dimensions of other cultural institutions. The problem, then, is how to maintain one's identity while at the same time immersing oneself in the world by living in and through a culture.[53]

The challenge of both belonging to the world and resisting aspects of the world faces every reflective person. In conducting this balancing act over a lifetime, Daniel Berrigan leans toward the "sect" model of the continuum.

Two Jesuits: Daniel Berrigan and John Kavanaugh

We would like to close with a comparison between Berrigan and Kavanaugh. John Kavanaugh, we believe, is the American Catholic philosopher most consonant with the thinking of his fellow Jesuit.[54] Though a generation separates the two men, the commonalities between them are broad and deep. The three themes of Berrigan's *Dead Men* that we explored above are integral to Kavanaugh's approach to faith and philosophy. Kavanaugh is perhaps unique among North American Catholic philosophers in offering a contemporary philosophical defense for the radicalized "seamless garment" doctrine that Berrigan and he espouse: no deliberate taking of human life can be justified.[55] In *Who Count as Persons?: Human Identity and the Ethics of Killing*, Kavanaugh develops the philosophical understanding of persons that inspires the writings and prophetic witness of Berrigan.[56] Berrigan admonishes, "Christians are called not only to give their lives, they're called to take no one's life. For whatever reason."[57] This doctrine rejects abortion (of which Berrigan says, "I call abortion a war on the unborn"), euthanasia, capital punishment, and war.[58] Both men are acquainted with the unpopularity of such a lineup of views. Berrigan recalls, "I well remember the fury that greeted me when I broke this mold [of expectations within radical circles], suggesting publicly that one was required to defend and foster life along its whole spectrum, prebirth to last gasp."[59] They offer powerful alternatives to the usual liberal understandings of freedom. We will draw out a number of the most striking commonalities of these exemplars of Catholic thought.

Berrigan and Kavanaugh are both deeply Christ-centered; each recognizes Jesus as the redeemer of all humanity and sees in Jesus our hope and the fullest revelation of what it is to be human. Berrigan exclaims, "Our hope is in the One who has undergone death on our behalf and has mysteriously and marvelously risen."[60] For Kavanaugh, the life of Jesus is the fullest revelation of what it means to be a person. He calls the Gospel "counter-cultural" and "revolutionary," and he turns to the life of Jesus as the embodiment of the personal form.[61] The Bible is a touchstone for both Berrigan and Kavanaugh. Kavanaugh concludes the preface to the first edition of *Following Christ* by identifying himself as "an evangelical Roman Catholic, whose final trust rests on the love of God made manifest to humanity in Jesus Christ."[62] Berrigan bemoans those scholars of the Bible who turn it to dust:

> To certain academics, almost any scriptural truth is regarded as grist for mere mortician skills . . . words, words are the point! Verify the word, codify it, explain its historical setting, its genesis in the cultural matrix, its influence on those times . . . Scripture is no more than a dead letter; and this even when its words are dead serious, direly urgent, words of fury, indignation, reproach, retribution.[63]

Faced with the alternative of being a bloodless academic or a fundamentalist, Berrigan would choose the fundamentalist.

When the Church does not witness to the transforming love of Christ, liberation comes up short. Berrigan writes in *Dead Men*:

> [T]he movements of mankind in the direction of human solidarity, justice, and peace are diminished. They lose their best substance. . . . No matter what it may accomplish in a human sphere, it cannot lead men to the transcendent freedom that Christ alone announces and confers. Deprived of His freedom, men still remain slaves, no matter what economic or political autonomy they may achieve. For the freedom of Christ is not in its substance the loosening of a specific human bondage at all; it is the release of man from the primordial slavery to sin and death, to the tyrannies of instinct and covetousness and lust.[64]

Nonetheless, both men warn against Catholic parochialism, which blinds itself to the faults of the faithful.

Over the decades Berrigan and Kavanaugh have watched while many friends and brothers left the Catholic Church, the priesthood, or the Society of Jesus. They stayed. Of those who left the Church, Berrigan observes, "Part of the trouble is that so few who walked out landed anywhere. Frying pan to fire; they left the church and the culture swallowed them whole. It seems better, as a rule, to hang around where one was born, trying as best one may to make it with a few friends, to do what one can in the common life: instead of launching out in the wilds, by and large wilder than the church."[65] The epigram that Kavanaugh chose for *Following Christ* comes from Dorothy Day, "When it comes to the Catholic church, I go to the right as far as I can go. But when it comes to labor, pacifism and civil rights, then I go as far as I can to the left."[66] Berrigan recounts as if it were yesterday the moment of his answering the call to become a Jesuit, "It comes to me again, as it struck me that day. It was 1939, I was in a darkened movie house, the bell tolled. I sensed the darkness, how thick it was. And I wept there for the renunciation that lay ahead, never to be revoked (not revoked, come hell and high water, to this day)."[67] Kavanaugh shares this fierce commitment to his vowed life as a Jesuit. As for priesthood, Berrigan says, "Priesthood? One could huff and puff about mystery, sacrament, sign, moments of grace. These I take to be realities. I am also consoled that they are out of our grasp, control, consuming."[68] These two men have found a lifetime of sustenance as vowed priests of the Society of Jesus.

Both Berrigan and Kavanaugh focus on the long haul: the need for faith life, prayer, and the sacraments: "You cannot survive in America without something better than America for a resource," Berrigan tells us; you need something more, "call it a tradition, a discipline of prayer, sacrament, the old words and realities worn smooth as David's pebbles. Palm them, press them, fling them."[69] These are words that Berrigan has taken to heart and lived by for decades. As for Kavanaugh, his conviction that the struggle for justice and peace would require the enduring personal and communal resources of a community of faith was a chief motivation for writing *Following Christ*, "Laboring for justice demands the support of a culture-transcending faith."[70] The faith to which Kavanaugh invites his readers "is found in the revelation of Jesus Christ and embodied in the deepest traditions of the Christian Church."[71]

The priceless dignity of the human person is central to Berrigan and Kavanaugh and constitutes the basis for their absolute prohibition on the taking of human life, yet both are acutely aware of the poverty of human persons. Through the poverty of human incompleteness the love of God is manifest. Human incompleteness allows for beauty and love; it is not the obstacle on our path. Berrigan writes of the "drama of man's incompleteness" and of "a poverty that, from the point of view of God and the neighbor, is simply a datum, a fact." This "drama of poverty," writes Berrigan, "opens before men the truth of their existence."[72] Kavanaugh concurs:

[H]umans find themselves in a condition of incompleteness, of being unfinished. This incompleteness is expressed in a striving for, a being

driven to, the realization of our potentialities in a mutuality of knowing
and loving. . . . The dynamic and structure of consciousness indicate
that our very "being" is a calling out for fullness, a "being-toward,"
a grand historical longing, a stretching out beyond the mere givenness
of our limits.[73]

It is no wonder, then, that Berrigan and Kavanaugh warn against an affluence that would cover up our poverty with "mountains of things." Of affluent societies Berrigan observes, "There, human faith and hope are placed
squarely in this world; men literally look to nothing beyond time; and
within their time capsule, comfort seeking, gadgetry, suburban childish-
ness, and the cult of the senses sharply reduce their potential for knowing
and acting upon a real world."[74] Kavanaugh's *Following Christ* is in large
part an examination of the depersonalization of human beings in the consumer society and how to resist it.

Daniel Berrigan makes no bones about either the importance he places
on moral consistency or the pride he takes in the life and the witness he and
his fellow nonviolent resisters keep giving.[75] "One woman I know has sat
in and been arrested at both abortion clinics and the Pentagon. Thus
enraging someone in both places. Her crime; an integrated conscience."[76]
At a New England meeting of the Catholic Peace Fellowship, Berrigan had
the temerity "to suggest that in Pentagon and abortion mill there existed
moral squalor and darkness, a common will to settle human difficulties in
the way of the quack; namely by disposing of humans themselves."[77] For
Berrigan, moral consistency requires a confession from the Church for
its treatment of women:

> Today the church is as uneasy and guilt-ridden as the circle of accusers,
> before the community of women. Women are regarded in the church,
> despite the manifest will of Christ, as those "taken in adultery": they
> are suspect, under judgment from birth, denied access to altar and
> pulpit, consigned to lowest places—pariahs whose only crime is their
> biology.[78]

Both Berrigan and Kavanaugh reject the justifications for war that have
been promulgated throughout history. Resistance to aggression is justified
but deliberate killing is not. The prohibition against killing is without
exception and includes targeting terrorists or enemy soldiers. Though a
pacifist, Kavanaugh has not followed Berrigan's path of nonviolent civil
disobedience. In a variety of ways, including his career in Catholic journalism, Kavanaugh keeps himself planted in the wider world. Uncompromising
in his own defense of human life, Kavanaugh is more likely to enter into

public deliberations and recognize the principles that his moral vision challenges. In his columns in *America*, he advises political candidates and evaluates proposed policies. Kavanaugh is more likely to acknowledge as morally relevant the distinctions raised by just war theorists concerning aggression, proportional response, last resort, or noncombatant immunity. These distinctions are familiar and constitute a shared moral vocabulary. The readiness to acknowledge them allows us to enter into public discussion and develop better responses.

Without giving up the Biblical basis of Catholic faith or the call to evangelization, we Catholics live in the secular city (or suburb) together with those who do not share our faith. Catholics must be able to address themselves to what serves the common good of a secular society. Berrigan has enunciated and lived the exacting norms of a prophetic stance. This prophetic vision, we believe, embodies the fullest truth of Scripture and human understanding. We worry, however, that dismissing the familiar distinctions of public morality contributes to general skepticism and isolates the prophetic voice. The "piety toward experience" so admired in *Dead Man* is lived out within this world that we share.

Berrigan Underground

Thomas Jeannot

The judge pounded his gavel and said, "Stop. You can't discuss that. This is getting to the heart of the matter."

Howard Zinn[1]

From April to August 1970 Daniel Berrigan, the "holy outlaw," went underground and eluded FBI capture.[2] Having lost the latest appeal of the Catonsville Nine—nine Catholic antiwar activists, who on May 17, 1968, poured homemade napalm over draft files outside the Selective Service Office in Catonsville, Maryland—the defendants were ordered to turn themselves in and begin their sentences in April 1970. On April 9 Berrigan disappeared. Four of his codefendants also went underground, including his brother Philip, who remained at large for ten days, and Mary Moylan, who remained at large for a decade until she turned herself in and served a year and a half of her three-year sentence.[3] Then, on August 12, 1970, Daniel Berrigan was apprehended at the Block Island home of William Stringfellow and Anthony Towne, after which he served eighteen months in the federal penitentiary at Danbury, Connecticut. From April 9 to

August 12, 1970, Berrigan underground violated the basic canons of the liberal doctrine of civil disobedience and transgressed the rule of law itself, calling into question the authority of the judiciary to adjudicate his case and the legitimacy of the state that adjudged him a criminal.

Just when Berrigan was acting to subvert the liberal doctrine and to call it into radical question, John Rawls gave it canonical form in *A Theory of Justice* (1971).[4] Looking back four decades later, it seems clear enough that in order to understand the dangerous memory of a criminal priest, we must situate him in the self-chosen wilderness of his sanctuary beyond positive statutory law and the safety, ease, and comfort of obedience. But this much American public life has always been able to accommodate. In retrospect, over the longer cycle, the classic examples of civil disobedience from Henry David Thoreau to Martin Luther King Jr. have even become icons of virtue in the American civil religion. Americans have managed to weave these profiles in courage into the fabric of their respect for the immense world-historical gain of the coming of the rule of law over the cult of personality. If Thoreau and King are American heroes, by the same token there are also American rogues. For example, between Berrigan's time then and our time now, the contrast between a lawless Richard M. Nixon and a lawless George W. Bush—each the architect of an imperial presidency, "executive privilege," and the blandly euphemistic doctrine of a so-called "unitary executive"—can only remind us of Marx's sardonic line, "the first time as tragedy, the second as farce."[5] Although the thesis of an American empire is uncontestable, elected statesmen like Nixon, Agnew, or Cheney and Bush have offended the reason and the sensibility of millions of Americans (and not merely among the remnants of the American left but just about anyone with a basic education in civics, American history, and the Constitution).[6]

But as I will argue, Berrigan underground is a more disturbing figure, who cannot be accommodated in the American narrative after the fashion of Thoreau on Walden Pond. We must understand him, if at all, along the path of a *via negativa*—a path of defiance, in fact, of the best American tradition of civil disobedience and of its philosophical justification. This tradition is of no avail and it offers no solace to Berrigan on the run. So he must disturb us in the way he disturbed a sober and thoughtful Robert Coles.[7] To understand the manner of Berrigan's defiance, hazy invocations of Thoreau or Gandhi or King will not suffice. What is required instead, if we want to take his great refusal seriously, is a clear grasp of the liberal doctrine he negated, the best contemporary articulation of which is Rawls's. The alternative is to view him as a stuntman trading on a certain celebrity—the epitome of the *cause célèbre*, by contrast, say, with the doomed and forgotten Mary Moylan—whose heroics were little more than a theater of vanities.[8] Shall we take Berrigan seriously, or shall we write him off as a less than merry prankster?

Rawls's Theory of Justice and Its Problems

Rawls works out a carefully circumscribed "constitutional theory of civil disobedience" still "within the limits of fidelity to law, although it is at the outer edge thereof."[9] His reasoning in sections 55 through 59 of chapter 6, "Duty and Obligation," marks his single descent in *A Theory of Justice* from "ideal" to "nonideal" theory.[10] The "ideal part" of the theory of justice envisions "strict compliance" with "an ideal conception of justice" and its principles (such as those that would be chosen by the parties in the original position); the "nonideal part" of the theory concerns the "less happy conditions" of "partial compliance."[11] "Existing institutions are to be judged in the light of [an ideal] conception [of a just society] and held to be unjust to the extent that they depart from it without sufficient reason . . . . Thus, as far as circumstances permit, we have a natural duty to remove any injustices . . . [But] the measure of departures from the ideal is left importantly to intuition."[12] Although Rawls is not an "intuitionist," he concedes that a "dependence on intuition" in ways that are relevant to ideal and nonideal theory cannot be entirely reduced from a theory of justice.[13]

With respect to ideal theory, the "ideal procedure" of legislation "stands in contrast to the ideal market process."[14] However dubiously, Rawls contends that the "ideal market is a perfect procedure with respect to efficiency," whereas, on the other hand, "even the ideal legislature is an imperfect procedure," so that there "seems to be no way to characterize a feasible procedure guaranteed to lead to just legislation."[15] Therefore, in the absence of a guarantee even in ideal theory, the relative justice of legislative enactments can be assessed only against the background, in part, of intuition, and in part the "connection between acting justly and natural attitudes,"[16] the "natural duty" of justice,[17] and a common or "the public's sense of justice," that is, "the sense of justice of the majority."[18] Rawls rightly recognizes that knowing what is just (both ideally and nonideally) is a matter of "reflective equilibrium," the "process of mutual adjustment of principles and considered judgments" (tempered by the various conceptions of justice handed down by "the tradition of moral philosophy").[19] Needless to say, there is no algorithm for this process: "it is obviously impossible to develop a substantive theory of justice founded solely on truths of logic and definition."[20] Therefore, Rawls appeals to an underlying "sense of justice" that is indispensable and that underwrites his argument as a whole. Through the process of reflective equilibrium, he acknowledges the possibility that "a person's sense of justice may . . . undergo a radical shift."[21] Yet in the nonideal theory of civil disobedience, the relevant sense of justice is the majority's.

The point for our purpose here is to take note of the amorphous, ambiguous, and shifting nature of these sands, even as a matter of ideal theory. This appears to be why Rawls insists that "while citizens normally submit their *conduct* to democratic authority, that is, recognize the outcome of a vote as establishing a binding rule, other things being equal, they do *not* submit their *judgment* to it," and that, "whereas a citizen may be bound to comply with the policies enacted, other things being equal, he is not required to think that these policies are just, and it would be mistaken of him to submit his judgment to the vote."[22] With respect to nonideal theory, then, for which "the problem of civil disobedience" is Rawls's "crucial test case for any theory of the moral basis of democracy," "the bounds of fidelity to law" are even hazier.[23]

Rawls's strategy for coping with such amorphous terrain as he concedes—assessing the justice of existing institutions as a matter of *nonideal* theory—is threefold. Civil disobedience is "the crucial test case." First, he draws a tight circle around the scope of his consideration. Second, he introduces the idea of an "overlapping consensus." Third, in the way he sets up his argument in sections 53 and 54, he adopts the essentially conservative view of defaulting to the *status quo ante*: granted the imperfect procedure of even an ideal legislative process and granted the virtual necessity of majority rule in a (nominally) democratic society, we "normally" have a duty to comply with unjust laws (even when we judge them to be unjust). Let's consider each of these strategies in turn.

First, Rawls's theory "is designed only for the special case of a nearly just society," such that the "problem . . . arises only within a more or less just democratic state for those citizens who recognize and accept the legitimacy of the constitution."[24] Accordingly, "The difficulty is one of a conflict of duties. At what point does the duty to comply with laws enacted by a legislative majority . . . cease to be binding in view of the right to defend one's liberties and the duty to oppose injustice?"[25] Within the bounds of fidelity to law and for a nearly just society, Rawls thinks civil disobedience is best understood as a form of "public speech" or a "mode of address."[26] He defines it "as a public, nonviolent, conscientious yet political act contrary to law usually done with the aim of bringing about a change in the law or policies of the government."[27] Within the scope of this narrow definition (by comparison, for example, with Howard Zinn's, which I will consider below[28]), Rawls distinguishes the act of civil disobedience from the conduct of "the militant" and "conscientious refusal."[29] In particular, the nonviolent character of civil disobedience is certified by its publicity and also because, although the law is broken, "fidelity to law is expressed by the . . . *willingness to accept the legal consequences of one's conduct.*"[30]

In the light of these commitments to nonviolence, publicity, and the willingness to accept the legal consequences, Rawls proceeds to outline three conditions, jointly sufficient, which should be satisfied in order to justify an act of civil disobedience as a mode of address to the sense of justice of the majority. First, it should be limited "to instances of substantial and clear injustice," so that "there is a presumption in favor of restricting civil disobedience to serious infringements of the first principle of justice, the principle of equal liberty, and to blatant violations of the second part of the second principle, the principle of fair equality of opportunity."[31] Rawls's explicit exclusion of the "difference principle" from the scope of his theory is striking: "infractions of the difference principle"—i.e. the *first part* of the second principle, which stipulates that "[social] and economic inequalities are to be arranged so that they are . . . to the greatest advantage of the least advantaged, consistent with the just savings principle"[32]—"are more difficult to ascertain," so that "they should not normally be protested by civil disobedience."[33] In this connection, Rawls flatly asserts that the "appeal [of the civilly disobedient person's mode of address] to the public's conception of justice is not sufficiently clear."[34] In other words, the exclusion of social and economic inequalities from the scope of civil disobedience is a monumental concession to the presumptive legitimacy of existing institutions in bourgeois, capitalist society, but it wears the disguise of a studied liberal agnosticism.

The second condition Rawls affirms for justified civil disobedience is "that the normal appeals to the political majority have already been made in good faith and that they have failed . . . . Since civil disobedience is a last resort, we should be sure that it is necessary."[35] Rawls's genteel assurance of necessity here belies the distance between the philosophy professor at Harvard and, for example, Malcolm X in Harlem ("by any means necessary").[36] The third justifying condition arises from Rawls's insistence that "the natural duty of justice may require a certain restraint."[37] A party (to use a Rawlsian term) contemplating civil disobedience should therefore consider (a) "that there is a limit on the extent to which civil disobedience can be engaged in without leading to a breakdown in the respect for law and the constitution, thereby setting in motion consequences unfortunate for all"; and (b) that there is "also an upper bound on the ability of the public forum to handle such forms of dissent."[38] "For one or both of these reasons, the effectiveness of civil disobedience as a form of protest declines beyond a certain point; and those contemplating it must consider these constraints."[39] Under these three conditions, then (and setting the difference principle aside)—the restriction to "serious infringements" of (civil, but not social and economic) justice, "last resort," and limited efficacy— the Rawlsian light turns green for civil disobedience, but it opens onto a narrow one-way street dead-ending at the courthouse and the jail.

Rawls's second strategy for coping with the ambiguities and uncertainties of his "crucial test case for any theory of the moral basis of democracy," uncertainties exacerbated by the descent to nonideal theory and into the swamps and dunes of "existing institutions," is to turn for the first time to the notion that became a prominent feature of his later thought, the idea of "overlapping rather than strict consensus."[40] He writes that the assumption that "in a nearly just society there is a public acceptance of the same principles of justice . . . is stronger than necessary."[41] Although there may be "considerable differences in citizens' conceptions of justice," "different premises can yield the same conclusion."[42] In overlapping consensus, then, what matters is convergence on "the same conclusion," whatever the premises may be.

However, Rawls's limit is "the point beyond which the requisite agreement in judgment breaks down and society splits into more or less distinct parts that hold diverse opinions on fundamental political questions. *In this case of strictly partitioned consensus, the basis for civil disobedience no longer obtains*."[43] In order to avoid this limit case, Rawls affirms that "[up] to a certain point it is better that the law and its interpretation be *settled* than that it be settled *rightly*."[44] In other words, granted that the legislative process is "an imperfect procedure," granted the slippery quality of "intuitions," and granted the intractability of divergent philosophical and religious opinions (the subject with which Rawls became more preoccupied after *A Theory of Justice*), he aims in this concluding discussion of the role of civil disobedience (section 59) to ward off the familiar and long-standing critic's fear that *any* justification could only be an invitation to "anarchy by encouraging everyone to decide for himself, and to abandon the public rendering of political principles."[45] For a tolerant society, this putative danger can only grow more acute in the face of the "intolerant," who threaten "the safety of free institutions."[46] "The majority is bound to feel that their allegiance to equal liberty is being exploited by [intolerant] others for unjust ends. This situation illustrates once again the fact that a common sense of justice is a great collective asset which requires the cooperation of many to maintain. The intolerant can be viewed as free-riders, as persons who seek the advantages of just institutions while not doing their share to uphold them."[47]

But here on the question of tolerance and intolerance, Rawls is not thinking, for example, of Mohammed Bouyeri's murder of Theo van Gogh on an Amsterdam sidewalk on November 2, 2004. Rather, he is thinking of the role of civil disobedience in a democratic society. The flank that concerns him in setting out his (severely restricted) justification is the right flank of law and order against the fear of anarchy. At this point, then, the question of Rawls's audience is unavoidably posed. The limit case of a "strictly partitioned consensus" (as, for example, under American apartheid in the era of Jim Crow) is just the circumstance Rawls hopes to ward off by making his apparently weakening concession to overlapping rather than strict consensus. He writes at first that the "reply" to the fear of anarchy is "that each person must indeed make his own decision."[48] Yet he immediately adds that "men . . . are always accountable for their deeds."[49] "The citizen is autonomous yet he is held responsible for what he does."[50] Rawls therefore retreats to the ground of his starting point: "in a state of near justice there is a presumption in favor of compliance [with law] in the absence of strong reasons to the contrary. The many free and reasoned decisions of individuals fit together in an orderly political regime."[51] In other words, although "each person must . . . make his own decision," it is the "orderly political regime" in the last analysis that matters: "while each person must decide for himself whether the circumstances justify civil disobedience, it does not follow that one is to decide as one pleases."[52]

Next Rawls proceeds to draw "parallels" with the "sciences," where there is likewise no "final authority," but "[we] are to assess theories and hypotheses in the light of the evidence by publicly recognized principles."[53] But the appeal to a parallel with the sciences is seriously diminished by the force of his earlier account of reflective equilibrium, where he writes that "there is a contrast, say, with physics. To take an extreme case, if we have an accurate account of the motions of heavenly bodies that we do not find appealing, we cannot alter these motions to conform to a more attractive theory. It is simply good fortune that the principles of celestial mechanics have their intellectual beauty."[54] Accordingly, within the broad framework of Rawls's proceduralism, the final court of appeal is not the objectivity of justice. Rather, "The final court of appeal is . . . the electorate as a whole.

The civilly disobedient appeal in a special way to this body. There is no danger of anarchy so long as there is a sufficient working agreement in citizens' conceptions of justice and the conditions for resorting to civil disobedience are respected."⁵⁵

Rawls concludes his discussion of civil disobedience by addressing the right-flank, law-and-order fear of the danger of anarchy, as if the liberal doctrine opened a floodgate rather than the narrow channel of his theory. In order to assuage this fear, he introduces the idea of overlapping consensus. By his own lights, this is a weakening condition, in order to make justified civil disobedience more rather than less reasonable. Yet when we stop to ask, reasonable to whom, we find that Rawls is plainly writing to law and order, the sense of justice of the majority, and the superiority in nonideal theory of settling the law over *settling it rightly*. In his singular foray into the field of nonideal theory where civil disobedience is the crucial test case, "the measure of departures from the ideal is left importantly to intuition." His theory is circumscribed by the confines of "a nearly just society," yet the anguish of intuitive nearness or farness is concealed in a two-pronged way: the common sense of justice, that is, the majoritarian view, is the arbiter of who is and who is not a "free-rider," and although "each person must decide for himself," the inference is unavoidable that accountability means "the willingness to accept the legal consequences of one's conduct" (whether or not one submits one's judgment to it).

On Rawls's theory, then, the free-rider Daniel Berrigan is irresponsible. He does not willingly accept. His "free and reasoned decision" does not fit into "an orderly political regime." Berrigan underground, who fails to satisfy the Rawlsian conditions for justified civil disobedience, may fall into the other categories Rawls leaves open, the "militant" or "conscientious refusal."⁵⁶ But Rawls's second strategy to cope with the hazy terrain of nonideal theory and existing institutions, which he thought to weaken the reins of justification, actually draws them tighter, in order to assuage the ever-present stake" and "it becomes a sacred duty to proclaim the standpoint of the nursery tale as the one thing fit for all age groups"⁵⁷ bourgeois anxiety that public protest against injustice must lead to anarchy, a shibboleth at least as old as Marx's *Eighteenth Brumaire of Louis Bonaparte*, which is apparently Rawls's anxiety as well. "Thus, if the government enacts a vague and harsh statute against treason, it would not be appropriate to commit treason as a way of objecting to it, and in any event, the penalty might be far more than one should reasonably be ready to accept."⁵⁸

Or in other words, in retrospect, the nonideal-theoretical liberalism of Rawls's theory is a critically dull blade "as soon as the question of property is at stake" and "it becomes a sacred duty to proclaim the standpoint of the nursery tale as the one thing fit for all age groups"[59]: if the specter of "anarchy" is the mortal threat to "an orderly political regime," the "Party of Order" stands ever ready to assert its doctrine of the unitary executive (up to and including the suspension of the writ of *habeas corpus*, the principle as ancient as the Magna Carta, upon which the very distinction is founded between the rule of law itself and naked tyranny), such as the world has just endured in one of the more bizarre annals of American history, with the rise and fall of the Bush administration. Whereas, at Catonsville, Berrigan had said:

> Our apologies, good friends, for the fracture of good order, the burning of napalm instead of children . . . . We could not, so help us God, do otherwise . . . We say: killing is disorder, life, and gentleness and community and unselfishness is the only order we recognize. For the sake of that order we risk our liberty, our good name. The time is past when good men can remain silent, when obedience can segregate men from public risk, when the poor can die without defense.[60]

The anguish of gauging the distance from a just society is palpable in the difference between the radical poet and priest and the liberal philosopher of civil disobedience.

Finally, Rawls's third strategy to navigate the foggy shoals of nonideal theory concerns the context within which he frames it. Section 53, "The Duty to Comply with an Unjust Law," and section 54, "The Status of Majority Rule," can be read as a preface to his theory of civil disobedience and conscientious refusal (sections 55–59). As I have demonstrated, Rawls first draws the distinction between "ideal" and "nonideal theory" in section 53, where he forecasts his aim to "take up but one fragment of partial compliance theory: namely, the problem of civil disobedience and conscientious refusal."[61] First, however, he must explain why "we normally have a duty to comply with unjust laws."[62] Even with a "just constitution," "procedural justice" will be "imperfect."[63] "Being required to support a just constitution, we must go along with one of its essential principles, that of majority rule. In a state of near justice, then, we normally have a duty to comply with unjust laws in virtue of our duty to support a just constitution."[64] Moreover, Rawls appeals to "a natural duty of civility not to invoke the faults of social arrangements as a too ready excuse for not complying with them . . . The duty of civility imposes a due acceptance of the defects of institutions and a certain restraint in taking advantage of them. Without some recognition of this duty mutual trust and confidence are liable to break down."[65] I have already considered how Rawls reinforces this argument in section 55 on majority rule, which "possesses a certain naturalness; for if minority rule is allowed, there is no obvious criterion to select which one is to decide and equality is violated."[66]

Moreover, "those with greater confidence in their opinion are not, it seems, more likely to be right . . . . The intensity of desire or the strength of conviction is irrelevant when questions of justice arise."[67] Yet as desires can be more or less intense and convictions stronger or weaker, so too do "intuitions" (whatever they may be) vary in intensity and strength and a variety of other ways, socially mediated, the reliability of which is without an algorithm, although desire, conviction, and intuition alike (not to mention experience, understanding, and judgment) enter into the "sense of justice" that Rawls presupposes in the argument of *A Theory of Justice* as a whole and in the absence of which his argument loses not only its illocutionary force and perlocutionary effect, but also its elementary locutionary sense. Having just argued for a duty to comply with unjust laws and the virtual necessity of the majority vote in order to create binding rules, it is perhaps too convenient and easy for Rawls to bleed out desire and conviction at just the moment he pitches his argument for obedience and submission. It is an inherently conservative argument in the sense that its presumption is with the *status quo ante* and the dominant social mood, before which a party contemplating disobedience and refusal must plead her case.[68] The upshot is that Rawls's liberal theory of justice (both ideal and nonideal) lacks a utopian dimension by design; its critical edge is blunted; and it leaves open only the smallest margin for the prophetic function characteristic of other prominent conceptions of justice in the same tradition of moral philosophy on which he himself draws. The theory is liberal rather than conservative, but its essentially conservative aspect shows up in its presumptions and defaults.

It is open to a Rawlsian to rejoin that this is all a misunderstanding, since the nonideal part of the theory presupposes "a nearly just society." But I have argued that this tidy formulation sweeps quite a bit of dirt under the rug. To the extent that it bears on "existing institutions," it is a fair question to ask which "nearly just" society Rawls has in mind. Although Rawls keeps his philosophical distance from a determinate answer, the textual clues in his presentation of the theory of civil disobedience and conscientious refusal warrant the inference that he is thinking of the historical circumstances of his own society in the 1960s and 1970s. In a note, he mentions Martin Luther King Jr.'s "Letter from Birmingham City Jail" (1963) and Howard Zinn's *Disobedience and Democracy* (1968).[69] His paradigm case of "conscientious refusal" ("noncompliance with a more or less direct legal injunction or administrative order"[70]) is the "refusal to engage in certain acts of war, or to serve in the armed forces," especially under the condition of "conscription" or a compulsory draft.[71] Evidently enough, he is thinking of the civil rights movement and of the anti–Vietnam War movement, both raging in American society at the time of his writing. It is not too far an inferential leap to conclude, as Zinn does, that the nearly just society he has in mind is his contemporary United States.

In *Declarations of Independence*, written years after the events in question, Zinn discusses Rawls's position on civil disobedience in a note. He writes that Rawls "worries about civil disobedience going so far as to bring about a general disrespect for law," which is not quite the same as Zinn's concern. "Rawls . . . confines his discussion to the situation in a 'nearly just constitutional regime' by which he seems to mean the United States. This exaggerates the justness in our system and, therefore, creates a basis for a more cautious and partial acceptance of civil disobedience."[72] I will return to Zinn below, but the point of quoting him here is to demonstrate Rawls's dilemma: if he is not thinking of the contemporaneous United States, then his theory is probably too abstract as nonideal theory to do the work that nonideal theory should do; but if he is thinking of the United States, then the anguish of gauging the nearness to or farness from a just society cannot be postponed by flat assertions of "near justice."

If a hermeneutic of suspicion is required in order to nail Rawls down to a time and place, Jeffrey Paris develops one in his bibliographical essay, "After Rawls."[73] Paris writes that "Rawls's writings are marked not by the simple avoidance of concrete political issues, but rather by the sublimation of the political into the theoretical, a process that obscures the origin of his thinking."[74] By tracing Rawls's development through five stages and reversing Rawls's direction by desublimating the theoretical into the political, Paris also tracks "the shifting fortunes of twentieth-century liberalism, all the way to its recent demise."[75] He contends that "liberalism's capacity to critique the existing order is tenuous at best; when it has its greatest hold on the principles governing society"—during the years that culminated in the publication of *A Theory of Justice*—"any critical edge is diminished."[76] Rawls takes a more critical turn after the neoconservative triumph of Reaganism, but Paris argues that his "more overt plaints against the decline in public, political reason in the 1980s are . . . made possible by the *lack* of any real possibility for a liberal recovery of any vestiges of tolerance and the sharing of social burdens that characterized its few centuries of political dominance."[77] Paris concedes that Rawlsian liberalism has a "moderate power . . . to critique deformities in the existing order," but it is generally ineffective "in promoting genuine social change. Thus . . .Rawls's greatest contribution to political philosophy—the public, political conception of the citizen implicit in the liberal democratic tradition—will prove," Paris thinks, "the most fruitless."[78] By the time of Rawls's 1993 essay "The Law of Peoples" (anticipating the book by the same name that came out in 1999), his implicit support for the First Gulf War (as Paris teases it out) presents a "direct example of . . . the sublimation effect. Existing political conditions and discourse are here directly incorporated into a theory that subsequently effaces those very conditions. It serves to give philosophical imprimatur to a new world order based on little more than naked aggression cloaked in a language of national security and global justice."[79] Paris therefore argues that Rawlsian liberalism "is ultimately unsustainable as a critical discourse."[80] He concludes:

> What Rawls could not account for, ultimately, was the failure of ideal theory to provide a genuine force against the direction of history. The limits of ideal theory, whether this be during a phase of total sublima-tion or one that can be critically suspicious, rest in its acceptance of the basic conditions of society, in the fact that it remains at best a model of that society . . . . After Rawls—that is, after the end of liberalism and the toleration of an existing state of affairs that promotes wanton destruction and cruel immiseration—we should exchange [Rawls's] reasonable faith ["in the real possibility of a just constitutional regime," i.e. liberal democracy] for something more powerful: a critical, if unreasonable, hope for a new organization of society.[81]

As Paris reads it, Rawls's liberal capitulation to the Reagan Revolution, now thirty years old, is already anticipated and forecasted by his treatment of civil disobedience.

Rawls had already worked out the basic idea of an "original position" by 1963, the year of King's "Letter from Birmingham City Jail," in his article, "Constitutional Liberty and the Concept of Justice." There Rawls argues that the liberty to protest against "the established institutions" depends on the "security of public order." Summarizing Rawls's argument and quoting from it, Paris writes, "Since any interference with this order threatens the liberty of all, the state has a legitimate right to limit the liberty of con-science 'at the boundary, however inexact, of the state's interest as expressed in the police power.'"[82] "Legal Obligation" (1964) "shows Rawls's abiding concern with any unruly interruption of the civic order; groups in protest must judge their circumstance 'reasonably (not irrationally)' and 'correctly.'

But it is precisely when the majority finds that conditions are already reasonable and just that civil protest emerges, as an attempt to change the general opinion and the practices that conform to that opinion. To judge protest unreasonable is the single most common means to discredit it, and thus Rawls's justification is strangely self-defeating."[83]

In Rawls's "The Justification of Civil Disobedience" (1969), Paris argues that the "self-defeating disciplinary approach is retained."[84] *A Theory of Justice* is just around the corner. Paris summarizes Rawls's position on civil disobedience this way: "If the decent, reasonable, normal way fails, then disobedience is appropriate, but do not actually threaten the established order, since it secures the basic liberties that make protest possible."[85] This summary is consistent with the account developed above of Rawls's high canonical presentation in *A Theory of Justice* itself. But the face of the holy outlaw staring out from the underground at his FBI pursuers on the pages of the *New York Times Magazine* in late June 1970 reflects a profoundly different sensibility concerning "the unruly interruption of civic order," what is "reasonable and correct," and what order of justice is actually threatened. We must now imagine the history professor Howard Zinn harboring a fugitive priest on the run from the FBI in Boston in the very same hours the Harvard philosophy professor must have been putting his final touches on what was soon to become the most celebrated book in American philosophy in half a century.

Zinn's Challenge to Rawls

The "boundary of the state's interest, however inexact" rarely has been more contested than it was by 1967 and 1968. On April 4, 1967, King broke his silence and spoke out, in his famous speech, "Beyond Vietnam" at the Riverside Church.[86] The distance between his "Letter from Birmingham City Jail" in 1963 and "Beyond Vietnam" in 1967 has the quality of a long march. A year later he was murdered, the Catonsville Nine carried out their action, and Zinn published *Disobedience and Democracy*, critically responding to Justice Abe Fortas's book published that same year, *Concerning Dissent and Civil Disobedience: "We Have an Alternative to Violence."* [87] The essential tension between Zinn and Fortas centers on the right relation between personal conscience and the rule of law in a democratic society: Fortas finally upholds legality over conscience; Zinn has just the opposite view.[88] Once King and Rawls, Coles and Berrigan, the long marches of Malcolm X and Stokely Carmichael[89], Black Power and the Weather Underground, join Fortas and Zinn in the conversation, matters become almost as bewilderingly tangled and complex as the late 1960s and early 1970s themselves.

For example, to this point, my discussion of civil disobedience has bracketed a consideration of the role of *nonviolent direct action* in its practice and justification. As I have argued, Rawls builds nonviolence into his definition, following the self-understanding of a Supreme Court Justice but on a higher level of abstraction with his fictionalization of a "nearly just" society. In the spirit of nonviolence of Rawls's definition, but more under the influence of Gandhi and the New Testament than American liberalism *per se*, King and Berrigan are fiercely dedicated pacifists. Yet Rawls is not a pacifist, and neither are Malcolm X and Stokely Carmichael.[90] Zinn too defines civil disobedience broadly enough to include at least the possibility of violence in principle, but this is the very point "beyond which," for Rawls, "dissent ceases to be civil disobedience."[91] The complexity if not irony of this circumstance—the nonpacifist Zinn (almost offhandedly quoting the revolutionist Thomas Jefferson's taste for "a little rebellion now and then . . . like a storm in the atmosphere"[92]) running cover for the ardently pacifist priest while the nonpacifist Rawls makes arguments the force of which must be to find the priest beyond the pale—can be partly disarticulated with respect to the state, the ruling-class interests it serves, and the government's monopoly on violence, police power, the use of coercive force, and the "right" of punishment (the crucial "right" at the basis of the Lockean social contract, which is the sole "natural right" an individual in a so-called "state of nature" forfeits for the sake of establishment).[93] For Fortas and Rawls, the constitutional state has *prima facie* legitimacy. For Zinn and Berrigan, Black Power and the Weathermen, and increasingly for the lionized King in his tormented passage from 1963 to 1967, the state is cast in the throes of a legitimation crisis.[94] The Rawlsian "state's interest as expressed in the police power" is not merely an "inexact boundary," but it was fundamentally contested by the rise of the New Left and the shock waves of civil unrest that then shook American society to its core.

Zinn finally disavows violence, but not because he follows Jesus of Nazareth; his disavowal is on pragmatic, strategic, and tactical grounds. He writes that we "face an enormous responsibility: How to achieve justice without massive violence. Whatever in the past has been the moral justification for violence . . . must now be accomplished by other means: It is the monumental moral and tactical challenge of our time."[95] With reference to the national King piety the net effect of which has been, perhaps, more to domesticate and trivialize his legacy, he writes that "King's phrase, and that of the southern civil rights movement, was not simply 'nonviolence,' but *nonviolent direct action*."[96] "Direct action does not deride using the political rights, the civil liberties, even the voting mechanisms in those societies where they are available (as in the United States), but it *recognizes the limitations of those controlled rights and goes beyond*."[97] Zinn continues, "Freedom and justice, which so often have been the excuses for violence, are still our goals. But the means for achieving them must change, because violence, however tempting in the quickness of its action, undermines those goals immediately, and also in the long run. The means for achieving social change must match, morally, the ends."[98] Finally, he writes, "It is true that human rights cannot be defended or advanced without *power*. But if we have learned anything useful from the carnage of [the twentieth] century, it is that true power does not—as the heads of states everywhere inspire us to believe—come out of the barrel of a gun, or out of a missile silo."[99] Although Zinn appeals to morality in these quotations, his appeal is not categorical, as it is for King and Berrigan. Moreover, it is not irrelevant that his arguments are secular rather than religious and theological (as King's and Berrigan's are). For him, nonviolence is not an end in itself; rather, it enters into the consideration of the best means for attaining the goals that *are* ends in themselves, freedom and justice (distinct from and higher than the rule of law). Unlike Fortas and Rawls, Zinn's end is not the rule of law *per se*, and still less public order and safety. Rather, his analysis of means and ends in relation to violence is closer to Malcolm X's speech of April 12, 1964, "The Ballot or the Bullet,"[100] than it is to Berrigan's or to King's in 1963 in the "Letter from Birmingham City Jail," and it is well beyond Rawls's theory of civil disobedience in *A Theory of Justice*.

Whereas Zinn contextualizes his account of civil disobedience within the framework of direct action, Rawls distinguishes his position from Zinn's on two counts: first, it is narrower; second, it excludes violence in principle.[101] In the end, this is not because Rawls is a pacifist, but because Rawlsian liberalism simply assigns a far greater weight to the duty of obedience (even to unjust laws, as I have shown) than the radical Zinn concedes. The author of *A People's History of the United States* systematically distinguishes between the state and institutions of government, on the one hand, and the people themselves on the other hand. Even within a constitutionally founded nation-state such as the United States, Zinn is systematically suspicious of the rule of law and the police power of the state to enforce it. He therefore qualifies as Rawls's "militant."

Because Rawls's theory of civil disobedience presupposes a nearly just society, he distinguishes it from the act of a militant: "Civil disobedience . . .

is clearly distinct from militant action and obstruction; it is far removed from organized forcible resistance. The militant . . . is much more deeply opposed to the existing political system."[102] "While [the militant's] action is conscientious on its own terms," Rawls insists by fiat that "[militancy] does not appeal to the sense of justice of the majority (or those having effective political power), since [the militant] thinks that their sense of justice is erroneous, or else without effect."[103] "Thus," Rawls continues, "the militant may try to *evade the penalty*, since he is *not prepared to accept the legal consequences* of his violation of the law . . . In this sense militant action is *not within the bounds of fidelity to law*, but represents a more profound opposition to the legal order."[104]

For as carefully reasoned a book as *A Theory of Justice*, it is modestly surprising that Rawls next asserts that the militant is one who tries "to prepare the way for radical and even revolutionary change" and that "this is to be done by trying to arouse the public to an awareness of the fundamental reforms that need to be made."[105] Not only does he blur the distinction between reform and "radical" or "revolutionary" change, but he concedes that militant action seeks "to arouse the public to . . . awareness" after he has just denied that it is the public sense of justice that is at stake in militancy (that is, in militant action as distinct from acts of terror). Finally, Rawls writes that "in certain circumstances militant action and other kinds of resistance are surely justified," but he declines to "consider these cases."[106]

That is, in 1971, against the backdrop of ongoing domestic social upheaval in the United States while the savage war against the people of Vietnam, Cambodia, and Laos wrought greater carnage still under the impact of Nixon's "madman strategy,"[107] Rawls nevertheless finds it necessary to distinguish between the genteel, law-abiding form of civil disobedience for which he finds justification within the scope of his narrow definition, and the militant action that Zinn includes within the scope of his broader definition. A Rawlsian might object once more that this is only on the presupposition of a nearly just society, but I have already argued that it is precisely this presupposition, in *nonideal* theory, which permits Rawls to evade the very urgent and pressing questions one might expect nonideal theory to take up if it is to be worth anything at all in its assessment of the justice of existing institutions. Instead, Rawls writes that militant action, as opposed to civil disobedience, presents a case that he shall not consider.

Meanwhile, we find the pacifist priest confounding categories altogether. In the tradition, civil disobedience goes together with nonviolence, and nonviolence traditionally includes the willing acceptance of the legal consequences of one's civilly disobedient act. On the other hand, by design, Zinn's more expansive view of civil disobedience does not require the willingness to cooperate peaceably with law enforcement and the criminal justice system, but neither is it *categorically* nonviolent or nonviolent in principle. Berrigan underground qualifies as a Rawlsian "militant," since he is not prepared to accept the legal consequences of his violation of the law, but he is militantly *nonviolent*, and unlike his friend Howard Zinn, he is a pacifist *in principle*. Berrigan throws the axes that coordinate civil disobedience with nonviolence and militancy with violence off the orbit of their steady rotation. In other words, we still lack a coherent explanation of the holy outlaw's criminality within the established sense-making categories.

Zinn Reads Berrigan and King

In *Declarations of Independence* (1990),[108] Zinn, who had traveled to Hanoi with Berrigan in early 1968 to secure the release of three American airmen only to be branded as "traitors" by then-FBI Director J. Edgar Hoover, challenges the liberal doctrine of civil disobedience through a reconsideration of Dr. Martin Luther King Jr.'s celebrated "Letter from Birmingham City Jail" (1963).[109] He writes that King's "Letter" "has been seriously misinterpreted."[110] King had written, "I submit that an individual who breaks a law that conscience tells him is unjust, and *willingly accepts the penalty* by staying in jail to arouse the conscience of the community over its injustices is in reality expressing the very highest respect for law."[111] In the liberal doctrine of civil disobedience, the law in question here is the positive statutory law of the state. However, in Zinn's rereading, "the 'law' that King respected . . . was not man-made law, neither segregation laws nor even laws approved by the Supreme Court nor decisions of the courts nor sentences meted out by judges. He meant respect for the higher law, the law of morality, of justice. To be 'one who willingly accepts' punishment is not the same as thinking it *right* to be punished for an act of conscience."[112]

In *Declarations of Independence*, Zinn engages his wide-ranging topics more in the style of a memoir than of philosophical argument, and he is welcome to the latitudes of his style. However, as a matter of philosophical argument, we should immediately observe two mistakes in his reasoning. First, as Rawls points out in one of his notes on Zinn, right after he records that Zinn "denies that civil disobedience need be nonviolent: Certainly one does not accept the punishment as right, that is, as deserved for a criminal act. Rather one is willing to undergo the legal consequences for the sake of fidelity to law, which is a different matter."[113] Second and more acutely, as Zinn recounts his personal involvement in harboring the fugitive priest, his rhetorical aim is to assimilate Berrigan underground to the case made by Dr. King in Birmingham in 1963. Not only is Zinn mistaken—for King, what is clearly at issue is respect for "man-made law"— but his rhetorical strategy slurs the crucial difference: even though Zinn contests the *liberal* doctrine of civil disobedience by subverting the presumptive sanctity of "fidelity to law" and by developing his more expansive view of civil disobedience as a modality of dissent and resistance, his account obscures the *radical* difference between Berrigan's conduct on the Atlantic Seaboard in 1970 and King's conduct in Birmingham in 1963. The difference between 1963 and 1970 is a world of difference.

It is understandable that Zinn would want to bathe Berrigan in the aura of King, and not merely as a rhetorical device in order to perfume the priest in the odor of King's sanctified place in the American civil religion (the plaster-of-Paris saint whom chambers of commerce from coast to coast annually co-opt on the national holiday). For not only do King and Berrigan share in Zinn's progressive, populist politics (vague as these terms are), but insofar as any lasting social transformations have eventuated at all from the turmoil of the social movements of what is called "the sixties" (however uncertain their true depth and breadth), the dedicated, principled nonviolence of the movements they led and inspired is an integral and vital part of the narrative of those times that must be brought front and center in our remembrance of their enduring legacy. Nor is it gratuitous to imagine that had King lived on past the darkness of 1968, by 1970 he might have given his imprimatur to Berrigan underground, just as Zinn suggests. But I have already noted King's long march from 1963 to 1967 and 1968, and with respect to the difference it makes, it is crucial to recognize that Rawls does greater justice to the "Letter from Birmingham City Jail" than does Zinn. Rawls is right to cite King's "Letter" as a paradigm case of the liberal doctrine of civil disobedience, and Zinn is wrong to play fast and loose with it.[114] After all, King addresses his "Letter" to his "dear Fellow Clergyman"; in particular, "eight prominent 'liberal' clergyman, all white," who had "published an open letter in January [1963] that called on King to allow the battle for integration to continue in the local and federal courts, and warned that King's nonviolent resistance would have the effect of inciting civil disturbances." In his masthead introduction to the "Letter," James M. Washington, the editor of a volume of King's collected writings and speeches, continues: "Dr. King wanted Christian ministers to see that the meaning of Christian discipleship was at the heart of the African American struggle for freedom, justice, and equality."[115]

Yet, Zinn is not entirely wrong in his grasp of King's spirit, if not the "Letter." Precisely because King's image has been coated in plaster of Paris and almost everyone invokes his name and stakes a claim on his legacy, it is still timely for Zinn to remind us of the radicalism of King's challenge to business as usual in American life. Before 1967, by virtue of his position of leadership in the Southern Christian Leadership Conference, King was widely perceived and even styled himself to be a moderate, especially by comparison with Malcolm X, Stokley Carmichael, and the emerging Black Power movement. The moderate spirit is epitomized in the "Letter from Birmingham City Jail": although he writes that he "gradually gained a bit of satisfaction from being considered an extremist," in that very context he is at his most canonical (in a letter saturated in references and allusions to the tradition he reasonably expected his interlocutors to share in common with him). He cites Jesus, Amos, Paul, Martin Luther, John Bunyan, Abraham Lincoln, and Thomas Jefferson in rapid succession, following which he goes on to record his disappointed "hope that the white moderate would see this."[116] Yet by 1967 and 1968, it is plain that the King of "Beyond Vietnam" who was gunned down in Memphis—where he had gone to support striking workers just as he was in the middle of organizing a Poor People's Campaign and planning a new march on Washington— was a different man than the King who declared, "I Have a Dream," on the Washington Mall in 1963, at least in the manner of his public self-presentation and in his strategy and tactics. The recovery of King's radicalism therefore remains an important and unfinished task to which Zinn makes an important contribution, and it may be that the core of King's being and message had been radicalism, rather than liberalism or moderation, virtually from the start, as Peter Hudis has recently argued: a radicalized and potentially revolutionary King appears at least as early as 1951, four years before the Montgomery bus boycott.[117] Still, it must be said that Zinn serves neither King nor Berrigan well by slurring two quite different occasions and acts.

In his chapter on "Law and Justice," Zinn succinctly states his principle: "The principle I am suggesting for civil disobedience is not that we must tolerate all disobedience to law, but that we refuse an absolute *obedience* to law. The ultimate test is not law, but justice."[118] Granted his disjunction between law and justice, it is fair to say that he holds the principle of "fidelity to law" (especially regarded as an end in itself) in low regard, as opposed to the high regard in which it is held by the liberal doctrine.

Concerning one's obligation to the state, he devotes a section of his chapter to a savage (if injudicious) critique of Plato's teaching in the *Crito*, the emblem of state paternalism. For Zinn, Plato's message is "Love it or leave it."[119] In the next section ("Accept Your Punishment!"), he writes, "King talks about 'staying in jail to arouse the conscience of the community over its injustice.' He does not speak of staying in jail because he *owes* that to the government and that (as Plato argues) he has a duty to obey whatever the government tells him to do . . . . He remains in jail *not for philosophical or moral reasons*, but for a practical purpose . . . Knowing King's life and thought, we can safely say that if the circumstances had been different, he might well have agreed (unlike Socrates) to escape from jail."[120]

The argument just quoted is as dubious as it is convenient for the next story Zinn tells, his recollection of his personal involvement in giving aid and comfort to a fugitive priest. "A few days after [Berrigan's] disappearance," he remembers, "I received a phone call at my home in Boston." He was invited to speak at a Catholic church on the Upper West Side of Manhattan, where it was rumored that Berrigan might show up. At the church, somebody slipped him a note, instructing him and a friend of the Berrigan brothers "to meet two nuns at a Spanish-Chinese restaurant . . . near Columbia University," where they "were given directions to New Jersey, to the house where Daniel was hiding out." They rented a car, nabbed Berrigan, and made their way back to Boston. "From that point on, for the next four months, he eluded and exasperated the FBI, staying underground, but surfacing from time to time, to deliver a sermon at a church in Philadelphia, to be interviewed on national television, to make public statements about the war, to make a film (*The Holy Outlaw*) about his actions against the war, both overt and underground."[121]

Zinn goes on to record that during "those four months, while helping take care of Dan Berrigan," he was teaching the *Crito* among other texts in his course on political theory at Boston University. Having already argued that King was no Plato's "Socrates," he writes, "I think it is a good guess, despite those often-quoted words of [King's] on 'accepting' punishment, that Martin Luther King Jr., would have supported Berrigan's actions. The principle is clear. If it is right to disobey unjust laws, it is right to disobey unjust punishment for breaking those laws."[122] This principle encapsulates the essential tension between Zinn's view of civil disobedience, and the view of Fortas, Rawls, and the traditional liberal justification.

However, in the "Letter from Birmingham City Jail," King himself had written:

You express a great deal of anxiety over our willingness to break laws. This is certainly a legitimate concern. Since we so diligently urge people to obey the Supreme Court's decision of 1954 outlawing segregation in the public schools, at first glance it may seem rather paradoxical for us consciously to break laws. One may well ask: "How can you advocate breaking some laws and obeying others?" The answer lies in the fact that there are two types of laws: just and unjust. I would be the first to advocate obeying just laws. One has not only a legal but a moral responsibility to obey just laws. Conversely, one has a moral responsibility to disobey unjust laws. I would agree with St. Augustine that "an unjust law is no law at all."[123]

At first blush, this quotation from King's "Letter," which is crucial to my argument in this essay, might appear to support Zinn's interpretation that King's true fidelity is to a "higher law." King's appeal to the authority of Augustine comes without citation, but its source is a young Augustine's dialogue *On Free Choice* (*De Libero Arbitrio*), which Aquinas cites nearly nine hundred years later in the context of working out his theory of the natural law (Zinn's "higher law" as it might be subject to a rigorous formulation).[124]

Zinn's argument notwithstanding, however, the Augustinian view that an unjust law cannot compel the obedience of a citizen is not *prima facie* inconsistent with the liberal doctrine of civil disobedience, inasmuch as King's appeal to it is equivocal. The distinction between just and unjust laws applies in retail, but its wholesale application remains unclarified by his willing acceptance of the penalty. His case does not unequivocally call into question the very sovereignty of the state over its subjects. Berrigan underground presents quite another case.

That neither the natural law nor Augustine nor Aquinas appear in the index of *A Theory of Justice* is not surprising. The theory of the natural law is explicitly theological and it explicitly belongs to the particular religious heritage of Christianity. It is predicated on the idea that the ultimate source of law is a Divine Lawgiver; specifically, the divinity of classical theism. While the Doctor of Divinity explicitly commits himself to this theological and religious heritage, the dedicated secularism of Rawls and Zinn requires them both to hold King's precise argument at arm's length.[125] While neither Rawls nor Zinn is a theologian, however, King is closer to Rawls than Zinn in his concern to address the bourgeois fear and loathing of the specter of anarchy, as when he writes of a great deal of anxiety over our willingness to break laws and his diligent urging of people to obey the Supreme

Court's decision of 1954 outlawing segregation in the public schools. In other words, his theological appeal to the distinction between just and unjust laws is carefully circumscribed by the liberal principle of fidelity to the positive statutory law of the constitutional state, and he invokes the distinction only in order to justify his *exception* to an otherwise binding rule, which coincides more or less exactly with Rawls's theory and explains why Rawls can take it as a *prima facie* illustration of justified civil disobedience. If the issue between Rawls and Zinn (or Plato and Zinn, Thoreau and Zinn, or Fortas and Zinn) is who has the better claim on King's "Letter," the compelling conclusion is that King in Birmingham in 1963 comports himself in both the spirit and the letter of liberalism (which, in the light of his most fundamental commitments, must have called upon him to exercise enormous restraint and self-discipline). In the case at hand, then, Zinn's "good guess" is not good enough. Even if Zinn's "clear principle" is correct, it does not reach to the radical question concerning the sovereignty, authority, and legitimacy of the state itself. Yet this is inescapably the question posed by Berrigan underground.

Berrigan and Coles

In 1971 a series of conversations between Berrigan and the psychiatrist Robert Coles was published as *The Geography of Faith: Conversations between Daniel Berrigan When Underground, and Robert Coles*.[126] Berrigan had spent most of his four months on the lam in the *Boston* area, where Coles was at Harvard along with Rawls at the same time Zinn was teaching Plato's dialogue to his students at Boston University.[127] In these conversations, Coles poses the very challenge that Zinn's account tends to obscure. Reasonably enough, Coles asks Berrigan to explain how his decision not to cooperate with the state authorities would differ with "those on the political right who would like the same kind of immunity from prosecution and the same kind of right to stay out of jail."[128] He offers the Ku Klux Klan as an example and then generalizes his point to include the Weather Underground, which was still making headlines in 1970. In the midst of this exchange, he invokes the name of Herbert Marcuse, who was then a celebrated doyen of the counterculture and the New Left as the author of *One-Dimensional Man* (1964) and *An Essay on Liberation* (1969), and who was about to publish *Counter-Revolution and Revolt* (1972).[129] If Zinn's attempt to assimilate Berrigan underground to King's "Letter" must be judged a failure despite its rhetorical deftness, Coles's glancing reference to Marcuse demonstrates the superior acuity of his own attempt to make sense of Berrigan's criminality: it has the character of Marcuse's "Great Refusal."[130]

The contrast between the great refusal and Rawls's "self-defeating, disciplinary" approach to civil disobedience at least has the virtue of being unequivocal. It forces us to acknowledge either that the difference between liberal and radical theories of civil disobedience has a sharp edge, or else that criminal conduct like Berrigan's should not be called "civil disobedience" in the first place.[131] In his exchange with Coles, Berrigan himself observes the irony, consistent with Marcuse's outlook, that whereas he had "never been able to look upon [himself] as a criminal . . . [we] tend to overlook the crimes of our political and business leaders. We don't send to jail Presidents and their advisers and certain congressmen and senators who talk like bloodthirsty mass murderers."[132] The great refusal includes the refusal to accept being criminally branded by a state so criminal it could be called a state of criminality.

Enter Coles, who cannot bring himself to see things this way, despite his disarming candor, his capacity for honest and unflinching self-criticism, his willingness to engage Berrigan in constructive dialogue, and his deeply felt admiration for the priest.[133] Precisely because he is unwilling to make the great refusal, he understands precisely what Berrigan's gesture entails, according it the full seriousness it deserves. In this respect, although he mocks this way of reading his exchange with Berrigan in advance, *he is a liberal who cannot bring himself to break with liberal ideology*, while Berrigan must be read as a *radical* whose very act constitutes a clear and decisive break with liberal ideology.[134] But liberal ideology correctly understood in its historical origins is the ideology of the bourgeois revolutions that brought the characteristically modern form of the nation-state into being, and as such it is the dominant ideology of bourgeois society.[135] Hence, we cannot avoid the conclusion that the perlocutionary effect of Berrigan's speech-act (that is, both the "mode of address" of his going underground and also his conversation with Coles) is to call the very foundations of bourgeois society itself into radical question. Therefore also terms like *progressivism* or *populism* as they were recently affixed to the Democratic Party and to the presidential campaign of President Obama cannot even begin to reach up to the implications of a deed like Berrigan's great refusal.

Marcuse himself broke with bourgeois society in post–World War I Germany and thereafter devoted his life's work to developing a critical theory intent on investigating, exposing, explaining, and criticizing it. The revolutionary character of such a break in Berrigan's deed as well cannot be overlooked. This is the profounder reason why it is a mistake to apprehend it through the lens of King's deed in 1963. Perhaps Coles's greatest virtue in his conversations with Berrigan is his clearheaded grasp of the stakes as he spends these hours speaking candidly with a man who is wanted by the FBI. The memory of Martin Luther King is practically invisible in their exchanges, despite Coles's extensive experience in the civil rights struggle.[136] Virtually taking King's place as the icons of resistance in their dialogue are Malcolm X, Stokely Carmichael, the Weather Underground, the antiwar Catholic left, ghetto youth, and radicalized youth on college and university campuses.[137] Throughout their conversations, Berrigan recurrently expresses his solidarity with them, while Coles is recurrently cautious and also doubtful that the rebellious youth of the sixties in whom Marcuse, for example, placed so much stock, were really capable of effecting any lasting transformation of American society.[138] (In retrospect, he seems to have been vindicated.)

When Berrigan renders one of his several apologies for the Weathermen (here, in contrast with Klansmen), Coles alludes to Marcuse in his reply. Berrigan says:

> I look upon the Weathermen as a very different phenomenon . . .
> I believe that their violent rhythm was induced by the violence of the
> society itself—and only after they struggled for a long time to be
> nonviolent. I don't think we can expect . . . passionate young people
> to be indefinitely nonviolent when *every* pressure put on them is one
> of violence—which I think describes the insanity of our society.

He goes on to say that he expects the Weathermen's violence to be "a temporary thing," hoping that it "will not take over and dominate them." Coles replies:

> This issue is a very important point, and I find it extremely difficult to
> deal with because . . . you're getting close to a position that Herbert
> Marcuse and others take: you feel that you have the right to decide
> what to "understand" and by implication be tolerant of, even approve,
> and what to condemn strongly or call "dangerous" at a given historical
> moment. You feel you have the right to judge what is a long-term
> ideological trend, and what isn't, and you also are judging one form of
> violence as temporary and perhaps cathartic and useful or certainly
> understandable . . . whereas another form of violence you rule out as
> automatically ideological. It isn't too long a step from that to a kind of
> elitism, if you'll forgive the expression—to an elitism that Marcuse
> exemplifies, in which he condones a self-elected group who have power
> and force behind them, who rule and outlaw others in the name of,

presumably, the "better world" that they advocate. There is something there that I find very arrogant and self-righteous and dangerous.[139]

Here Coles challenges Berrigan, renowned Catholic pacifist, along the double fronts of violence and elitism that converge in the transgression against state authority, once conscience becomes a law unto itself and individuals or groups situate themselves as outlaws, "holy" or otherwise.

Such terrain is a wilderness beyond the protections of the liberal doctrine of civil disobedience, such as Hegel had foreseen two hundred years ago in *Phenomenology of Spirit* as a cartographer of "conscience," charting the map that led from the primacy of personal conscience to "absolute freedom and terror" in the aftermath of the French Revolution, that uncertain landscape between the Augustinian Martin Luther and the terrorist Robespierre.[140] Because Hegel, the eminent philosopher of state power, is not quite a liberal or a "Kantian" in the sense in which Rawls is both, his thought does not suffer from the abstract formalism and ahistoricism from which even Rawls's brief foray into nonideal theory suffers. Rawls is no help to Coles, whose concerns are not with a possibly or a nearly just society but with the prospects and possibilities of American society as it is. As opposed to a broadly "Kantian" orientation, Hegel insists on the concreteness and actuality modeled by Aristotle, rather than the otherworldly "Platonism" of Kant and Rawls. But his "Aristotelian" emphasis on actuality brings him philosophically closer to the orbit of conversation between Coles and Berrigan, whose topics are intensely real. Coles's anxieties, hesitations, and doubts about Berrigan's course are profoundly Hegelian concerns.

Situating Marcuse in just this terrain beyond the liberal principle of fidelity to law, Coles confesses the extreme difficulty he has upon finding Daniel Berrigan there too, across the fences and safeguards by means of which the rule of law would dispose evenhandedly of the Klan and the Weather Underground alike. We can readily accommodate the Catonsville Nine to the doctrine of civil disobedience upheld by philosophy from Plato to Thoreau and Rawls. In Berrigan underground, however, we find "civil disobedience" *in extremis*, the limit situation of Coles's anxiety, which Berrigan's own disavowal of violence does not quite comfort.

Berrigan replies:

O.K. Well, let's agree to differ on that, maybe from the point of view of a certain risk that I am willing to take in regard to those young people—a risk that I would be much less willing to take in regard to something as long-term as the Klan. But there is always danger in

taking these risks, and the only way in which I can keep reasonably free
of that danger is by saying in public and to myself that the Weatherman
[*sic*] ideology (for instance) is going to meet up with people who are
going to be very harshly and severely critical of it, as I have been and
will be; in fact, at the point in which their rhetoric expresses disregard
of human life and human dignity, I stand aside and I say no, as I will say
no to the war machine. But I discern changes in our radical youth,
including the Weathermen. And again I have hope for them, hope they
will not be wedded to violence. [141]

On the one hand, Berrigan answers Coles by acknowledging the "danger"
and reaffirming the principled nonviolence that underwrites his direct
action of resistance to the pervasive violence of "the war machine." Yet on
the other hand, being underground too, he does not neatly sever himself
from the Weathermen (as he does without hesitation from the Klan).
Rather, he offers a gesture of solidarity and hope, not conceding to
the force of Coles's argument but agreeing to disagree. He knows what
Coles is asking from him, aid and comfort to liberalism. He does not
give it.

Soon enough, then, the conversation turns directly to the crucial question of state power itself. Coles says, "you feel American power is uniquely
dangerous to the world. I do not agree."[142] He mentions "Soviet power"
and "rising Chinese power." Berrigan replies, "I am arguing that we are
particularly dangerous as a nation—because of the nuclear resources and
armaments we possess, and also because of the ideological frenzy induced
in us by 20 years of a 'cold war.' I would never deny that other nations are
also dangerous . . . I never expect decent activity from great power, whether
it be church power or state power."[143] In an astonishingly personal moment,
he secures Coles's confession that Coles is "cautious" only because he is "a
husband and a father," so that, in Coles's own words, he "carefully, maybe
semiconsciously, calibrate[s] how far 'out' I dare go politically."[144] Berrigan
is relentless. He says, "I think marriage as we understand it and family life
as we understand it in this culture both tend to define people in a far more
suffocating and totalizing way than we want to acknowledge. There is a
very nearly universal supposition that after one marries one ought to cool
off with regard to political activism and compassion—as compared to one's
student days, one's 'young' days."[145] The holy outlaw heads in the direction
of a totalizing critique, evoking Coles's summary.

Coles: You are saying that our institutions are not fit institutions and
therefore have no right to exercise their authority as institutions and

determine, for instance, how to deal with violence, whether it be from the Klan or from the Weatherman. But if those institutions don't have such authority, which institutions, which people do?

Berrigan: *We* do.

Coles: Who is we?

Berrigan: Well, *we* are that small and assailed and powerless group of people who are nonviolent in principle and who are willing to suffer for our beliefs in the hope of creating something very different for those who will follow us. It is we who feel compelled to ask, along with, let's say, Bonhoeffer or Socrates or Jesus, how man is to live as a human being and how his communities are to form and to proliferate as instruments of human change and of human justice; and it is we who struggle to do more than pose the questions—but rather, live as though the questions were all-important, even though they cannot be immediately answered.[146]

Coles's rhetorical question—"Who is we?"—brings us to the heart of the matter. The liberal doctrine of civil disobedience stops well short of a totalizing critique of the basic institutions of society. As opposed to this liberal doctrine, Berrigan extends his criticism of the inherent violence of the state as a "war machine" to the institutions of family life and civil society themselves. Coles and Berrigan alike grasp how truly dangerous is the outlaw ground on which the priest then stands, out on the other side not only of the "Letter from Birmingham City Jail" but of the Baltimore Four and the Catonsville Nine and of the many Plowshares actions since.

Hegel's meditation on a like geography finds safe passage in the movement from *Phenomenology of Spirit* to *Philosophy of Right*. *Moralität* gives way to *Sittlichkeit*.[147] Retreating in alarm from the threshold of terror, a revolutionary Hegel reconciles himself to the sovereignty, authority, and legitimacy of state power, the sole means of healing the breach depicted in Sophocles's play between the just claim of Creon and the just claim of Antigone.[148] One senses Coles reaching out for the Hegelian solution in his poignant cry, "Who is we?" Yet Berrigan underground has divested himself from every trapping of bourgeois society: "we" are neither the private comforts of hearth and home nor the public security assured by the state monopoly on violence. That state monopoly leads only to a war machine the grim necessity of which Hegel found himself soberly willing to affirm as the price that could yet still be glorious to the cause of a post-Restoration nation-state yet to be constructed in the heady days between 1814 and the failed revolutions of 1848.

In other words, still envisioning that war could be affordable when the battlefield still looked like Waterloo, the philosopher Hegel had no inkling of what was to come on the slaughter-bench of history: the American Civil War, World Wars I and II, the English invention of the concentration camp, Stalin's gulag archipelago, Hiroshima and Nagasaki, the epoch of weapons of mass destruction and the total mobilization of society for war, the mass carnage of Southeast Asia, the Congo, Iraq, Afghanistan, and Gaza.

Berrigan underground in 1970 saw that the state as a war machine could only be a mass murderer, with which the comforts of civic privatism could only be in collusion.

Hence, the radicalism of Berrigan's answer to Coles: "we" are that "small and powerless group" in the company of Bonhoeffer, Socrates, and Jesus, who "live as though the questions were all-important, even though they cannot be immediately answered." Coles had told Berrigan that he, like Marcuse, was an "elitist." Yet the hallmark of "elitism" is the certainty of an answer, such as the philosopher of state power is compelled to find in a solution such as the *Philosophy of Right*. What Berrigan underground reveals is the untenability of this reply in the light of the nightmare of the twentieth century and the horror of the American war against the people of Vietnam. In the face of this horror, perhaps it is easier for the poet than the husband and father or the philosopher of the state to "live as though the questions were all-important."

Lonergan and Berrigan: Two Radical and Visionary Jesuits

Patrick D. Brown

My thesis is simple and, I trust, audacious: each of the prophets . . . is an "other" of Yahweh. As God's compassionate and clairvoyant image, each prophet strives for a divine (which is to say, truly human) breakthrough in the human tribe. Lacerating, intemperate, relentless, each of the prophets raise the question again and again, in images furious and glorious, poetic and demanding: What is a human being? We are unready for God; we are hardly more ready for one another. And yet, and yet . . . Through the prophets, Yahweh strives mightily for a breakthrough on the human landscape of history, to bring light to our unenlightened human tribe, to speak the truth, unwelcome as it is, of who we are, who we are called to become: friends, sisters, brothers of one another.

—Daniel Berrigan[1]

The choice does not lie between the good conscience of a self which has kept all its laws and the bad conscience of the transgressor, but between the dull conscience which does not discern the greatness of the [divine] other and the loftiness of his demands, the agonized conscience of the awakened,

183

and the consoled conscience of one who in the company of the spirit seeks
to fulfill the infinite demands of the infinite other.

—H. Richard Niebuhr[2]

In the ordinary conventional view of things, there appears to be little that
unites Bernard Lonergan and Daniel Berrigan other than their mutual
membership in the Society of Jesus, their devotion to both Catholicism
and intelligence,[3] their dedication to what has been called "the difficult
good,"[4] their nuanced opposition to what Josef Pieper named the "secular-
ized, bourgeois optimism" which induces an ostensibly enlightened liberalism to close "its eyes to the evil in the world,"[5] and their shared and
unconditional commitment to Christ and to justice. Such a commitment,
of course, is always already a commitment to the radical transformation
of persons and societies called for by the Gospel, and so involves a deep
and abiding concern for those who suffer under nearly universal unjust
economic and social structures and distorted cultural systems.[6]

Very early on in their lives as hearers and doers of the Word,[7] both these
Jesuits somehow sensed the horror of the fact that "the conventional mind
is our situation."[8] Each became uncomfortably aware that "the inertia coef-
ficient of the human mind"[9] is disturbingly high in personal life, in the
dynamics of groups, and in institutional settings. And so, in their different
ways, both Lonergan and Berrigan set about attempting to engage in serious and sustained acts of resistance against the entrenched and systemic
corruption of contemporary economy, society, and culture.[10]

This assertion, however, may seem something of an overstatement, at
least with regard to Lonergan. For conventionally Lonergan is regarded as
a "transcendental Thomist,"[11] and by a kind of immediate and thoughtless
process of association, he must be somehow implicated in what is commonly taken to be the defensive inertia and out-dated conservatism that
dominated Catholic thinking in the wake of the Reformation and Counter-
Reformation. To echo Tertullian's famous question, what has a radical like
Berrigan to do with a devotee of Thomas? What has Lonergan's seemingly
traditional philosophy and theology to do with the contemporary recognition of the need for liberation and praxis?

But I want to suggest that this view is itself the product of the inertial
thinking characteristic of "the conventional mind," that it profoundly mis-
interprets and misrepresents Lonergan, and that a more adequate, accurate, and supple view shows basic affinities between the radical and
visionary projects of Berrigan and Lonergan.[12]

My thesis, then, is simple and, I trust, audacious. For all their differences, both Lonergan and Berrigan are, in their own unique ways, prophetic,

visionary, and radical in striving to promote "a divine (which is to say, truly human) breakthrough in the human tribe." Each "tries to pay and to encourage others to pay the high price of orthodoxy in a social climate so antagonistic to the Christian story of living and suffering; or again, in a Church many of whose 'pillars' may have misconstrued and so abused the Christian story by perhaps tacitly subordinating it to quite alien and alienating stories."[13] Each raises in different ways the most demanding, insistent, relentless question, "What is a human being?" And each answers—not only in his thinking and writing but by his very life—that the human being is an *imago Dei*, an image of God, which is to say "that a capacity for truth is the glory of our humanity; perhaps the first glory of all. To seek the truth—passionately, persistently, and thereby to come on it and announce it in the world—is simply to name ourselves as human, and therefore godly."[14]

But both know, as well, that the divine image in us is marred, scarred, eclipsed, and obscured by a world in which the refusal of grace and growth has continuous and cumulative personal, social, cultural, economic, political, and institutional consequences.[15] We live, in other words, in a sin-warped world, twisted by ideology and poisoned by alienation, a world of distraction, distortion, destruction, violence, and suffering, a world of "wars, transplanted populations, refugees, displaced persons, unemployment, outrageous inequalities in living standards . . . and the vast but somewhat hidden numbers of the destitute."[16]

And so instead of the liberation and progress that might be engendered by "the continuously adaptive interplay in which the voluntary cooperation and the personal responsibility of each contribute to the personal life and development of all,"[17] we live in a world dominated by destructive disorientations organized and perpetuated on a mass social, economic, political, and cultural scale, resulting in "a regimentation of human living, a mechanization of human activity, a leveling down of human aspirations."[18] Rather than "the free unfolding of human vitality," we are left instead with "the economic and political determinism" that result when "egoistic practicality [is] given free rein."[19] Instead of welcoming the reign of the Prince of Peace, we let slip the snarling dogs of war, aggression, greed, vanity, venality, vengeance, and violence—not the Kingdom of God, then, but a "despotism of darkness"[20] drawing its force and strength from "the objectively organized lie of ideology in a trans-Marxian sense."[21]

In such a world, it is nothing less than the duty of Christian conscience to reject "complicity with a culture and a power structure which idolizes power and privilege, and degrades human life."[22] What Christianity demands, then, is not a dull or complacent conscience but an agonized and ultimately consoled conscience sharpened by the infinite demands of the infinite divine other. What Christianity demands in our time are acts of resistance against the deeply distorted self-images of our age.[23] As Berrigan's friend Thomas Merton said, quoting Berdyaev, in our times Christian faith "turns into an accusation of the age in which I live and into a command to be human in this most inhuman of ages, to guard the image of man for it is the image of God."[24]

I do not propose to undertake here anything like an adequate dialectical comparison and contrast of Berrigan and Lonergan in their mutual projects of fostering and cooperating with "a divine . . . breakthrough in the human tribe"[25] and of guarding the images of the human and the divine in an inhuman and alienated age.[26] That would be a very large effort indeed,[27] reflecting many areas of agreement and disagreement on many topics.

Instead, on this occasion I want to honor Daniel Berrigan for a lifetime devoted to the Gospel, justice, peace, and service. I could perhaps do so best simply by quoting a remark Aquinas makes in the course of commenting on the reward promised peacemakers in the Beatitudes. "Establishing peace, either in oneself or among others, shows a man to be an imitator of God, who is a God of unity and peace. Therefore the reward given to such a one is the glory of divine sonship, which consists in perfect union with God through consummate wisdom."[28]

As appropriate as it would be to honor Berrigan for his efforts in the service of peacemaking, though, I wish instead to take a somewhat different tack, and to honor him by what might seem a peculiar theme: sin. Although it may initially seem an odd assertion, I would venture to say that one of the great merits of Berrigan's life and thought has been his relentless focus on the reality of sin as it stalks the lives of each and all of us, in personal, social, cultural, economic, political, historical, and institutional forms—certainly the horrific forms it has assumed in the last one hundred years, but perhaps also forms we have not yet seriously noticed. The same can be said of Lonergan. I want to take up this theme as a way of exploring the contributions of these radical and visionary Jesuits—and Jeremiahs—Bernard Lonergan and Daniel Berrigan.

The Prophetic Critique of Sin and Culture

Yet contemporary peacemaking must go far beyond acknowledgement
of failure to one's God and one's community, as the High Holy
Days require; or the personal love that Francis lived. It must resist
the powers of this world, the institutions of domination and their

chieftains, whose wealth and position give them control over the resources of the world and the lives and deaths of human beings.

—Daniel Berrigan[29]

I begin with this passage not only because it is vintage Berrigan but also because it focuses so clearly the problem of Christian praxis in a world dominated by sin. Despite its obvious Pauline overtones, however, the last sentence of the passage no doubt makes some people nervous—is it not somehow dangerously antinomian? Yet rather than representing a wild-eyed and free-floating antinomianism, as some might suspect, I think Berrigan's sentence is poignantly calling attention to the obvious and enormously important fact, accepted by almost all Christian thinkers, that not all power is legitimate power, that not all legitimate power is used legitimately, and that illegitimate power can be capable of great evil.[30] His position is, I think, radical and orthodox—indeed, one might say radically orthodox.[31]

It is radical in the sense that it goes to the roots of Christianity. Phrased otherwise, it is no more radical (or perhaps I should say, no less radical) than Jesus. It is no more radical, and no less, than Aquinas's position on the relation between natural and positive law.[32] The sentence is no more, and no less, radical than Augustine's rather prophetic critique of the false gods of the empire of his time:

But the worshippers and admirers of these gods delight in imitating their scandalous iniquities, and are nowise concerned that the republic be less depraved and licentious. Only let it remain undefeated, they say, only let it flourish and abound in resources; let it be glorious by its victories, or still better, secure in peace; and what matters it to us? This is our concern, that every man be able to increase his wealth so as to supply his daily prodigalities, and so that the powerful may subject the weak for their own purposes. Let the poor court the rich for a living, and that under their protection they may enjoy a sluggish tranquility; and let the rich abuse the poor as their dependents, to minister to their pride. . . . Let the laws take cognizance rather of the injury done to another man's property, than of that done to one's own person. . . . Let there be erected houses of the largest and most ornate description . . . If such happiness is distasteful to any, let him be branded as a public enemy; and if any attempt to modify or put an end to it, let him be silenced, banished, put an end to. Let these be reckoned the true gods, who procure for the people this condition of things, and preserve it when once possessed.[33]

Silenced, banished, branded a public enemy—there are worse fates, such as active or passive personal complicity in "the despotism of darkness" that makes humans its slaves.[34] Yet it is not so easy to escape this despotism, for it is within us as well as around us; it is the cumulative product of the basic and permanent human tension between limitation and transcendence, between sin and grace, and "this inner tension and ambivalence are reflected and heightened in the social sphere."[35] Within its many manifestations in the personal, social, economic, political, and cultural spheres, we live and move and have our nonbeing.[36]

In any event, Catholic teaching on solidarity insists, against the overwhelming individualism of American culture,[37] that we are "members of one another," that we are in this together.[38] Even the old *Baltimore Catechism*, not exactly an embodiment of contemporary concern about social and cultural sin, got this right. "Who is my neighbor? My neighbor is all mankind." And how are we to love our neighbor? There are many paths, some of them involving simple and sustained *caritas*. But surely one of them involves practicing the justice that Aquinas teaches is the preeminent moral virtue.[39] In the Catholic and Christian worldview, after all, "Christian love of neighbor and justice cannot be separated. For love implies an absolute demand for justice, namely, a recognition of the dignity and rights of one's neighbor."[40] One might even say that, in the limit, effectively loving one's neighbor requires taking a stand against, as Lonergan puts it, "the monster that has stood forth in our time."[41]

Yet while Berrigan is, I think, deeply traditional[42] and orthodox[43] in his radical concern for the poor, the marginalized, and the victims of sins against justice, as well as in his indictment of the sins of the powerful,[44] he is also keenly interested in transposing the traditional and the orthodox into terms that both respect the Christian tradition and also make sense in the modern and postmodern contexts. The same, I think, must be said of Lonergan's basic project.[45]

One might say that each engages in a kind of hand-to-hand combat with what Lonergan once pointedly called "the sin of backwardness, of the cultures, the authorities, the individuals that fail to live on the level of their times."[46] Each engages in a sustained attempt to develop our understanding of what it means to be human and Christian "in this most inhuman of ages."[47] And each in his own way attained an uncomfortable awareness that "without developed understanding . . . truths become uncomprehended formulas, moral precepts narrow down to lists of prohibitions, and human living settles into a helpless routine without a capacity for vital adaptation

and without the power of knowledge that inspires and directs the movement from real possibility to concrete achievement."[48]

One can, of course, understand sin in different ways, and the Christian
tradition has not always been wholly successful in avoiding the reduction of
the whole range of ethics and morals into lists of prohibitions, and then
thinking of sin as coextensive with such lists. "A capacity for vital adaptation" this is not, and it inhibits rather than inspires the movement from
real moral or ethical possibility to concrete achievement. Nonetheless, sin
is real (in a manner to be qualified in the next section) and quite concrete—
a twisted kind of "concrete universal," to use Hegel's phrase. Its immensity
is intimated with some intensity in Barth's contention that:

> The revelation of God in Jesus Christ, necessarily means the discovery
> of the darkness which is man, of the plight in which he exists and the
> depths to which he has sunk, and this disclosure is what sharply
> contradicts his creation, the glory of God and his own glory. . . . What
> is discovered here is not something which he *lacks* but who and what he
> *is*. Here he has nothing to complain about, but complaint is made
> against him.[49]

By "sin," therefore, I do not mean "sin" in the sense in which it has been
co-opted by the various forms of religious legalism, for even at its best
legalism appeals only to "the good conscience of a self which has kept all its
laws and the bad conscience of the transgressor." [50] I do not mean sin in its
merely individual sense, although that is real and harrowing enough to
anyone who is not yet filled with that complacent self-regard so characteristic of our times as to be considered a contemporary virtue.[51] I do not
even mean sin in the larger sense in which we now speak of "sinful social
structures."[52]

I mean sin in a broader sense still; perhaps one can refer to it under the
wider and strangely neglected rubric of "sinful cultural structures."[53] The
integrity, adequacy, truth, and depth of the meanings and values by which
we collectively constitute and orient ourselves are not some automatic
given. Rather, our currently effective cultural meanings and values are a
precarious, mixed, and often muddled achievement.[54] They can be riddled
with all the ambiguous development-and-decline of the technical, social,
economic, and political layers of a society.[55] Yet though it is fed by, and
feeds into, those prior layers, cultural distortion is a distinct level.[56] Cultural
distortion degrades the operative and constitutive meanings and values
informing the way of life of a community.[57] And as affecting or afflicting

those meanings and values, sinful cultural structures can include not only deeply embedded disorientations such as the idolatry of individualism and consumerism or an ultimately blasphemous faith in technology, but also what rightly has been called "the culture of death."[58] The dimensions of that life-denying culture, that necrophiliac culture, are large and growing. I would venture to claim that, in some crucial sense, Lonergan did his level and painful best for decades to resist it, and Berrigan for decades has consistently and faithfully refused to participate in normalizing and legitimating the abnormal and hideous features of the culture of death.

The range of the culture of death is vast, and illustrations are abundant. One might begin with "the unrelenting assault on human dignity" that is pervasive violence, together with the casual acceptance of violence as entertainment.[59] Or one might consider the contemporary emancipation of mimetic greed, which begins in a kind of culturally acceptable status-whoring involving the accumulation of possessions and commodities for the sake of burnishing one's own ego, and culminates in "a public spectacle of brutish economics, military muscle, and governments in service to mammon and its godlings."[60] Or as Lonergan describes it, "the body social becomes the victim of warring egoisms and blundering shortsightedness."[61] What is worse, we can begin to take this aberrant condition for granted; we can come to accept it as normal. "We, all of us, took Cold War lunacies, well underway, as inevitable as changes of the moon, even as God-given ingredients of our world."[62]

This "normalizing of the abnormal" creates a situation in which—absent some effective intervention in the process—each new generation is stamped with the image of the distorted situation into which it was born in a kind of demented decalcomania.[63] Because "it is only with respect to the available common meanings that the individual grows in experience, understanding, judgment, and so comes to find out for himself what to make of himself,"[64] the taken-for-granted reality of warring egoisms, or an unnoticed poverty or a massive distortion in the fund of common meanings and values, can have disastrous ripple effects throughout a society and culture.

One can note, too, the steady inroads of mechanomorphic thought, "the social imaginary" by which humans increasingly envision themselves in terms of their tools and technology.[65] But the disease goes beyond that. It lies far beneath the tip of the iceberg manifested in blinking Bluetooth earpieces, "management cybernetics,"[66] and contemporary "death fashion."[67] It threads through institutions, and it worms its way into our tacit self-images.[68] It can colonize the common meanings and values operative in a culture, and twist self-understanding in its deadening image. It can make an attentive, reverent, and humane stance toward human self-mystery—and, as well, the mystery of the other—well-nigh impossible,[69] and thereby mutilate and distort our relationship with ultimate mystery.[70]

Nor is the culture of death something one can simply set aside in a flurry of good will and good intentions. For, in the end, all such cumulative "distortion is not merely some abstract grievance waiting on mere good will and polite words to be set right: it is the concrete and almost irradicable form of achievements, institutions, habits, customs, mentalities, characters."[71] In such a culture, "the meanings and values of human living are impoverished . . . . Where once there were joys and sorrows, now there are just pleasures and pains. The culture has become a slum."[72] And, one might add, the slum is becoming global.

Perhaps even today there are those who think that such talk somehow dilutes or minimizes the reality of individual sin. But I would make the opposite claim. Dilating on individual sin considered only in an individual context disguises and diminishes the full scope and horror of the cumulative human refusal of God and grace. It can blind us to the fact that, as individual sin is an injustice against ourselves, a betrayal of our own possibilities of advance or development in spirit and in truth, so injustice is a sin against others, a betrayal of their possibilities of development and of the advance of human solidarity and progress. It can blind us to the "runaway nightmare"[73] that is the cumulative effect of the refusals of God and grace, the sigma of sin that is our situation. For our contemporary situation is nothing less than "the cumulative product of centuries of ambiguous change . . . of civil and cultural development-and-decline, solidified in assumptions, mentalities, interpretations, philosophies, tastes, habits, hopes, fears."[74] So, though we are lavishly gifted with grace, we are also relentlessly colonized by sin; and it is solidified and concretized and transmitted and perpetuated in ways that go far beyond individual sin.[75] We are the unfortunate and often unconscious heirs of what the philosopher Eric Voegelin referred to as "the murderous grotesque of our time."[76] "We have come out of the second millennium in an axial crisis of stupidity and schizothymia and evil."[77]

I mean *sin*, then, in its full horror, amplitude, ubiquity, and concreteness. I mean it in a sense that resonates with the condemnations of the ancient Hebrew prophets, with the falling-empire reflections of Augustine, with the medieval efforts of Aquinas, with the contemporary struggles of a Barth or Lonergan or Berrigan.[78]

My first suggestion, then, is that Berrigan's writings fall squarely within the whole trajectory of Judeo-Christian thought on sin and injustice.

Aquinas, after all, wrote a treatise on "sins against justice,"[79] and Augustine held that "injustice occurs in every case where a person loves as a goal something which should be desired only as a means to an end, or seeks for the sake of something else things which ought to be loved for themselves."[80] Injustice, in that sense, has become for us virtually a way of life (or rather, a way of death). And so "we have the socializing of sin, its mimetic power, the passage of quite normal, quotidian activities into perilous areas: the normalization of the abnormal . . . . And above all and permeating all, we note with horror (or we do not) the normalizing of violence, near and far, as a matter of daily record. A matter inevitably claiming us, our souls in servitude to a cannibal, spoliating beast."[81]

My second suggestion is that Berrigan's writings fall squarely within the Judeo-Christian tradition of prophecy. To be sure, the adjective *prophetic* has been bandied about, and almost emptied of meaning, by those who merely mean by it that someone wholeheartedly agrees with them and therefore deserves to be praised. But it can mean something more than reflexive and mindless approbation. I take the realm of the prophetic to be intimately related to "genuineness" in Lonergan's technical and very demanding sense of the term. It relates to the personal, social, and cultural negotiation of the tension between limitation and transcendence, "and it is no vague tension between limitation in general and transcendence in general, but an unwelcome invasion of consciousness by opposed apprehensions of oneself as one is and as one concretely is to be."[82] The "prophetic" can refer, then, to the careful, prayerful, insightful, and endlessly repentant sifting not only of future alternative possibilities but also of depressingly present actualities, by one who has the intellectual, moral, and religious standing and wisdom to do so—siftings of the way we are all of us failing in one way or another to live deeply and consistently in the light.

As in individual life, so in a culture, sin festers all the more feverishly the more it remains unnoticed. Prophecy is at least in part a matter of naming the fever of sin in a society.[83] "The prophet was an individual who said "no" to his society, condemning its habits and assumptions, its complacency, waywardness, and syncretism."[84] As Berrigan glosses the "handwriting on the wall" scene in the Book of Daniel:

> Shortly, the prophet issues an ethical summons. His words are, in the closest sense, prophetic, a revelation, an epiphany, in two stages. First, the cultural analysis of things as they are: the orgy as evidence of cultural anomie, appetite and greed on a rampage. Then, the judgment: here, now, the human vocation is violated and scorned, along with creation itself.[85]

By the same token, prophecy involves deep suffering and heartbreak, for the prophet "was often compelled to proclaim the very opposite of what his heart expected."[86] The grief of a Jeremiah "is incurable, my heart is sick within me."[87]

In the Hebrew tradition, the prophet's very "existence is participation in the suffering of God,"[88] and in the prophet's utterances, "the justice of God was at stake."[89] So a prophet may prophesize in "the sense that he tells his audience, at risk of their displeasure, the secrets of their own hearts."[90] In that sense, even art can serve a prophetic function. "As spokesman of his community, the secrets he must utter are theirs. The reason why they need him is that no community altogether knows its own heart; and by failing in this knowledge a community deceives itself on the one subject concerning which ignorance means death."[91] As Collingwood noted in the very last sentence of his great work on the philosophy of art, "Art is the community's medicine for the worst disease of mind, the corruption of consciousness,"[92] and one might say the same of genuine prophecy.

No one, I think, has put this point about the relation between faith, art, and prophecy better than Flannery O'Connor.

> My own feeling is that writers who see by the light of their Christian faith will have, in these times, the sharpest eyes for the grotesque, for the perverse, and for the unacceptable. . . . Redemption is meaningless unless there is cause for it in the actual life we live, and for the last few centuries there has been operating in our culture the secular belief that there is no such cause. The novelist with Christian concerns will find in modern life distortions which are repugnant to him, and his problem will be to make these appear *as distortions* to an audience which is used to seeing them *as natural*; and he may well be forced to take ever more violent means to get his vision across to this hostile audience.[93]

This passage, for me, incisively names the nature of Berrigan's life's work. Not that Berrigan has ever taken "violent means" to get his vision across— although in the inverted cultural world in which we live, nonviolent civil disobedience seems oddly violent to a culture that is increasingly debased by violence.

Berrigan's faith has given him very sharp eyes indeed "for the grotesque, for the perverse, for the unacceptable." We are far too used to seeing the distortions of war and violence, poverty and imprisonment, as natural, just as we are far too used to seeing abortion and capital punishment as normal. A thinker who rejects the *Realpolitik* of war as normal or natural will find a hostile audience on the right. A thinker who rejects the *Realpolitik* of abortion as normal or natural will find a hostile audience on the left. A thinker who rejects both will find himself simply surrounded—surrounded, that is, by grotesqueries desperately in need of being named as distortions "to an audience which is used to seeing them as natural."[94]

I think it is fair to say, in this connection, that Berrigan has consistently attempted to resist the kind of "narcotized receptivity"[95] which has come to characterize American culture under the reign of the false facts brought about by cumulative sin.[96] That is to say, he has done everything in his power to make these distortions appear as distortions to a culture that insists on viewing them as utterly natural.

Berrigan has been, in many ways, ahead of his times—in his art of poetry and essays, in sermons and in scriptural commentaries, in protest and in peacemaking—in his grasp of the magnitude and amplitude of sin, in his sense of the way it honeycombs through our personal and collective lives, and in his willingness to say a prophetic "no," condemning the community's complacency and waywardness, the many varieties of its corruption of consciousness.

A genuine condemnation of the corruptions of contemporary consciousness can be conveyed through artistry and prophetic utterance, through prayer and the study of scripture,[97] through a lifetime of commitment and action, of faith and service, of contemplation and resistance to contemporary forms of evil, through persistently and insistently calling attention to the suffering of God in the sufferings of God's people, through a calling-to-account for the sake of, and in service to, the Gospel. Yet the corruptions cannot be fully and adequately diagnosed on those levels alone. Put simply, unless some creative cultural minority is struggling to develop and expand what Lonergan calls the theoretic differentiation of consciousness, our efforts to foster an adequate contemporary movement "toward the enlargement of the attainable human good"[98] ultimately will be stunted and stymied. And that is where I have found Lonergan's massive labors in the realm of theory to be of enormous value, and that is why I find Lonergan in so many areas and on so many levels to be far ahead of his times.

I cannot possibly begin to justify that conviction here.[99] But I think it will shed light on Berrigan's project to take a clue from the young, energetic, and radical Lonergan. And so I propose to investigate, very briefly, the early Lonergan's transposition of the traditional understanding of sin as *non ens*, as what he calls "false facts" or "objective falsity," to the levels of economics, politics, society, culture, and history.

The Reign of Sin as False Fact in Society, Economy, Culture, and History

I saw the oppression that is done under the sun, and the tears of the innocent. And they had no comforter: and they were not able to resist this violence being destitute of help.

—Lonergan, quoting *Ecclesiastes*, circa 1933[100]

Was this not simply what a Jesuit was called to, supposing the worth of a task and the competence and conscience of the doer? They had a great saying, often repeated: Jesuits belonged "at the cutting edge, not the soft center."

—Berrigan, *To Dwell in Peace*[101]

Lonergan's early works on history, unknown and unpublished during his lifetime,[102] are a complicated affair,[103] and I can do no more here than offer a few key intimations and implications. Yet whatever their complexity, it is clear that in those efforts the young Lonergan was striving to "keep pace with the times,"[104] struggling to overcome "the antinomy between a merely traditional mentality and a mentality that is thinking in terms of the future and of problems of which the mere traditionalist has not the ghost of a notion,"[105] and straining to be at the cutting edge, very far from the soft center. In fact, in a private and obviously exuberant moment, he expressed the view in 1935 that his theory of history and economics would "throw Hegel and Marx, despite the enormity of their influence on this very account, into the shade"[106]—at the very "cutting edge" indeed.[107]

When Lonergan wrote in 1977 that it "has long been my conviction that if Catholics and, in particular, if Jesuits are to live and operate on the level of the times, they must not only know about theories of history but also work out their own,"[108] very few readers would have realized how long a period he was referring to; he had in fact held that conviction for at least forty-five years.[109] In fact, he began working on economics in 1930, when he was twenty-five, and kept working on it steadily for the next fourteen years. That work evidently drew him into broader concerns regarding the dynamics of history, an expansion of his initial project very possibly given additional momentum by *Quadragesimo Anno*'s call for a reconstruction of the social order in 1931.

Lonergan's concern was, of course, political as well: his "Essay on Fundamental Sociology" takes as its epigraph the famous passage in Plato's *Republic* which contends that unless political power and love of wisdom coincide, there will be no end of troubles for political communities.[110]

Like many intellectuals in the early 1930s, Lonergan was concerned with the conditions of the possibility of the survival of democracy. As he framed the matter in stark and simple terms in 1931, "Democracy is faced with the alternative of teaching thought or meeting its decline and fall."[111]

But by the "teaching of thought" required for democracy's survival, Lonergan evidently meant something other than mindlessly transmitting the philosophical anthropology of Hobbes, the decayed and distorted tradition of nineteenth century liberalism, or the nostrums of then-ascendant communism. For him, even at that early stage, thinking on the level of the times[112] meant thinking on the level of history. Nor was the solution a matter of analyzing power as though it were by itself somehow normative and not, as is frequently the case, the result of sin, injustice, or decline. "A philosopher cannot be content to ask of history, Who holds the power? He must ask whether this incidence of power is for human progress or for human extinction."[113]

In short, any solution to the mess of modern history had to go beyond the distortions of *Realpolitik*; it had to operate on the level of a theory and a dialectic of history; and it had to involve a moral and religious revolution against entrenched and settled patterns of egoistic and class interests. As Lonergan would later write in 1941:

> I think we can find a lesson in Leon Trotsky's gospel of perpetual revolution. This visionary clearly saw that the only effect of Bolshevism was to create a new bourgeoisie, a new pattern of egoisms to be the real antitheses of an ideal world. But if revolution must be perpetual, it is not the revolution of violence and bloodshed, of terrorism, torture chambers, proscribed classes, and cultural nullity; it is the inner revolution in the heart of men that must be constant; it is the illumination of his understanding and the purification of his will that must ever be effected. "If any man will come after me, let him deny himself and take up his cross daily and follow me" (Luke 9:23). There is indeed an immediate and imperious necessity to rid the world of Hitler and all he stands for; but there is a deeper and more long-standing need for an inner victory, for the dethronement of the petty Hitlers in the hearts of us all.[114]

It seems clear, at any rate, that Lonergan in the 1930s believed that the "reconstruction of the social order" called for by *Quadragesimo Anno*—were the effort to be adequate to the task—required a *Summa Sociologica*,[115] an accurate economic theory, a philosophy of history, a view of the possibility of an "essential renaissance" or "a new order" based on Christian faith,[116] and a critique of the conventional notions that had been handed to the twentieth century by the nineteenth, especially nineteenth century liberalism and its antithesis in communism. Such a complex and comprehensive effort, Lonergan believed, "is imperative if man is to solve the modern political-economic entanglement."[117]

"History," Stephen Dedalus famously said, "is a nightmare from which I am trying to awake."[118] For the early Lonergan, too, the modern political-economic entanglement is something of a nightmare, and he is not afraid to name it. "Thus the heritage of intellectual vacuity and social chaos given by the nineteenth century to the twentieth century is the real reason why the twentieth century is such a mess."[119] Nor was Lonergan's fierce critique of the mess the product of some inertial, sedentary, or nostalgic conservatism. "Despite the cries of obscurantists to the contrary, there is as a matter of fact such a thing as progress. It is further manifest that progress is the fundamental concept in any theory of the external flow [of history], the effective solidarity of mankind."[120] But Lonergan has harsh words for the neglect of solidarity and history by nineteenth-century liberalism and its correlative political economy.

Nineteenth-century liberal individualism centered on enlightened self-interest. But as Lonergan pointed out, "self-interest is not enlightened because it is not objective; it centers the world in the 'ego' of the individual or class and neither is the centre."[121] Liberal individualism had no real way to acknowledge the effective solidarity of humankind in history, no serious way to account for the past flow of meanings and actions that "integrate into the reality of the present . . . . It had no concern for the differentials of flow in virtue of an asinine confidence in political economists. It has landed the twentieth century in an earthly hell."[122]

For the early Lonergan, then, genuine progress is not merely a matter of good will; it is much more centrally a matter of good theory, of theory adequate to the complexity of social, economic, and historical process. "All the good intentions in the world are compatible with all the blunders conceivable. The nineteenth century was a century of good wills and bad intellects. The combination is fatal."[123] To understand the complex weave of progress and sin that is our historical situation, "what is needed is a metaphysic of history, a differential calculus of progress,"[124] a theory of the dialectic of history that could take into account the solidarity of humankind in both the genuine progress and the real sin that accumulate in the historical process.

It is worth noting the implications of Lonergan's theory of solidarity on the level of class or group bias. On the positive side, Lonergan evokes

Marx's notion of class-consciousness. In the course of his exposition of the differences between, first, spontaneous, unguided historical process, second, the historical period characterized by the emergence of theory in "reflex thought," and third, a future history involving the deliberate application of theory of history to guide historical process in what he calls "reflex history," Lonergan remarks that "The 'class consciousness' advocated by the communists is perhaps the clearest expression of the transition from reflex thought to reflex history."[125]

On the negative side, one can, of course, relate this theme not only to the theme of human solidarity but also to the later theme of group bias in *Insight*.[126] The seriousness with which the early Lonergan engaged the problem of class or group bias in his early theory of history is manifest in his treatment of the "false fact" of class bias. As he describes the bias of practical thought in one of the historical manuscripts, that bias

> transforms the distinction of those who govern and those who are governed into a distinction between the privileged and the depressed. The latter distinction in time becomes an abyss: its mechanism would seem as follows. Insensibly the privileged find the solution to the antitheses of their own well-being and progress. Too easily they pronounce nonexistent or insoluble the antitheses that militate against the well-being of the depressed. Thus it is that with the course of time, the privileged enjoy a rapid but narrowly extended expansion of progress, and meanwhile the depressed are not merely left behind but are more or less degraded by the set of palliatives invented to prevent their envy bursting into the flame of anger and revolution. The total result is an objective disorder: both the progress of the few and the backwardness of the many are distorted; the former by its unnatural exclusiveness, the latter by the senseless palliatives. And this distortion is not merely some abstract grievance waiting on mere good will and polite words to be set right: it is the concrete and almost irradicable form of achievements, institutions, habits, customs, mentalities, characters.[127]

Or as he noted in a draft for the same paper, "The bourgeois is full of the milk of human kindness: but this [class or group] bias in outlook makes him pronounce non-existent or insoluble the antitheses that do not directly affect him."[128] Lonergan takes up the same theme in an explicit way in his account of sin in his lectures on education in 1959. There he notes of the good of order:

> It develops under a bias in favor of the powerful, the rich, or the most numerous class . . . This division of classes gives rise . . . in those that

have the better end of the stick, to haughtiness, arrogance, disdain, criticism of "sloth," of "lack of initiative," or "shortsightedness," or in earlier times, of "lowly birth." Thus in the very process of the development of the civilizational order, there result from sin a bias in favor of certain groups and against other groups, class opposition, the emotional charging of that opposition, and the organization of those emotions and that opposition in mutual recrimination and criticism. . . . Sin as a component in the social process lets the material development go ahead, and at the same time takes out of it its soul.[129]

Much more could be said about the brilliance and audacity of the early Lonergan's theory of the dialectic of history and his critique of the "night-mare"[130] of our present, including his analysis of peace under the conditions of decline.[131] But here it will suffice simply to note that his treatment of the traditional notion of sin as a privation of the good, a nonbeing, or what he calls "a false fact" or "objective falsity,"[132] transposes it from the individual level to the levels of economics, society, culture, and historical process.

Since the time of Augustine, theologians and philosophers have struggled with the peculiar status in reality of sin.[133] Augustine understood sin as something that ultimately "removes the sinner from being."[134] For Aquinas, sin is *non ens*, nonbeing, "the privation of a due perfection."[135] As Lonergan later put it, "Sin is nothing, a negation," yet it is "the basis of decline in human society."[136]

In a complicated and elusive way, the nothing, the negation, the removal from being, the privation of a perfection or development otherwise due, nonetheless creates enormous and significant ripple effects in the political, economic, social, and cultural spheres. How can this be? How can a nothing give rise to something? That is a complex philosophical and theological question. But at least one may say that for the early Lonergan, "the blunders and the sins of men create objective situations that should never exist and that easily become intolerable, whether we consider the microcosmic tragedies of passion and cruelty and suicide or the more terrible fruits of so-called economic and political forces."[137] This preclusion of an advance otherwise due,[138] and the resulting concretization and embodiment of sin in personal life and society, become a basis for the earliest version of Lonergan's notion of the dialectic of history. Rather than entering into the complexities of the history and development of that notion here, however, let me simply note that the notion of sin as *non ens* was the baseline for Lonergan's treatment of the category of sin in his early historical manuscripts. Yet he lifts and extends it into the categories of economic, social, political, and cultural process. The fruits of that "vast enlargement of the theoretical horizon"[139] would later find expression in *Insight*'s category of "the social surd."[140] But the seeds of it were present in his early efforts, and although *Insight* places that notion in a much larger theoretic perspective, the pattern of expression in *Insight* tends to lack some of the immediacy and directness of Lonergan's language in the historical manuscripts.

What, then, is the result of taking seriously the fact that social, economic, political, and cultural processes can be constituted in part by false facts? It is a difficult question, raising as it does further questions—ultimately, religious and theological questions—that concern whether or how human beings may be able to reverse the objective irrationality or "the objective falsity"[141] that has been injected into the humanly made world by humans.[142] One result, certainly, is a heightened attention to, and concern for, the concrete historical and cultural transmission of sin and its massive implications and ramifications. In one of the early manuscripts, Lonergan framed this in stark and memorable terms:

> the greatest evil in the world is the evil that is concretised in the historic flow, the capital of injustice that hangs like a pall over every brilliant thing, that makes men and nations groan over others' glory, that provokes anger and suicide and dire wars, that culminates in the dull mind and sluggish body of the enslaved people or the decayed culture.[143]

Lonergan treats this concretization of evil in the historic flow in a number of ways in the historical manuscripts. Obviously it relates to economic, social, cultural, and even political sin. But one of the taproots of these forms of sin, for Lonergan, is the dominance of the modern ideology of "realism," of *Realpolitik*.[144] On that topic, Lonergan is rather vehement and eloquent, in these manuscripts and in his later writings. As the result of centuries of ambiguous change, the modern world (and there is no reason to think the postmodern world is any different) is heir to a distorted tradition of political, economic, and social "realism."[145] To the distortions of accumulated sin, "realism" adds a distorted notion of practicality which, in turn, only accelerates the original distortions. As Lonergan described this distorted stance in 1951, "For men to be truly practical is for them to favor the common good of order at the expense of private advantage; but, in fact, to be practical is taken to mean that one is cool and calculating and, when necessary, moderately unscrupulous in getting what one wants."[146] He considered this dominant distorted practicality as the product of a series of ever less comprehensive syntheses in historical process, and he regarded a serious understanding of that series as a key component of any contemporary attempt to reverse the decline wrought by cumulative sin.

The notion of a succession of less comprehensive syntheses is more complex than it may at first appear. Lonergan deploys it as a kind of genealogy of the emergence of modernity as the product of a series of lower syntheses, and it plays a central role in his diagnosis of the malaise of modernity. The notion makes its first appearance in compact form in the historical manuscripts in the context of what Lonergan calls the dialectic of fact and the dialectic of sin.

> First, the dialectic of fact. The objective situation gives a phantasm which specifies an idea. The idea is an incomplete act of intellect but it is put into execution as though it were complete: the result is a false historic situation which reveals the incompleteness of the old idea and leads to the emergence of a compensating idea. Second, there is the dialectic of sin. False situations may be created not only by following incomplete acts of intellect as though they were complete but also by not following intellect at all. Thus . . . the theory of liberalism is a consequent of the sixteenth century heresy with the consequent religious wars while the theory of communism is a consequent of the pharisaical religiosity of capitalist exploitation and oppression.[147]

Again, one could go into much greater detail on the development of this notion in Lonergan's thought on history. But his genealogy of communism seems an appropriate introduction to the early Lonergan's efforts at an economic theory on the level of the times. For distorted economic process can be a source of "the evil concretised in the historic flow," an instance of sin as "false fact" with an enormous range of implications. Thus, one result of taking seriously "the evil that is concretised in the historic flow" would be to compel attention to the need for economic development and economic justice over against the despair generated by "the inherited capital of injustice."[148] As Lonergan notes on the very last page of his manuscript fragment on the philosophy of history:

> The function of progress is to increase leisure that men may have more time to learn, to conquer material evil in privation and sickness that men may have less occasion to fear the merely factual and that they may have more confidence in the rule of intellect, to struggle against the inherited capital of injustice which creates such objective situations that men cannot be truly just unless first the objective situation is changed, and, finally, I am not certain I speak wildly, out of the very progress

itself to produce a mildness of manners and temperament which will support and imitate and extend the mighty power of Christian charity. This then is the virtue of progress, the virtue of social justice, by which man directs his action so that it will be easier for his neighbors and his posterity to know and to do what is right and just.[149]

It is quite a vision of the power of faith and intelligence as linked in the generation of justice. But he goes further. The fragment of the manuscript that survives ends with a Biblical passage and a comment. The passage is from *Isaiah* 2:2–4: "And they shall turn their swords into ploughshares and their spears into sickles. Nation shall not lift up sword against nation: neither shall they be exercised any more to war." The comment is Lonergan's own, a poignant hope in the darkness of the 1930s, and perhaps also in our own time: "Is this to be taken literally or is it figure? It would be fair and fine indeed to think it no figure."[150]

Lonergan's Radical Breakthrough in Economics

Why does the proletariat today include almost everyone? Why is the control of industry in the hands of fewer and fewer? Radically it is our own fault. We leave our affairs to others, because we are too indolent and too stupid to get to work and run them ourselves.

—Lonergan, 1941[151]

It must be added, as a matter of truthfulness, they were helpless by choice. They chose to be impeded, in the way of most of us, when unpleasant demands arise . . .

—Berrigan[152]

A radical new beginning has to be found.

—Lonergan, 1942[153]

No intimation of the early Lonergan's breadth and radicality of vision would be complete without some reference to his massive labors in economic theory. Just as he had long been convinced that if Catholics, and in particular, Jesuits were to live on the level of their times, they would need to think out a theory of history,[154] so I think he had long been of the opinion that "the basic step in aiding [the poor] in a notable manner is a matter of spending one's nights and days in a deep and prolonged study of economic analysis."[155]

Yet it is difficult even to make an entry into this formidable and craggy domain of remote but brilliant theory. The two economics volumes in the *Collected Works* "are principally foundational works: grimly difficult reading, then, for someone seeking a beginning view."[156] Few indeed are the cragsmen who can view those volumes, with their complicated analyses and their fifty-odd complex equations, with something less than fear and trembling.[157] Yet we have Lonergan's own veiled testimony to the importance of his economic labor: "The most influential man in the twentieth century—the strongest candidate, at least—is Karl Marx, and he spent years in the British Museum writing books that everyone laughed at."[158] We are no longer laughing at Marx, because his Toynbean withdrawal for the sake of theory was matched with a relentless return for the sake of praxis. But perhaps it is true to say that we have not yet begun to read Lonergan, and that it would be progress if the standard economic establishment were at least laughing at his books.[159]

It is, I think, worth spending some time pondering Lonergan's remark on Marx: "There is a terrific hatred in Marx, and it is a hatred of sin."[160] This comment relates, of course, to his remark in the historical manuscripts on the origin of communism in "the pharisaical religiosity of capitalist exploitation and oppression."[161] One might also contemplate this remark in the context of the later Lonergan's position on "the sin of backwardness," relate it back to his stark claim regarding the universalization of the proletariat, and relate it forward again to his later blunt comments on multinational corporations as well as social alienation.[162] One could relate Lonergan's comment, as well, to his references to privileged and depressed classes.[163] One could relate it also to his early concern about democracy as having become a functional oligarchy.[164]

In any case, Lonergan worked steadily on economic theory from 1930 to 1944. Somehow he also found time to write his extraordinary study on *Grace and Freedom* in Aquinas—there are fragments of his economic theory typed on the reverse side of a typescript of his dissertation[165]—and in the bargain he worked out his various manuscripts concerning fundamental sociology, the analytic concept of history, and the dialectic of history.

While I cannot introduce the basic notions of his economic theory here, it is fair to say that Lonergan's analysis of the cyclic pulsing of the productive process was far ahead of its time, and still is.[166] He was convinced that he had discovered "a new science" of economics,[167] a generalization of prior capitalist and socialist efforts that left those older efforts in the same unenviable position in which the new physics had left Ptolemy and Newton.[168] Like any successful serious scientific generalization, he claimed, it effected "an integral transformation of the whole previous position." [169] And that transformation has radical implications. "A generalization will postulate a transformation not only of the old guard and its abuses but also of the reformers and their reforms; it will move to a higher synthesis that eliminates at a stroke both the problem of wages and the complementary problem of trade unions" and a host of further traditionally inveterate problems.[170]

Lonergan's mention of "a transformation not only of the old guard and its abuses but also of the reformers and their reforms" calls attention to the relation of his economic theory to capitalism and to socialism. As James Marsh remarks, Lonergan's analysis in some sense argues "for a plague on the houses of both late capitalism and state socialism."[171] Specifying in what precise sense that is true would entail a lengthy and difficult analysis. But it is at least safe to say that Lonergan's economic theory is radically innovative and novel in a way that the standard theories underlying late capitalism and state socialism are not.

To begin with, his analysis takes place at a level prior to "the juridical concepts of property and exchange."[172] It reaches "behind the psychology of property and the laws of exchange to form a more basic concept and develop a more general theory."[173] It critiques "the classical assumption that profits are the measure of soundness,"[174] not by means of what he would later call "moral precepts that are not technically specific,"[175] but by reference to a functional analysis of four distinct phases of the productive process, which he names the capitalist, the materialist, the static, and the cultural phases, each with different sets of implications for action and hence different precepts.[176]

Although Lonergan ultimately believes in the superiority of what is conventionally called a free enterprise system overagainst socialist planning or bureaucratic management of the economy,[177] his analysis gives a quite different and radically unconventional meaning to the phrase *free enterprise*. As he pointedly insists, "One has to refuse to mean by free enterprise what has been going on in the West for the last two hundred years."[178] It is also fair to say Lonergan's functional analysis of the phases of the productive process entails a distribution of blame across traditional lines. "Just as one might make a locomotive leap off the tracks to the right or the left by blocking the steam conduits to the pistons on this side or that, so the economic process can be wrecked by the stupidity of capital or by the stupidity of labor, by the demand for high profits or high wages out of due season."[179] Similarly, the distinct requirements of each phase cut across the traditional battle lines of capitalism and socialism. As Lonergan remarks concerning one component of his analysis, "Obviously, there is no necessary correspondence between this law and either the classical view that profits are due to intelligence, enterprise, or risk, or the Marxian view that profits are due to reckless exploitation of labor."[180]

Again, precisely where Lonergan agrees and disagrees with Marx requires careful and detailed study. But there appears to be little doubt that their roads diverge significantly on the question of the nature of *surplus value*.

> I agree with Marx inasmuch as I find intrinsic to the developing economy a surplus. I disagree inasmuch as I have no doubt that it is a blunder to conceive this surplus as surplus value; it is to be understood and conceived, not in terms of marginal analysis, but in terms of macroeconomic analysis. Again, I agree with Marx inasmuch as he finds the fact of surplus a source for moral indignation, but I disagree with him on his interpretation of the fact of surplus and on the moral conclusions he draws.[181]

This is not a matter of dueling *a priorist* ideologies, then, but of the comparative adequacy of functional macrodynamic analysis.[182] Similarly, Lonergan's analysis discerns "a radical flaw in the classical theory of prices"[183] with enormous implications. The nature of his diagnosis may be complicated, but its implications are clear enough:

> the classical price mechanism . . . isolates the individual in the narrowest and lowest of his interests, and then leaves it to labor organizations and strikes, to interlocking directorates and monopolies and lockouts, to state intervention and lobbying and tariffs and subsidies, to nationalism and armaments and economic imperialism and wars, to fight out unjustly and stupidly and even brutally the issues which should be settled by a competent theory of prices and properly developed price system.[184]

These few and scattered intimations of Lonergan's labors in economic theory cannot, of course, begin to give any real account of Lonergan's "new science" of economics. But I hope to have given some flavor of its radical innovations and implications.[185] As to its possible and precarious future implementation, that depends on whether the economics establishment chooses to live on the level of the times or becomes instead a massive and ultimately appalling instance of "the sin of backwardness." In any case, as Lonergan says, "The task will be vast, so vast that only the creative imagination of all individuals in all democracies will be able to construct at once the full conception and the full realization of the new order."[186]

Conclusion

> The determinism and pressures of every kind, resulting from the
> cumulative surd of unintelligent policies and actions, can be withstood
> only through a hope that is transcendent and so does not depend on
> any human prop. Finally, only within the context of higher truths
> accepted on faith can human intelligence and reasonableness be
> liberated from the charge of irrelevance to the realities produced by
> human waywardness.
>
> —Lonergan[187]

> In faith and hope, the stories converged.
>
> —Berrigan[188]

The efforts of Lonergan and Berrigan to resist contemporary sinful social,
economic, and cultural structures, each in their own ways, may strike some
as quixotic at best, naïve at worst. But I would claim that one of the radical
displacements called for by a contemporary, adequate self-knowledge
concerns precisely the status of "the complacent practicality"[189] of a distorted common sense in each of us, an inertial complacency which "easily
twists to the view that, as insistent desires and contracting fears necessitate
and justify the realization of ideas, so ideas without that warrant are a
matter of indifference."[190] What if this "apparently hard-headed practicality and realism"[191] is one of the very roots of our collective failure consistently to stand in faith against injustice and oppression, consistently to
stand in love and solidarity with its victims, insistently to lean forward
in hope toward a world transformed by transcendent faith, hope, and
love?

What if this complacent subpracticality and pseudo-realism are really a
neurosis-like refusal to face the corruptions of contemporary consciousness, or the corruptions of our own, a refusal to work courageously and
painfully toward their accurate diagnosis and eventual healing? What if
Lonergan is correct in the diagnosis he offers? "Just as the biased intelligence of the psychoneurotic sets up an ingenious, plausible, self-adapting
resistance to the efforts of the analyst, so men of practical common sense
become warped by the situation in which they live and regard as starry-
eyed idealism and silly impracticality any proposal that would lay the axe to
the root of the social surd."[192] What if "that practicality is the root of the
trouble," [193] and what if it has caused our civilization to drift "through
successive less comprehensive syntheses to the sterility of the objectively
unintelligible situation and to the coercion of economic pressures, political

forces, and psychological conditioning"?[194] What if we ourselves are products of that drift? What if we are its drones and clones? Can we really avoid complicity on the excuse that we consider ourselves supremely practical? Isn't that narrow-minded and small-souled practicality part of the complicity?

What if that stance is related to the madness of blandly and unconsciously assuming the Machiavellian project of modernity in our daily struggles? What if that stance can be critiqued for "the plausibility it lends to the Machiavellian argument that true answers to the question of how we ought to live are so far removed from how we do in fact live as to be practically or politically irrelevant; and to the consequence of completely separating politics and morality"?[195] Is that stance in the end not perhaps an instance and a product of "the dull conscience which does not discern the greatness of the [divine] other and the loftiness of his demands"?[196]

Lonergan and Berrigan are radical and visionary Jesuits, one in the realms of theory, interiority, and method, and the other in the realms of conscience, contemplation, and resistance. Both are united in a Christian faith that makes radical demands in an age that is dominated by all manner of injustice, oppression, and distortion. Both take their stand on the truth of Christian revelation and on the dignity of the human person overagainst an all-too-palpable reign of sin. That truth is radical, and that truth matters. It also has radical social, economic, political, and cultural consequences.

I began by suggesting that Lonergan and Berrigan are united by something more than their status as serious and committed Christians and Jesuits. I have sketched a range of additional affinities. Perhaps in conclusion I may briefly allude to those here by suggesting that both Lonergan and Berrigan are, in their very different ways, united in anguish and care-filled struggle "to prevent dominant groups from deluding mankind by the rationalization of their sins,"[197] "to protect the future against the rationalization of abuses,"[198] "to prevent the falsification of history,"[199] and to assist the oppressed, for "they were not able to resist this violence being destitute of help."[200] They are united as suffering servants of the emergent yet eschatological kingdom of God. They are against the settled reign of ideology, the destructive dominance of pervasive false facts and false values deeply embedded and "concretised in the historic flow"[201] in the form of "achievements, institutions, habits, customs, mentalities, characters,"[202] and transmitted through "assumptions, mentalities, interpretations, philosophies, tastes, habits, hopes, fears."[203] They are united in resistance against dominant and accepted "claptrap,"[204] united against "the day's loud lying," to quote the poet Patrick Kavanagh,[205] or more generally, the loud lying of our times.

Berrigan once remarked that "the unmasking of the Big Lie is a characteristic of Christian society in bad times: or ought to be,"[206] and Lonergan
spoke of "the lies of decadent culture"[207] and of "the objectively organized
lie"[208] of ideologies that seek "to defend, justify, legitimate, an iniquitous
style of living, of economic arrangements, of political government, of any
of the organized forms of human activity."[209] Both take their stand on the
transcendent truth of Christian faith overagainst the reign of organized lies
of ideology and alienation. Both take their stand on a transcendent hope in
the face of the despair generated by the seemingly insurmountable moun-
tain of accumulated sin, injustice, hatred, ignorance, complacency, stupidity, ideology, alienation, greed, violence, and oppression. And both take
their stand on the power of transcendent love as a wellspring and a force
for resistance and peace. "As alienation and ideology are destructive of
community, so the self-sacrificing love that is Christian charity reconciles
man to his true being, and undoes the mischief initiated by alienation and
consolidated by ideology."[210] Both know in their bones, in the very roots of
their being, that although sin is pervasive in our personal lives, in our institutions, in society, culture, economy, and history, nonetheless grace is
abundant, and Christ is mysteriously present in a suffering world. "We are
unready for God; we are hardly more ready for one another. And yet, and
yet . . ."[211]

> . . . Christ plays in ten thousand places,
> Lovely in limbs, and lovely in eyes not his
> To the Father through the features of men's faces.[212]

Government by Fear, and How Activists of Faith Resist Fear

Gail M. Presbey

Fear and courage are perennial topics of discussions in moral philosophy. From Aristotle's analysis of the courage of the soldier on the battlefield, we have inherited the idea that courage, as with any virtue, requires two parts. First, we have to know what to fear, and what not to fear. Second, when confronted with what we should not fear, we should become fearless, so that we can be courageous. Courage is connected to values worth upholding.

Recent books, like Corey Robin's *Fear: The History of a Political Idea*, and former US Vice President Al Gore's book *Assault on Reason*, have focused upon the uses and abuses of fear in politics. Both books speak of how the former Bush administration had been manipulating US citizens' fear so as to keep itself in power. By the Bush administration's using a certain style of rhetoric, inflammatory ad campaigns, and draconian laws, some US citizens have been frightened into thinking that only the Bush administration and its policies can keep them safe from attack by terrorists. The Robin book has a broader historical scope, suggesting that the problem of the manipulation of fear by elites has a long history. He focuses on the McCarthy years of finding and prosecuting "communists" and their sympathizers as a precursor to today's "war on terror." He also charts how civil society in the United States magnifies any attempts by government to instill fear. Often the private sector does the work of the government, threatening its workers with firing, or actually firing them if they do not tow the party line. Members of society mirror and reinforce government's judgments by shunning those who receive bad publicity, in effect becoming the enforcers of government's wishes.

This essay looks at the life and works of Daniel Berrigan, long-time peace activist, poet, and author of books and essays. Berrigan has shed light on the distorting effects of both Church and State on our moral sensibilities. What we should fear, and what we should not fear, are clarified by Berrigan. We should fear having stones for hearts. We should fear becoming a nation of murderers. We should reach out to those whom we are told to fear. Not only does Berrigan demonstrate the clarity of discernment but he demonstrates the moral virtue of courage in his acts of speaking out as well as civil disobedience. He knows first hand the instruments used by government and civil society in encouraging conformity and discouraging dissent. Yet his connection in compassion to the suffering of others has made him willing to take personal risks to address the well-being of the larger whole. His background as a member of the Catholic clergy allows him to shed light on that other arm of government within civil society (given slight mention in Robin's book)—organized religion.

This essay focuses on four key stages of Berrigan's life, recounting the challenges he faced in each and how he engaged in courageous action. The theories of Robin and Gore, as well as the moral analysis of Aristotle, Martha Nussbaum, and other philosophers will be brought in at each stage to show the significance of the struggles in which Berrigan was engaged. "Berrigan Learns to Speak Up" follows Robin's theme of fear in the workplace to discern Berrigan's early challenges within the Catholic Church and his religious order, the Jesuits. "The Catonsville Action" looks at courage in the specific example of Berrigan's civil disobedience action, in Catonsville, Maryland, against the Vietnam War, including prosecution by J. Edgar Hoover that parallels the earlier political show trials of McCarthyism covered in Robin's book. "Berrigan and Plowshares Disarmament in 1980" follows his Plowshares action in King of Prussia, Pennsylvania, against nuclear weapons proliferation. "Other, more recent forms of resistance" recounts other more recent ways in which Berrigan has countered fear with courage: responding to the AIDS epidemic, "Star Wars" research projects in Manhattan, and the 9/11 attacks in his home city of New York. All four parts of his life are filled with examples of moral discernment (intellectual virtue) as well as courageous action (moral virtue). The conclusion will draw together some key insights about fear and courage.

Berrigan Learns to Speak Up

In his autobiography, *To Dwell in Peace*, Daniel Berrigan talks of growing up in a family where his parents often quarreled and fought, with seemingly no awareness that their witnessed and overheard quarrels might adversely affect their children. He went to Catholic schools, where a young nun, unprepared for her role, used cruelty and terror against the students. Berrigan considered her a "victim bound to victimize."[1] The lessons of childhood seemed to be that the large dog eats the small dog. The brothers of the family threatened each other unless they were threatened from the outside, at which point they would gather in unity. He remembered with considerable shuddering the witnessing of parents drowning stray kittens, and the later bloodier occasion of the slaughter of the fattened pig. This violence was very uncomfortable but considered by others to be normal.

In 1932 he was glad to find a new teacher, Sister Mary Lua, who cared for the hungry, spoke up to the male hierarchy, and taught him to love the Eucharist. He refers to her as a great light, as quenching water brought to his desert. Later, in high school, another sister who was his French teacher encouraged him to become a priest.[2] Berrigan entered the Jesuits in 1939 and spent his first fifteen years in "formation."[3] Priests were exempt from military service. The Church kept out of trouble by its silence and its blessing of war. He says the young Jesuits lived like cozy piglets in a brick-and-mortar house, while the Big Bad Wolf (World War II) huffed and puffed outside.[4] The young Jesuit trainees were told to devote themselves to the life of the mind; in their apolitical stance, Berrigan charges, "moral men clot and form an immoral society."[5] A fellow Jesuit, John L'Heureux, wrote of Jesuit formation of the time, "Theology had nothing whatsoever to do with society, or, for that matter, with the living.[6] Yet Berrigan kept himself busy with feats of academic study and religious observations, just to keep up with and fit in with the order.[7] He was ordered to study philosophy at Woodstock, and considered the whole ordeal an endurance test. While they were learning Aquinas's five arguments for the existence of God, a new god was being created: the Bomb.

When Berrigan read Knox's *God and the Atom*, he was enthusiastic about its critique of the US bombing of Hiroshima and Nagasaki. But his classmates were horrified at the argument, and defended US actions. They said Berrigan didn't know the facts. "With considerable heat I was informed that I scarcely knew my arse from my elbow, a bomb from a berry."[8] He then realized that people could spend years learning about Christian ritual, sacraments, and theology, and then "go off to war, in apparent good conscience." This lack of conscience was stretched to encompass mass murder, even destruction of all the living.

The Jesuits then sent him to France. During 1954, the area was in the midst of inner conflict. Rome had issued condemnations of the French worker-priests, and told them they had to give up their jobs in factories and return to regular priestly duties, or be excommunicated. (They were later rehabilitated during Vatican II). He witnessed the town he lived in to be divided in two. One half were the "unholy" poor workers, and the other half were "the religious and their holy indifference and secure livings and noses on high."[9] From there he was assigned to a military chaplaincy in West Germany for forty days (during 1954). He was awestruck in retrospect, as he noted that he naively went around exhorting soldiers to observe their faith as if everything were normal.[10] From there he was assigned to teach at Brooklyn Prep. There his mind was invaded by "second thoughts worthy of a Hamlet"—about whether the work the Jesuits did with these youths was merely preparing them to take the reins of power in a class society.[11] Berrigan was already beginning to develop the trait of critiquing his church, and his society.

But it was in 1957, shortly after he had been assigned to teach theology at LeMoyne College in Syracuse, that he "stumbled on a live wire." Something would happen that would forever change him. He met Karl Meyer, who came to Syracuse fresh from jail. Meyer had served a sentence for refusing to pay war taxes. He wanted to stay and open a Catholic Worker house there, inspired by Dorothy Day's example. Impressed with Meyer, Berrigan decided to write the bishop of Syracuse about the planned house. The bishop phoned Berrigan with complete disapproval of the project. The bishop condemned Karl Meyer's witness as going against Pope Pius XII's doctrine of Just War, which (in Berrigan's paraphrase) "clearly blessed the defensive guns of the virtuous, together with their virtuous explosion in the flesh of the unvirtuous."[12] The bishop went further to assert that Berrigan, by admiring Meyer's witness, had proven himself unfit to teach theology at LeMoyne. President Perkins of LeMoyne resisted the bishop's pressure to remove Berrigan for five years.

Berrigan said that he learned a lot from this encounter with power. Both Church and State suffer from the "disease of power." Each decides that

their view is "God's will." In the following years Berrigan was often shuf-
fled around and removed by powers who insisted that it was he who was
out of step with God's will. Over the years, he mastered a way of dealing
with unjust treatment by authorities. He found a way to see God's message
to him (a sign pointing the way) in even the most heavy-handed of treatment. After all, he explains, God is not "mayor of a heavenly Dullsville."[13]

Here we see Berrigan getting an ecclesiastical version of Robin's "Fear,
American Style" (which I will explain shortly below). While most workers
in America serve an employer at will and can be dismissed without cause, a
Jesuit who joins an order and takes the vow of obedience is in a different
relationship to his superiors. They have invested in him, through many
years of education and spiritual direction. He is like family. They don't
want to dismiss him lightly. But they can call on the fact that he has taken
a vow to obey them. That vow can be called upon by Church superiors
when they think an individual has said something wrong, done something
daring—just like an employer. The mere fear that a superior could do such
a thing keeps many Jesuits and other religious in order on a daily basis. But
in certain situations, the clergy member is called in for a serious discussion.
The act of power gets conflated with an interpretation of the power relationship as "God's will," which makes the direct order even harder to
resist.

The examples of what happens to Berrigan also illustrate the intersec-
tions of power in the Catholic Church, between bishops and cardinals,
members of the Catholic hierarchy, on the one hand, and the Jesuit Order
itself and other religious orders, on the other hand. Orders have limited
autonomy but they are not sovereign. They would usually prefer to be left
alone without limits by the hierarchy, but they realize that to preserve their
limited autonomy they must observe certain limits. Into the mix come
other employers such as universities.

Berrigan found out, to his chagrin, that his Church was content to be
the handmaiden of the state. Money is always scarce, and Catholic universities can get funds working on military contracts. He used a metaphor:
Church and State are like hand and glove. It's cold, so it's best for the hand
to stay warm in the glove. Everyone understands that. And, every once in
awhile, the gloved hand will kill in war, and bless the killing. That is considered normal.[14]

Berrigan noted that war commandeered the Church's conscience and
the loyalty of its believers. The Church cooperated because its properties
were not threatened. Likewise he notes, with perhaps some cutting
humor, that Americans were willing to give their sons to war, but if the

government had asked to commandeer their cars for the war, they would have rebelled.[15] His point was that the Church had squandered something precious—its gospel mission—in order to fit in and prosper in a worldly fashion. Is this not how Robin said fear is exercised "American Style"? Complicity is bought with promises of flourishing.

To understand how fear is instilled, and complicity is won, in many power situations, political theorist Corey Robin traced an argument back to Thomas Hobbes. Unlike other accounts (which see fear as irrational and uncontrollable), Hobbes emphasizes the control of fear by reason. Remember that Hobbes fled England during the Cromwell-led Puritan's attack on the monarchy there. Being a monarchist, Hobbes's work, *The Leviathan*, was intended to convince people that they were better off meekly submitting to a monarch who could ensure peace, than to try to take power into their own hands and risk all the difficulties and insecurities of civil war. Hobbes analyzed human nature and decided that humans quarrel (and fight) for three reasons: gain, diffidence (security), and reputation. In his works, he ridiculed those who fight for reputation, saying they fought over "trifles." He thought it made more sense to put concerns for reputation aside, and give oneself over to calculation of one's own gain and security.[16] Now, the word *reputation* might not capture all the meaning we intend here. Robin explains that Hobbes knew that people would sometimes fight for a cause because they believed in it. If they felt their group had been wronged, they would put self-interest aside and fight, knowingly risking their lives. Hobbes thought that in order to rein in people's reckless tendencies to fight for various causes, they had to be encouraged to learn to think "rationally," which, for Hobbes, meant to care for their individual survival above all else.[17]

Hobbes knew that people didn't naturally care about their own survival as the highest good, but he thought that through education, they could learn to become this kind of human. Hobbes reasoned in this way: in order to enjoy any aspect of life (family, wealth, nature, good health and so on), one must be alive in order to experience it. So, self-survival is necessarily the highest good. Whatever one must do in order to survive is justified. The pursuit of safety is therefore rational. Within the secure confines of safety, one would then be free to pursue gain (of a variety of goods, as well as human relationships).[18]

Once one has become the kind of person who decides that self-survival is the highest good, it is a small and "reasonable" step to calculate that the way in which one can be most safe is to submit one's self (and hand over one's freedom) to a very powerful sovereign who can then protect oneself, and secure a context of law in which gain is possible. If a person is hesitant to enter such a contract, Hobbes points out to them that they are being unreasonable. By risking their lives in staying outside of such a contract, they jeopardize all that they hold dear.[19] These same themes, with a bit of a different emphasis, were covered in Arendt's book, *Eichmann in Jerusalem*. Why did Adolf Eichmann, a mid-level bureaucrat in the Nazi Party, engage in schemes of great evil? He was an ambitious person, motivated by concern for his career. Collaborators are in a vulnerable position, Robin explains. They desire advancement, but are susceptible to being dismissed by their employers for even slight exhibitions of disagreement.[20] Robin explains that the terror that most Americans feel on a daily basis is related to the workplace. Seventy-six percent of Americans are employed at will, meaning that they can be dismissed without cause. Courts have upheld the decisions of employers who have dismissed employees for legal behavior outside of the workplace that the employers find distasteful. Many employers engage in discouraging the unionizing efforts of their workers. While it is possible to sue to be reinstated to one's job if one is dismissed for union activity, there is no penalty levied against the employer for having done so, and 80 percent of those who are reinstated lose their jobs again within one year. Robin also points out that all federal employees of the Department of Homeland Security have no union organizing rights and no job security.[21]

Robin's book ends up with an ironic portrayal of America: it's the land of the free and the home of the brave, but each individual American is terrorized by fear that they will lose their job. With little social safety net, Americans really fear losing employment. Employers ask for total loyalty and suppress dissent.[22] While the fear of a Jesuit in an order is a little different from the average worker whose employer feels no loyalty, nevertheless clergy experience pressure from their superiors and fear being thrown out of their communities, or banished to obscurity within their communities.

Berrigan would be banished, transferred, and demoted many times, on his way to eventually being incarcerated for civil disobedience. As he explained, the Vietnam War turned his world upside down. Others thought the war was normal, and that what was disgraceful were priests—such as he and his brother Philip—protesting the war. As he explains, "The courts and jails, off limits to decent folk like ourselves . . . at most, places one visited from time to time as a supporter or counselor of others . . . their doors swung wide. And we, turned about, were tumbled into their maw, to be judged, found guilty, and locked up."[23]

Daniel's brother Philip Berrigan had been a priest with the Josephites and had been teaching in Newburgh, New York, when he lost his job due to his protests against the war. He was reassigned, without consultation, to a poor neighborhood in Baltimore, Maryland. Daniel Berrigan empathizes with the frustration of his being "plucked from his work." As Robin explains, people find meaning in their lives by developing their special talents. Being reassigned to more marginal work is a common fate for those who do not follow orders at work.

Soon Daniel himself would be ousted from his work at the Jesuit Mission in New York. He had dared to say something commemorative about the death of Roger LaPorte. LaPorte had set himself on fire in front of the United Nations as a protest of the war. The official Catholic view was that it was a suicide that could not be condoned by the Church. Berrigan was upset about LaPorte's lost life. But he thought it unfair to call it a simple suicide and do nothing but condemn it. He said that whether God would consider it a sacrifice and not a suicide is something that we don't know with certainty. When his statements were publicized, he was abruptly told by his religious superiors that he was to pack his bags. He was being sent to Latin America with no date of return.[24]

Through these actions, Berrigan demonstrated that he would not give in to fear. He did not want to live the life of toning down truth as he saw it in order to pursue a non-ruffled career. He could not have seen his banishment coming, and it was hard for him to bear packing up and leaving New York City, as yet unsure of what lay in store for him in Latin America. But in retrospect he realizes that his being sent to Latin America was a godsend, and he learned many important lessons there. He saw an imperial Catholic church on the side of the rich, as well as those within the church challenging that unholy alliance.[25]

Berrigan had been banished by New York's Cardinal Spellman, who had pressured Berrigan's Jesuit superiors to have him sent away. The banishment had given others a chance to exercise their courage. Biographers Murray Polner and Jim O'Grady explain that students across US campuses were protesting and even engaging in fasts in support of Berrigan. Supporters among the clergy organized a full page ad in *The New York Times* in support of Berrigan. Joseph Mulholland explained that it wasn't easy to encourage clergy to sign the ad since they feared the retaliation of Spellman. He met with Jesuits at Fordham University as well as Jesuits in formation at Woodstock theological seminary. Some were only encouraged to sign it when Mulholland explained that the more signatures gathered, the less the chance that any one person would be singled out by the cardinal for retaliation. Jesuit superiors put pressure on novices forbidding them to sign, but some signed anyway. In the end there were one thousand signatures, seventy-five from clergy.[26]

Undaunted by the support for Berrigan, the cardinal not only did not rescind the banishment, but went to Vietnam to minister to the troops there, and was quoted as saying "My Country, Right or Wrong."[27] As Daniel's brother Philip would say, the frustrating thing about the Catholic Church is that its leaders are always speaking against war, but never against *this* war—that is, the war at hand, the war being waged by their country in the present tense.[28] Thus we see a whole hierarchy of pressures, not only on Berrigan but on the whole Catholic Church, to cooperate with the government's agenda. Likewise, parishioners who witness their cardinal supporting the war may think twice before speaking out against it. Or perhaps their conscience will be lulled by his example so that the question of the morality of war won't even be raised as an issue.

The Catonsville Action

When he came back to the United States after his banishment to Latin America, Berrigan got a job at Cornell University as associate director for service. He led students in anti–Vietnam War protests. He was frustrated by the timidity or apathy of most faculty members over the pressing issues of the war. He explained that the Vietnam War was the longest war in US history, and that more bombs were dropped on Vietnam than the total used in World War II. Yet Cornell's President Perkins explained to Berrigan that the goal of the university is to help the government. Berrigan was undoubtedly frustrated with his limited role on campus. How to stop a war and protect the lives of innocents?[29]

Berrigan described his first arrest in a civil disobedience action blockading the Pentagon. The participants were protesting the Vietnam War. He hadn't planned ahead of time on getting arrested. When police told protestors to disperse or risk arrest, he explained: "My friends, of course, chose to remain. And so, by force of example, did I."[30] He said the moral pressure he felt well up inside of him was due to his own sensitivity toward the "perils descending on my friends."[31] He cared about the issues at stake as much as they did, and he didn't want to be exempt from their sacrifice. But he notes that his own act of arrest was low-cost in comparison to the simultaneous act of the Baltimore Four, where his brother Philip Berrigan and others were pouring blood on draft documents to protest the

Vietnam War. There, Philip Berrigan and friends were "seized by the great Seizer . . . . They had dared muck up the exquisite order of his necrophilic files, where the names of the soon to be killed, or the soon to kill, or both, were preserved."[32] Their act was perceived as more daring, more destructive, and more deserving of longer prison sentences than his own simpler act of blockading the Pentagon building. A writer covering the Baltimore Four's action and conviction said of Philip Berrigan: "He is devoid of all the fears, the cautions, the proprieties that motivate normal men."[33]

But Daniel Berrigan would soon have a chance to take on great risks for peace. He received a request to travel to Hanoi, with Howard Zinn, to receive three US pilots who had been taken prisoner. The North Vietnamese had agreed to release them to members of the peace movement. While in Hanoi, the city shook from falling American bombs. Berrigan explains, "Being under American bombs was an education without parallel."[34] It helped him get a first-person perspective of what it must feel to be terrorized by the thought that one or one's loved ones might at any moment fall victim in such a large explosion. It was this experience of the fragility of life, and the sensed scale of the emergency, that radically opened Berrigan to confront more risk in a civil disobedience action like his brother Philip's. Upon returning from Hanoi, when he was asked to join the Catonsville Nine action, he agreed.[35]

It was this concern about napalm's destructive capabilities that led himself, his brother Phil, and seven others to concoct their own homemade "napalm," and then to pour it, not on people but on draft files. As he explained in his famous passage from *The Trial of the Catonsville Nine*, "Apologies, good friends, for the fracture of good order, the burning of paper instead of lives."[36]

How did he overcome the fear that most would have regarding engaging in such a risky protest during wartime? He explains, "Instead of sight, or evidence, or logic, there was something better to go by—a hand in mine, someone to walk with."[37] With this company, he felt a new calm. He explained that he arrived at his choice not through an academic sort of logic that tells professors they should do anything for "tenure"—the ultimate of fixity. He had some sense that he may very well be jeopardizing his chances for a career in academia. Instead Berrigan realized he was "fixed nowhere, except in the lives of those I loved."[38] They engaged in their action, mixing kerosene and soap to make homemade "napalm" and pouring it on draft files, to set them alight. Practically, thousands of young men could not easily be called in the draft with their files destroyed. But the act was largely symbolic. Berrigan states, self-deprecatingly, "The act was pitiful, a tiny flare amid the consuming fires of war."[39] But luckily, the act's importance caught on. In the following years, seventy draft boards were entered by protestors, and draft files were shredded, burned, scattered, and in one case mailed back to each draftee.[40]

Berrigan was mostly concerned with the extreme problems—where people were dying. And of course, in the days of nuclear weapons, there are fears that local, conventional wars could escalate to become nuclear wars. And here is where it's clear that Berrigan's thinking departs from Hobbes. For while Hobbes has his rational actor care only for self-survival, Berrigan is empathically connected to other humans. When he finds out that someone else is dying, he wants to do something to stop the killing, and nurse the wounded. Hobbes did not create a role for caring and empathy in his system. He even reduced the mother-child relationship to a social contract. He presumed that "human nature" meant that one did not care for others. But Berrigan could not stand the participation in cruel acts. As he watched the Vietnam War unfold, he was mortified by the stories of napalm burning fields of food crops as well as people's bodies. How could US forces use such cruel measures, not to mention in a war fought for unclear and ideological motives? Who would care about the children in harm's way?

In her analysis of compassion, Martha Nussbaum outlines four factors that encourage us to feel compassion for others, or not. Compassion is not just a feeling, it is also guided by reason. To feel compassion, we make the following judgments. First, that another person is experiencing serious harm or pain. Second, that the person suffering does not fully deserve the pain. Third, that the person suffering shares similar vulnerabilities as we do. Fourth, that the person suffering is somehow related in an important way to ourselves or to our projects.[41]

Since these various ingredients are needed to feel compassion, Nussbaum notes that compassion can "go wrong" if we don't make good and accurate judgments in all the above cases. For example, we could decide that someone deserves their suffering (even when they don't) and therefore not be moved to compassion when we hear of their sufferings. We may also be moved to sympathize with those whom we should not sympathize with. We may get the judgment of seriousness wrong, and care about limited sufferings while ignoring large suffering. Often our biggest problem, according to Nussbaum, is that those who are suffering don't seem related to our lives or our projects. In those cases we may find our attention span short-lived. We hear about their misfortune on our news programs, we feel bad for them, and then immediately forget the whole problem so that we can refocus on what is important in our lives.[42]

For Berrigan, the experience of going to Hanoi made the suffering of North Vietnamese people very real to himself. By sharing their fate of being the possible victims of American bombs, he was able to care for their vulnerability. He saw the extent of their suffering, and he knew that they did not deserve their suffering. It was still a decision to allow that experience to influence him so that his concern for them would become central to his own life. He could have considered the Hanoi trip a harrowing experience, which he wanted to blot out of his memory. But he let the suffering of others touch him deeply. He then became able to risk his own safety in order to secure theirs.

There is a self-interested aspect in caring about others, in wanting to keep them out of harm's way. It has to do with concern for moral integrity. One does not, as an individual, want to participate or lend support through even unwitting cooperation (like paying war taxes) to an atrocity. But it isn't merely a concern for individual moral integrity that Berrigan exhibits. He is always concerned just as much with the moral integrity of the Church and the nation. How can our Church be so content to be complicit in government atrocities? How can our government so blithely pursue inhumane methods to reach its calculated goals? Is it really good for the nation to try to achieve world "dominance" at the expense of losing the good will of other nations?

While they had to go to trial for their Catonsville action, he noted that "the war, those who waged it, were never to stand trial."[43] The war went on. So when it was time to turn themselves in to begin serving their sentences, some of those found guilty, including Berrigan, decided not to comply.[44] He evaded police, giving short public speeches or appearances when such could be organized with quick getaways, until he was finally apprehended and imprisoned. His daring in consenting to appear in public, to boost the morale of peace activists as well as to give guidance to the movement, is also rich with examples of courage—perhaps even a daring aspect that drove Hoover and the FBI crazy, since it gave the country the impression that the FBI was being outwitted by peace activists.[45]

Fellow civil resister David Eberhardt described his own fear of prosecution, imprisonment, and even fear of being attacked by other prisoners. He said he was amazed at the calm demeanor of Daniel and Philip Berrigan, who called the years of the Catonsville trial and their subsequent imprisonment "the happiest days of our lives." Eberhardt called Philip Berrigan a model of courage and sacrifice.[46]

There were critics of their action among members of the peace community. Thomas Merton criticized the Catonsville action, saying that its lawlessness frightened an already terrified American public that was jittery after the assassinations of Kennedy and King. Rosemary Radford Reuther said she would not join in such an act because it had an us-against-the-world mentality. Other critics worried that such actions would alienate average Americans or that the actions departed from strict Gandhian guidelines insofar as they were secretive and perhaps not completely non-violent. Barbara Deming eventually distanced herself from the Catonsville supporters, saying she was troubled by their "intrigue and Quixotic romanticism." Others wondered if civil disobedience was a sign of rejection of democracy.[47]

But the bigger challenge was to come from J. Edgar Hoover, head of the Federal Bureau of Investigation. While in prison for their action, Hoover announced in November 1970 that he would indict and try the Berrigan brothers for belonging to an anarchist group, the "East Coast Conspiracy to Save Lives," which planned to kidnap a government official (later identified as Henry Kissinger) and destroy underground steam pipes in Washington, D.C. These were fabricated charges. The charges were later reduced to conspiracy to destroy selective service records. This indictment was part of an overall strategy of Hoover to whip up fear of communists and internal enemies among average US citizens. He wanted media coverage to glorify the FBI's ability to find and destroy such enemies. He had used his power to target other critics of US foreign and domestic policy such as Martin Luther King Jr., the Black Panther Party, Vietnam Veterans against the War, Daniel Ellsberg, Students for a Democratic Society, and Clergy and Laity Concerned. Polner and O'Grady explain: "So active was the FBI in probing every war resister organization and leading personality that it eventually kept files on hundreds of thousands of Americans, transforming the agency into a kind of federal thought police, and to all intents and purposes a political arm of the White House."[48]

Philip Berrigan, Liz McAlister, and others were indicted and Daniel Berrigan was an unindicted coconspirator. The trial was held in Harrisburg, Pennsylvania, in 1972. The case rested on the testimony of Boyd Douglass, a prisoner informant, "a victim deftly transformed into a victimizer,"[49] Berrigan explained. By using that description, we can see that Berrigan had already come to an analysis of the situation similar to one that Robin would many years later articulate. Douglas was an example of what Corey Robin had described as the old McCarthy-style abuse of people pushed to become informants.

Boyd Douglas was a prison inmate who came from a broken home. He committed a string of various crimes as a teenager. At age nineteen he was given the choice of prison time or joining the service. He chose the latter, but deserted twice, and finally received a six year sentence for a fake check scam.[50] This landed him in Lewisburg Penitentiary, and Philip Berrigan met him there. Douglas was given permission to leave the prison to attend Bucknell University. Once at Bucknell, Douglas joined the antiwar movement, and told people he was in prison for not cooperating with war plans. People in the peace movement found him charming, and used him as an example of a war maker who could have had a conversion to peace-making.[51]

Philip was anxious to communicate with Liz McAlister without prison censors reading their mail. He trusted Boyd Douglas to carry their correspondence. Some other inmates, as well as peace activists suspicious of Douglas, warned Liz and Philip that Douglas might be working for the government, but Philip checked him out and believed his sincerity, dismissing the rumors about Douglas.[52]

In the meantime, Liz was missing Philip and wanting to write him all the things on her mind. One day Liz and other nonviolent activists were sitting on a porch, brainstorming and daydreaming, wondering aloud what they could do to stop the war. One person wondered whether they could stage a nonviolent "citizens' arrest" of Henry Kissinger. They quickly dismissed the idea as a pipe dream. But Liz wrote of the conversation in a letter to Philip while he was in jail. Philip actually wrote back liking the idea and offering some concrete suggestions as to how it could be done. McAlister explained later that she was trying to keep up Philip's morale while he was in jail. All along, Douglas had been turning over their correspondence to the FBI. This correspondence was then used in the indictment.[53]

Why did Douglas agree to be a government agent? During cross-examination at the trial, Douglas revealed that he was a paid informer for the FBI. But how did he first decide to do it? Douglas's own account is that he had already begun smuggling the mail between Philip and Liz when he was caught by prison authorities. He had started to pass the letters because he had really admired Philip. Philip was convinced that he really was beginning to reach Douglas, changing his heart. When caught, the assistant warden called Douglas into his office, and the FBI agents there told Douglas that he could be sentenced to ten years in prison for his role in the smuggling, or he could cooperate with them.[54]

After fourteen days on the witness stand and after much cross-examination, Douglas revealed that he had demanded $50,000 and an honorable discharge from the army in exchange for his agreement to testify at the trial. He had earlier, upon revealing the Kissinger plot, received payment of

$3,800 from the FBI which he used to buy a new car. After the trial, Douglas disappeared into "an early version of the government witness protection program, name and identity changed forever."[55]

Daniel Berrigan had been out on parole while Philip Berrigan was still in jail, during the trial. Philip was led to the courtroom each day in prisoner's shackles. Daniel watched the court proceedings, and then visited with his brother in his prison cell each evening to talk about the day's court events. Both brothers felt some sympathy for Boyd Douglas, "a rag doll of a human," used by the government as their collaborator.[56] Daniel described the court during Douglas's testimony as "the sadness he spread about the court, like a fog machine making fog."[57] While this collaborator was to be pitied as a victim, he had to be resisted as a paid helper of the government.

News of Douglas's cooperation with the FBI may have led to jurors casting doubt on his testimony. The government did not win its case. The jury would not comply, and the case was declared a mistrial by the judge, leading, in Berrigan's estimation, to "Hoover's demise." Hoover had tried to traumatize and crush the spirits of dissenters, but he could not do so because "friends came together, strengthened, sturdier of purpose."[58]

The FBI harassment of the peace movement in the 1970s was not new. It had a precursor in the harassment of communists during the McCarthy era. Robin shows that the strategic thinking of Hobbes is not remote from what has happened in the United States. As Robin explains, Senator Joseph McCarthy, who led the House on Un-American Activities interrogations (working with big business, the Republican Party and the FBI), realized that the United States would have to have a propaganda campaign to convince Americans that they should fear the Soviets. After all, they had been our allies just a few years earlier in World War II. By putting individual communists on trial, Americans could be led to believe that communism is dangerous.[59]

At the beginning of the attacks on Hollywood, actors and film directors responded in unison against such charges. But the government then decided to proceed by arresting individuals. Cut off from other support, the government's goal was to isolate each individual, so that they would feel that they were a lone self up against an overwhelming power. Under such conditions, it would seem reasonable to capitulate.[60] During interrogations, questioners would emphasize that it would be good for the family of the person on trial if they were to decide to collaborate with the court by naming other actors and writers who were members of the Communist Party. Those who decided to cooperate and name names, did so, according to Robin, because they were convinced that such actions would enable them to support their families. Some informants, like Roy Higgins, saw their responsibility to their families primarily as financial responsibility. In order to make a living to support their families, they named names. Higgins was also encouraged to consider his naming of names to be a service to his country, as it strengthened the State.[61]

There was another main motive for people in Hollywood to name names so as to stay off the blacklist. They experienced fulfillment in their work, their careers. They were creative persons. While they could have scraped by in manual labor jobs, they didn't want to have to give up their careers, because using their special talents gave meaning to their lives.[62] Examples like this abounded in Hollywood, located in a liberal democratic milieu. Across the ocean, in Eastern European countries, professionals were also put into a similar vice grip by their communist governments. This dilemma was recently dramatized in the film *The Lives of Others* (2007). In the film, a highly talented stage director and composer, Jerska, is black-listed for political reasons. The film demonstrates the pain he feels on being deprived of the opportunity to make his artistic contribution to the world. While he refuses to compromise on his political views so as to have the ban against him lifted, he feels he can't go on living in such circum-stances, and he takes his own life. Jerska's choice is (seemingly) contrasted to the talented actress Christa-Maria, who compromises herself by agree-ing to have sexual liaisons with a powerful Communist Party member (whom she personally abhors) in order to have permission to continue her career. Her lover, Georg Dreyman, a talented writer, temporarily bolsters her resolve to resist such blackmail. But under government interrogation, when her interrogator, Captain Gerd Wiesler, makes plain to her that she must collaborate with the government and betray her lover in order to secure her career, she capitulates. The interrogator, who by now is reluc-tant to do his own job (but is watched by superiors so that he must carry out orders), knows exactly what he has to say in order to make his subject break. He knows she is someone who lives to practice her art. One gains collaborators by threatening the things that they hold dear in life.

By the end of the film, Wiesler the interrogator, despite his exquisite skills in interrogation methods, refuses to practice his skills when he realizes they are being used to crush two good people. He betrays his com-munist overseers by protecting those he is supposed to expose. He is then reassigned to the menial work of the mail room, in retaliation for his insub-ordination. One gets the feeling that Wiesler accepts this demotion, find-ing fulfillment in his act, knowing that his insubordination saved at least one good person (the writer, Dreyman) from his demise.

If one did not care about the good that the government threatened to withhold or destroy, one would not be so psychologically tortured by the threat of its removal or destruction. In Czech author Milan Kundera's novel *The Unbearable Lightness of Being*, the main character, Tomas, a doctor, loses his ability to practice medicine because he signs a statement criticizing the communist government of Czechoslavakia. He is relegated to window washing, and later moved to a farm.[63] But the novel takes a surprising twist (if I understand it correctly). Tomas learns to appreciate his various occupations and settings. He does not torture himself with reflecting upon the frustration he must feel in being deprived of his career. He learns to love the simple things. Luckily, he is not deprived of the company of the woman he loves. Robin clarifies that to ask someone to betray family in order to gain some other good, as in *The Lives of Others*, is always a risky business. More often, an interrogator will gain cooperation of others by suggesting to them that their family will be safe if they cooperate with the government.

In a situation where powerful government figures want to discredit the peace movement, active citizens like Daniel and Philip Berrigan can be caught in the maws of a giant apparatus using the courts and negative media to destroy an individual's integrity. No wonder, under situations like these, individuals may decide to agree to silence or complicity to be spared the harsh publicity that threatens to destroy their lives. A recent film covering the same era is *The US vs. John Lennon*, a 2006 documentary by David Leaf and John Scheinfeld. When John Lennon and Yoko Ono spoke up for peace and announced their solidarity with other strident political activists like John Sinclair in the early 1970s, the US government began deportation proceedings against them, dredging up minor infractions of the law committed by Lennon many years earlier as the supposed grounds for deportation. While the court case dragged on forever, Lennon and Ono felt pressure to become silent on a range of political issues in order not to jeopardize their court case.[64] This is exactly the kind of silencing that Robin has outlined that was used by McCarthy. That the Berrigans were victim of this kind of pressure tactic but nevertheless committed themselves to continued resistance is a mark of their courage in very difficult circumstances.

Berrigan and Plowshares Disarmament in 1980

When it comes to the topic of nuclear weapons in general, and the US stockpile of such weapons in particular, we can ask ourselves, what kind of fears are rational, and which are irrational? Perhaps in this context, to have no fears may be irrational.

As Aristotle has explained, there are two parts to virtue. One must first be able to discern right from wrong (intellectual virtue), and then one must be able to act upon the right (moral virtue). I will focus first on discernment. Reason has to be able to evaluate the situation in order to discern what right action should be. In this case, a rational person must be able to discern what the genuine and most dire dangers are. To discern this, one must notice that something is wrong, and then seek out and get information. So many dangers, threats, dire emergency situations exist in the world. How to prioritize, how to decide which is most important?

As you will remember, for Hobbes, self-survival is the utmost goal of a person, because, without survival, one cannot enjoy any other goals or ends. But one can ask, why is individual survival the utmost importance? What if there was a threat of omnicide, the killing of all that lives in the world? Would this not be a larger danger? Without the world, I can't have my individual life either. Certainly all my goals, whether to do good in the world, to have progeny, to amass wealth, or to build up the Church and have more Catholics in the world, would all be brought to naught if the entire world were destroyed. And yet, there is evidence to show that the destruction of the entire world is possible. Governments and their citizens have developed technology, devoted the monetary resources, and produced weaponry that is on alert. Countries have mutually threatened each other with the technology and continue to do so. Even if only a fraction of the existing nuclear weapons were to be detonated, the combination of explosions and debris fallout would make our planet uninhabitable. So, to consider the control and reduction of the weapons, as well as the risk of their being used, as one's utmost life priority, makes rational sense.[65]

And yet, most Americans are far from spending their life in this way. For most Americans, the threat of nuclear war, and the will to engage in disarmament, is way down the list of fears. It could be that the mind-boggling extent of destruction that would be unleashed by even one nuclear warhead (a fire cloud two miles in diameter, incineration of all people and buildings at heats of thousands of degrees, severe skin burns and nuclear fallout causing radiation sickness and cancer) makes the human imagination cringe at the thought of the weapons' use. The severity of its use, combined with the fact that a large nuclear bomb has not yet been used and the smaller scale atomic bombs of Hiroshima and Nagasaki have become a distant memory, could lead people to decide that, although it would be terrible, there is nothing to fear, because competent government controls are in place to ensure an attack will not happen.

Berrigan had his own ways of describing those who would rationalize the building of so many destructive weapons as a system of "defense" for our country. He called it "Eichmania" (after Eichmann's close-minded carrying out of Hitler's orders). He calls it "ideologically closed insanity." Professionals who all claim expert competence in creating such a system of "defense" and the church and secular ideologues who justify the system are playing an "academic-ecclesial game of scrabble." Who is sane, who is insane? Illness and "rotten power" are disguised as good reason. He thinks that reason and rationality had long fled the scene.[66]

The avoidance of nuclear war was an utmost imperative for Berrigan. While weapons are being built, the work and risks needed to stop their production and deployment must be done by someone, somewhere, somehow. If all citizens pass the buck, the deadly work continues. But how is one to decide if oneself is the one that needs to stop the work, and at what time?

Berrigan described his decision in 1980 to participate in a Plowshares disarmament action at the General Electric plant at King of Prussia, Pennsylvania. In the statement of their group, he said:

> We commit civil disobedience at General Electric because this genocidal entity is the fifth leading producer of weaponry in the US To maintain this position, GE drains $3 million a day from the public treasury, an enormous larceny against the poor.
>
> We wish also to challenge the lethal lie spun by GE through its motto, "We bring good things to life." As manufacturers of the Mark 12A reentry vehicle, GE actually prepares to bring good things to death.[67]

They did not know what the criminal justice system would do to them. But I suggest that their days in prayer were practices in courage. Much of it had to do with the preliminary intellectual clarity. One becomes sure in one's mind that the protest against the weapons is the right thing to do. This certainty is reinforced by group discernment. One feels more confident if others agree with one's analysis. This community of faith is needed especially in the case where others outside of the community would consider the action to be wrong-headed or the dangers undertaken foolhardy.

And yet the group does not cut itself off from the outside world by its prayerful retreat. Rather, other people are drawn in through prayer, and the resisters gain their confidence by knowing that they act due to their love and concern of other people, both Americans and those from other countries, both current and future generations. It is due to this deep association between themselves and others that the actor can freely risk many personal goods. Here the parallel with Aristotle is apt. He uses the example of the courage of a soldier on the battlefield. I will also draw upon Michelle E. Brady's analysis of Aristotle. The courageous and virtuous soldier does not fear death. But that's not because the soldier does not value his or her life. The soldier, like Hobbes's self-interested individual, knows that without life, one cannot fulfill any other personal goals. But the soldier has identified his or her own life with that of the polis or political community. Caring for the survival of the community, they consider the loss of their own personal goals or chances for personal enjoyment as unimportant. It is the fact that the soldier, in Aristotle's example, has become the sort of person who cares more for the good of the polis that makes us call them courageous and honorable when they offer their lives for a cause.

Brady, at the end of her analysis of Aristotle, alludes to the possibility that while Aristotle used the example of the courageous person on the battlefield as his paradigm of courage, it may be that a courageous person could refuse to fight. For, she explains, "a truly virtuous person is only synonymous with a good citizen in the best of regimes."[68] She explains that a virtuous person ultimately concerned with the flourishing of a community may in some cases argue against participation in battle if it does "not serve the end of preserving a community that encourages human flourishing."[69] I would argue that Berrigan fits that model. He discerned that his own country was engaging in acts against the flourishing of his own countrymen and women as well as those from other countries. He then discerned ways to bravely act against the wrong-headed plans, so as to speak out for a more humane world.

Berrigan explains that the group spent several days in prayer. This prayerful discernment gave them confidence about their action. Berrigan admits he spent the night before the action in a mostly sleepless state, going in and out of dreams and nightmares.[70] Was this fear? Was it, rather, related to all the uncertainties of the undertaking? Would they get into the plant, so that they could enact their symbolic disarmament on the missiles there? And if they succeeded, what would be the reactions of others? The responses of other agents are always, to a certain extent, unpredictable. The sleeplessness, in any case, was not related to any doubts about undertaking the action. Berrigan explained in his autobiography, "Everyone stood to lose—nearly everything except our lives: years in prison, family rupture, our good name, our good work in the world."[71] It is this fear of loss of values each person holds dear that would, under the influence of Hobbesean logic, counsel capitulation to the State's (Leviathan's) demands.

Going against the grain as Berrigan did took a lot of courage. To return to the King of Prussia Plowshares example, it takes courage to enter a nuclear facility. It takes courage to break laws, trespassing on GE's property beyond signs warning, "Do not enter." The trespasser first encounters guards and police, and does not know if he or she is in danger of being detained, beaten, or shot. The person does not know ahead of time the consequences he or she will reap from the action. Will it be understood? Popularized? Or demonized? Will such an activist receive a long prison sentence as punishment? Berrigan described many naysayers, as well as people who thought they were generally concerned for the resisters, in pointing out the grave dangers of the action, and becoming enveloped in fear for the participants. Berrigan thinks their fears were uncalled for. He said that both pity and fear aroused in others by their sacrifice were not useful, because sympathizers got the emphasis wrong. Their own imprisonment, trial and conviction were not the issues at stake. The real issue was stopping the corporate crimes of General Electric which fuel the "the race toward oblivion."[72]

He did say that it took strength and courage to maintain equanimity once in custody of the police. The police and media tried to paint them as "violent crazies" who had "gone on a rampage." They charged them with "assault . . . reckless endangerment, criminal mischief, terroristic threats, harassment, criminal coercion . . . . Talk about overkill! We sat in court, transfixed, gazing on our images in the crazy mirrors of the state fun house. It takes a large measure of good sense to stand firm at such moments."[73] The court case, instead of focusing on the faces and testimony of the defendants (where "mirrors of conscience" could be discerned), focused instead on the implements they used on the day of the action: the hammers they used to beat upon the weapons, and the empty blood bottles they used when pouring their own blood on the weapons. "They will be compared, subtly, openly, to the tools of safecrackers, to bloodied knives and guns. What if such implements became the common tools of so-called conscience? What if all citizens . . . took up such tools . . . against the law of the State?"[74] Members of the jury were led to believe that it was the defendants, those who engaged in conscientious civil disobedience to disarm the weapons, who were the real danger to society—not the weapons themselves, or the company that produced them for profit, which were seen as the protectors of society.

Aristotle explained that there are some things that are rightfully to be feared, and that one who does not fear them is not really courageous. For example, he states, one should fear disgrace, "for he who fears this is a good man and has a sense of honor, and he who does not fear it is shameless."[75] However, "disgrace" and "shame" are not unproblematic. Even Socrates had to dispute the popular ideas of disgrace and shame in ancient Athens during his trial. When Socrates was condemned to death, he noted that some people would suggest that he, being found guilty by the jury, should be ashamed of himself. But Socrates countered that he did not feel shame because he had an inner conviction that he had only done good. Although he could not prove that there would be a reward for him in an afterlife for his good deeds, he at least felt blessed by a clear conscience. And he had a feeling of certainty, beyond what could be proven, that something good would come of his principled action.[76] It is the same kind of confidence that buoys up Berrigan and his compatriots in their moments of difficulty in the courts, and later in prison. Some of the courage clearly necessary to engage in an act of disarmament like that is to brave the scorn of those who misunderstand or disagree.

Drawing on Aristotle, as well as Brady's treatment of Aristotle, I think it is important to contrast the civil resister's courage in engaging in acts of disarmament, despite unknown severity of punishment, with the carefree courage of citizens who either don't realize the scale of danger involved in current weapons systems, or the "patriotic" who have confidence that the United States would prevail in any war, making fear unnecessary. Aristotle explains that confidence, based on one's assurance of one's own expertise or strength advantage, is not the same as virtuous courage per se. A trained soldier (perhaps a mercenary) may with confidence engage in battle with untrained or under-armed troops, not because they have controlled their fear of death, but because they presume that they have the advantage, and so can win and come away unscathed.[77] As Brady explains, the willingness to fight of a soldier who expects to win "depends on the assumption that real loss can be avoided."[78] This is not real courage, for courage fights even while realizing real loss is possible, perhaps even likely.

In this nuclear war scenario, distinctions between soldiers and civilians melt away, as the civilian population becomes the target, literally on the front lines of battle. Many Americans may presume that there is nothing to lose in current nuclear policy, because the government will protect them from loss. The carefree attitude that is the fruit of this conviction lies in ignoring real dangers and refusal to comprehend the losses at stake in a dangerous policy. There is also a hardening of the heart toward any from other countries who might be at the receiving end of US warheads. For example, any who would counsel preemptive use of nuclear "bunker-buster" weapons to destroy Iran's nuclear capability years before any real weapons capability (or professed desire to build them) is a person who has decided ahead of time that killing civilians (undoubtedly harmed even when targeting "military" sites in Iran) is an acceptable loss.

Berrigan concludes his autobiography by pondering the toll taken on Americans who are stuck worshiping "Lord Nuke." The dependence on these terrible weapons for "security" induces helplessness, stalemate, and paralysis of will. The Plowshares actions, based on the model of their action at the GE King of Prussia plant, had many imitators. In 1987, he could say that twenty Plowshares actions had followed theirs. By 2003 Art Laffin calculated that one hundred and fifty people had participated in seventy Plowshares actions of disarmament.[79]

More Recent Forms of Resistance

Berrigan's Plowshares action in 1980 was not his only or his last act of civil disobedience. While residing in New York City, he realized that a building on 42nd Street housed Riverside Research Institute (RRI). RRI was related to the earlier Manhattan Project, which had helped design nuclear weapons. During the Reagan years, RRI was competing for and winning defense contracts to design an antiballistic missile shield, nicknamed "Star Wars." It promised to make Americans safe from nuclear bombs. But it would also clearly destabilize the nuclear stalemate between the United States and the former Union of Soviet Socialist Republics (USSR). Berrigan led opponents in blockades of the entranceway to the corporation. These acts of civil disobedience would happen several times a year, on holy days and other holidays such as Good Friday, Hiroshima Day, or Martin Luther King Day. Berrigan never tired of year after year being part of that blockade. That is where I first encountered Berrigan. He cheerily faced repeated arrests, in line with his personal convictions.

While this essay has focused upon Berrigan's fearlessness in his civil disobedience actions, there is another way in which he has been fearless. He has embraced members of society who have been ostracized due to fear and scorn—the homeless and AIDS patients. He has drawn them close, and cared for them, in a way similar to how he felt near to the victims of

US bombing in Vietnam. He was not of them, but he felt that their safety and comfort were central to him. Berrigan explained that he visited AIDS patients at St. Vincent's Hospital in New York. Most were gay Catholics, shunned and condemned by their own Church. In 1987 he asserted that AIDS was our current plague. He noted that the Jesuit Order was called to service of plague victims. Yet AIDS patients were being treated as if they were lepers. Berrigan said that the Catholic Church's stance on homosexuality was cruel to people in giving them celibacy as their only option for a pious life.[80]

Berrigan would have another occasion to draw close to the suffering in New York City. When the Twin Towers were hit on September 11, 2001, he cared for those who had been harmed. He also pondered on the significance of his community's suffering harm on such a large scale. He gathered his reflections on the topic into a book called *Lamentations*, which was also a reflection on that book of the Old Testament.

Pollsters noted that good will toward Americans was very high soon after the 9/11 attacks. Despite any past cruelties the US government might have dished out, people were genuinely concerned about the safety of Americans caught in the Twin Towers and the Pentagon. They felt their families' pain. Berrigan is not alone in noticing that the United States squandered that good will. While the United States could have responded by pursuing bin Laden and other al-Qaeda members through police raids into Afghanistan, they decided to attack the country, blaming the whole country for harboring terrorists. While the Taliban government was not immediately enthusiastic about giving access to US forces for such missions, they could possibly have been convinced if given a bit more time. But Bush and some Americans were anxious to do something decisive against their enemy, so they did not wait for such permission. They went in, and many Afghani civilians got caught in the crossfire. (They are still dying at the hands of US soldiers to date, and in great numbers.)

Berrigan devotes his book *Lamentations* to the topic of the 9/11 attacks and the aftermath of the Afghanistan war. He analyzes what he thought would have been a more humane and productive response to the attacks. He mourns the loss of life in the war in Afghanistan. And he expresses his horror that his own Church went along with this war, blessing it and calling it just. He calls the Church the "Grand Inquisitor," counseling the advantages of power.[81] Of Church and State he says, "The Twin Towers turned to rubble. The Twin Powers turned to war."[82] By agreeing to fight the war in Afghanistan, the Church helped to *create* widows and orphans, and turned strangers into enemies. What was really needed after the 9/11 attacks was trust, friendship, and repairing.[83]

During peacetime, Church and State teach about just war theory, in which there are careful moral rules for war. We learn that women, children, hospital patients, the innocent, should be protected. But during war, we are told to stop the "prattle" of rules. Aerial bombs, aimed at al-Qaeda or the Taliban, hit other innocent people regularly, yet the bombs are not stopped. Berrigan reminds us that the gate that leads to damnation is wide. The gate that leads to life is narrow.[84]

He calls President Bush's "war on terror" a war "drowned in cliché and contradiction." "Terror" is "a polluted word." He reminds us of the statistics that say forty million people a year die of hunger. He says that is like three hundred and twenty jumbo jets crashing daily. Do we keep these larger, ongoing atrocities in mind on a daily basis? [85]

Berrigan dares to speak of what no one else will mention: the background of the attacks. The United States has created a hideous world, he charges. The war-making super-State uses its economic advantage to turn the whole world into "a gigantic sweatshop" made up of "those who sweat, and those who shop."[86] He quotes Arundhati Roy, who lists America's misadventures including "its gunboat diplomacy, its nuclear arsenal, its vulgarly stated policy of 'full-spectrum dominance,' its chilling disregard for non-American lives."[87] Berrigan sums it up:

> After bombing eighteen countries in the last decades, after incursions
> and manipulations and lethal sanctions and the seizure of world
> markets and the reduction of multitudes to economic enslavement—
> after all this, the towers were struck, ejecting their human cargo like
> rubbish. And the Pentagon was breached. . . . How vulnerable are
> the mighty.[88]

But despite these grave sins, it is taboo to ask the question whether we Americans did anything to bring on this terrible attack? Confession of our own sin became unthinkable. The myth of the unprovoked, gratuitous evil reigned.[89] The attack showed Americans that their country's motives and behavior were being questioned, and they responded with blind and pitiless reprisal, "in the image of our tormentors."[90] Americans did not spend any time contemplating the fact that others around the world had suffered worse fates at the hands of US forces, both military and economic. The US media paid loving tribute to the dead of 9/11, but not to the Afghan casualties.[91]

Robin's book is filled with recent examples of the same tactics of the political use of fear in the war on terrorism. Robin peppers his book with multiple examples of how reporters and newscasters felt pressure from their employers to cover the events of 9/11 and the Afghanistan and Iraq wars in a certain way, to seem most "patriotic" and uncritical of the United States. Such coverage meant that reporters were told not to cover civilian casualties in Afghanistan, or if they were ever to do so, they must cut quickly to scenes of Americans dying in the 9/11 disasters. Reporters cooperated because they wanted to save their jobs, their careers.[92] Berrigan has shown that he will not be cowed by threats. He still speaks truth to power, even during the war on terror. He continues to challenge church and state, while comforting the afflicted.

Conclusion

Berrigan came a long way from his beginnings, where the Church and his faith gave him the feeling of a warm and safe insulation from the troubles of the world. This faith of childhood has to be questioned and deepened. Berrigan's experience reminds me of his fellow Jesuit, James Carney, who ended up as a martyr struggling with the landless peasants of Honduras. Carney said that as a teen he thought that if he personally refrained from sin, that God would reward him by letting his football team win. As he got older, he realized, that is not how God works. He realized that he had feared offending God (by engaging in sin) because he feared losing God's help. (In this scenario, it seems that God also plays the role of enforcer of conformity through fear.) Carney wanted to win the football game; he had internalized the competitiveness of his culture. But he later reflected, "Now that I know better the only true God revealed in Jesus Christ, the god crucified for seeking justice and the liberation of the poor, I know that God rewards those closest to him with trials and sufferings in order to sanctify them."[93] Certainly Berrigan had also experienced such suffering as he drew closer to his God, his liberatory God.

Clearly, Berrigan is not the first Christian to go through an ordeal like this. Our Church history is filled with the stories of martyrs for the faith. So many martyrs faced difficult situations, willing to risk their lives because they were inspired and challenged by their God, Jesus, who in human form died a painful death on a cross. In fact, Berrigan did not face death, only ostracism and imprisonment. But his hardships are large in a comparative context, if we think that the choice for priesthood as a vocation is usually one of safety and lack of controversy.

Søren Kierkegaard expressed frustrations such as these in his days. Around 1854–1855 in Denmark, he realized that young men were drawn toward the idea of becoming reverends and pastors in the "state religion" of Denmark because of the offer of stable payment and pension. Kierkegaard considered this longing for safety the exact opposite of the call of Christianity. In a collection of his works called *Attack Upon Christendom*, he recounts the ways in which Jesus and those who truly followed him by speaking truth to the powers that be suffered: "unappreciated, hated, abhorred, and then derided, insulted, mocked . . . scourged, maltreated, dragged from one prison to the other, and then at last . . . crucified, or beheaded, or burnt . . . his lifeless body thrown by the executioner in an out-of-the-way place."[94] But in Kierkegaard's time, the young man who decides to follow Jesus by becoming a reverend in the state church of Denmark wants "to have all worldly goods and advantages . . . and then at the same time to be a witness to the truth . . . . Such a witness to the truth is not merely a monster but impossibility."[95]

Such a person will, instead of following Christ's example, pervert the example into its opposite:

> When in His Word He talks about preaching the Word in poverty, we understand thereby some thousands yearly in stipend; when in His Word He talks about preaching the Word in lowliness, we understand it as making a career, becoming Your Excellency; and by heterogeneity to this world we understand a royal functionary, a man of consequence; by abhorrence for the use and employment of worldly power, by suffering for the doctrine we understand using the police against others; and by renunciation of everything we understand getting everything, the most exquisite refinements, for which the heathen has in vain licked his fingers—and at the same time we are witnesses to the truth.[96]

This harsh lampoon was meant to wake up a complacent and hypocritical Church to the message of Christ. Certainly, this form of clergy and Church stands ready to reap the benefits of conformity to this world, rather than to fidelity to the message and example of Christ.

We can learn from Berrigan's example. We can learn that, with community and compassion, people can resist succumbing to the politics of fear.

They can decide that giving over their power to a sovereign Leviathan and renouncing solidarity with others does not lead to flourishing. Standing together, in community, risking their own personal safety for the collective safety of a larger group, is a way to find meaning in life, connection, and fulfillment.

Announcing the Impossible

Christopher Harless

In the spring of 1998, Fordham University invited Father Daniel Berrigan to teach a class on poetry related to social justice. The class, which I had the great privilege of taking, focused on works by poets who, through their art, sought to remember and bear witness to violence and political suffering around the world—works by the likes of Bertolt Brecht, Pablo Neruda, Primo Levi, Anna Świrszczyńska, and many others. With these poets' heart-wrenching and horrifying experiences on our minds and with Berrigan's own commitment to nonviolent direct action before us as an example, I remember the class repeatedly raised a particular, burning question: What exactly can ordinary folks do in response to the violence in our culture? More specifically, should people still be engaging in the kinds of public actions for which the Berrigan brothers became household names several years ago? What point is there, after all, in protesting and continually making oneself vulnerable to the powerful purveyors of violence in our society when it is all but assured that such protests will fall on deaf ears? What good does it do to keep getting arrested as Berrigan has done, year after year, for protesting not only current military engagements but also things like the symbolic significance of the military museum aboard the

USS *Intrepid*, given that no one in power seems to care or even notice? I will never forget the answer Berrigan gave one particular day when a question like these was asked. He stood and wrote two words on the blackboard: Best and Good. Then, altering a phrase from Voltaire, he said, "Never let the Best be the enemy of the Good."

At the time I did not really see how this answered the question. In ordinary contexts, the phrase means one should not allow perfectionism to keep one from doing something good. It is typically meant as an admonition not to give in to tendencies toward inaction and paralysis, even in the face of near-constant reminders that one's actions are always compromised by context and that things rarely turn out exactly the way one wants. So, when someone encounters her own powerlessness in the quest for a perfect society, she should not let it stop her from doing what can be done, here and now, to make things better. In the context of the question, though, this seemed to miss the point. At least for me, the question was not about whether one should do something good when it seems like the final goal is out of reach. Rather, the question was precisely about the goodness of the proposed action itself. Indeed, if the goodness of a particular action—say, a protest that ends in arrest—can be assumed, then it would make sense to appeal to a kind of Kantian morality that obligates one to do things simply because they are right, without regard to consequences. But how does one know the action is good? It would seem that an action involving such a public form of communication (for example, acts of witness, resistance, speaking truth to power) can only be considered good in relation to the change it engenders in the recipients of the message (policy makers, bystanders, other peacemakers and citizens, the press, police, judges). The question the students were asking, then, was more about why people of conscience should continue to protest and risk their lives when no one seems to be listening, or when those that are can already be counted among the converted. Why should anyone keep doing it if it doesn't seem to matter?

If Berrigan sidestepped the question that those twenty-somethings were asking, perhaps it is because, for him, the goodness of public resistance against violence and violent institutions is a given. In the years since that class, as I have become more acquainted with the radical and prophetic nature of Berrigan's vision, I have come to appreciate the spiritual aspect of his political actions and to believe that only in that light is it possible to understand why Berrigan does what he does. To put it simply, Berrigan's radical actions and the sense of urgency he feels toward them are driven more by his spiritual calling and his Christology than by his practical shrewdness.

For Berrigan, resistance and getting arrested for a cause are not merely tactics, and cannot be judged solely on that level. They are not simply strategic means for accomplishing political goals, though they often function as such as well. Rather, for him, the good of nonviolent direct action has as much to do with the change that it incites in the protester or resister as it does with the change it creates in society. If they accomplish nothing else, actions like those undertaken by the Catonsville Nine present a chance for the actors to undo a bit of the stranglehold that a violent culture has exerted over the thoughts and habits of individuals. They also effectively place the actor on the side of life and sanity in a world that's thoroughly gone mad in its lust for death. Another way to put this is to say that they are means to becoming fully human, or to realizing a suppressed human potential.

I do not mean here to reduce Berrigan-style activism to a program for personal piety, as if it were merely a way to bolster one's own righteousness, creating a kind of island in a sea of wickedness. In fact, it would be wrong (maybe obviously) to conclude that his methods aim primarily at self-improvement, as opposed to being directed ultimately at the achievement of some perfect end that would encompass everyone. I do, however, wish to point out that Berrigan's ethics of nonviolent direct action is founded on a vision of human potential, a future way of being human, that can only be brought closer to reality when people make it present in their own selves. Thus, to answer the question posed by the Fordham students, his actions really are founded on the hope that they will be efficacious in creating a better world. It's just that sometimes this means causing the transformation to happen within oneself, in the realm of subjective spirit, before seeking corresponding change in the objective spirit of one's culture.

Still, the original question can be made more acute. Why should I participate in a particular act of civil disobedience? What exactly is the transformation that Berrigan hopes to achieve, and how would engaging in this or that action contribute to it? More pointedly, what is Berrigan's own motivation for engaging in such acts, and can this be communicated to others?

In an open letter that he wrote to members of the Weathermen in 1970 while he was in hiding from the FBI, Berrigan suggests the following rule of thumb when deciding on actions: "Do only that which one cannot not do."[1] Essentially, Berrigan leaves it to each person's conscience to decide what must be done, but the implication is that sometimes there are situations that call for immediate action, some way of crying out, "No, not in our name!" There are times when we must act because it has become impossible for us not to act—not to act and still be human, that is.

For Berrigan, the decision to engage in civil disobedience or protest is not made casually. Through several decades of writing and walking resolutely against the prevailing winds of a violent culture, Berrigan has borne witness to a necessity that lays claim to his life, a call that is more of a demand than an invitation. This demand is simply always to act now, while the time is ripe, in a way that ushers in the new humanity. This sense of urgent necessity, I submit, springs from Berrigan's religious faith and his belief in a God who is active in history. In its purest form, it is a common trait of the prophets from whom Berrigan derives inspiration. Consider, for example, Berrigan's reflections on Isaiah:

> Isaiah, and those who live in his tradition, announce the impossible: "They will beat their swords into plowshares." The necessary must somehow be fused with the impossible. Something new, something beyond all effort or genius or ecstatic longing or even imagining, must come to be. The historically impossible must happen to the inconvertible, the imperium, to those obsessed with violence and arms and the misuse of resources and the wanton expending of lives.
>   The truth of this transformation oracle, "swords into plowshares," is absolutely crucial to the prospering of nations and cultures, to the survival of individuals, of children and the elderly and the ill. It is crucial to honor, to religious faith, to a civilized sense of the human— crucial to the fate of the earth.[2]

"They will beat their swords into plowshares" means for Berrigan, "They must . . ." It is simultaneously a statement about the future and an imperative for the present. It must happen, because it is "crucial" to all humanity and all things human. Picking up on Berrigan's language, one could even say that it is crucial as the crucifix itself is crucial to salvation. Berrigan's point is that, despite the impossibility of the task, the certainty of the prophesied future entails the necessity of action in the present. Berrigan continues:

> Those who have worked hardily against the war-making state know well the impossibility of the task. . . .
>   And yet the word of Isaiah must come to pass: "They will beat their swords into plowshares." The words surpass the human even

while they engage the human in its deepest longings, in the lives of saints and martyrs and mystics. The words commit, invite, command, exact vows, demand conversion—of hearts as well as swords.[3]

This prophetic command is not only directed at others, that is, the powerful, the oppressors, the wielders of swords. It is directed at all of us: "It cannot be done, yet it must be done. If it is to be done, it must be done—by ourselves."[4] Here we see the root of that grave urgency one so often senses behind Berrigan's writings and acts of nonviolent resistance. The key to the strength and tenor of Berrigan's commitment to peace activism surely lies here, in the way he has internalized and appropriated this prophetic injunction.

For Berrigan, to be a peacemaker is to announce and bring to fruition the future envisioned by Isaiah—which is also that of Jeremiah, and Jesus, and Gandhi, and a host of other prophets (Hebraic and otherwise). This involves both words and actions: "The nonviolent man does not announce that something new is going to happen in the future; he announces that something new is currently happening. Or, better still, he is making it happen."[5] So, through the activity of the nonviolent peacemaker, the future breaks into the present. The new creation happens now.

But what are the contents of this new creation? We need to understand more fully this vision of transformation and its relation to our present situation in order finally to grasp—to the extent that this is possible—Berrigan's motivation for action.

As already mentioned, Berrigan says that the object of his pursuit as a peacemaker is to bring into being a new humanity. In a sense, his ethics is founded on a humanistic hope, namely, that the ills of society might one day be remedied so as to enable all people to live a fully human life. Such a pursuit requires both a long-range vision and a belief in the possibility of human perfection, however impossible it may seem. Further, it involves an awareness of the interconnectedness of systems of violence and war such that it becomes possible to imagine replacing the whole regime with a new system of nonviolent relations. Berrigan writes:

> But the consciousness of the radical man [in contrast to that of the liberal] is integrated. He knows that everything leads to everything else. So while he works for the end of the war, for the end of poverty, or for the end of American racism, he knows also that every war is symptomatic of every other war. Vietnam to Laos and on to Thailand, and across the world to Guatemala, and across all wars to his own heart. What he is finally looking for is not a solution (knowing as he does that

human history has not offered solutions). He is really working for a new creation: a new man in a new society.[6]

If a new society is needed, it is because the current one hinders people's ability to be fully human. As Berrigan sees it, all the systems of our society have been rotted beyond useful functioning by the cancer of violence. "The law profession, I submit, is one among several professions that, in the larger world of men, are simply acting against the human."[7] Speaking of himself and the others of the Catonsville Nine, Berrigan furthers the thought:

> Our act was a denial that American institutions were presently functioning in a way that good men could approve or sanction. We were denying that the law, medicine, education, and systems of social welfare . . . were serving the people, were including the needy, or might be expected to change in accord with changing needs, that these could enlist or embody the resources of good men—imagination, moral suppleness, pragmatism, or compassion.[8]

Thus, without rehearsing their reasons here, the judgment of the Nine was that, contrary to popular consensus, the basic institutions of American society are not supportive of human ends. Therefore, a new society is needed, corresponding to a new humanity.

Whatever may be entailed in creating this new society, Berrigan warns against thinking such change can be achieved through some program of gradual reform. The cancer runs too deep, and so the whole organism must pass away and make way for a new one. According to Berrigan, this is the meaning of the judgment issued by God through Jeremiah:

> But the word spoken to Jeremiah is an enemy to all gradualism, all theories of history based upon the escalation of goodness. No, God implies, there are times so evil that the first and indeed the only genuinely prophetic function is to cast down the images of injustice and death that claim man as victim. . . . [T]he times were judged by God; evil beyond cure. Only a new beginning would suffice.[9]

After the above quote, Berrigan hesitates to say that our times are as bad as Jeremiah's. Yet, it is clear enough that he thinks they are close.[10]

The traditional name for doing away with an old order and establishing a new one is revolution. There is certainly a revolutionary strain in Berrigan's writings, but it is balanced by frequent reflections on the failure of Utopian ideals and the universal degeneration of revolutions into reigns of terror. If revolution is the proper word, it is a revolution of the heart, a conversion, that he seeks. Most importantly, it is a revolution that undoes the cycles of violence in the present system. In the letter to the Weathermen referenced above, Berrigan writes:

> A revolution is interesting insofar as it avoids like the plague the plague it promised to heal. Ultimately, if we want to define the plague as death (a good definition), a prohuman movement will neither put people to death nor fill the prisons nor inhibit freedoms nor brainwash nor torture enemies nor be mendacious nor exploit women, children, Blacks, the poor.[11]

While he does not categorically renounce all forms of violence in that letter, notably violence against property, he does reject all killing: "No principle is worth the sacrifice of a single human being."[12] This is because the use of violent means always undermines in some way the sought-after end. For Berrigan, the end as the birth of a nonviolent humanity must always be kept in mind, and this means maintaining an unrelenting commitment to nonviolence. The new humanity must begin with us: "We are to strive to become such men and women as may, in a new world, be nonviolent."[13]

Nonviolent revolution does not happen overnight. It cannot be forced, but will come about slowly and will require much sacrifice on the way. So we have here a bit of a paradox (is not paradox always a companion to prophecy?). On the one hand, the new humanity is announced by the prophet and peacemaker as present, here and now, and not in some far-off, distant future. On the other hand, the arrival of the new humanity will take place through an unbearably slow process of conversion to nonviolence—and the peacemaker's work has just begun; indeed, it seems always to be just beginning. To unravel this paradox, it is necessary to delve a little deeper into the notion of time involved in the prophetic announcement that Berrigan references. What does it mean, after all, to say that the new humanity is present when it is also in the process of coming into being? The answer to this, it seems to me, lies in a proper understanding of the messianic mystery itself, particularly in its Christian form. Jesus announced that the "kingdom of God is at hand," and yet Christians continue to long for the coming of the kingdom. Christ came and lived among us; Christ is present "where two or three are gathered together in [his] name;"[14] and yet Christians wait for him to come again. Reflecting on this relationship to time as it is expressed in the book of Revelations, Berrigan writes:

> It might be worth noting that time in the Book of Revelation is defined as a state of "relation." That is to say, one is truly within time insofar as he is related, in faith and in fact, to Someone. And this Someone is the

very hinge upon whom time itself turns. Relationship, friendship, community with Him define events as past, present, and future. He is Himself "the Happening" par excellence. Jesus is the One Who was, Who is, Who comes again.[15]

Berrigan writes further that "the 'coming again' of the Lord Jesus, as promised, makes a future an assured one, an event, a meeting of persons, defined and understood as the consummation of history itself."[16] Thus, to understand the Christian's relationship to time, one must adopt an apocalyptic imagination that sees the end of history as already somehow established in the present, through Christ. Berrigan explains:

> Apocalyptic time is a mode of consciousness that includes the present and the future, but always embodied. . . . It is the property of vision to eradicate the distinctions between present and future, and to set forth, in a single moment of ecstasy, the future, precisely as *present*.[17]

So, the Christian is capable of seeing current events through the lens of this apocalyptic imagination, which casts everything in light of the consummation of history that has already been secured, but is also always still to come. That is to say, the Christian is able to see present actions as having meaning in relation to a very long arc of history, one in which the end shall be the fulfillment of what was given in the beginning. To be more explicit, for the Christian, Jesus's life, death, and resurrection, as well as the hope that this affords, make history meaningful. Thus, the Christian's ability to apply an apocalyptic imagination to current happenings deeply depends on his or her understanding of who Christ is (and was and is to come).

In Berrigan's case, his own apocalyptic imagination is clearly informed by his contemplation of Christ, for his writings are rife with references to Jesus and interpretations of his nonviolent message and example. Indeed, the core of Berrigan's own teaching and example is intelligible only in light of his Christology and religious faith. Any reflection, therefore, on the motivations behind his actions, or their relation to the ultimate goal he envisions, must take this into account. Given this, the next question to ask would be, to what extent is Berrigan's vision and motivation for action communicable to others, such as that group of students in his poetry class? Must one be a Christian to get it?

To some extent I think the answer must surely be yes, one does have to be a Christian, or at least grounded in a religious tradition that emphasizes the virtue of sacrifice, to fully understand and follow Berrigan's example of thoroughgoing pacifism and sacrificial resistance to violence. This is because the way is so long and the price often so high that Berrigan-style pacifism becomes indefensible without some such grounding. Is not this the reason that even the most high-minded revolutionaries find themselves tempted to use violent means to accomplish their objectives? The hope is usually that the application of violence in the present will make it possible for a nonviolent future to come into being—once the dust has settled.

This is the sort of thinking that, for example, led Jean-Paul Sartre to consider revolutionary violence to be justified under certain circumstances. Near the end of his life, Sartre, who in many ways shared Berrigan's general outlook on politics, continued to believe that violence against oppression is sometimes necessary for "break[ing] up a certain state of enslavement that . . . mak[es] it impossible for people to become human beings."[18] Sartre maintained this position even though by then, like Berrigan, he posited the ultimate end of political activity to be a future humanity in which everyone would enjoy fully ethical relations in a spirit of "fraternity."[19] "Violence," he recognized, "is not going to speed up the pace of history and draw humanity together,"[20] but he clearly thought it had a place in paving the way for that which could.

And why shouldn't Sartre think that way, given that he did not believe in God? Of course, there is never any guarantee that a revolution will be successful or effect any positive change, but to ask someone to continue to accept suffering when it seems it could be alleviated by a swift application of violence is to ask something that demands justification. What other justification could there be than adoption of a long view of history and an appeal to the certainty of the ultimate outcome? How else can this be granted but through faith in a promise given by God Himself?

Through the years, Berrigan has reflected on this very question in his writings. For example, in a piece he published in 1970 on some key terms in Albert Camus's work, Berrigan writes:

> The deeper question of whether or not [Camus] saw in his heart the drama and death of God, and buried Him out of sight, out of mind, is colored by at least one fact. That is, Camus declared a consistent nonviolence to be impossible without the postulate of the existence of God. In this rigorous judgment, he seemed mysteriously to have joined hands with the spirit of Gandhi, who had often and overtly stated the same convictions; a man could only embrace a lifelong nonviolent position if he was in touch with the living God.[21]

To be in touch with the living God, then, is a prerequisite to avoiding utter despair while embracing nonviolence in the face of the absurd. This is because the most sober and lucid analysis of our situation can only produce one conclusion: to speak metaphorically, we are headed for a long dark night that permits almost no glimmer of hope. Berrigan puts it thus:

> Everything from Vietnam to Lewisburg suggests to me that those who hope at this point for other directions than further repression, further wars, more jailings of resisters, are whistling into the prevailing winds. To expect the worst, to prepare our souls, prophetically or cowardly, for the worst, is the only realism worth talking about. For we are going, downhill and pell-mell, into a dark age, a progress led by Neanderthals armed to the teeth.[22]

Though these words were written nearly forty years ago, it seems little has changed that would soften Berrigan's judgment. Since Vietnam, the United States has engaged in at least ten military interventions to protect and expand its economic and political hegemony. The wheels of war roll ever on. And so, in 2002, just after the terrorist attacks of 2001 and the US invasion of Afghanistan, Berrigan again invoked in his writings the dark visions of the prophet Jeremiah, lamenting, like him, the sins of his country and the destruction it has rendered.[23] But, Berrigan reminds us that the book of Lamentations is not only about remorse, repentance, and woe, but also about hope for reconciliation.[24] In the context of the grief and chaos described by Jeremiah, such hope would seem foolish, were it not for the promise of God. This promise, which was given first to Israel and later appropriated by Christianity, provides a firm foundation for the believer's hope. Thus, at the end of one essay on this theme, Berrigan calls to mind the particular form that this promise takes for the Christian: "For Christians, at a stroke someone has answered: 'Yes. Stand confident, befriended.' Someone has healed and reconciled and died, that the Yes! may live on."[25]

Berrigan's justification for nonviolence, therefore, ultimately resolves to a hope, grounded in faith, secured by a promise. He does not recommend it primarily because it works, or because it is an effective way of achieving results. His commitment to nonviolence goes far beyond pragmatism to a kind of hope against hope.[26] This is important because the strongest argument people tend to raise against nonviolence is that it does not work, or at least not in all circumstances. Conservatives are wont to point out, for example, that while Gandhi's strategies may have been successful against the British, they certainly would not have worked against a dictator like Hitler or Saddam Hussein.[27] Such arguments are usually far too abstract and hypothetical to be worth engaging, but they raise an important question about the advisability of rejecting all violence. From the point of view of prudence, a dogmatic commitment to nonviolence is patently absurd.

But for Berrigan, none of this matters. He has his sights set on an end that is more sublime than what practical reason judges to be possible, one which he knows he cannot secure by his own effort but which he is willing to risk a great deal for on the hope that it might still one day burst on the scene.

To return to an earlier question, is this a vision that can be communicated to others, especially non-Christians or even nonreligious? It seems to me that the humanistic element in the future that Berrigan longs for is indeed compelling and offers a hook for forging links of solidarity with radicals and progressives of other stripes. However, even if the end is agreed upon, it is not clear to me that Berrigan's level of commitment to the means of nonviolence can be sustained without a corresponding level of faith. Where such faith exists, though, people like Berrigan have tremendous resources for undertaking risky ventures and for hoping for the impossible. This kind of infinite hope, together with a steely determination to accept all shorter-term outcomes, is fully necessary for a peacemaker in the current situation. In a recent interview with Chris Hedges, Berrigan confirms this idea and, incidentally, gives as good an answer as can be found to the questions raised in that poetry class at Fordham University:

> The good is to be done because it is good, not because it goes somewhere. . . . I believe if it is done in that spirit it will go somewhere, but I don't know where. I don't think the Bible grants us to know where goodness goes, what direction, what force. I have never been seriously interested in the outcome. I was interested in trying to do it humanly and carefully and nonviolently and let it go.[28]

The "Global War on Terror":
Who Wins? Who Loses?

G. Simon Harak, SJ

We have to struggle with the old enemies of peace—business and financial monopoly, speculation, reckless banking, class antagonism, sectionalism, war profiteering. They had begun to consider the Government of the United States as a mere appendage to their own affairs. We know now that government by organized money is just as dangerous as government by organized mob.

—Franklin D. Roosevelt[1]

Money has taken on an ominous pseudo life, a new name: Mammon. It is a though the imperial face on coins were speaking aloud, instructing their handlers as to whose pockets they would line. *Accumulation*—the buzzword.

—Daniel Berrigan[2]

On May 17, 1968, Daniel Berrigan and his brother Philip joined seven other Catholic protesters[3] at the Catonsville, Maryland, draft board. They went into the draft board (housed in the Catholic Knights of Columbus building), removed 378 draft files, brought them out to the parking lot and burned them with homemade napalm. The action marked a major turning point in the antiwar movement and has been immortalized by a play,[4] a movie,[5] and more recently, a documentary.[6]

Dan Berrigan explained their use of "homemade" napalm with these words:

> Our apologies, good friends, for the fracture of good order, the burning of paper instead of children, the angering of the orderlies in the front parlor of the charnal house. We could not, so help us God, do otherwise, for we are sick at heart. Our hearts give us no rest for thinking of the land of burning children. We say, killing is disorder, life and gentleness and community and unselfishness is the only order we recognize. The time is past when good people may be silent, when obedience can segregate us from public risk, when the poor can die without defense. How many indeed must die before our voices are heard? How many must be tortured, dislocated, starved, maddened? How long must the world's resources be raped in the service of legalized murder? When, at what point, will you say no to the war? We have chosen to say with the gift of our liberty, if necessary our lives: the violence stops here, the death stops here, the suppression of the truth stops here, the war stops here![7]

In this essay I want to explore one aspect of the use of napalm as a multivalent symbol of the evil of war. Berrigan indicates this investigation when he challenges: "How long must the world's resources be raped in the service of legalized murder?" Specifically, I want to examine war profiteering, starting with napalm in Vietnam, and moving to the current state of war profiteering in the "global war on terror." Along the way, I hope to show how war profiteering has changed from Vietnam until now.

Dow Chemical's Napalm: The "Girl in the Picture"

On June 8, 1972, the Vietnamese village of Trang Bang was bombed with napalm. Among the people fleeing in terror from the burning village was nine-year-old Phan Thi Kim Phuc. Her naked (literally) terror was captured by photographer Huynh Cong "Nick" Ut, who brought her to a hospital in Saigon where she defied prognoses and lived.[8] Ut's photo helped raise consciousness of the horrors that war weapons produced and stirred further public resistance to the war.

Developed by a group of chemists from Harvard, led by Louis Feisner, napalm is a generic name for any flammable liquid that has been turned into a gel, thus enabled to stick to a target, whether material or human. A major ingredient for the stickiness of napalm is polystyrene.

In 1965, as the Vietnam War was heating up, the Pentagon requested bids from the seventeen US companies that made polystyrene. Dow Chemical of Midland, Michigan, won the contract and became the sole producer of napalm for the US military at its Torrance, California, plant.

Dow was already a major weapons producer for the US government. It produced twenty tons of mustard gas a day during World War I, along with phenol, an important explosive ingredient. After World War I, Dow continued and increased its manufacturing of chemicals for the military, also improving its phenol formula. Leading up to World War II, "Dow was by far the fastest growing of the nation's large chemical firms, averaging 26 percent in annual growth during a period when one expert estimated growth for the top ten firms in the industry at an average of 3.2 percent yearly, and much of Dow's growth was in products that were to be key to the war, such as magnesium and styrene."[9]

Having won the contract for napalm production in 1966, Dow continued to work on the product. Their "improvements" were succinctly and cavalierly recounted by a soldier in a conversation with photojournalist Philip Jones Griffiths:

> We sure are pleased with those backroom boys at Dow. The original product wasn't so hot—if the gooks were quick they could scrape it off. So the boys started adding polystyrene—now it sticks like shit to a blanket. But then if the gooks jumped under water it stopped burning, so they started adding Willie Peter [WP—white phosphorous] so's to make it burn better. It'll even burn under water now. And just one drop is enough, it'll keep on burning right down to the bone so they die anyway from phosphorous poisoning.[10]

As hideous as it was, napalm was one of the least examples[11] of Dow Chemical's valuing profits over people and earnings over the environment. Dow was also one of the manufacturers of Agent Orange, one of whose chemicals, dioxin, had been shown to cause birth defects in mice with concentrations of 0.25 parts per trillion solution.[12] In *Trespass against Us*, investigative reporter Jack Doyle recounts Dow's involvement in various tragedies, such as Bhopal (through its subsidiary, Union Carbide),[13] its production and false advertising of safety claims for Dursban,[14] and the scandal of silicone breast implants (internal memos later revealed that the "leakage problem" was known to company officials even before they began marketing the implants).

Dow Chemical continues to be pursued for its chemical warfare. It has for the most part, however, escaped legal consequences for its actions.[15]

Dow's legal battles have produced three benefits for the company, and for future chemical and weapons manufacturers. First, Dow's out of court settlements forestalled government's passing of laws against negligent and criminal practices. Second, such settlements meant that Dow cannot be legally compelled to clean up the environmental damages. Finally, during the course of these trials (in 1974), Dow succeeded in shifting the burden of proof to the government: the government had to prove that the chemicals were harmful, whereas previously the manufacturers had to prove that the chemical was safe.

Dow's far-reaching success in the legal system was shown in March 2005 when US District Judge Jack B. Weinstein dismissed a lawsuit filed on behalf of over three million Vietnamese against Dow and more than thirty other companies for the use of Agent Orange in Vietnam. In his opinion, Weinstein stated that the plaintiffs failed to prove Agent Orange caused their injuries.[16] If upheld, the case would have required not only personal damages but environmental cleanup in Vietnam. The case has recently gone to federal appeals court, where former US Solicitor General Seth Waxman, arguing for the chemical companies, noted a lack of legal precedent for punishing the use of poisons in war and warned of harming US battlefield decisions if judges find the suit can proceed. "This does affect our ongoing diplomacy," he said, citing the use of depleted uranium shells by US forces in Iraq.[17] The irony of equating battlefield poisons and radioactivity with diplomacy seems to have escaped the defense lawyer.

In the past two decades, there have been other significant economic and political shifts that have, if imaginable, transmogrified war profiteering into an even deeper affliction upon people and the environment.

The Defense Policy Board

In 1985, during the presidency of George Bush, the US government formed the Defense Policy Board Advisory Committee, otherwise known as the Defense Policy Board (DPB). Selected by the Under Secretary of Defense for Policy[18] with the approval of the Secretary of Defense, its duties are to:

> Review and assess: (a) the long-term, strategic implication of defense policies in various regions of the world; (b) the policy implications of current and prospective weapons classes; (c) the impact of our defense policies on alliance military issues; and (d) other major areas as identified by the Under Secretary of Defense for Policy.

Analyze selected, short-term policy issues identified by the Secretary of
   Defense, Deputy Secretary or Under Secretary of Defense for Policy
   and present the results to the requesting official.
Serve as individual advisors to the Under Secretary of Defense for Policy
   as required.
When required, the Under Secretary of Defense for Policy may direct
   that specific, time-sensitive subjects be examined by ad hoc panels of
   regular and/or associate Committee members.[19]

Here, even in the title, we sense a change. Since 1956 the US Department
of Defense has been advised by the Defense Science Board, whose members "are selected on the basis of their preeminence in the fields of science,
technology and its application to military operations, research, engineering, manufacturing and acquisition process."[20] This relatively new board is
not just about research, development or acquisitions. It concerns itself with
policy. The members of this powerful advisory committee are drawn mostly
from the "private sector" (only four members can be active in government),
from people who are deemed to have expertise in national security matters.
They meet at least four times a year with the under secretary and members
of the Defense Department.

Who Are the Members of the DPB?

Christopher Williams is the former acting Under Secretary of Defense for
Policy, member of the George W. Bush transition team, and special assistant to Donald Rumsfeld. (A list of DPB Members [July 11, 2007] can be
found at http://tinyurl.com/dpb-members [under "Members"], accessed
August 15, 2011.) When he left that last position in 2001, he joined
Johnston & Associates, a Washington, D.C.–based lobbying firm, started
by former Senator J. Bennett Johnston.[21] Williams is also a former member
of the Project for the New American Century[22] and the Committee for the
Liberation of Iraq.[23]

Williams sat on the DPB during the entire military buildup of the global
war on terror (August 16, 2001–June 4, 2007). At the same time, as a registered lobbyist, Williams was being paid between $100,000 and $300,000
a year to lobby for such defense contractors as Boeing and Northrop-
Grumman.

During that same period, John J. "Jack" Sheehan served on the DPB.
Sheehan retired as a General in the Marine Corps, and was Supreme Commander of NATO forces in the Atlantic region (1963–1997). After his

retirement, Sheehan joined the Bechtel Group, first as manager for Europe, Africa, Middle East, and Southwest Asia (1998–2000), then as senior vice president for Europe, Africa, Middle East, and Southwest Asia (2001–present).

Bechtel is the largest construction company in the world. Its history began in the early twentieth century with the construction of the Bowman Lake Dam in California. It later joined with five other companies to build and complete the Hoover Dam two years ahead of schedule. In 1972 Bechtel completed the Bay Area Rapid Transit System (BART).

Recently, however, Bechtel's reputation has become tarnished. Bechtel botched the 1963 construction of a nuclear power plant in San Onofre, California. Their participation in the privatization of water in Cochabamba, Bolivia, prompted demonstrations when the price of water rose 200 percent. To quell those demonstrations, the Bolivian government fired upon the crowds, killing at least six people, and wounding many more. Bechtel is the primary architect in Boston's "Big Dig,"[24] which is currently nine years and twelve billion dollars over budget. In July of 2006, a portion of the tunnel collapsed upon a car driven by newlyweds Angel and Melina Delvalle, killing Melina. "There's no reason why we in the state of Massachusetts should have spent $16.8 billion and counting to have someone lose a life in Massachusetts. Doesn't make any sense," said former State Inspector General Robert Cerasoli.[25]

Finally, Bechtel has won nearly three billion dollars in contracts to "rebuild" Iraq. We must use quotes there, because the average household in Iraq now gets about two hours of electricity a day. Iraq unemployment runs about 70 percent. Sixty-eight percent of Iraqis have no access to clean drinking water. Eighty-one percent of Iraqis have no access to sewage treatment.[26]

Bechtel withdrew from Iraq on October 31, 2006. In their forty-month stay in Iraq, fifty-two of their workers were killed, forty-seven of whom were Iraqis. And yet, according to Bechtel President Cliff Mumm, "We provided training to thousands of Iraqi professionals and craft workers. And we accomplished all this with a safety record that would be the envy of any firm operating in the United States." He added, "We are proud of our record in Iraq."[27]

Sheehan was a member of the DPB. At the same time, he was senior vice president at Bechtel. Sheehan left the DPB about the same time Bechtel left Iraq.

Richard Bowman Meyers is a retired US Air Force General. He was Chair of the Joint Chiefs of Staff throughout the buildup for, invasion and occupation of Iraq (October 1, 2001–September 30, 2005). Meyers is extraordinarily well connected. Prior to becoming chairman, he served as the vice chairman of the Joint Chiefs of Staff from March 2000 to September 2001. As vice chairman, General Myers served as the chairman of the Joint Requirements Oversight Council, vice chairman of the Defense Acquisition Board, and as a member of the National Security Council Deputies Committee and the Nuclear Weapons Council. In addition, he acted for the chairman in all aspects of the planning, programming and budgeting system including participation in the Defense Resources Board. He also served as commander-in-chief of the North American Aerospace Defense Command and US Space Command; commander of the Air Force Space Command; and Department of Defense manager of the space transportation system contingency support at Peterson Air Force Base, Colorado. Shortly after his retirement, he joined the board of directors of Northrup-Grumman, the world's third-largest weapons contractor. He presently sits on the DPB.

Also in 2005, Vernon Clark retired from his position as admiral in the Navy and joined the Board of Directors of Raytheon. According to *CNNMoney.com*, "Raytheon specializes in defense, homeland security and other government markets throughout the world. With a history of innovation spanning 85 years, Raytheon provides state-of-the-art electronics, mission systems integration and other capabilities in the areas of sensing; effects; and command, control, communications and intelligence systems, as well as a broad range of mission support services." In 2006, Clark joined the DPB. In that year, Raytheon announced over $20 billion in military contracts.

Sheehan, Williams, Myers, Clark and other members of the DPB would advise the defense department on defense policy: what weapons systems to buy, what countries are "threats," and need (with the new US doctrine) to suffer preemptive military strikes. Yet they and other members of the DPB work for, and are highly paid by, corporations that will directly benefit if the United States does go to war, remains at war, and persists in occupation.

In *War Made Easy*, Norman Solomon recounts how many different corporations have profited from the "global war on terror": Orbit International, Engineered Support Systems, Inc., Northrup Grumman, et al. A typical quote from one of the companies' reports reads, "We are heavily dependent upon military spending as a source of revenues and income. Accordingly, any substantial future reductions in overall military spending by the U.S. government could have a material adverse effect on our sales and earnings."[28]

Pentagon officials argue that they need to seek out experts in the field of defense to advise them. But we might also wonder: Is it possible that there is a conflict of interest here? Employed and highly paid by such corporations, is the security of the United States the only thing that's on their mind as they advise the Pentagon and government officials on war-making policy? Members of the board reveal their business associations to the Pentagon, but those associations are not revealed to the public, leaving the Pentagon as the sole arbiter of their ethical propriety.

Keeping the DPB in mind, let us turn to other ways that companies have access to government decision-making when it comes to war. By the end of this chapter, through our description of the confluence of such avenues, a clearer picture will emerge of the extent of corporate influence on US war-making policy.

PR Firms and Media Blitzes

From a marketing point of view, you don't introduce new products in August.

—Andrew H. Card[29]

See, in my line of work you got to keep repeating things over and over and over again for the truth to sink in, to kind of catapult the propaganda.

—George W. Bush[30]

GULF WAR I

We can easily transition from the power of the DPB to the power of PR firms by noting that Devon Gaffney Cross[31] and Victoria "Torie" Clarke are members of the DPB. Cross is an adviser to the Lincoln Group. The Lincoln Group of Washington, DC, is a PR firm—and more. In 2005 it "was awarded an indefinite delivery, indefinite quantity contract, with a potential maximum value of $100,000,000, for media approach planning, prototype product development, commercial quality product development, product distribution and dissemination, and media effects analysis for the Joint Psychological Operations Support element and other government agencies. The work will be performed CONUS and OCONUS and task orders may be issued from June 7, 2005–June 6, 2010."[32] The acronyms are ominous: they stand for "Continental United States," and "Outside the

Continental United States." This means that the firm has been give enormous resources to perform its operations in the United States.

A small portion ($6 million) of that contract was given to Iraqex, a newly formed subsidiary of the Lincoln Group, to do PR for the Coalition Forces in Iraq.

On November 30, 2005, the *Los Angeles Times* reported that the US military was paying Iraqi newspapers to publish articles produced by the Lincoln Group.

> The articles, written by U.S. military information operations troops, are translated into Arabic and placed in Baghdad newspapers with the help of a defense contractor, according to U.S. military officials and documents obtained by the Los Angeles Times.
>
> Many of the articles are presented in the Iraqi press as unbiased news accounts written and reported by independent journalists. The stories trumpet the work of U.S. and Iraqi troops, denounce insurgents and tout U.S.-led efforts to rebuild the country.[33]

The authors of the article articulate a theme which I hope the reader can see emerging in this article: "The arrangement with Lincoln Group is evidence of how far the Pentagon has moved to blur the traditional boundaries between military public affairs—the dissemination of factual information to the media—and psychological and information operations, which use propaganda and sometimes misleading information to advance the objectives of a military campaign."[34]

On the other hand, one can understand Daniel Berrigan's life and work as an effort to bear witness to the truth—more precisely, to the Truth of the Gospel. And for Berrigan, the central truth of the Gospel is the nonviolence of the Sermon on the Mount, "Love your enemies." Berrigan is aware of the image-making (or rather, image-distorting) power of the dominant culture. Crucially, he speaks of how the Empire has coopted the image of Christ.

> Christ, it goes without saying, is no longer shown as the accused and abused suffering Servant Hailed before Pilate. Now He is the friend and advocate and beneficiary of Pilate.
>
> The change hardly stops with the later images, the God of "power and might." Images always go far beyond themselves; they urge new attitudes and behavior, celebrate new social structures. Icons became signs of immense social change, celebrating a new and prosperous status of the Holy vis-à-vis secular power.[35]

Jesus's claim that he is "The way, the truth and the life" gives Berrigan a useful hermeneutic for analyzing the PR that leads to war. For Berrigan, truth leads to life. Conversely, killing requires lying. "Whenever we find an insistence on killing, the death of the poor is inevitable," that, for Berrigan, is the supreme departure from the truth of Jesus. In his commemoration of Dorothy Day, he writes:

> What had she seen? The tragedy of the victim was by no means accidental, nor was it in any way to be equated with the will of God for humans.
>   Something else was at work, something eminently sinful. Choices against, overwhelmingly against, multitudes of the living. Caught in the gun sights of war and cut down; war being a simple and appalling synonym for the modern world, its main horrific work and business-for-profit.[36]

Cross's link to Lincoln shows us only one aspect of how PR firms profit from war. We can find even more dramatic cases, one leading up to the first Gulf War in 1991, and another leading up to the 1993 invasion of Iraq.

In 1990, Victoria "Torie" Clarke was general manager of what was then the world's largest PR firm, Hill & Knowlton. In 1990, after Iraq's invasion of Kuwait, the Kuwait's emirs hired Hill & Knowlton to help "sell" the war to the American people. They paid them between $12 million (according to "60 Minutes") and $20 million (according to "20/20"). Their main coup, as recounted by Solomon and others, perpetrated by Tom Lantos (D-CA), who brought in "Nayirah" to tell the tale of how Iraqi soldiers had thrown Kuwaiti babies out of incubators. The story was false and Tom Lantos knew it. Nayirah was the daughter of the Kuwaiti Ambassador to the United States. It is doubtful that Nayirah was even in Kuwait at the time of the invasion, and certainly not in the hospital[37] since the al-Sabah family had fled Kuwait in advance of Hussein's invasion.

Nevertheless, the "incubator story" was repeated over and over by President Bush and the media, and even accepted by Amnesty International. Crucially,

> The final decision to go to war was made on January 12, 1991 in a Senate vote of 52 to 47 (a margin of 3). Before passing this resolution, six pro-war senators specifically brought forth the baby incubator allegations in their speeches supporting the resolution. Without the incubator allegations the margin of victory within the Senate would likely not have been sufficient for the war to be approved.[38]

It is important to note that Hill & Knowlton profited from *promoting* war. That echoes our suspicions of the conflict of interest in the DPB (of which Clarke is currently a member): that the members represent corporations that will profit if they "advise" the United States to go to war.

In the lead-up to the 1991 attacks on Iraq, the media mostly followed the lead of the "hired PR guns." For example, Solomon notes that "major American news outlets printed and aired comparisons between Saddam Hussein and Hitler at an average rate of several times each day during the five-and-a-half months that led up to the Gulf War in mid-January 1991. Yet Hussein's dictatorship had been known and supported by the United States for many years."[39]

During the 1991 war, the media almost wholly abandoned objective reporting. Writing about that coverage, *The New York Times*'s Chris Hedges said:

> It gave us media-manufactured heroes and a heady pride in our military superiority and technology. It made war fun . . . It was war as spectacle, war as entertainment. The images and stories were designed to make us feel good about our nation, about ourselves. The Iraqi families and soldiers being blown to bits by huge iron fragmentation bombs just over the border in Iraq were faceless and nameless phantoms.
>
> . . .
>
> The notion that the press was used in the war is incorrect. The press wanted to be used. It saw itself as part of the war effort . . . For we not only believe the myth of war and feed recklessly off the drug but also embrace the cause. We may do it with more skepticism. We certainly expose more lies and misconception. But we believe. We all believe.[40]

Between the wars, the media were unimaginably remiss in reporting the effects of the *sanctions* on the Iraqi people. In Gulf War I, most of the bombs were dropped on the civilian infrastructure of Iraq, resulting in the loss of electric power and critically, clean water delivery and sewage treatment systems. That specific targeting unleashed water-borne diseases like acute dehydrating diarrhea (cholera), prolonged febrile illness with abdominal symptoms (typhoid fever), acute bloody diarrhea (dysentery), and chronic diarrhea (Brainerd diarrhea) which, as the Defense Intelligence Agency had predicted before the war, reached epidemic proportions within six months.

Deprived by the sanctions of any means of treating these illnesses, or of repairing the damage that unleashed them, the Iraqis began to die in their tens of thousands, then hundreds of thousands, starting with the weakest. The most authoritative book on this topic to date is by UN Humanitarian Coordinator in Iraq, Hans von Sponeck.[41] I know of only few commentators who include this twelve-year genocidal policy in their analysis of the present situation in Iraq.[42]

Gulf War II

We have many books and articles about how the "fourth estate" failed to challenge the Bush Administration's "case" for the invasion of Iraq in 2003.[43] I'd like to cull some of these resources to examine some of the strategy used by the US government to "sell" the war on Iraq.

When it was time to convince the US public to invade Iraq after 9/11, the government PR apparatus had become even more sophisticated, and "Torie" Clarke was part of that push as well. Even before 9/11, Donald Rumsfeld had invited Clarke to the Pentagon as the Assistant Secretary of Defense for Public Affairs, the public spokeswoman for the Pentagon. After 9/11, Rumsfeld gave Clarke the task of "selling" the invasion of Iraq.

> Almost immediately upon taking up her new gig, Clarke convened regular meetings with a select group of Washington's top private PR specialists and lobbyists to develop a marketing plan for the Pentagon's forthcoming terror wars. The group was filled with heavy-hitters and was strikingly bipartisan in composition. She called it the Rumsfeld Group and it included PR executive Sheila Tate, columnist Rich Lowry, and Republican political consultant Rich Galen.[44]

In addition to orchestrating the Defense Department's propaganda leading up to the 2003 invasion, Clarke created the idea of "embedded reporters" during the invasion.[45]

On another media front, on January 21, 2002, by Executive Order 13283, President George W. Bush "established within the White House Office an Office of Global Communications (the 'Office') to be headed by a Deputy Assistant to the President for Global Communications."[46] Its mission was

> to advise the President, the heads of appropriate offices within the Executive Office of the President, and the heads of executive departments and agencies on utilization of the most effective means for the United States Government to ensure consistency in messages that will

promote the interests of the United States abroad, prevent misunderstanding, build support for and among coalition partners of the United
States, and inform international audiences.

To accomplish this, one of its principle functions was to

> assess the methods and strategies used by the United States
> Government (other than special activities as defined in Executive
> Order 12333 of December 4, 1981) to deliver information to
> audiences abroad. The Office shall coordinate the formulation among
> appropriate agencies of messages that reflect the strategic communica-
> tions framework and priorities of the United States, and shall facilitate
> the development of a strategy among the appropriate agencies to
> effectively communicate such messages.[47]

One of the duties of the "Office" is to publish the daily "Global Messenger,"
sent out to all US ambassadors abroad and favorable contacts in the media.
It gives the government's position on various events, and thus ensures that
everyone is repeating the government's message. *The New Yorker* observed
the lock-step effect of such a PR strategy:

> During the six months or so prior to and encompassing the nomination
> and confirmation of John Roberts as Chief Justice of the United States,
> one phrase was on every Republican senatorial lip. "All of the
> President's nominees, both now and in the future, deserve a fair
> up-or-down vote," said Sam Brownback, of Kansas. "Every nominee,
> no matter if the President is Democrat or Republican, deserves an
> up-or-down vote," said Jim DeMint, of South Carolina. "We must take
> action to insure President Bush's nominees are getting the up-or-down
> vote they deserve," said Kay Bailey Hutchison, of Texas. "Since the day
> I came to the U.S. Senate," said Pete Domenici, of New Mexico,
> "I have believed strongly that every nominee deserves an up-or-down
> vote." The conservative commentariat was equally of one mind about
> the sanctity of verticality. "The American people," wrote John
> Podhoretz, in the *Post*, "won't understand why a candidate should be
> denied an up-or-down vote." The White House, naturally, agreed. "We
> believe that every judicial nominee deserves an up-or-down vote," said
> Karl Rove.[48]

That constant repetition of "sound bites" is characteristic of PR. That they
come from so many quarters should concern us.

Further, in a by now characteristic move, the government "Office"
outsourced the task of selling the war. One of the firms hired was the

Rendon Group. The Rendon Group had also been active in selling Gulf War I, since "during Desert Storm [John] Rendon pulled in $100,000 a month from the Kuwaiti royal family. He followed this up with a $23 million contract from the CIA to produce anti-Saddam propaganda in the region."[49] (Note that in April 2005, the Office of Global Communications was disbanded, but its duties were taken up directly by the National Security Council.)

As reported in *Weapons of Mass Deception*, PR firms have now become so sophisticated that they attach electrodes to members of "focus groups," in order to measure the most minute reactions to their advertisements. What John Rendon and his associates discovered was that people were not much moved, for example, by the fact that Saddam Hussein was a brutal dictator (perhaps they were lulled by all those years that the United States supported his activities), or that there was torture in Iraq (something most Americans—especially in the Justice Department—seem callous toward). What *did* get people upset was "weapons of mass destruction." After 9/11, they had another angle: they could link Saddam Hussein with the terrorist attacks.

Once they had their selling points, the Rendon Group went to work. They assembled a stable of speakers and trained them in the techniques of what Chomsky would call "manufacturing consent." For example, they were trained, whenever they mentioned 9/11, to say "Saddam Hussein," or "Iraq" in the same sentence—whether or not they made a causal relationship. Association was enough, because all that was required was what Nicholas J. O'Shaughnessy calls "emotional proof."

> [Emotional proof] is where we feel intuitively that there is a causal connection which is highly significant to the creation of some event and yet which cannot easily be pinned down, but where we believe this thing to be true because we have a deep emotional need for it to be true.[50]

The Rendon group earned their money. "By the start of the war, 66 percent of Americans thought Saddam Hussein was behind 9/11 and 79 percent thought he was close to having a nuclear weapon."[51] The propaganda was even more successful among the military. "[A] Zogby survey of 944 military personnel in Iraq, finds that 85 percent of U.S. troops in . . . Mesopotamia think they are there to avenge Saddam Hussein's role in the 9/11 jetliner attacks.[52] Seventy-seven percent think the U.S. invaded to stop Saddam from helping al Qaeda."

Just to be clear: these were not mistakes in intelligence; they were lies.[53]

During the war, PR and psy-ops were needed more than ever.

In Qatar, a stage-set headquarters was set up—under the design of a Hollywood art director who had also worked with illusionist David Blaine—which would accommodate journalists and provide them with representations of conflict through the wizardry of advanced techno-logical communications.[54]

Furthermore, during "major combat operations," the "embedded" reporters "still presented a largely bloodless—but action-packed—view of the Iraq war to American audiences,"[55] where the dead were virtually never shown, especially on FNC [Fox News Channel] and where only about 2 percent of shots showed people killed in the war. Even more rare (only 4 shots in 600 hours of coverage) were pictures taken in close enough proximity or with an angle that allowed the audience to see the victim's face. Instead, the dead were seen at a distance, covered by a sheet, or through a surrogate (most commonly a coffin and very rarely anything as graphic as a pool of blood).[56]

The effect was predictable:

This carefully controlled and choreographed environment produced round-the-clock information which effectively minimized any opposi-tional reports emerging and was used to restrict the scope for journalis-tic interpretations which departed from military lines. By filling airtime with propaganda, the Bush administration and the military succeeded in keeping Iraqi reports from infiltrating coverage and thus helped to maintain the illusion that the war was progressing in much the same way as a Hollywood cinematic experience with America fulfilling its mythic role as a civilizing force bringing freedom to those subject to barbarism.[57]

As the above quote indicates, there is, beneath all this PR activity, a deep confusion inherent in the United States that justifies its wars—especially in the case of Iraq, where the United States wants to present itself as a "civi-lizing force" to the very birthplace of civilization. This deep confusion per-meates all areas of official governmental and corporate reporting on Iraq. Perhaps it also explains the "logic" in President Bush's famous statement, "I just want you to know that, when we talk about war, we're really talking about peace."[58] More humorously, I recently saw a bumper sticker that read: "Be nice to America—or we will bring you democracy."

After the occupation of Iraq was more established, the Rendon Group was awarded a $6.4 million contract to report the war from Baghdad.[59] Here, then, is a move that I believe is a pattern for corporations in their dealings with the US government: They sell the war, then profit from it. In tandem with PR firms like Rendon and Lincoln, the Pentagon engaged its own (governmental) "Combat Camera" which gave us the manufactured story of the "rescue" of Private Jessica Lynch:

> The Lynch story was fed to the eager press by a Pentagon operation called Combat Camera, the Army network of photographers, videographers and editors that sends 800 photos and 25 video clips a day to the media. The editors at Combat Camera carefully culled the footage to present the Pentagon's montage of the war, eliding such unsettling images as collateral damage, cluster bombs, dead children and US soldiers, napalm strikes and disgruntled troops.[60]

We should note that on its website,[61] one of the duties that "Combat Camera" tasks itself with is "information warfare."

To close this section, I'd like to note that John Rendon and the Rendon Group have an interesting history of working with the government in its war-making policies. Information desks at the CIA have also been outsourced to private companies, with the result that employees from the Rendon Group have taken over jobs long reserved for the CIA. "According to one senior administration official involved in intelligence-budget decisions, half of the CIA's work is now performed by private contractors."[62] This is further disturbing evidence of corporate takeover of government functions, but the more so because in 1991, the CIA hired John Rendon to "create the conditions for the removal of Saddam Hussein from power."[63] Since his firm is being paid for that purpose, what will a Rendon employee do when information comes across his CIA desk?

In the most recent exposé, R. J. Hillhouse discovers other sources inside the CIA that confirm the 50 percent outsourcing figure, then points out another disturbing dimension of this shift:

> The contractors in charge of espionage are still chiefly CIA alumni who have absorbed its public service values. But as the center of gravity shifts from the public sector to the private, more than one independent intelligence firm has developed plans to "raise" succeeding generations of officers within its own training systems. These corporate-grown agents will be inculcated with corporate values and ethics, not those of public service.[64]

Campaign Contributions

It should be obvious that campaign contributions influence the voting of policy-makers in the government.[65] But in 2002 the Center for Responsive Politics (CRP) put out a chart that "graphically" demonstrates the relationship with regard to weapons companies (see Figure 1).

While we await an updated chart from the CRP, I might point out two things about this one. The first is contained in the comment on the chart itself: "This means that 90% of the variation in defense contract size is accounted for by campaign contribution size." Please note that this chart deals with the size of the contract. Actually getting access to the contract is a story that will unfold in the course of this essay.

The second is that the defense contractors are getting a tremendous bargain for their money. For example, Lockheed Martin is the largest

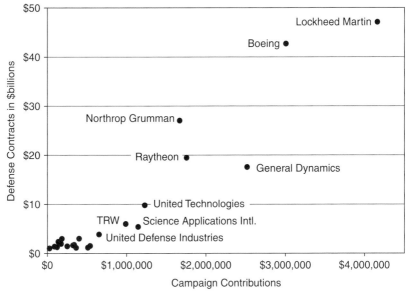

Includes 24 public and private defense contractors with $1 billion or more in 2000–02 contracts for which the Defense Department accounted for more than 10% of total sales in 2002. "Campaign contributions" include soft-money and Political Action Committee contributions. $R^2 = .8997$. This means that 90% of the variation in defense contract size is accounted for by campaign contribution size.

Figure 1 Campaign contributions and defense contracts, 2000–2002.

weapons manufacturer in the world. When one looks at the campaign contributions of Lockheed Martin for the period charted, one sees that they contributed over $4 million dollars to various campaigns. That is a great deal of money. But compare that amount to the dollar amount in the contracts awarded to Lockheed Martin during that time: about $48 billion. Please note the ratio: contributions in the millions reaped contracts in the tens of billions—a huge return on investment (ROI).

A comparison might help to better grasp the enormity of that ROI. Imagine those millions invested and billions returned not in terms of dollars, but in terms of seconds. If you spent $1 every second, it would take eleven days to spend one million dollars. At the same rate, it would take thirty-one years to spend one billion dollars. And recall that Lockheed-Martin's contracts are in the *tens of billions* of dollars. Then, returning to the chart in Figure 1, one can see that defense contractors "earned" about $12,000 for every $1 they "invested" in political campaigns.

Other companies that profit from war also follow a similar pattern of "investment." I will discuss Blackwater later in this chapter. But when Erik Prince was the CEO of Blackwater, he gave about $250,000 to federal campaigns, and "not a dime to Democrats"[66] That was not because the Democrats were too peaceful, but because the Republicans were in power when the contracts for mercenaries were being outsourced.

With the power of the DPB, of PR firms with access to CIA desks, and the weight of campaign contributions, I hope a pattern of influence with the war profiteers emerges. I would venture to say that there has been a paradigm shift since the days of the Berrigan protests. Whereas it is still true to say that these corporations profit from war now, because of their great influence on war-making policy, it might be more accurate to say that *they make war for profit.*[67]

We know that in the past, corporations have influenced governments to buy weapons systems. We know that in the days of the British Empire, corporations influenced the government to go to war to pacify areas or to gain access to cheap labor and resources. We know that in 1935, Marine Major General Smedley Butler published *War Is a Racket,*[68] describing how industrialists profit from war. But now, along with those dimensions, we see that war itself is profitable, that the whole endeavor is a profit-making venture. From the people who "sell" it, and then go to Iraq to "report it," from the weapons manufacturers who destroy, to the reconstruction companies who "rebuild," from the people who "equip" the US military to the people who provide medical care for the returning veterans—twenty-first century US war is a profit-making cycle.

Thus the capitalist standard of profitmaking penetrates into war making as well, giving it a new form. Some years after his Catonsville action, Berrigan in *Whereon We Stand* discussed the all-consuming nature of profitmaking, using religious grammar to describe its omnipresence: "Business as a form of religion, the undeniable religious aura of business, the profane elevated to the sacramental."[69] Tellingly in the same work, Berrigan proceeds from his analysis of the "peace" struck between religion and greed, to the idolization of Mars, the god of war. He recasts Demetrius's words in defense of Artemis (the goddess whose silver statue reigned in Ephesus), placing them in the mouths of the present-day defenders of war: "Great and loyal and worthy of all support is our work, great are the factories, laboratories, bunkers and bases of Mars. It is though these that our country flourishes unparalleled in the world!"[70]

With "making war for profit" as a working hypothesis, I would like to make explicit another area where corporations have a profound influence on war-making policy in the United States: the so-called "revolving door" between military contractors and positions in the US government.

The Revolving Door

> From the moment the Bush team took power, the Pentagon was stacked with ideologues like Paul Wolfowitz, Douglas Feith . . . and with former corporate executives, many from large weapons manufacturers, like Under Secretary of Defense Pete Aldridge (Aerospace Corporation), Army Secretary Thomas White (Enron), Navy Secretary Gordon England (General Dynamics), and Air Force Secretary James Roche (Northrop Grumman).
>
> —Jeremy Scahill[71]

I have suggested that corporate representatives influence decision-making through the DPB. The DPB, however, is still technically an advisory group. With what is called the "revolving door," government policy-makers and -enforcers become members of corporations who use their contacts and access to enrich the corporations (and themselves). Then they return to government positions with their vision of national security colored (at best) by their corporate experience. Then they return to the corporate world with even more influence, and then return to government, and so on.

I will give several examples of this, but my prime example is former Vice President Dick Cheney. In 1989 Cheney was appointed Secretary of

Defense for George H. W. Bush, overseeing, in part, Gulf War I. After the war, Cheney hired a private firm to cap the oil well fires in Kuwait. The name of the firm was Halliburton. In 1992, Cheney paid a private firm $9 million to determine whether the outsourcing of military logistics would be economically feasible. After nearly a year, the private firm said that outsourcing to private firms would indeed be the way to go. The name of the private firm was Brown and Root (later, KBR), a wholly owned subsidiary of Halliburton.

When Cheney left office in 1995, he had no experience working in corporate management structures. Nevertheless, he was hired by Halliburton and became their CEO. Then Brown and Root won a five-year contract to provide logistics for the US Army Corp of Engineers all over the globe. Over the next five years, Halliburton doubled the number of contracts it received from the US government. "At Halliburton, Cheney exploited his government and international contracts to boost Halliburton's government-guaranteed loans from $100 million to 1.5 billion in less than 5 years. He also created 35 offshore, tax-free subsidiaries."[72] And in the decade following KBR's "findings" for the government, 3,000 government contracts were outsourced to private firms. Halliburton received 750 of those contracts.[73]

Working for the government (or more accurately, vice versa) has other benefits beside guaranteed profits. In 1998, Halliburton paid $302 million in taxes. In 1999, it paid nothing. In fact, in 1999 Halliburton received a tax refund of $85 million.[74] Such "tax breaks" are not uncommon. As Antonia Juhasz reports, "The Arms Trade Resource Center determined that almost 80 percent of Lockheed's 2004 earnings were paid for by U.S. taxpayers . . . Moreover, the Resource Center found that in 2002 Lockheed paid so few taxes that it was effectively taxed at just 7.7 percent, compared to the average American's tax rate of about 20 to 35 percent."[75] Not only that, but a recent GAO report revealed that more than 60,000 contractors with the US federal government that owe more than $7.7 billion in back taxes, including 27,000 Department of Defense contractors.[76]

There seems to be a further advantage in this government-corporation weddedness: contracts can be gained through contacts, rather than through competitive bidding. Thus, Representative Waxman reports:

> Last year's [2006] report found that no-bid contracts and other forms of contracts awarded without full and open competition had risen from $67.5 billion in 2000 to $145.1 billion in 2005. This year's report finds that spending on these no-bid and limited-competition contracts

surged over $60 billion to $206.9 billion in 2006, the largest single-year increase ever. The value of federal contracts awarded without full and open competition has more than tripled since 2000. For the first time on record, more than half of federal procurement spending was awarded through no-bid and limited-competition contracts in 2006.[77]

In 2000 George W. Bush asked Cheney to help him find a suitable vice-presidential candidate. After interviewing a dozen people, Cheney submitted his own name, and Bush accepted. He immediately resumed outsourcing. In 1997 KBR had lost its contract because of fraudulent billing practices in Bosnia. But in 2001, when Cheney was back in government, KBR got its contract back—"just in time for the invasions of Afghanistan and Iraq."[78]

Before he became vice president, Cheney had to sell off his Halliburton stocks to avoid a conflict of interest. He made about $35 million from the sale. However, he left with a "compensation package" of 433,000 stock options in Halliburton. As with all corporations, Halliburton has made moves to assure that its stock remains robust. For example, in 2002 Halliburton realized a $25 million profit by cutting in half the pensions of people it had forced into early retirement.[79] Now Halliburton is leaving Texas to establish its main offices in Dubai, centering itself at the crossroads of the Middle East–Asian oil trade, and escaping whatever vestiges of control that might still be exerted by the US government.

Cheney's compensation package included five years of deferred payments from Halliburton. These payments were detailed in a press release from Senator Frank Lautenberg's office on September 15, 2005.[80] It might be helpful to place those amounts received from Halliburton in comparison with Cheney's salary as vice president (see table).

Cheney's Salary

	As Vice President	From Halliburton
2001	$175,400	$205,298
2002	$175,400	$162,392
2003	$198,600	$178.437
2004	$198,600	$194,852

Might there be a conflict of interest there? Is national security and public service the only thing influencing Cheney as he makes his policy decisions?[81]

Oddly, Cheney's official biography from the vice president's site neglected to mention his five-year term at Halliburton. Also unmentioned is that until 2001, Cheney's wife Lynne served on the board of Lockheed Martin. Or that Cheney's son-in-law Philip J. Perry had Lockheed Martin as a client in his law firm, and that he worked as a registered lobbyist for Lockheed Martin in 2003 and 2004.[82]

Speaking of Lockheed Martin, and continuing in the theme of the revolving door, let us examine the case of James B. Comey. In 2002 George W. Bush appointed Comey as Deputy Attorney General of the United States, the second highest office in the Department of Justice. In 2005 Comey left governmental service and took a job as the General Counsel and Senior Vice President at Lockheed Martin, overseeing their stable of 140 lawyers. Commenting on the hire, Charles W. Garrison of District-based Garrison & Sisson Inc., a recruiter, said Comey was "pretty much able to write his own ticket," given his credibility and his longstanding contacts within federal agencies. "While Lockheed Martin hasn't had a lot of problems, it's probably a very good defensive acquisition for them, and an offensive acquisition for them as far as Comey being able to open doors."[83]

> Nor is Comey alone in joining the ranks of Lockheed Martin. Johnson and Witte point out that Lockheed Martin's board of directors is well-stocked with prominent former government officials, including E. C. "Pete" Aldridge Jr., former undersecretary of defense; Gen. Joseph W. Ralston, former vice chairman of the Joint Chiefs of Staff; Adm. James O. Ellis Jr., former commander of the U.S. Strategic Command; Gwendolyn S. King, former commissioner of the Social Security Administration. The company also has many of former government officials in its executive ranks and has hired numerous former members of the House and Senate to lobby on its behalf.[84]

All this—"advisory committees" like the DPB, the power of PR firms hired by the government, the impact of campaign contributions, the access of "revolving doors" —points to the profound influence, one might venture to say control, that corporations have over governmental policy, especially in war making. Time to look at the effects of this corporate-dictated policy, especially in Iraq.

"Winning" on the Ground in Iraq

Following the aforementioned twelve years of genocidal sanctions, the US invasion of Iraq in March 2003, and the subsequent occupation, is a moral, diplomatic and military disaster. Most analysts say (neglecting the fact that the invasion was based on lies and greed) that the United States went in without a plan for post-invasion Iraq. But in a well-researched and important work, Antonia Juhasz writes:

> It has been said so often that it is now repeated as gospel that the Bush administration had no plan for post-conflict Iraq. But the gospel is not correct. There was at least one clear plan—an economic plan—the blueprint for which was ready and in Bush administration hands at least two months prior to the invasion.

She goes on to point to the origins of that plan—predictably, with an enormous government payment to another private corporation, which "provides analysis and assessment for undertaking a "mass privatization" of Iraq's state-owned industries:[85]

> The 107-page three-year contract between the Bush administration and Bearing Point, Inc. of McLean, Virginia, lays out the president's economic agenda in Iraq. In return for $250 million, Bearing Point provides "technical assistance" to the U.S. Agency for International Development on the restructuring of the Iraqi economy to meet Bush administration goals.[86]

To this end, the Bush administration brought in Paul Bremer to be the director of Reconstruction and Humanitarian Assistance for post-war Iraq. After a stint in the Foreign Service, Bremer also served for a while as the managing director of Kissinger and Associates, a worldwide consulting firm founded by Henry Kissinger. Coincidentally, Kissinger is a member of the DPB. In his role as head of the Coalition Provisional Authority, Bremer reported primarily to Donald Rumsfeld, the US Secretary of Defense, and for approximately one year, exercised absolute authority over Iraq's civil administration.

The amount of money that has been poured into the corporations to maintain the Global War on Terror (GWOT) is literally unimaginable. The most recent report from the Congressional Research Service reveals that Congress has appropriated $610 billion in war-related money since the 9/11 terror assaults. This is about the same amount spent on the entire Vietnam War. All by itself, the Iraq invasion and occupation has put nearly half a trillion dollars into the hands of the war-makers. When Congress approved President Bush's pending request for another $147 billion for the budget year starting October 1, 2008, the total bill for the war on terror since September 11 reached more than three-fourths of a trillion dollars, with appropriations for Iraq reaching $567 billion. Also, if the increase in war tempo continues beyond September, the Pentagon's request "would presumably be inadequate," CRS said.

> The Congressional Budget Office estimates that additional war costs for the next 10 years could total about $472 billion if troop levels fall to 30,000 by 2010, or $919 billion if troop levels fall to 70,000 by about 2013. If these estimates are added to already appropriated amounts, total funding for Iraq and the GWOT could reach from about $980 billion to $1.4 trillion by 2017.[87]

More recently, Nobel Prize laureate in economics Joseph Stiglitz presented a more detailed analysis of the costs of the war, submitting that a "moderate" estimate would be three *trillion* dollars.[88]

Of course, to establish and maintain the US occupation and to profit from it, the government needed weapons, lots of them. And then, of course the weapons and vehicles have to be replaced. So, as might be expected, weapons companies profited from the "boom" of warfare. Listed on the "CorpWatch" site are the major weapons manufacturers in the United States, and how they've benefited from war. Lockheed Martin is averaging around $20 billion a year in contracts, a significant increase from before the so-called global war on terror. Other weapons manufacturers like Boeing, Northrup Grumman, General Dynamics, and Raytheon show a similar growth patterns.

One company, ATK in Minnesota, has the contract to manufacture all the bullets for the US military. It has had to outsource its contract to an Israeli company, however, because ATK cannot keep up with demand. It can only produce about four million bullets a day.[89]

But once the weapons have destroyed the country, the reconstruction companies have to come in to "rebuild" it, another turn of the profit cycle. We have already heard something of how Bechtel gained access for its nearly $3 billion of contracts in Iraq, and its "success" there. "According to the U.S. State Department of 249 water and sewage projects originally planned [by Bechtel], only 64 have been completed."[90] Sometimes Bechtel's PR graces us with photos of gleaming water plants in Iraq. But the several water plants that have been completed have no pipes to connect them to the houses. Further, "None of the 19 electrical facilities that has undergone U.S.-funded repair work is being run correctly."[91]

Other companies are no better. Parsons, which had the contract to repair the health care system in Iraq, once, before Gulf War I, the sanctions and Gulf War II, the envy of the Arab world, "won" $3.3 million in profit for its work. "And that is in addition to the $186 million that U.S. taxpayers shelled out to Parsons to build dozens of clinics that have yet to dispense a single aspirin."[92] Though contracting for 120 health care centers, Parsons and the Army Corps of engineers actually only built four. And of those four none was opened. The World Health Organization called this situation "shocking."[93]

Halliburton, as mentioned above, first went into the war area after Gulf War I, under Cheney's Department of Defense. In 1992 its subsidiary, won a $2 billion KBR Logistics Civil Augmentation Program (LOGCAP) contract to supply logistical support for the military in any theater it went to. But under Cheney's vice presidency, Halliburton returned to the Iraq theater with a vengeance. KBR received a $23 billion contract for military logistics in Iraq.

Recently, even though Stewart Bowen, the special investigator general for Iraq reconstruction, reported that KBR had been unable to account for how much fuel had been delivered, or not delivered. It had overcharged $4.5 million for food, and the report "found numerous errors in KBR's automated billeting tracking tool"[94] (which is used for tracking and assigning housing). Nevertheless, the military awarded KBR an additional $50 billion for logistical support, to be shared with Fluor and DynCorp.

Interestingly, the Pentagon has hired *another* private firm, SERCO, to oversee the work of those three private firms, thus putting them another level away from government reach. The "oversight" contract specifically states that SERCO has no enforcement or punitive powers.[95] In response to that, Cray points out:

> No company can be expected to provide this kind of accountability, companies are designed to make money for themselves and their shareholders, not safeguard the taxpayers. The buck ultimately stops somewhere in the Pentagon's chain of command where, instead of overseeing the actual work (keep in mind that KBR has some 200 subcontractors working in Kuwait and Iraq), they will spend increasingly more time evaluating SERCO's work. And even then, SERCO has influence over the process. (See page 31 of SERCO's contract "Contractors Self-Assessment.")[96]

Overall, by June 2005, "the Defense Department had 149 "prime contracts" with seventy-seven contractors in Iraq worth approximately $42.1 billion. According to Pentagon auditors, Halliburton 'alone represent[ed] 52% of the total contract value.'"[97] In addition, Halliburton received a no-bid, $30 million contract from the Navy to repair oilrigs destroyed in the Gulf of Mexico by hurricane Katrina.[98] In 2007, Halliburton "spun off" KBR, so that it could "focus more on energy."

Jeremy Scahill provides us with an in-depth look at other "winners" in the Iraq war: private security firms, principally Blackwater. Even the General Accounting Office admitted in December 2006 "that the military had no effective system of oversight and that 'officials were unable to determine how many contractors were deployed to bases in Iraq.' "[99] Scahill, however, estimates the number of mercenaries in Iraq at 48,000.[100] Even more surprising, Scahill reveals that Britain has sent more mercenaries to serve in Iraq than it has its own military personnel: "By October 2006, there were an estimated twenty-one thousand mercenaries working for British firms in Iraq, compared to seventy-two hundred active duty British troops."[101]

Worldwide, the mercenaries are a $100 billion-a-year business. Particularly in Iraq, mercenaries are needed to protect the corporations that have invested in Iraq. Indeed, the fact that the military has outsourced so many of its tasks to private firms creates a greater need for mercenaries to protect those firms. As a result, more and more of the "reconstruction" money is being siphoned off to pay for these security firms. These mercenaries are hired both with official "government" funds (read: US taxpayer money), with stolen Iraqi money,[102] and by the corporations themselves. Halliburton, for example, hires security guards from Blackwater and Triple Canopy. Thus:

> When Bremer left Iraq in June 2004, there were more than twenty thousand private soldiers inside the country's borders and Iraq had become known as a "Wild West" with no sheriff. Those mercenaries officially hired by the occupation would be contracted for more than $2 billion of security work by the end of the "Bremer year" and would account for upwards of 30 percent of the Iraq "reconstruction" budget.[103]

That, of course, does not take into account the private entities that widely hired mercenaries in Iraq.

In fact, the war has created a greater need for mercenaries in the United States itself. First, as Jeffrey St. Clair points out, moving all those military police from US bases to Iraq and Afghanistan prisons means that there are fewer soldiers left on the bases. So now the Pentagon has to outsource military police positions in the US to private corporations. For example, Chenega and Alutiiq received $500 million to provide 4,385 private security guards. They subcontracted this out to other companies.[104] Second,

"After Katrina in 2005, hundreds of heavily armed Blackwater mercenaries—some fresh from deployment in Iraq—fanned out into the disaster zone. Within a week, they were officially hired by the Department of Homeland Security to operate in the US Gulf, billing the federal government $950 a day per Blackwater soldier. In less than a year, the company had raked in more than $70 million in federal hurricane-related contracts—about $243,000 a day.[105]

More ominously, private security firms like Titan and CACI have participated in the interrogation and torture of prisoners in Iraq and elsewhere.[106] Yet even after the Abu Ghraib scandal, the Pentagon responded by renewing a $16 billion contract with CACI and awarded Titan a new contract worth up to $164 million with options.[107]

It also goes without saying that the mercenaries are paid better than the government's military. Often they are better equipped. This creates a temptation for governmental soldiers to leave government service and join private security firms. Scahill reports:

> There is slang in Iraq now for this jump. It is called "Going Blackwater." To put it bluntly, these private forces create a system where national duty is outbid by profits. And yet these forces are being used for mission-critical activities. Indeed, in January Gen. David Petraeus admitted that on his last tour in Iraq, he himself was protected not by the active-duty military but by private "contract security."[108]

So, we might add, was Paul Bremer during his stay in Iraq. "Once Blackwater started recruiting for its first big job, guarding Paul Bremer, the rate shot up to $600 a day [from $300 a day]."[109]

There are a number of profound difficulties with this increasing turn toward mercenaries to support the US military ventures. Two problems are noted by Michael Ratner, president of the Center for Constitutional Rights in an email to Scahill. First:

> The increasing use of contractors, private forces or as some would say "mercenaries" makes wars easier to begin and to fight—it just takes money and not the citizenry. To the extent a population is called upon to go to war, there is resistance, a necessary resistance to prevent wars of self-aggrandizement, foolish wars and in the case of the United States, hegemonic imperialist wars. Private forces are almost a necessity for a United States bent on retaining its declining empire.

Second, Ratner notes, "Likewise, here at home in the United States. Controlling an angry, abused population with a police force bound to obey the Constitution can be difficult—private forces can solve this 'problem.'"[110]

Finally I would like to add a third observation from my own studies of Rome. A turning point in the Roman Republic came when Rome changed the law that said that you had to be a Roman citizen to serve in the Roman military. This limitation had to be removed as Rome extended its empire farther. How, then, might one get noncitizens to fight for Rome? By paying them. But this brought about a crucial change in the motivation of the military. They were not so much fighting for Rome as they were for the person who paid them. Their loyalties shifted. The men, or "triumvirates," who could pay the most, had the bigger and better army. When Caesar's troops "crossed the Rubicon" in violation of Roman law, it was because they had more loyalty to him than to Rome. Such a shift of loyalty and power was a major factor in ending the Roman Republic and ushering in the dictatorship (the word is Roman in origin) of the emperors.

Analogously, as mercenaries grow more powerful both in the United States and abroad, their power will accrue to those who can pay them most. In the future, that will be not one person, but the corporations. Ironically, the corporations will have been empowered first by taxpayer money, as we are seeing now. Then having had their wealth swelled by public coffers, they will become powerful enough to rule over the very people and governments whom they purport to serve. We have seen that already, corporations are paying for mercenaries. Recently, Lockheed Martin bought its own mercenary company, Sytek. I do not think that the day is very far off in the future when mercenaries from one corporation will be fighting mercenaries of another, for control of territory, resources and labor.

How big the "win" was for corporations in Iraq is best described in Antonia Juhasz's excellent work, *The Bush Agenda*. She draws our attention to the extent to which the quarter-million-dollar "Bearing Point" plan which "provides analysis and assessment for undertaking a 'mass privatization' of Iraq's state-owned industries."[111]

The scope of the plan to transform the Iraqi economy is, she writes, "astonishing." "The company specifies changes in every sector of the Iraqi economy—from trade rules to banking and financial services, to public services, agriculture, housing, media, elections, and the structure of the government itself. It even specifies propaganda tools to sell these policies to the Iraqi public."[112]

In one of his steps to implement this plan, Bremer disbanded the Iraqi army, placing over half a million armed men into the streets with no work, and with families to support. He handed their work over to US contractors. He eliminated benefits to war widows and disabled veterans who were party members. But in a by-now predictable turn, the plan for demobilization was handed over to a private US corporation. "On March 14, 2003, three days before the invasion, Ronco Consulting Corporation of Washington D.C. was awarded a $419,000 U.S. Defense Department contract to develop a plan to 'disarm, demobilize and reintegrate the Iraqi armed forces.'"[113] Juhasz also notes that the lack of a viable military is one of the primary justifications the Bush administration gives for not being able to pull out of Iraq.

During his tenure in Iraq, through a series of one hundred orders, Bremer re-shaped the country according to the Bearing Point model. Juhasz takes us through several of those orders and explores their ramifications for Iraq. For example, Order 12 removed all protective tariffs, customs duties, licensing fees, and so on. This allowed local labor and products (so damaged by Gulf War I, the sanctions, and Gulf War II) to be overrun with foreign goods and resources.

Order 17 "granted full immunity from Iraqi laws and the Iraqi legal system to Coalition military forces and all foreign contractors, including private security firms." The same order gave "foreign contractors freedom from all income from all income taxes, corporate taxes, and sales taxes, and denies Iraqis the ability to inspect contractor vehicles or require any sort of licensing or registration fees. Contractors do not have to pay tolls and are granted 'freedom of movement without delay throughout Iraq.'"[114]

Most significant are Orders 39 and 94. The latter allows for 100 percent foreign ownership of Iraqi banks. The former, the "Foreign Direct Investment Law," allows unrestricted, 100 percent foreign ownership of all "economic sectors in Iraq" except oil, and allows 100 percent removal of their profits out of Iraq "without delay."

This, truly, is "astonishing." *All* economic activity in Iraq: telecommunications, road building, transportation, garbage collection, hula hoops, everything can be foreign owned, and all the profits can be taken out of Iraq. Bremer also made sure that such economic policies were ensconced in the new Iraqi Constitution (he had veto power over any aspect of it). They can only be acted upon by a parliament that, even if it weren't a puppet government and even if it actually *could* fully assemble, would still need a two-thirds majority to revoke them. When Michael Lampres, vice president of insurance for the Overseas Private Investment Corporation

(OPIC) said in 2003 that "Iraq is open for business," perhaps he should have said, "up for sale."

This shift seems to have been predicted by Berrigan when he wrote, six years before 9/11:

> Let us suppose that an international crisis has arisen; the possibility, then the probability of war.
>
> Special, altogether urgent interests are now involved and converge. The trough is filled; the appetites are voracious. A huge investment of money and talent has been mounted in view of (indeed if truth were told, in hope of) one contingency: war.
>
> No need to underscore the provocation offered by prior, mostly secret arrangements; all those weapons, all those soldiers (otherwise unemployed and possibly dangerous to law and order) all those weapons experts. Get things moving! Test the weapons, prove the sound nature of the permanent war economy in a "dangerous world."[115]

At this point, one might want to reflect on the corporate motivations of the invasion and occupation of Iraq as discussed above. It seems that the wishes of the corporations have borne full fruit in the passage of Bremer's laws. And I invite the reader to reflect on a statement that a researcher made as he pored through this information at the War Resisters League: "The corporations have conscripted the US military to effect a hostile takeover of an entire nation."

Of course the major economic prize in Iraq is its oil. Before January 2004, Halliburton had the contract to develop all the oil fields in Iraq. In 2004 the northern oil fields were given to Parsons to develop. Historians point out that during the Bush administration, for the first time in US history that the president, the vice president and the secretary of state are all former oil officials. We might mention that Robert Gates, the past secretary of defense, served on the board of Parker Drilling Company, an American company that owns offshore oil drilling rigs.

This oil cartel in the highest ranks of US government might give us further insight into motivations for the invasion and occupation of Iraq. It might also help to explain Executive Order 13303 (May 22, 2003) that, about the same time as Bremer's Order 17, granted complete legal immunity to all transnational oil companies operating in Iraq.

Investigative reporter Greg Palast has suggested that the oil companies' "control" of Iraqi oil was to keep the oil *off* the market so that the price of oil might increase. Whatever the reason, we see that in the last few years, the profits of the oil companies have been staggering. In one year, from 2004 to 2005, ExxonMobil announced that its profits had risen 42 percent to $36.13 *billion* dollars. And again, this is *profit*. The next year, 2005–6, ExxonMobil's profits rose again, this time to $39.5 billion dollars. For the *first quarter* of 2007, its profits were $9.28 billion—up 10 percent from the previous year's first quarter.[116] Other oil companies have followed suit. Chevron, for example, set a 125-year record for profits in 2005. They broke it the next year.

Recently, the United States has developed a plan for Iraqi oil distribution. It has passed through the House and Senate, and been sent to Iraq to be passed by its parliament. The proposed petrochemical bill, however, is deeply flawed. In "The Struggle for Iraqi Oil," Michael Schwartz provides a history of the US pursuit of Middle Eastern Oil.[117] He then turns to the new Petrochemical Bill:

> The Iraq National Oil Company would have exclusive control of just seventeen of Iraq's eighty known oil fields, leaving two-thirds of known—and all of its as yet undiscovered—reserves open to foreign control.
>
> The law also grants foreign oil companies "national treatment," which means that the Iraqi government cannot give preference to Iraqi oil companies (whether public or privately owned) over foreign-owned companies when it chooses contractors.
>
> The law sets no minimum standard for the extent to which foreign companies would not have to invest their earnings in the Iraqi economy, partner with Iraqi companies, hire Iraqi workers or share new technologies.

Schwartz notes that the resistance to the new bill is strong, and spread throughout Iraqi society. First, the Iraqi Parliament itself kept deferring discussions on the bill, and now its provisional acceptance has been challenged by the Kurds, who said they had had no part in the discussion. Next, the Iraqi ministers of oil (who would actually implement the law) are opposed, resenting the interference of outsiders in their oil. The Iraqi Federation of Oil Unions has opposed the new law and has undertaken labor strikes against it.[118] Further, there is armed resistance to the implementation of the law. This was demonstrated, sadly, by the assassination of Vice President Adel Abdul Mahdi, a major advocate of the law, on the day the bill was made public. In addition, the law has been opposed in a formal statement by six women Nobel Prize recipients.[119]

The Obama Administration and the New Congress

With Barack Obama's election being supported by so many in the peace movement, and with polls indicating that the ousting of the Republican majority in Congress was due to popular resistance to the war, one might expect that the situation might improve. However, the penetration of corporate profiteering into the policymaking of our government has become systemic. Of itself, the government is no longer able to change this system. If the peace movement is to succeed in the twenty-first century, it must embrace and develop the second dimension (resistance to government being the first dimension) of the protest of the Catonsville Nine—the corporations themselves. Without a conscious, continuous, and direct focus on the corporations who press us to make war for profit, the peace movement will never succeed in defeating the United States' forced addiction to war making.

Early actions of the new administration and congress indicate the unwillingness, or better, their inability, to change this structure. Note, for example, that Robert Gates was initially kept as secretary of defense, with his history of serving on the board of the Parker Drilling Company (whose significant customer was Halliburton), and his service on the Board of SAIC, another company that profits from war making.[120] During the years 2002–8, Obama's Deputy Secretary of Defense, William Lynn, oversaw a team of lobbyists who won $54 billion in contracts for Raytheon. Further investigations of Obama's appointees will reveal that the business-politics revolving door is still spinning.

Then, too, note that on February 25, 2009, House Democrats killed a resolution that would have called for an ethics committee inquiry into the relationship between campaign contributions and earmarks.[121] Tim Holden (D-Pa.), who presided over the House during the vote, received more than $57,000 in campaign contributions from PMA's political action committee (a major defense lobbying group) from 2001 to 2008.[122] Holden secured $3.2 million in earmarks for clients represented by the PMA Group in the fiscal 2008 defense appropriations law. Congressmen who were overseeing the defense budget received $8 million from the PMA Group and its clients. In particular, John Murtha (D-Pa). Chair of the Defense Appropriations Subcommittee, received $2.4 million from the PMA Group and in turn earmarked over $300 million for PMA's clients in the most recent Defense Appropriation Bill.[123] The power of corporate campaign contributions still reigns, it seems, in Congress.

At the same time, Obama has chosen to escalate the war and the number of troops in Afghanistan. Some 90 percent of the spending for Afghanistan in the Obama administration's current supplemental bill is military. Nor does the Obama administration scruple about attacking Pakistan with bombs and Hellfire missiles fired from MQ-9 Reaper and MQ-1 Predator drones.

And while Obama promises to reduce US troop presence in Iraq, the "withdrawal" of US troops is from the cities, and into rural bases just outside the cities. At the same time, his administration has increased the number of military contractors in both Iraq and Afghanistan. As Jeremy Scahill reports:

> According to new statistics released by the Pentagon, with Barack Obama as commander in chief, there has been a 23% increase in the number of "Private Security Contractors" working for the Department of Defense in Iraq in the second quarter of 2009 and a 29% increase in Afghanistan, which correlates to the build up of forces in the country. These numbers relate explicitly to DoD security conractors. Companies like Blackwater and its successor Triple Canopy work on State Department contracts and it is unclear if these contractors are included in the over-all statistics. This means, the number of individual security contractors could be quite higher, as could the scope of their expansion.[124]

The power of the military contractors has increased under the Obama administration, with the additional effect of obscuring the actual military presence and misleading the American public about the extent of the US commitment to an armed presence in Iraq and Afghanistan.

Finally, we cannot ignore the growing number of robot soldiers on the ground in Afghanistan, and especially in Iraq. As P. W. Singer reports, "When U.S. forces went into Iraq in 2003, they had zero robotic units on the ground. By the end of 2004, the number was up to 150. By the end of 2005 it was 2,400, and it more than doubled the next year. By the end of 2008, it was projected to reach as high as 12,000."[125]

After US troops and military contractors, these robot soldiers comprise the third largest army in Iraq. Together with the massive increase in unmanned aerial vehicles (UAVs) again, their presence further serves to mask, and mislead the public about, the US commitment to military dominance. This roboticization of the battlefield once again illustrates the new theory of war profiteering we have been proposing in this chapter. The corporations develop the technology and then sell that technology in order to profit from, and perpetuate, the war they have promoted.

While we can acknowledge that the use of such unmanned vehicles reduces the number of US troops being killed, there are long-term consequences that we need to examine. For example, if the "pilot" is at home in the United States in an office or university or research facility, would it not be legitimate to attack the pilot there? If research for such robots is being conducted (among many other projects) in a university, would it not make that university, with all its personnel, a legitimate military target? Or take another tack: the electromagnetic pulse (EMP) from a nuclear weapon detonated over a battlefield would instantly decommission all such unmanned vehicles. Would the deployment of such robotic weaponry, with such vulnerability, require the development of nuclear weaponry as defense?

In short, every development of weaponry in war has led to countermeasures. As researcher Eric Stoner puts it, "When it comes to killer robots, the stakes are high. If activists don't work to stop this robotics revolution in its tracks, science fiction has warned us about our potential fate."[126]

The Lost

I cannot close here without first honoring what we have lost and are losing by surrendering to the greed of the corporations. By the time this chapter is published, we will most probably have nearly 5,000 US military dead, and tens of thousands wounded. Nor will there be adequate care for the veterans who return. A recent report by Physicians for a National Health Program stated that already by 2004 there were 1.7 million veterans without health insurance, access to government hospitals, or clinics for veterans.

One reason for this (and the recent reports of scandalous health care for vets) is again, that health care for the military has been outsourced to private firms. Health Net, for example, was a private firm that was losing money in the public sphere. Once they were given a military contract, they experienced a $285 million increase in profits in 2005. In this regard, recall that Berrigan has written:

> The motto of the "Baals" [false gods in early Hebrew literature], here excoriated, comes to this: Everything has its price. Baal is, among other things, a market god.
>
> "Everything," including humankind, exists only "as priced." Indeed, the price tagged upon humans is their only reality.

> Humans are on sale, precious as jewels or gold, their price inflated
> or reduced, remaindered, expendable as slave labor, or to be discarded
> if unproductive, the disabled, the aged, dwellers in-utero, the
> condemned on death row.[127]

And to that we might now add, US veterans and the Iraqi people.

For all the veterans, there are spiritual and psychological wounds as well.[128] These are particularly difficult to heal because of the reluctance of any military person to admit that he or she is "weak." In addition, military "treatment" sometimes calls for personnel suffering from post-traumatic stress disorder (PTSD) to be treated in the war theater—with the supposed assumption that getting back into combat would signify a cure. Finally, when the warrior returns, the military asks if they feel they might be suffering from PTSD. If so, they should stay on the base and be treated. What might their answer be, when their families are waiting for them just outside the fence? And with all this, the US military still reports a 25 percent incidence of PTSD.

And in a larger sense, what will all of us Americans do as our civil and human rights, and our humanity itself, crumble under the ictus of war?

I speak of these first because, as Plato said long ago, "It is better to suffer harm than to do it." So we turn to the suffering of the Iraqi people. I have already indicated the losses Iraq suffered during the twelve-year sanction regime. I have spent most of this chapter speaking about the loss of economic, political, and personal independence by Iraqis.

Finally, I note that in October 2006, the *Lancet* published a well-researched, peer-reviewed study estimating conservatively that the invasion and occupation had taken the lives of 655,000 Iraqis.[129] One can only imagine the trauma for the survivors—especially the children. In one news story we heard from [Child psychiatrist Dr. Ali] Hameed that there isn't enough money or manpower to treat the million or more of Iraq's children he estimates are deeply traumatized, much less the millions of children learning to live—and die—by the gun.

> "So they are being trained to be killers?" asked [CBS News correspondent Kimberly] Dozier.
> "I'm sorry to say that I think yes," Hameed answered.[130]

"[I]t is decreed by the temple god that little children suffer and die for the sins of the mighty," writes Berrigan in a passage that is both remorsefully retrospective and painfully prescient.[131]

Once in our New York Jesuit community, we were discussing our reactions to 9/11. I told of how my first (and second) reaction was denial. Older in the movement, much wiser and more sorrowful, Daniel said that his reaction was, "So . . . it's come home at last."

What shall we do when all—or even a fraction of—this horror we've visited upon these peoples "comes home?" Will we excoriate "the Arabs?" Tell of how "Islam is a violent religion?" Torture ever more people? Turn again to the very violence that brought us to this pass in the first place? As Kathy Kelly and Brian Terrell write about their protest of the drone attacks on Pakistan, "In the past few days, the Taliban have responded to US drone attacks with attacks of their own and with threats of further retaliation which have provoked renewed drone attacks by the United States. Are we to believe that the predictable spiral of violence is the only way forward?"[132]

By now I hope the reader sees that, like Daniel Berrigan and his companions, we must join together in nonviolent opposition, but this time in resistance to the increasing encroachment of corporations on governance. One effective strategy is a "corporate counter-recruitment" campaign, similar to the military counter-recruitment campaigns in schools. That is, nonviolent activists could identify war profiteers and block their recruitment efforts in colleges and universities. Activists could educate job candidates about the war profiteering practices of certain companies, then get candidates to sign a pledge that they will not work for those companies, and will discourage their friends from working there as well. These pledges can be sent directly to the CEO of the war profiteer. Finally, "Catonsville Nine" style direct actions can be directed against corporations since, more and more, that is where the "recruitment" for war is taking place.

And in a larger sense, we must adopt more nonviolent lifestyles. The United States consumes about 20.7 million barrels of oil a day. That's the equivalent of the oil consumption of China, Japan, Germany, Russia, and India—*combined*! The US military alone consumes about 365,000 barrels of oil a day—almost double the daily consumption of the entire country of Ireland.

That is just one example. Overall, the United States is 5 percent of the world's people, consuming 25 percent of the world's goods. This disparity, this injustice to the rest of the world, does not occur voluntarily. The "American way of life" (which our politicians are always urging us to defend) is enforced by the most lethal military in the history of the world. In just one measure: if the dollar amounts of military expenditures are totaled correctly, the United States will spend about $647 billion in 2008[133]—more than the *rest of the world combined*. Economically, such violence is unsustainable, as our current recession should indicate to us. Most seriously, our planet earth cannot bear such violence.

The boldness and originality of the action of the Catonsville Nine were unprecedented in their resistance to the destruction of life, land, and community. Unless we wish to "perish together as fools," we will need similar visionary activists to turn us from the path of corporate profiteering toward building of the beloved community.

A Conversation with Daniel Berrigan

Anna J. Brown and James L. Marsh

Editors' Note: Anna Brown (AB) and James Marsh (JM) met with Daniel Berrigan (DB) during the summer of 2008 in his apartment. The point of the meeting was to allow for Berrigan to have the "final word" in this volume. What follows is an edited transcription of their conversation.

AB: I have been acutely aware of and, perhaps more so, challenged by certain anniversaries this year. Throughout 2008, for example, there is the 40th anniversary of the assassination of Dr. Martin Luther King Jr., the 40th anniversary of the Catonsville Nine; the 75th anniversary of Dorothy Day and Peter Maurin's founding of the Catholic Worker; and the 40th anniversary of the death of Thomas Merton. My sense is that most people are not aware of what these folks said and were trying to say, and that we need to hear these voices more than ever. I am wondering if you have been thinking about any of these anniversaries and of the ways in which a justice- and faith-bound people might rightfully commemorate them?

DB: My role in all of this, the 40th, the 75th, etc. In one sense, it's been quite passive because of my health. In another sense, it's been very spiritual and very active in trying to carry the memories and not let them die in an era of nostalgia, which I think is always a temptation. It is as though we are seeking to recreate better times by just hauling out the memories of friends, people, and events. It seems to me that to be true to memory is to reproduce the essential goodness and truth telling that mark these lives and this work, all of which we are still trying to understand and walk with today. So, I was thinking especially of Merton's anniversary because in a sense his death crowned the year, coming in the dead of winter and in the last month of the year. And out of all of these figures, it seems to me, his influence has grown most markedly. His work is still being published, particularly his work on war and peace. This is the work that we anguished over because it had just been tossed by the wayside by the authorities of the Church. Suddenly that work is before us again and sounding really as fresh as yesterday or this morning. He urges us, for example, to take seriously this whole business of saving the earth, of saving the human community, etc. So it's very heartening to know that his voice is still vibrant and of the moment. It's also heartening to know that the *Trial of the Catonsville Nine* is still being produced around the country and around the world. These are very hard blessings. They are blessings but they are very harsh because they speak of unfinished work and unfinished humanity and unfinished Christianity, and to take it one step further is crucial.

AB: Yes, that is why I said "challenged," because there is nothing that you can really be at ease with in these anniversaries. As you have said, we can't just mark them; we must live them, we must get in to what's essential about them so that we may be sane in these insane times.

JM: I was thinking along the lines of the Catonsville Nine, having in mind, more specifically, the meaning of Catonsville forty years later. What's changed, what's remained the same, and what's gotten worse? What obvious ways, for example, have things gotten worse within the nation and the international community since the 1960s and the destructiveness unleashed then by the American empire? Looking back on that now— that era compared to now—it certainly wasn't an idyllic time but it somehow seems to have been much more of an innocent and hopeful time. Do you agree with that? Things are a lot worse; I know, in terms of the amount of the world we are trying to control, the Middle East, Latin and Central America, etc.

DB: I think it's always helpful for me in a quiet way, perhaps in a very small way, to reflect on the meaning of "we" or "ourselves," "we are," etc., because it gets kind of amorphous. People tend to mix identity, whether it's Christianity or citizenship, and which is subject to change, modification, politics, etc. But I think often I have to help clarify that in front of an audience, especially, questions like: What are we to do? What are we allowed to do? What are we forbidden to do? Is everything that is allowed as Christians allowed as American citizens, or is there a very sharp distinction between behavior and ethos so that we can recognize in a time of crisis like this the fact that not everything is allowed. And the very fact of being at war is a call to Christians to say "no" instead of internalizing or romanticizing or melding this whole question. When that's done, we become part of an ethic that says, "Well, what's going on is allowed and it's allowed because it's going on," and so the hideously abnormal gets normalized and we end up, it seems to me, faceless and voiceless. The mass of our people are victimized by politics and by the media. It's a very tough situation. We are called to be sensible and realistic about the state of our world without being completely absorbed into it so that we have nothing to say about it, nothing to do about it. We're too involved. We have nowhere to go with or without it. We must grapple with the questions of where do we go, what do we do, and what can be realistically expected given the world and given whom we are. I think, if we stop with just the analysis of how bad things are, we miss the point of the Gospel which is saying to us in various ways, in all sorts of ways, what is to be done.

JM: The message of Catonsville forty years later, as you said, is one of hope and resolve.

DB: I think so. And for me and certainly for Anna and for all these events that have occurred around Kairos, in the Social Justice House at Saint Peter's College, and in the young people joining in the peace movement, etc., that hope is being verified in very modest ways, but in real ways because people are not just languishing, not giving up. They're saying, "Let's move it, let's do this, let's try this, on to the next action, etc." Sure, there's hope, there's hope.

AB: This book brings together a series of essays—some of which were presented at the 2005 American Catholic Philosophical Association's meeting at the University of Notre Dame—that examine the ways in which your thought and action have challenged and deepened Catholic social teaching. Our readers, we suspect, will be fellow academics. With that community in mind, can you speak about your decision to leave

Cornell University in 1968, and to leave what you loved—your teaching and your students—temporarily behind, so that you could be part of the Catonsville action. For those of us who are wrestling with how to live the academic-activist life, can you speak to what brought you to Catonsville and how you negotiate life amidst two goods, the good of the academic life and the good of the activist life, whose demands and responsibilities often conflict with one another?

DB: Well, I think the influences were many; some of them were very modest and some very proximate and pressing. The latter, of course, was the trip to Hanoi in February of 1968 and the visit of Philip [Berrigan] in April of that same year. And those two converging was a huge kind of calling. I was sort of carrying the burden of Hanoi and not knowing where to go with it: what I had seen there, the daily dose of bombing, the contempt shown by American politicos and the military for our effort to get the pilots home, etc. It was very difficult to come home with that bag full of horror because I couldn't just dump it somewhere and then go on as usual at Cornell. And then Philip arrived and things clarified. He proposed something absolutely audacious, as was his wont. He said, and I'll paraphrase, "Tom Lewis and the rest of us are already in trouble for the Baltimore Four, and we're proposing to do it again while we're still out on appeal. It looks as though it would be a simple fire rather than a blood pouring and you're invited in." So, in true Jesuit fashion, I said, "Well, give me a couple of days because I want to put down the 'pros' and the 'cons' and have some meditative time." I knew it was a very serious undertaking. I did my discernment, and much to my chagrin, the "pros" outweighed the "cons." Then I said, "Oh dear, here we go." Though that kind of simplifies it, that's what happened.

JM: When I think about Catonsville in the context of that time, I think about that action in relationship to the Catholic Church and to American universities in the 1960s. The early part of those years was filled with Vatican II, John Kennedy being elected President, and the the American Catholic Church discovering America or, perhaps better said, America discovering it. Catholic universities, like Fordham, were consciously trying to move from being what they perceived as narrow, Thomist enclaves to being more a part of the mainstream. All of this was done, as I remember, very triumphalistically and very positively. There was the sense that this movement was all well and good. The Catholic Church becomes integrated with America, the Catholic universities become integrated with America and then, out of the blue in 1968, comes Catonsville as the big "no," or at least a question mark.

DB: Well, there was a question mark in the Ivy League, too. There was an escalating development in the resistance movement to the war in the Ivy League, a nonreligious lot. And that was a mixed blessing; it became the Weather people [Weathermen]. In this development, the hidden tendency toward violent reprisal was set loose; the seduction of violence came to the fore. On the other hand, there was much working in our favor. I think, though much against his will, the president of Cornell University said—at the time of our trial for Catonsville—that he was trying to stem the tide of approval and blessing that was surrounding the Catonsville Nine among the students and the faculty. He also said, however, that those who attended the trial in Baltimore would certainly not be penalized in any way, which was quite a concession because the trial was to begin a week before the academic term was to begin.

I think, as far as the Catholic community's response to Catonsville, there was shock—and initial sense of disbelief—and I remember saying to Philip, when we were all finally released on appeal, that we were going to have to have a couple of years to talk with the Catholic community. He agreed with me. I think we were in agreement, too, in our anticipation that this was going to be our toughest audience and the one that would be the most easily angered. It took a long time before the changes in the Church began to take hold and we had to learn how to stand, if you will, before a Catholic audience. Were we there simply to put down any people who were "pro-war"? It shortly became clear that that kind of stance was useless and that we could talk to anyone in the Church, including large numbers of veterans, as long as we told our story of being a Catholic family who were up to our neck in war, not the Vietnam War, of course, but certainly the World War II. It seemed that kind of honesty, rightness, and fraternity on the war question was a great kind of way of entering into their lives in a way that was not threatening or morally superior.

JM: Why do you think it was Catholics that were the hardest to talk to? Do you have any sense of that? Was it Cardinal Spellman and the Church in New York with its Cold War, anti-Russian rhetoric?

DB: I think it was more the supposition about the priesthood that made this scandalous and shocking. More so, it was a sense of betrayal. Our priests have betrayed us by getting into this kind of messy no-person land while putting the Church on trial and disgracing the priesthood. We felt a great deal about that; we heard a great deal about that.

AB: As I was reading through *Lights Out in the House of the Dead*, where you write about your time in prison for the Catonsville action, I was wondering if you would recommend that experience to my fellow academics. If so, why do we need to go there? Why do we need to join folks in jail? What did you see there? What did you learn while in prison?

DB: Well, let's step back a bit. The question that you bring up, Anna, became quite the question in South Africa when I was there after Sharpesville. The Catholic community was so very tightly bound up with apartheid, at least by way of ignorance, by way of distancing, by the "sweetness" of the white skin, by suburban living and by being middle class. They were just not hearing anything, by and large, about the horrors that were just next-door and about what people were enduring, right up to the slaughter.

I tried to awaken Catholics in parishes that the bishop set out for me. I tried to say the forbidden words, and to talk about the violence of apartheid, and tried to get a real response. It took the form of telling about everything, from Selma to Catonsville. I sensed a kind of shock running through the crowd, and the response being: "Well, if we get in trouble, what happens to our children?" I responded, "We've learned to put that question in a different way and, perhaps, even more powerfully: What happens to our children if we don't get into trouble?" I can't be sure, but it seemed to be a moment for sowing seeds in a very tight environment. I was certainly under the aegis of a great bishop in Johannesburg. He was actually, at one point, indicted for some statements that we coauthored, but they didn't dare bring him to trial. He was very anxious that I be exposed to the Catholic community, and I was quite pleased to do so. I didn't have the sense going in that we would solve the problem—that would be absurd, but at least that we were trying and that we had something to offer. We tried to reach out, to do something.

JM: Would you say that the impact of your thought and actions have been international in scope?

DB: I think so.

AB: As well as local, and "human," I would add. Would you speak to your meeting with the doctor last summer, whose draft file, apparently, was burned during the Catonsville action?

DB: Yes, that meeting occurred during a medical adventure a year ago. In June I was taken to the emergency room for an infection in my hip, and in a lot of pain. We were hardly getting any kind of medical attention there but toward the evening the medical person on charge of the whole chaotic scene pointed to my alcove and directed a doctor toward me. Over he came, and he said something like, "Are you the real Dan Berrigan?" And I said (laughing), "Oh, I think so." He then said, "Well, I want to thank you. In 1968 I was bound for Vietnam and you saved me." He didn't say, "You burned my draft card." What he said, in fact, was quite interesting: "You saved me from the slaughter. I went to medical school instead, and I am here to take care of you."

JM: That's an incredible story.

DB: I am sure he was referring to Catonsville, because he said '68, and that was the year of the action, of course. He did take care of me. He was very skilled and he was an excellent surgeon. So, once again, we see that crime pays off!

JM: Well, there have to be just countless numbers of people and groups of people, some of them you don't know but whom you have affected positively.

DB: I suppose that may be true.

JM: We who have felt the fire and heat of Catonsville, and by "we" I mean the Church, the nation, your own action at the time, etc. Now, however, it's a different time and there is a different Church, a different scene. You have, for example, the changes in the Church implemented after Vatican II; you have Catholic universities, like Boston College and Fordham University, who are confident, in the mainstream, etc. But then you have something like Boston College inviting former Secretary of State Condoleezza Rice to be its commencement speaker in the spring of 2006, only to have them follow up by inviting former Attorney General Michael Mukesey to give an address at their Law School. Both Rice and Mukesey, as we know, were part of the inner circle of former President George W. Bush and gave the "green light" for our nation's use of torture. Torture, aside from being banned under international law, is a gross violation of Catholic social teaching. Your message, moreover, stressed the incompatibility of Christianity with war and with empire and with militarism. In my own work, I call this tendency that of "cozying up to empire." And I find it incredible that, forty years later, the Church and Catholic universities are still cozying up to empire.

DB: Well, much of the vitality of these campuses depends upon a relationship with peace communities, like the relationship between Kairos and Saint Peter's College, for example. The peace communities make an effort to salvage something of a genuine article by a manifestation of [Christian] faith: the Sermon on the Mount, love your enemies, don't go to war or engage in these periodic military ventures in broken countries, etc. It just seems to me that the best things in the Catholic campuses are happening off campus in many ways. I take great help from the martyrs, but the real thing is modest.

AB: In an article published by the Catholic Worker in 1982, "What Is Yet Lacking?" you write about your brother Jerry and about an action that he did at the Pentagon for which he went to jail. What did the example set by Jerry, who was a professor of literature at the time, mean to you? How may his example speak to other academics?

DB: Jerry was one of the few that I have noted in my own checkered career who used tenure in a very creative way. The college couldn't really get rid of him. He would go and do these things and then serve thirty days or whatever it was. Yet he always did it with great care for his students, who, he made sure, knew what he was up to and why he had done it. He always made sure he had a competent substitute so the class wouldn't be marooned. That had a great impact on his campus, and it was very new for an academic to take that kind of risk. Though the world seems not very condoning of this kind of thing, still, here it was. Jerry was kind of the "unsung third," but he kept at it beautifully and still does. He was arrested a couple of weeks ago in Syracuse, by the way. The great number of people who showed up at my brother John's funeral, well that was really a tribute to Jerry. Local peace people came in large numbers. There is such a vibrant Catholic community of peacemakers up there; it's just marvelous. It was so difficult for so many years.

JM: That strikes me as another kind of influence or impact of your work, because that kind of vibrant Catholic peacemaking community wasn't around in the 1950s or 1960s. I read yours and Thomas Merton's and Dorothy Day's writings from that period and your voices were those crying in the wilderness. Now, in different ways, small and very modest ways, seeds have been sown.

DB: Yes, seeds have been sown.

AB: In a recent issue of the Agitator, published by the Los Angeles Catholic Worker, there is an article that claims that the Catholic Worker Movement is actually growing these days. The author also says something quite beautiful about Dorothy Day, which is that she didn't set out to start a movement. What Day did instead was set out to befriend people. She simply befriended people in the community; she was steadfast and loyal in her friendships. From that base—and not with a concern for results—the movement actually grew.

DB: Dorothy always had a few steadfast Jesuit friends, many around *America* magazine, and the one who stood by her the most was John LaFarge. Of course, he was moving in so many directions, but always well, very well. I had been frequenting the Catholic Worker and I hadn't yet been ordained, though I was always bringing students down. This was in the late 1940s, and I was slowly getting a little bit of light on the spiritual and intellectual connections Dorothy made about war, the poor, the war on the Bowery, the homeless, etc. And I started bringing up these connections in summer school and in various Jesuit apostolates and there was a very mixed response. Essentially, it came down to something very simple: this woman was admirable as long as she was in her backyard cleaning up the Bowery. I am using a metaphor, but she's "gone public" on the streets of New York, she's in Union Square, etc. and she's proclaiming something that is outside of her competence, this business about war.

JM: That sounds like sexism, Jesuit sexism.

DB: Oh, a lot of that. But also this kind of territory, the territory that belongs to the experts, like political scientists and such. "We're going to tell her where she belongs because we're the experts," that kind of talk. It made me "worse" than ever when I heard this stuff going on! I said, "There's more here than meets the ear."

JM: She should be seen, I suppose, and not heard!

DB: The four watercolors on the wall over by the door, those were done by Tom Lewis. He did the same scene of a tree in Massachusetts in four different seasons. This large watercolor is also his, and this woodcut, which has a Chinese quality to it, is also his.

AB: He came down to the Saint Peter's Social Justice House for Liz McAlister's seminar on nonviolence, and he saw his artwork all over the house, as well as Elmer Maas's picture. To see all of that all was wonderful for him.

DB: I may have told Anna this, but I was sitting here about two weeks ago reading a letter from him, though his writing was almost incomprehensible. He said that he was overjoyed that there was going to be a great exhibition of his work of fifty-two years in Worcester. No wonder he was rejoicing; he's never had anything like this before. Later in the day the phone rang and I found out that he had died in his sleep the night before. It was that close.

JM: Isn't that something. Is the exhibit still going to take place?

DB: Oh, yes, it has already started. Amazing.

INTRODUCTION

1. Daniel Berrigan, *And the Risen Bread*, ed. John Dear (New York: Fordham University Press, 1998), 144.

2. Daniel Berrigan, *Poetry, Drama, Prose*, ed. Michael True (Maryknoll, N.Y.: Orbis, 1988), 6.

3. Daniel Berrigan, *Testimony: The Word Made Fresh* (Maryknoll, N.Y.: Orbis, 2004), 202.

4. George Anderson, "Looking Back in Gratitude: A Conversation with Daniel Berrigan," *America* 201, no. 1 (July 6, 2009), accessed August 15, 2011, http://tinyurl.com/looking-back-in-gratitude.

5. Berrigan, *Poetry*, 7.

6. Ibid., 8.

7. Berrigan, *Testimony*, 91.

8. Daniel Berrigan, *To Dwell in Peace* (San Francisco: Harper & Row, 1986), 142.

9. Daniel Berrigan, *The Trial of the Catonsville Nine* (Boston: Beacon, 1970), 84–85.

10. Berrigan, *Poetry*, 11.

11. Ibid., 12.

12. Berrigan, *Trial of the Catonsville Nine*, 87.

13. Daniel Berrigan, *Night Flight to Hanoi: War Diary with 11 Poems* (New York: Harper & Row, 1968), 56.

14. Ibid., 129.

15. Berrigan, *Poetry*, 49.

16. Berrigan, *Trial of the Catonsville Nine*, 93–94.

17. Daniel Berrigan, *The Nightmare of God* (Marion, S.D.: Rose Hill, 1999), 3.

18. Isaiah 2:4 (New Revised Standard Edition).

19. Berrigan, *And the Risen Bread*, 360.

20. Daniel Berrigan, *Ten Commandments for the Long Haul* (Nashville, Tenn.: Abingdon, 1981), 25.

21. Ibid., 113 and 117.

22. William Griffin, "Book Review: Gandhi & Jesus: The Saving Power of Nonviolence," *The Catholic Worker* LXXVL, no. 4 (June/July 2009): 5.

23. Daniel Berrigan, "What Is Yet Lacking?" *The Catholic Worker* XLIX, no. 3 (August 1982): 1.

24. Berrigan, *To Dwell in Peace*, 100.

25. Chris Hedges, "Forty Years After Catonsville," *The Nation* (June 2, 2008), accessed August 15, 2011, http://tinyurl.com/berrigan-forty.

26. Ibid.

27. Daniel Berrigan, *Minor Prophets, Major Themes* (Marion, S. Dak.: Fortkamp, 1995), 48.

28. Pope Benedict XVI, "*Caritas In Veritate*" (section 21), http://tinyurl .com/caritas-in-verite.

29. Ibid., section 22.

30. Daniel Berrigan, *Exodus: Let My People Go* (Eugene, Ore.: Cascade, 2008),155.

PHILOSOPHY AND THE PROPHETIC CHALLENGE

Martin J. De Nys

1. See Bernard Lonergan, *Method in Theology* (New York: Herder and Herder, 1973), for a discussion of being in love as completing the process of self-transcendence.

2. G. W. F. Hegel, *Phenomenology of Spirit*, trans. A. V. Miller, (Oxford: Clarendon Press, 1977), 16.

3. Lonergan, *Method in Theology*, 20.

4. Bernard Lonergan, *Insight: A Study of Human Understanding*, (Toronto: University of Toronto Press, 1997), 209–10, 244–360.

5. Ibid., 372–75.

6. Ibid., 196–267.

7. See Lonergan, *Method in Theology*, 105. Lonergan is fond of citing Rom. 5,5, which he does here by speaking of "God's love flooding our hearts through the Holy Spirit given to us."

8. Thomas Merton, *New Seeds of Contemplation*, (New York: New Directions, 1972), 25.

9. Ibid., 64.

10. Ibid., 203.

11. Ibid., 120.

12. " . . . we must begin again to unwind and unlearn, if we are to have anything new to offer the times. It will be necessary that some, perhaps even wasting time, become contemplatives, that is to say, men of profound and available sanity." Daniel Berrigan, *No Bars to Manhood* (New York: Doubleday, 1970), 63.

13. Daniel Berrigan, *Jeremiah: The World, the Wound of God* (Minneapolis: Fortress Press, 1999), xi–xii.

14. William Stringfellow, *An Ethic for Christians and Other Aliens in a Strange Land*, (Waco, Tex.: Word Books, 1978), 55.

15. Ibid.,56.

16. Berrigan, *Jeremiah*, 40.

17. Ibid., 51.

18. Ibid., 45.

19. Ibid., 115–24.

20. Berrigan, *No Bars to Manhood*, 97. These comments appear in the chapter that deals with Jeremiah.

21. Ibid.,176.

22. Ibid.,161.

23. Ibid., 31.

DANIEL BERRIGAN'S THEOLOGY: RETRIEVING THE PROPHETIC AND
PROCLAIMING THE RESURRECTION
Robert A. Ludwig

1. Bernard Lonergan, *Method in Theology* (New York: Herder and Herder, 1972).

2. David Tracy, *Blessed Rage for Order: The New Pluralism in Theology* (New York: Seabury Press, 1975), and *The Analogical Imagination: Christian Theology and the Culture of Pluralism* (New York: Crossroad, 1981).

3. Daniel Berrigan, *Minor Prophets, Major Themes* (Marion, S.Dak.: Fortkamp Publishing, 1995).

4. Daniel Berrigan, *Isaiah: Spirit of Courage, Gift of Tears* (Minneapolis: Fortress, 1996).

5. Daniel Berrigan, *Ezekiel: Vision in the Dust* (Maryknoll, N.Y.: Orbis Books, 1997).

6. Daniel Berrigan, *Jeremiah: The World, the Wound of God* (Minneapolis: Fortress, 1999).

7. Daniel Berrigan, *Daniel: Under the Siege of the Divine* (Farmington, Pa.: The Plough Publishing House, 1998).

8. Daniel Berrigan, *Job: And Death No Dominion* (Franklin, Wisc.: Sheed & Ward, 2000).

9. Daniel Berrigan, *Wisdom: The Feminine Face of God* (Franklin, Wisc.: Sheed & Ward, 2002).

10. Daniel Berrigan, *Lamentations: From New York to Kabul and Beyond* (Franklin, Wisc.: Sheed & Ward, 2002).

11. Daniel Berrigan, *Whereon to Stand: Acts of the Apostles* (Marion, S.Dak.: Fortkamp Publishing, 1991).

12. Daniel Berrigan, *Nightmare of God* (Portland, Oreg.: Sunburst Press, 1982).

13. Walter Brueggemann, *The Prophetic Imagination* (Minneapolis: Fortress Press, 2001).

14. Berrigan, *Minor Prophets, Major Themes*, viii–ix.

15. Berrigan, *Jeremiah*, xi–xii.

16. Ibid., vii–viii.

17. Berrigan, *Ezekiel*, xx.

18. Daniel Berrigan, *Testimony: The Word Made Flesh* (Maryknoll, N.Y.: Orbis Books, 2004), ix.

19. Ibid., xi–xii.

20. Ibid., 220.

21. Berrigan spoke about this Caravaggio painting in a retreat at Kirkridge in September 2003, and again in a lecture at Loyola University of Chicago in October 2005.

22. Daniel Berrigan homily, May 5, 2006.

THE STATE OF RESISTANCE: ON THE RELEVANCE OF
DANIEL BERRIGAN'S WORK TO CATHOLIC SOCIAL THOUGHT
Michael Baxter

1. Daniel Berrigan, foreword to *Quotations From Chairman Jesus* by David Kirk (New York: Bantam, 1971); *The Trial of the Catonsville Nine* (Boston: Beacon Press, 1970); *The Dark Night of Resistance* (New York: Doubleday, 1971).

2. Berrigan, *Dark Night*, 2.

3. Pope Leo XIII, *Rerum Novarum*, n. 22. *Social Wellsprings: Fourteen Epochal Documents by Pope Leo XIII*, ed. Joseph Husslein, SJ (Milwaukee, Wisc.: Bruce Publishing Company, 1940), 183.

4. Pope Leo XIII, *Aeterni Patris*, n. 12. *Social Wellsprings: Fourteen Epochal Documents by Pope Leo XIII*, ed. Joseph Husslein, SJ (Milwaukee, Wisc.: Bruce Publishing Company, 1940), 257.

5. William M. Halsey, *The Survival of American Innocence: Catholicism in an Era of Disillusionment*, 1920–1940 (Notre Dame: University of Notre Dame Press, 1980). Philip Gleason, *Contending with Modernity: Catholic Higher Education in the Twentieth Century* (New York: Oxford, 1995).

6. Gleason, *Contending*, 105–66.

7. *Proceedings of the American Catholic Philosophical Association* 1 (January 5, 1926): 9. See Halsey, *Survival*, 145.

8. *Ibid.*, 13–14.

9. Moorhouse F. X. Millar, SJ, "The History and Development of the Democratic Theory of Government in Christian Tradition," "Modern 'Practical Liberty' and Common Sense," and "Our Medieval Inheritance of Liberty," in *The State and the Church*, ed. Moorhouse F. X. Millar, SJ and John A. Ryan (New York: MacMillan 1922), 99–194. (Incidentally, in a letter to me in 2003, Daniel recalled crossing paths with Father Millar while in formation, "during the salad course" as he put it.)

10. Halsey, *Survival*, 61–83.

11. Ernan McMullin, "Presidential Address: Who Are We?" in *Proceedings of the American Catholic Philosophical Association* 1967 (Washington, D.C.: n.p., 1967), 4.

12. For more on this argument, see Michael J. Baxter, "John Courtney Murray," in *The Blackwell Companion to Political Theology* (Maldan, Mass.: Blackwell Publishing, 2004), 150–64.

13. In noting the similarity between Murray's account of public philosophy and his successors' account of public theology, I am drawing on an argument made by Joseph Komonchak, "John Courtney Murray and the Redemption of History: Natural Law and Theology," in *John Courtney Murray and the Growth of Tradition*, ed. J. Leon Hooper, SJ, and Todd David Whitmore (Kansas City: Sheed & Ward, 1996), 60–81.

14. Regarding these last two figures, see, for example, George Weigel, *Tranquillitas Ordinis* (New York: Oxford University Press, 1987) and David Hollenbach, *Justice, Peace, and Human Rights* (New York: Crossroad, 1988).

15. The phrase comes from Richard John Neuhaus, *The Catholic Moment* (San Francisco: Harper & Row, 1987). A brief, incisive statement of how Neuhaus's "Catholic moment" was anticipated by Murray thirty years before can be found in Michael Budde, *The Two Churches: Catholicism and Capitalism in the World System* (Durham, N.C.: Duke University Press, 1992), 102–25. Given the trajectory that Budde sketches, going back to John Ryan, combined with the intellectual agenda of Catholic scholars after World War I, one can say that the Catholic moment in some sense was anticipated sixty years before. Indeed, as Budde hints, this theme is wrapped up with aspects of US Catholic nationalism that can be found in the writings of two nineteenth-century Catholic figures, Orestes Brownson and Isaac Hecker. See Budde, *Two Churches*, 74–86.

16. National Conference of Catholic Bishops, *Peace and Vietnam*, in quoted in Ronald Musto, *The Catholic Peace Tradition* (Maryknoll, N.Y.: Orbis, 1986), 255n188. National Conference of Catholic Bishops, *The Challenge of Peace: God's Promise and Our Response. A Pastoral Letter on War and Peace*, May 3, 1983 (Washington, D.C.: United States Catholic Conference, 1983), para 186.

17. G. E. M. Anscombe, "War and Murder" and "Mr. Truman's Degree," in *Ethics, Religion and Politics: Collected Philosophical Papers* (Oxford: Basil Blackwell, 1981), 3:51–71. John Finnis, Joseph Boyle, and Germain Grisez, *Nuclear Deterrence, Morality and Realism* (Oxford: Clarendon Press, 1987). Alasdair MacIntyre, *Dependent Rational Animals* (Chicago: Open Court, 1999), 131–33.

18. Alasdair MacIntyre, *After Virtue*, 2nd ed. (Notre Dame: University of Notre Dame Press, 1984), 263.

19. The retreat was given by Daniel Berrigan on December 6–8, 1987. A tape of it is on file with the author. For a book gathering together these themes, see Daniel Berrigan, *Whereon to Stand: The Acts of the Apostles and Ourselves* (Baltimore, Md.: Fortkamp, 1991).

20. For a brief summary of the theological context that shaped Berrigan's thought, see Michael J. Baxter, foreword to *Wisdom: The Feminine Face of God*, by Daniel Berrigan (Chicago: Sheed & Ward, 2001).

21. Peter Maurin, *Easy Essays* (Chicago: Franciscan Herald Press, 1977), 37.

22. Berrigan, *Dark Night of Resistance*, 172.

FATHER BERRIGAN AND THE MARXIST-COMMUNIST "MENACE"
William L. McBride

1. "There can be no just war. There never was one."—Daniel Berrigan, "Love Your Enemies: There Is No Just War; the Gospel Is Always Relevant," in *Testimony: The Word Made Fresh* (Maryknoll, N.Y.: Orbis Books, 2004), 61.

2. *Capital: A Critical Analysis of Capitalist Production* (Moscow: Foreign Languages Publishing House, 1961), 1:751. In the very next sentence, Marx cites an author, William Howitt, writing about the "Christian colonial system," stating that "the barbarities and desperate outrages of the so-called Christian race, throughout every region of the world, and upon every people they have been able to subdue, are not to be paralleled by those of any other race, however fierce, however untaught, and however reckless of mercy and of shame, in any age of the earth."

3. Daniel Berrigan, *To Dwell in Peace* (New York: Harper & Row, 1987), 69.

4. Ibid., 70.

5. See Garaudy, *Mon tour du siècle en solitaire: Mémoires* (Paris: Éditions Robert Laffont, 1989). For his account of the St. Louis adventure, see 222–24; it took place, remarkably, in 1966, as anxieties over the war in Vietnam were mounting.

THE LANGUAGE OF THE INCANDESCENT HEART: DANIEL BERRIGAN'S
AND ETTY HILLESUM'S RESPONSES TO A CULTURE OF DEATH
Anna J. Brown

1. The Kairos community, cofounded by Berrigan in 1978, is an ecumenically faith-based community of resistance. Its primary focus has been nuclear disarmament and nonviolent peacemaking. Its New York City–based members meet biweekly for prayer, reflection, fellowship and nonviolent acts of protest and civil disobedience.

2. "How are we to live our lives?" is a question that comes up repeatedly in *The Dark Night of Resistance*, a book Berrigan wrote while on the lam from the FBI following the Catonsville Nine trial See Daniel Berrigan, *The Dark Night of Resistance* (New York: Doubleday, 1971).

3. Johannes Paulus PP II, *Evangelium vitae*: To the Bishops, Priests, and Deacons, Men and Women religious, lay faithful and all people of Good Will on the Value and Inviolability of Human Life." March 3, 1995, accessed August 15, 2011, http://tinyurl.com/evangelium-v.

4. Ibid.

5. Ibid.

6. Ibid.

7. Pope Benedict XVI, "On the Revolution of Love," February 18, 2007, http://tinyurl.com/revolution-love (accessed August 15, 2011).

8. Ibid.

9. Ibid.

10. Ibid.

11. Catholic Peace Fellowship. "The Moral Compass of Benedict XVI: Where Will His Commitment to Peace Lead Us?" *Sign of Peace* 5, no. 1 (Spring 2006): 17, accessed August 15, 2011, http://tinyurl.com/commitment-to-peace.

12. In 2003, Pope Benedict XVI condemned the Iraq war as one that was "illegal, immoral and unjust." The war did not meet the right reasons and proportionality criteria of just war theory. In addition, he noted that "the concept of 'preventive war' does not appear in the *Catechism of the Catholic Church*." See "The Moral Compass of Benedict XVI," 17.

13. For information on the number of dead and refugees, see Tom Englehardt. "Escalation by the Numbers: What progress Really Means," *Tom Dispatch*, August 13, 2007, http://tinyurl.com/escalation-numbers (accessed August 15, 2011). For the cost of the war in Iraq, see "The Three Trillion Dollar War: Nobel Laureate Joseph Stiglitz and Harvard Economist Linda Bilmes on the True Cost of the U.S. Invasion and Occupation of Iraq," *Democracy Now*, February 29, 2008, accessed August 15, 2011, http://tinyurl.com/three-trillion-war. For an accounting of the shredding of civil liberties

and the use of torture, see Barbara J. Oshlansky. *Democracy Detained: Secret Unconstitutional* Practices *in the U.S. War on Terror* (New York: Seven Stories Press, 2007).

14. Daniel Berrigan, "America Is Hard to Find," in *And the Risen Bread: Selected Poems, 1957–1997,* ed. John Dear, SJ (New York: Fordham University Press, 1998), 143.

15. Ibid., 143.

16. Fyodor Dostoevsky, *The Brothers Karamazov*, trans. Richard Pevear and Larissa Volokhonsky (New York: Vintage, 1991), 53.

17. Ibid., 56.

18. Ibid., 58.

19. Ibid., 58.

20. Ibid., 58.

21. Ibid., 58.

22. Berrigan reformulates St. John of the Cross's classic work, *Dark Night of the Soul*, to reflect upon the work and journey of the peacemaker.

23. On May 17, 1968, Berrigan and eight others (including his brother, Philip) entered a draft board office in Catonsville, Maryland, and removed approximately 378 A-1 draft records. They burned the files using homemade napalm in the parking lot outside of the office. All nine were arrested for the action, were found guilty of all charges in a court of law, and were sentenced to prison for two to three years. Five of the nine defendants, including Daniel Berrigan, decided not to cooperate with the FBI and did not show up on the date they were to begin their prison terms. Daniel Berrigan was "underground" for about ten months and was eventually captured by the FBI on Block Island, Rhode Island, in August 1969.

24. Berrigan, *The Dark Night of Resistance*, 12.

25. Berrigan, "Etty Hillesum," in *And the Risen Bread*, 300

26. Ettly Hillesum, *An Interrupted Life* and *Letters from Westerbork*, trans. and ed. Eva Hoffman (New York: Henry Holt, 1996), 199.

27. Berrigan, *The Dark Night of Resistance*, 2. The line "Of Deeper Origin" is found in Berrigan's poem "Zen Shovel" in *And the Risen Bread*, 233.

28. Ibid., 3.

29. Berrigan, "My Name," in *And the Risen Bread*, 117.

30. Daniel Berrigan, "Living as Though the Text Were True" in *Testimony: The Word Made Fresh* (Maryknoll, N.Y.: Orbis, 2004), 168.

31. Berrigan, *The Dark Night of Resistance*, 24–25.

32. Ibid., 18–19.

33. Ibid., 93.

34. Ibid.

35. For an account of what he witnessed while in Vietnam, see his book, *Night Flight to Hanoi: War Diary with 11 Poems. New York: Harper,* 1968.

36. Berrigan, *The Dark Night of Resistance,* 93.

37. Ibid.

38. Ibid., 94.

39. Ibid.

40. Berrigan, "Etty Hillesum" in *And the Risen Bread,* 299–300

41. Etty Hillesum, *Letters from Westerbork* (London: Jonathan Cape, 1987), 102.

42. Ibid.

43. Ibid.

44. Ibid., 40–41.

45. Carol Lee Flinders, *Enduring Lives: Portraits of Women of Faith and Action* (New York: Penguin, 2006), 52.

46. Hillesum, *Letters from Westerbork,* 32.

47. Alexandra Pleshoyano, "Etty Hillesum: For God and With God," *The Way* 44, no. 1 (January 2005): 8.

48. Hillesum, *Etty: The Letters and Diaries of Etty Hillesum,* 87.

49. Ibid., 479.

50. Ibid.

51. *Zen Flesh, Zen Bones: A Collection of Zen and Pre-Zen Writings,* ed. and trans. Paul Reps and Nygoen Senzaki (Boston: Tuttle, 1998), 19.

52. Hillesum, *Etty: The Letters and Diaries of Etty Hillesum,* 465.

53. Hillesum, *Letters from Westerbork,* 43.

54. Ibid.

55. Daniel Berrigan, *Lights On in the House of the Dead* (New York: Doubleday, 1974), 27–28.

56. Ibid., 18.

57. Hillesum, *Letters from Westerbork,* 12.

58. Hillesum, *Etty: The Letters and Diaries of Etty Hillesum,* 505.

59. Daniel Berrigan, *The Nightmare of God* (Marion, S.Dak.: Rosehill, 1999), 3. (Emphasis added.)

60. Berrigan, *Lights On in the House of the Dead,* 121.

61. Ibid.

62. Ibid., 111.

63. Daniel Berrigan, *Uncommon Prayer: A Book of Parables* (New York: Seabury, 1978), 69.

64. Ibid., 67.

65. Daniel Berrigan, *Prison Poems* (Greensboro, N.C.: Unicorn, 1973), 105–6.

66. Berrigan, *Lights On in the House of the Dead*, 13.

67. Ibid.

68. Ibid.

69. Ibid., 125.

70. Ibid.

71. Ibid.

72. Ibid., 169.

73. Ibid.

74. Ibid.

75. Ibid., 114.

76. Ibid.

77. Martin Luther King, "A Knock at Midnight," in *A Testament of Hope: The Essential Writings and Speeches of Martin Luther King, Jr.*, ed. James M. Washington (New York: Harper, 1986), 500–1.

78. Berrigan, *Lights On in the House of the Dead*, 10–11.

79. Daniel Berrigan, *American Is Hard to Find* (New York: Doubleday, 1972), 95.

80. Berrigan, *Lights On in the House of the Dead*, 11–12.

81. Daniel Berrigan, "An Ethic of Resurrection," in *Testimony*, 221.

82. Ibid., 221.

83. Hillesum, *The Letters and Diaries of Etty Hillesum*, 307.

84. Ibid., 581.

85. Ibid., 542.

86. Ibid., 526.

87. Ibid., 550.

88. Ibid., 489.

89. Ibid., 488.

90. Ibid., 494.

91. Ibid.

92. Ibid., 53.

93. Ibid., 245.

94. Ibid.

95. Ibid., 21.

96. Ibid., 90.

97. Ibid., 91.

98. Ibid., 459.

99. Ibid., 461.

100. Berrigan, *Lights On in the House of the Dead*, 280.

101. Ibid.

102. In *Ten Commandments for the Long Haul*, Berrigan notes, for example, that a life of resistance does not easily make "friends of an enemy"; there is too much of the "disturbance of the good order" and affliction of

the comfortable." See Daniel Berrigan, *Ten Commandments for the Long Haul* (Nashville, Tenn.: Abingdon, 1981), 79.

103. See Philip Berrigan's foreword in Berrigan, *Prison Poems*, 1.

104. Hillesum, *The Letters and Diaries of Etty Hillesum*, 19.

105. Ibid., 104.

106. Ibid., 543.

107. Ibid., 522.

108. Ibid., 524.

109. Daniel Berrigan and Thich Nhat Hahn, *The Raft Is Not the Shore* (Maryknoll, N.Y.: Orbis, 2001), 123.

110. Ibid., 128.

111. Ibid., 128–29.

112. Ibid., 130.

113. Berrigan, *Ten Commandments for the Long Haul*, 67.

114. Daniel Berrigan, "Etty Hillesum" in *Prayers for the Morning Headlines* (Baltimore, Md.: Apprentice House, 2007), 64.

SELF-APPROPRIATION AND LIBERATION:
PHILOSOPHIZING IN THE LIGHT OF CATONSVILLE
James L. Marsh

This essay was delivered at the meeting of the American Catholic Philosophical Association, and discusses events in the United States and the world occurring since 2000, and especially from the time of the Iraq War that began on March 20, 2003.

1. Daniel Berrigan, *The Trial of the Catonsville Nine* (New York: Fordham University Press, 2004). This piece of Marsh's first appeared in the Proceedings of the American Catholic Philosophical Association: *Social Justice: Its Theory and Practice* (Charlottesville, Va.: Philosophy Documentation Center, 2006), 79:1–18.

2. Jack Nelson Pallmeyer, *Brave New World Order* (Maryknoll, N.Y.: Orbis Books, 1992), 4–5. Doug Henwood, *After the New Economy* (New York: The New Press, 2003), 129.

3. James L. Marsh, "Justice, Difference, and the Possibility of Metaphysics: Toward a North American Philosophy of Liberation," *Proceedings of the American Catholic Philosophical Association* (New York: National Office of the American Catholic Philosophical Association, Fordham University), 76:57–76.

4. James L. Marsh, *Radical Fragments* (New York: Peter Lang, 1992), 13.

5. See Daniel Berrigan, *The Nightmare of God* (Portland, Oreg.: Sunburst Press, 1983), 49–50.

6. James L. Marsh, *Post-Cartesian Meditations* (New York: Fordham University Press, 1988), 106–14.

7. Noam Chomsky, *Pirates and Emperors, Old and New: International Terrorism in the Real World* (Cambridge, Mass.: South End Press, 2002), vii.

8. Berrigan, *The Nightmare of God*, 48–49.

9. William Appelman Williams, *Empire as Way of Life* (New York: Oxford University Press, 1980).

10. Noam Chomsky, *Turning the Tide* (Boston: South End Press, 1985), 47.

11. Enrique Dussel, *Ethics and Community*, trans. Robert Barr (Maryknoll, N.Y.: Orbis Books, 1988), 139.

12. James L. Marsh, *Critique, Action, and Liberation* (Albany, N.Y.: SUNY Press, 1995).

13. Larry Everest, "The Selling of Peru," *Z Magazine* 7 (September 1994): 35–36.

14. Daniel Berrigan, *Minor Prophets, Major Themes* (Marion, S.Dak.: Fortkamp Books, 1985), 49–50.

15. Daniel Berrigan, *To Dwell in Peace: An Autobiography* (New York: Harper & Row, 1987), 334. For Marx on "universal prostitution," see *The Grundrisse*, trans. Martin Nicolaus (New York: Vintage, 1973), 163.

16. Daniel Berrigan, *Lamentations: From New York to Kabul and Beyond* (Lanham, Md.: Sheed and Ward, 2002), 13.

17. Ibid., 313–30.

18. Bernard Lonergan, *Insight: A Study of Human Understanding*, ed. Frederick Crowe and Bob Doran (Toronto: The University of Toronto Press, 1992), 721–22; Daniel Berrigan, *Jesus Christ* (Garden City, N.Y.: Doubleday and Company, 1973); Bob Doran, *Theology and the Dialectics of History* (Toronto: The University of Toronto Press, 1989), 113–15, 198–206.

19. Marsh, *Critique, Action, and Liberation*, 113–24.

20. Ibid., 313–30.

21. James L. Marsh, *Process, Praxis, and Transcendence* (Albany, N.Y.: SUNY, 1989), 298–320.

22. Juliet Schor, *The Overspent American: Upscaling, Downshifting, and the New Consumer* (New York: Basic Books, 1998), 111–42.

23. Marsh, *Process, Praxis, and Transcendence*, 318.

24. Ibid., 21–29.

25. Berrigan, *The Trial of the Catonsville Nine*, 95.

CONSECRATING PEACE: REFLECTING ON
DANIEL BERRIGAN AND WITNESS
William Desmond

1. Daniel Berrigan, *America Is Hard to Find* (Garden City, N.Y.: Doubleday, 1972); *Prison Poems* (New York: Viking Press, 1973); *To Dwell in Peace: An Autobiography* (San Francisco: Harper & Row, 1987).

2. Berrigan *To Dwell in Peace*, 121–22.

3. See also his challenging Presidential address to the American Catholic Philosophical Association, "Self-appropriation and Liberation; Philosophizing in the Light of Catonsville," in *Social Justice: Its Theory and Practice, Proceedings of the American Catholic Philosophical Association* (2005), 79:1–18. I suppose the tilt of my own thinking is towards keeping free space for the practice of the lost arts of contemplation. See note 4 below.

4. See my study of this in *Is There a Sabbath for Thought? Between Religion and Philosophy* (New York: Fordham University Press, 2005), chapter 6.

5. Berrigan, *To Dwell in Peace*, 340.

6. "The time will shortly be upon us, if it is not already here, when the pursuit of contemplation becomes a strictly subversive activity. This is the deepest and at the time, I think, the most sensible way of expressing the trouble into which my brother and I have fallen" (Berrigan, *America Is Hard to Find*, 77).

"I am convinced that contemplation, including the common worship of the believing, is a political act of the highest value, implying the riskiest of consequences to those taking part. Union with the Father leads us, in a sense charged with legal jeopardy, to resistance against false, corrupting, coercive, imperialist policy . . . The saints were right: their best moments were on the run, in jail, at the edge of social acceptability" (ibid, 78). See also William Desmond, "Doing Justice and the Practice of Philosophy," in *Social Justice: Its Theory and Practice, Proceedings of the American Catholic Philosophical Association* (2005), 79:41–59.

7. Berrigan, *To Dwell in Peace*, 347.

8. Ibid., 164–73.

9. Ibid., 234.

10. Daniel Berrigan, *Prison Poems* (Greensboro, N.C.: Unicorn Press, 1973), 50.

11. See Berrigan, *To Dwell in Peace*, 143–47. On the "disease of power"; see Berrigan, *America Is Hard to Find*, 292, on Caiaphas and the corrupt high priest "faithful to the usual interests."

12. Berrigan, *To Dwell in Peace*, 225–29, 247; "Letter to the Weathermen" in *America Is Hard to Find*, 92–98.

13. Berrigan, *To Dwell in Peace*, 227–29.

14. William Butler Yeats, *The Collected Poems of W.B. Yeats*, ed. Richard J. Finneran, 2nd edition (New York: Simon & Schuster, 1996), 312

15. See Berrigan, *To Dwell in Peace*, 69–73, 171–73 on Dorothy Day; the book opens with a reflection on a painting of St. Francis and the wolf of Gubbio. On religion and the poverty of philosophy, see chapter 3 of *Is there a Sabbath for Thought?*

16. Berrigan, *To Dwell in Peace*, 334–36.

17. See Berrigan, *To Dwell in Peace*, 43.

18. On the different communities of erotic sovereignty and agapeic service, see William Desmond, *Ethics and the Between* (Albany: SUNY Press, 2001), chapters 14 and 15.

19. I particularly think of those for whom this separation means that the final judge is the state. We see this in the French Revolution. We find it in diverse thinkers like Hobbes and Spinoza. We see it in Hegel for whom the State becomes god on earth. The Church is a merely spiritual community, while the State embodies worldly freedom in the immanent sphere—and this is the fullest realization of freedom, Hegel thinks. This is a separation that puts the Church beneath the State when it comes to the most important things. The Nazis were very suspicious of the churches for that reason—the idolization of the *Volk* cannot but seem blasphemous to one who believes that God alone is God—and not all churches escaped the idolatry. The temptation of this idolatry worried Berrigan about the American churches during the Vietnam War, and perhaps still does.

20. See Berrigan, *To Dwell in Peace*, 262–66.

21. Berrigan, *Prison Poems*, 19.

22. Berrigan, *America Is Hard to Find*, 103; ibid., Letter to the Jesuits: "We are not criminals, but we choose to be exiles in our own land" 35.

23. See Berrigan, *To Dwell in Peace*, chapter 11, and Fyodor Dostoevsky, *The House of the Dead* (New York: Penguin Classics, 1986).

24. See Berrigan, *To Dwell in Peace*, especially chapter 18; "A certain freedom here. He walked free from the need of self-justifying or of debate, whether modish or rancorous. And at the same time, Christian symbols and images came to life. He approached, he reached a point, at once dazzling and darksome. The point being the political and social consequences of the cross of Jesus" (348). See also, Berrigan, *America is Hard to Find*; writing on April 10, 1970, Berrigan speaks of a "mood of peace, of rightness, all the horrors and honors at some distance. I feel strongly suspended in mind . . . my life has anchored in a great simplicity" (47).

25. A matter also relevant to the vocation of the philosopher. See William Desmond, "Consecrated Thought: Between the Priest and the Philosopher," *Louvain Studies* 30 (2005): 92–106

26. See William Desmond, "Consecrated Love: A Philosophical Reflection on Marriage," *INTAMS Review* 11 (Spring 2005): 4–17.

BERNARD LONERGAN AND DANIEL BERRIGAN
Robert M. Doran

1. Berrigan's reflections on his ministry with AIDS patients are recorded in Daniel Berrigan, *Sorrow Built a Bridge: Friendship and AIDS* (Baltimore, Md.: Fortkamp, 1989). For my own reflections, see Robert M. Doran,

"AIDS Ministry as a Praxis of Hope," in *Jesus Crucified and Risen: Essays in Spirituality and Theology in Honor of Dom Sebastian Moore*, ed. William P. Loewe and Vernon J. Gregson (Collegeville, Minn.: Glazier, 1998) 177–93.

2. See Eric Voegelin, *Israel and Revelation*, and *Plato and Aristotle*, vols. 1 and 3, respectively, of *Order and History* (Baton Rouge: Louisiana State University Press, 1956/1957).

3. In attempting to track down what I remember reading and then quoting in a homily, I found the likely source in the piece entitled "Letter to the Jesuits," dated April 10, 1970, in Daniel Berrigan, *America Is Hard to Find* (New York: Doubleday, 1972), 36–37. Berrigan writes: "The real question of the times is not the conversion of cardinals or presidents, but the conversion of each of us . . . . There are few American Jesuits who, if their speech is to be trusted, are unaccepting of change Most of us are obsessed with its inevitability. We talk persuasively of it, we grasp at new forms and styles. And yet the suspicion remains; very few of us have the courage to measure our passion for moral change against the sacrifice of what lies closest to our hearts—our good name, our comfort, our security, our professional status. And yet, until such things are placed in jeopardy, *nothing changes*" (emphasis added). I am sure this is the source of the memory that I am reporting here.

4. Lonergan's *Collected Works* are being published in twenty-five volumes by University of Toronto Press. Fourteen volumes have been published to date.

5. Robert M. Doran, *Theology and the Dialectics of History* (Toronto: University of Toronto Press, 1990).

6. Bernard Lonergan, *Method in Theology* (Toronto: University of Toronto Press, 2003), 31–32.

7. On the development of the scale, see Doran, *Theology and the Dialectics of History*, chapter 4; on the Church, ibid., chapter 5.

8. See Bernard Lonergan, "Natural Right and Historical Mindedness," in *A Third Collection*, ed. Frederick E. Crowe (Mahwah, N.J.: Paulist Press, 1985), 169.

9. Lonergan, *Method in Theology*, xii.

10. Joseph Schumpter, *Imperialism / Social Classes: Two Essays*, trans. Heinz Norden (New York: New American Library, 1951), 6. See the index in *Theology and the Dialectics of History*, "Imperialism," for the numerous references to the topic.

11. Bernard Lonergan, *The Triune God: Systematics*, trans. Michael G. Shields, ed. Robert M. Doran and H. Daniel Monsour (Toronto: University of Toronto Press), 139.

12. Richard Golsan, *René Girard and Myth* (New York: Routledge, 2002), 1. Golsan's book is an excellent introduction to Girard's work.

Also recommended are Chris Fleming, *René Girard: Violence and Mimesis* (Cambridge, U.K.: Polity Press, 2004), and Michael Kirwan, *Discovering Girard* (Cambridge, Mass.: Cowley, 2005).

13. Helpful here are Raymund Schwager, *Must There Be Scapegoats? Violence and Redemption in the Bible* (New York: Crossroad, 2000) and Gil Baillie, *Violence Unveiled: Humanity at the Crossroads* (New York: Crossroad, 1995).

14. See Lonergan, *Method in Theology*, 33.

15. René Girard, *I See Satan Fall Like Lightning*, trans. James G. Williams (Maryknoll, N.Y.: sOrbis, 2002) 189.

16. Ibid., 189–90.

17. See Lonergan, *The Triune God*, 470–73.

18. The depths of that ignorance are reflected both in Berrigan's references to "Lord Nuke" in the last chapter of his autobiography, *To Dwell in Peace* (San Francisco: Harper & Row, 1987) and in Lonergan's references to the climax of the "longer cycle of decline" in *Insight: A Study of Human Understanding* in *Collected Works of Bernard Lonergan*, ed. Frederick E. Crowe and Robert M. Doran, vol. 3 (Toronto: University of Toronto Press, 1992). That climax is described as follows: "Reality is the economic development, the military equipment, and the political dominance of the all-inclusive state. Its ends justify all means. Its means include not merely every technique of indoctrination and propaganda, every tactic of economic and diplomatic pressure, every device for breaking down the moral conscience and exploiting the secret affects of civilized man, but also the terrorism of a political police, of prisons and torture, of concentration camps, of transported or extirpated minorities, and of total war" (257). Again, only at the page-proof stage was the following conclusion to chapter 20 of *Insight* removed, possibly not by Lonergan but by the publisher: "the dispassionate, unrelenting at-oneness with all the true, the real, the good, that outlasts the fire-ball of the atom bomb and immeasurably exceeds its power to change the living of man" (see www.bernardlonergan.com at 37200DTE050, the very end of the entry).

A KIND OF PIETY TOWARD EXPERIENCE: HOPE IN NUCLEAR TIMES
Patrick Murray and Jeanne Schuler

This first part of the autobiographical preface is authored by Patrick Murray. Beginning with "Three Seminal Themes in Berrigan's Thought," the remaining sections of the chapter are coauthored by Patrick Murray and Jeanne Schuler.

1. Daniel Berrigan, *To Dwell in Peace: An Autobiography* (San Francisco: Harper & Row, Publishers, 1987), 178–79. Then a Lutheran minister, Neuhaus would later convert to Catholicism, become a priest, and found the journal *First Things*.

2. Berrigan, *To Dwell in Peace*, 187.

3. Sr. Corita designed the cover to Berrigan's book, *They Call Us Dead Men: Reflections on Life and Conscience* (New York: The Macmillan Company, 1962). See his tribute to her in *Testimony: the Word Made Fresh* (New York: Orbis Books, 2004), 113–122.

4. Berrigan wrote of Bill Farmer's art, "So merciless and sensitive an art is an act of liberation of the highest order; it diagnoses man's wretchedness with surgical skill and compassion—always as the indispensable prelude to healing."

5. Torres's turn to violence appalled Berrigan. He writes of first seeing a Camilo Torres collage, "In the first image, the priest is attired in a soutane, in the second in a business suit, in the third in commando fatigues, a submachine gun in his embrace . . . . The image stopped my heart. It gathered in one the nearly unbearable ironies of my life." Daniel Berrigan, *Ten Commandments for the Long Haul* (Nashville, Tenn.: Abingdon, 1981), 41).

6. See David Dellinger's memoir, *More Power than We Know* (Garden City, N.Y.: Anchor Books, 1975) for an inside account of these times.

7. Berrigan's dear friend William Stringfellow, at whose home Berrigan was captured when he was underground, was a leading American advocate of Ellul's work; he wrote the introduction to Ellul's *The Presence of the Kingdom*, trans. Olive Wyon (New York: The Seabury Press, 1967).

8. This second and last part of the autobiographical preface is coauthored by Patrick Murray and Jeanne Schuler.

9. Myles Connolly, *Mr. Blue* (New York: Macmillan, 1928).

10. The title refers to 2 Corinthians 6:8–9; *They Call Us Dead Men* was printed in 1962, 1963, 1964, 1965, and 1966, when William Stringfellow contributed an introduction. The book was dedicated to Jim and Sally Douglass. The Rev. Terrence J. Cooke, later the cardinal of New York City, gave the Imprimatur.

11. "Pastoral Constitution on the Church in the Modern World (*Gaudium et Spes*)" may be found in *The Documents of Vatican II*, ed. Walter M. Abbott, SJ (New York: America Press, 1966).

12. Berrigan, *They Call Us Dead Men*, 41. Berrigan finds this notion of piety in Gabriel Marcel, "What Gabriel Marcel calls a 'deep sense of piety toward life' " (162), and John Dewey, "What Dewey calls 'piety toward experience' " (171).

13. Ibid., 128.

14. Ibid., 129.

15. Ibid.

16. Giovanni Battista Montini (Pope Paul VI), *On the Development of Peoples (Populorum Progressio)* (Washington, D.C.: Office of Publishing Services, United States Catholic Conference, 1967).

17. Berrigan, *They Call Us Dead Men*, 146.
18. Berrigan, *Ten Commandments*, 124.
19. Berrigan, *They Call Us Dead Men*, 49.
20. *Ibid.*, 160.
21. Berrigan, *Ten Commandments*, 115. Earlier in the book, Berrigan writes of "the stony unlikelihood of any future at all" (68).
22. Berrigan, *They Call Us Dead Men*, 56.
23. *Ibid.*, 51. Several of the great twentieth-century philosophers already felt this need acutely. Consider, for example, these works: Edmund Husserl, *The Crisis of the European Sciences*, trans. David Carr (Evanston: Northwestern University Press, 1970); Martin Heidegger, *Being and Time: A Translation of Sein und Zeit*, trans. Joan Stambaugh (Albany: State University of New York Press, 1996) and "Letter on Humanism," in *Martin Heidegger: Basic Writings*, ed. David Farrell Krell (New York: Harper & Row, Publishers), 193–244; and John Dewey, *Reconstruction in Philosophy*, enlarged edition (Boston: Beacon Press, 1948).
24. Berrigan, *They Call Us Dead Men*, 53.
25. *Ibid.*, 52. "Who is man?" and "What is his destiny?" are, respectively, the fourth and third critical questions of Kant. The first two are: "What can I know?" and "What ought I do?"
26. *Ibid.*, 55. G. E. M. Anscombe, "Modern Moral Philosophy," in *Ethics, Religion and Politics*, vol. 3, *G. E. M. Anscombe Collected Philosophical Papers* (Minneapolis: University of Minnesota Press, 1981). This article originally appeared in *Philosophy* 33 (1958). Alasdair MacIntyre, *After Virtue*, 2nd ed. (Notre Dame: University of Notre Dame Press, 1984 [1981]). See also Patrick Murray and Jeanne Schuler, "Marx, Subjectivism, and Modern Moral Philosophy," *The Modern Schoolman*, LXXXIII (March 2006), 173–96.
27. Berrigan, *To Dwell in Peace*, 118.
28. Berrigan, *They Call Us Dead Men*, 51.
29. *Ibid.*, 43.
30. On the former see the section of the *Phenomenology* called "Absolute Freedom and Terror," and on the latter see the "civil society" section of the *Philosophy of Right*.
31. In *They Call Us Dead Men*, Berrigan specifically called for "a new openness with Marxists" (110). Being open, though, need not mean being in agreement.
32. Berrigan, *Ten Commandments*, 71. See also 141–42. All the same, Berrigan maintained good personal relations with Gustavo Gutierrez and Paulo Freire.
33. See Berrigan, *Ten Commandments*, 72–75.
34. *Ibid.*, 74.

35. Ibid., 141–42.

36. Karl Marx, *Grundrisse*, trans. Martin Nicolaus (Harmondsworth: Penguin, 1973), 331.

37. See Patrick Murray and Jeanne Schuler, "Recognizing Capital: Some Barriers to Public Discourse about Capital," in *Race, Class, and National Identity*, ed. Andrew Light and Mecke Nagel (Amherst, N.Y.: Humanity Books, 2000), 101–16.

38. In his *First Philosophy of Spirit*, Hegel gave Adam Smith's "Invisible Hand" a more ominous appearance: "Need and labor, elevated into this universality, then form on their own account a monstrous system of community and mutual interdependence in a great people; a life of the dead body, that moves itself within itself, one which ebbs and flows in its motion blindly, like the elements, and which requires continual strict dominance and taming like a wild beast." G. W. F. Hegel, *System of Ethical Life (1802/3)* and *First Philosophy of Spirit (Part III of the System of Speculative Philosophy 1803/4)*, ed. and trans. by H. S. Harris and T. M. Knox (Albany: State University of New York Press, 1979), 249.

39. Marx, *Capital*, 1:280.

40. Ibid.

41. National Conference of Catholic Bishops. *Economic Justice for All: Pastoral Letter on Catholic Social Teaching and the U.S. Economy* (Washington, D.C.: United States Catholic Conference, 1986).

42. See Max Horkheimer, *The Eclipse of Reason* (New York: Seabury Press, 1974).

43. Tony Smith points out that Max Weber, a leading proponent of the conception of instrumental reason, recognized its dependence upon the capital-wage labor relation, "Weber himself admitted that technical or formal rationality can become fully institutionalized only after labor has been made a formally calculable factor of production," that is, after "labor itself has taken on the commodity form." Tony Smith, *The Logic of Marx's* Capital (Albany: State University of New York Press, 1991), 198.

44. Marx, *Grundrisse*, 248–49.

45. Berrigan, *To Dwell in Peace*, 2.

46. It is not surprising, then, that Berrigan should begin this meditation by describing Francis's embrace of the wolf as a "Pascalian wager" (*To Dwell in Peace*, 1). Pascal was a Christian Skeptic and took a similar view of human wolfishness.

47. Ibid., 3.

48. We remember discussing this line of Hegel's thinking with James Marsh in the 1970s, not in connection with Berrigan but with certain aspects of the counterculture.

49. Berrigan, *To Dwell in Peace*, 3.

50. At the end of the introduction Berrigan again emphasizes the alleged disconnect between action and outcome, "Play the game according to the rules of the game, for love of the game. Win, lose, draw, the game is the thing" (4). But to play a game well is to play to win; determining how one is playing cannot be disassociated from outcomes.

51. Berrigan offers this counterpoint: "To pray for His intervention is to imply my own . . . That is why I am arrested again and again, and will never give up . . . . I believe further, that it is not the method of God to intervene in events, not miraculously. This is the evidence I gather from the Bible, as from those who live with their eyes open . . . . So believing, I deny to the politicians, the researchers, the generals, their way in the world. They will not prevail" (Berrigan, *Ten Commandments*, 117).

52. Berrigan, *To Dwell in Peace*, 3–4.

53. John F. Kavanaugh, SJ, *Following Christ in a Consumer Society*, 25th anniversary edition (Maryknoll, N.Y.: Orbis Books, 2006), 133. The criticisms that Father Michael Baxter makes of Father John Courtney Murray may be expressed in these terms: Baxter, drawn to the "sect" model, criticizes Murray for affirming the "natural institution" model. See Baxter's PhD dissertation, "In Service to the Nation: A Critical Analysis of the Formation of the Americanist Tradition in Catholic Social Ethics" (University of Notre Dame, 1996).

54. In many respects, James Marsh, once a philosophy colleague of Kavanaugh at St. Louis University, is very close to Berrigan's vision. See, for example, his *Critique, Action, and Liberation* (Albany: State University of New York Press, 1995) and his essay "Self-Appropriation and Liberation: Philosophizing in the Light of Catonsville," in *Social Justice: Its Theory and Practice*, *Proceedings of the American Catholic Philosophical Association*, vol. 79 (2005).

55. Cardinal Bernardin of Chicago popularized a version of the "seamless garment" doctrine that did not include a prohibition of war.

56. See *Who Count as Persons?: Human Identity and the Ethics of Killing* (Washington, D.C.: Georgetown University Press, 2001). This book is Kavanaugh's answer to Berrigan's call in *They Call Us Dead Men* for "a profound change in the structure of the thought of modern man" that could address the "appalling moral vacuum" he observed.

57. Berrigan, *Ten Commandments*, 134. See also 30 and 132.

58. Ibid., 150.

59. Ibid., 149. Here is a more recent statement of Berrigan's radicalized "seamless garment" principle: "Don't kill. Have no part in killing, either enemy or criminal or the aged or the disabled or the unborn" (Berrigan,

Testimony, 17). See also "The Strange Case of the Man Who Could Not Please Anyone," in *Testimony*, 197–99.

60. Berrigan, *They Call Us Dead Men*, 99.

61. Kavanaugh structures *Following Christ* around the contrast between the Commodity Form and the Personal Form.

62. Kavanaugh, *Following Christ*, xvii.

63. Berrigan, *Ten Commandments*, 122.

64. Berrigan, *They Call Us Dead Men*, 66–67.

65. Berrigan, *Ten Commandments*, 150.

66. Kavanaugh, *Following Christ*, iv.

67. Berrigan, *Ten Commandments*, 56–57.

68. Ibid., 142.

69. Ibid., 13. See also 16 and 59.

70. Kavanaugh, *Following Christ*, xii.

71. Ibid., xii.

72. Berrigan, *They Call Us Dead Men*, 24.

73. Kavanaugh, *Following Christ*, 77.

74. Berrigan, *They Call Us Dead Men*, 53.

75. "What I am proud of is the consistency that binds the last twenty years in a coherent and even exciting unity . . . . Let the record show, we paid up. And continue to do so" (*Ten Commandments*, 102).

76. Berrigan, *Ten Commandments*, 149.

77. Ibid., 30. See also 150.

78. Ibid., 111.

BERRIGAN UNDERGROUND
Thomas Jeannot

1. Howard Zinn, *Declarations of Independence: Cross-Examining American Ideology* (New York: HarperCollins Publishers, 1990), 134. Zinn tells the story in the first person: "not long after I got back from Hanoi . . . I was asked to testify at a trial in Milwaukee. Fourteen people, many of them Catholic priests and nuns, had invaded a draft board and destroyed documents to protest the war. I was to testify as a so-called expert witness, to tell the judge and jury about the history of civil disobedience in the United States, to show its honorable roots in the American Revolution, and its achievements for economic justice and racial equality. I started out talking about the Declaration of Independence and then about Thoreau's civil disobedience, and then gave a brief history of civil disobedience in the United States. The judge pounded his gavel and said, 'Stop. You can't discuss that. This is getting to the heart of the matter.'"

2. *The Holy Outlaw* is the title of Lee Lockwood's 1970 documentary profiling Berrigan on the lam.

3. Berrigan wrote his famous play, *The Trial of the Catonsville Nine*, in 1970. He also wrote the screenplay for the film version directed by Gordon Davidson in 1972. A new edition of the play was published by Fordham University Press in 2004 with a preface and afterword by Robin Anderson and a second afterword by James Marsh. Mary Moylan died in 1995. For a moving and disturbing obituary, see Rosemary Radford Ruether, "To Mary Moylan, another casualty of war," in the *National Catholic Reporter* (November 10, 1995; available online at http://tinyurl.com/mary-moylan, accessed August 15, 2011). Ruether's own involvement in the events in question can be discovered from a press release she wrote protesting the solitary confinement of Philip Berrigan and David Eberhardt in the Lewisburg Federal Penitentiary while Daniel Berrigan and Mary Moylan were still at large. Among other details, she reports: "On June 27 [1970] approximately a hundred FBI agents, supported by a fleet of some 25 radioed cars and walkie-talkies invaded a wedding in a Lutheran church in Baltimore . . . looking for Father Daniel Berrigan," only to find the "next day, Father Daniel Berrigan staring at the FBI from the pages of the Sunday [*New York*] *Times* [*Magazine*]." Ruether's statement appears in Daniel Berrigan and Robert Coles, *The Geography of Faith: Conversations between Daniel Berrigan, when underground, and Robert Coles* (Boston: Beacon Press, 1971), 3–5. In 2001 Skylight Paths Publishing brought out an expanded edition, *The Geography of Faith: Underground Conversations on Religious, Political and Social Change* (Woodstock, Vt.: Skylight Paths Publishing, 2001). I will come back to *The Geography of Faith* below. The disturbing quality of Ruether's obituary for Moylan comes out in lines like these: "Mary Moylan's decision to surface, to go to jail, was barely noticed . . . . [Friends] told us she was embittered, that she did not want to hear from former friends . . . . She remained bitter against her former comrades and refused to attend the 25-year anniversary celebration of the Catonsville Nine's action. When Mary was found dead in her apartment of unknown, probably alcohol-related causes, few of us were notified . . . . [Most] in the Catholic left to whom I have made inquiries, never heard of her . . . . Perhaps we should have had the foresight to warn you against trying to rival the Berrigans, to take your jail term in 1970 and get on with your life. But we did not know how to question these heroics. We lacked the experience to see that a gesture that provided a stage and pulpit for them would be a black hole for you, an unknown woman . . . . You, indeed, laid your life on the line for justice and were broken by it."

4. See Rawls, *A Theory of Justice* (Cambridge, Mass.: Harvard University Press, 1971), 363–91. Rawls's discussion of "civil disobedience" and

"conscientious refusal" appears in "Part Two. Institutions," chapter 6, "Duty and Obligation," sections 55–59, immediately after his discussion of "The Duty to Comply with an Unjust Law" in section 53 (350–55) and "The Status of Majority Rule" in section 54 (356–62). Hereafter cited as *ATJ*.

5. Karl Marx, *The Eighteenth Brumaire of Louis Bonaparte*, complete in Robert Tucker, ed., *The Marx-Engels Reader* 2nd ed. (New York: Norton, 1978), 594.

6. While John Conyers's House Judiciary Committee lacked the backbone of Peter Rodino's Committee during the Nixon impeachment hearings, in the country at large the movement to impeach Bush and Cheney was only gaining momentum as this rogues' gallery was finally turned out of office and they scurried away like rats from a sinking ship. Although you would not know it from corporate media, millions of Americans hold the former administration in contempt. As of this writing, there is a vigorous public debate, which the Obama administration would like to put out of bounds, as to the extent of the criminal liability of the previous regime and the remedies available to hold its key figures accountable. For a sense of the sentiment across the political spectrum concerning the lawlessness of the Bush administration and the mandate for impeachment, see, for example, the broadcast of the PBS program *Bill Moyers Journal* of July 13, 2007, featuring a conversation with John Nichols, a writer for *The Nation* and other publications, and Bruce Fein, the conservative constitutional scholar who once served in the Justice Department of the Reagan Administration (accessed August 15, 2011, http://tinyurl.com/tough-talk-impeachment).

7. See Berrigan and Coles, *The Geography of Faith*, briefly discussed in section "Berrigan and Coles" below.

8. See note 3 above.

9. Rawls, *ATJ*, 363, 366.

10. Ibid., see 351, 391.

11. Ibid., 246.

12. Ibid., 245–46.

13. Ibid., 44. Rawls's basic discussion of "intuitionism" appears under the heading of "The Priority Problem," 40–45.

14. Ibid., see 359–62.

15. Ibid., 359–60.

16. Ibid., 570.

17. Ibid., see 334–37.

18. Ibid., 367.

19. Ibid., 20.

20. Ibid., 51.

21. Ibid., 49.

22. Ibid., 357, 360 (emphasis added).

23. Ibid., 363, 367.

24. Ibid., 363.

25. Ibid., 363.

26. Ibid., 366.

27. Ibid., 364.

28. Ibid., 364n19 and 366n22 for the comparison with Zinn. Rawls quotes Zinn's definition from *Disobedience and Democracy* (1968) in the first of these notes: civil disobedience is "the deliberate, discriminate violation of law for a vital social purpose." Also see notes 87 and 88 below. In *Declarations of Independence*, Zinn foreshortens the definition: it is "the deliberate violation of a law for a social purpose" (107).

29. Ibid., see 367–68 for "the militant," 368–71 for "the definition of conscientious refusal," and 377–82 for "the justification of conscientious refusal."

30. Ibid., 366 (emphasis added).

31. Ibid., 372.

32. Ibid., 302 (in the context of "the final statement of the two principles of justice for institutions").

33. Ibid., 372.

34. Ibid., 372.

35. Ibid., 373.

36. In his famous speech from June 1964, establishing the Charter of the Organization of Afro-American Unity, Malcolm X declared "our right on this earth . . . to be a human being, to be respected as a human being, to be given the rights of a human being in this society, on this earth, in this day, which we intend to bring into existence *by any means necessary*" (http://malcolmxfiles. blogspot.com/). It should be emphasized that Malcolm X frames his speech within the framework of the Charter of the United Nations, the Universal Declaration of Human Rights, the Constitution of the United States, the Bill of Rights, and the Declaration of Independence, that is, essentially the same framework as Rawls envisions for nonideal theory, although it is difficult to say where the "overlapping consensus" between Malcolm X and Rawls might be.

37. Rawls, *ATJ*, 373.

38. Ibid., 374.

39. Ibid., 374.

40. Ibid., see 388–91. The importance of an "overlapping consensus" to the sustainability of liberal institutions and to the viability of liberalism's underlying "social contract" view of social relations first came to prominence

in Rawls's thought in his famous essay, "Justice as Fairness: Political not Metaphysical," in *Philosophy and Public Affairs* 14 (1985): 223–51. Following Jeffrey Paris below, I will situate Rawls in his social and historical context, where the difference between 1971 and 1985 can be summarized by the Reagan Revolution. In "Justice as Fairness: Political not Metaphysical," Rawls writes, "since justice as fairness is intended as a political conception of justice for a democratic society"—that is, rather than as an epistemological or a metaphysical one, and, in view of seemingly intractable philosophical differences, as a matter of political and moral "theory" rather than political and moral "philosophy" *per se*—"it tries to draw solely upon basic intuitive ideas that are embedded in the political institutions of a constitutional democratic regime and the public traditions of their interpretation . . . . We hope that this political conception of justice may at least be supported by what we may call an 'overlapping consensus,' that is, by a consensus that includes all opposing philosophical and religious doctrines likely to persist and to gain adherents in a more or less just constitutional democratic society" (225–26). In a note, Rawls continues: "This idea was introduced in [*A Theory of Justice*], pp. 387f., as a way to weaken the conditions for the reasonableness of civil disobedience in a nearly just democratic society. Here and later [in 'Justice as Fairness: Political not Metaphysical'] in Secs. VI and VII it is used in a wider context" (226n5). Whereas Rawls claims that the notion of overlapping consensus in *A Theory of Justice* aims to "weaken the conditions for the reasonableness of civil disobedience," I will argue just the opposite: Rawls's account in *A Theory of Justice* actually makes the recourse to civil disobedience *more unreasonable*.

41. Ibid., 387.
42. Ibid., 387–88.
43. Ibid., 388 (emphasis added).
44. Ibid., 389 (emphasis added).
45. Ibid.
46. Ibid., 388.
47. Ibid.
48. Ibid., 389.
49. Ibid.
50. Ibid.
51. Ibid.
52. Ibid.
53. Ibid., see 389–90.
54. Ibid., 49.
55. Ibid., 390.
56. Ibid.; for the page citations, see note 29 above.

57. See Marx, *The Eighteenth Brumaire of Louis Bonaparte*, 594–617. For example, Marx writes: "The defeat of the June insurgents, to be sure, had now prepared and leveled the ground on which the bourgeois republic could be founded and built up, but it had shown at the same time that in Europe there are other questions involved than that of 'republic or monarchy.' It had revealed that here *bourgeois republic* signifies the unlimited despotism of one class over other classes. It had proved that in lands with an old civilization, with a developed formation of classes, with modern conditions of production and with an intellectual consciousness into which all traditional ideas have been absorbed by the work of centuries, *the republic* signifies *in general only the political form of the revolution of bourgeois society* and not its *conservative form of life*, as, for example, in the United States of North America, where though classes, indeed, already exist, they have not yet become fixed . . . During the June day all classes and parties had united in the *Party of Order* against the proletarian class as the *party of anarchy*, of socialism, of communism. They had 'saved' society from '*the enemies of society*.' They had given out the watchwords of the old society, '*property, family, religion, order,*' to their army as passwords and had proclaimed to the counter-revolutionary crusaders: 'In this sign you will conquer!' " (602). What is a good bourgeois to do when "anarchy" threatens? The "Party of Order" is always already ready-to-hand.

58. Ibid., 365.

59. Here I interpolate lines extrapolated from chapter 26, "The Secret of Primitive Accumulation," of Marx's *Capital*, translated by Ben Fowkes, vol. 1 (New York: Penguin Books, 1976). It may be objected that my interjection of property relations is unfair to Rawls in *ATJ*, who argues among other things, in his discussion of "Economic Systems," that "there is no *essential* tie between the use of free markets and private ownership of the means of production" (271, emphasis added). Rawls's opening to a form of market socialism has not gone unnoticed, of course, but of course "markets" are no more "free" than "competition" is "perfect" in the "market process," "ideal" or otherwise. Here, however, pursuing Marx's construction of the integral relation between "the sphere of circulation" and "the sphere of production," which are related to one another precisely as appearance to *essence*, would lead too far afield from the subject matter.

60. Berrigan, as quoted in Zinn, *Declarations of Independence*, 120. Zinn quotes from a pamphlet "distributed by the Catonsville Nine Defense Committee in 1968" (316n19).

61. Rawls, *ATJ*, 351.

62. Ibid., 353.

63. Ibid.

64. Ibid., 354.

65. Ibid., 355.
66. Ibid., 356.
67. Ibid., 361.
68. Having just mentioned "the dominant social mood," which would probably best be clarified with reference to Gramsci's theory of hegemony, I need to introduce a note of caution in my critique of Rawls's majoritarianism. Surely any theory of democracy worth its salt includes the notion of popular sovereignty. Especially for class-conscious theory and philosophy, what the people think, desire, and aspire to matters substantively and significantly. ("All power to the people!") Moreover, as Noam Chomsky points out so frequently it defies citation, public opinion as it appears through scientific polling on matters of domestic and foreign policy ranging from health care to the current wars is often and nearly systematically at odds with the government and the interests of the ruling class. Yet on the other hand, Chomsky is the coauthor with Edward Herman of *Manufacturing Consent* (New York: Pantheon Books, 1988), and the role of propaganda in discursive and nondiscursive will-formation cannot be overestimated. While theories that imply that people in general are stupid are reprehensible, it also seems true that a junk food diet for the mind breeds and disseminates junk ideas. Moreover, time and again, government and the ruling class demonstrate their capacity and willingness to mobilize, manipulate, regiment, and discipline the popular will, and they are aided and abetted by a culture industry, public relations, marketing and advertising, a dazzling array of strategies of cooptation, and the mass production of overawing mass media the behavioral and psychodynamic efficacy of which have been well studied and documented by countless sources. The Neo-Marxian tradition of Critical Theory has been exemplary in this respect; for example, Horkheimer and Adorno's *The Dialectic of Enlightenment* (1947; repr. New York: Continuum, 1976) and Marcuse's *One-Dimensional Man: Studies in the Ideology of Advanced Industrial Society* (1964; repr., Boston: Beacon Press, 1991). These first-generation Frankfurt School thinkers were thinking in part under the impact of Kierkegaard, Nietzsche, and Heidegger. Habermas, the leading second-generation representative of what has become of critical theory, draws his metaphor of "the colonization of the lifeworld" in the second volume of *The Theory of Communicative Action* (Boston: Beacon Press, 1987) under the impact of Max Weber's allusions to an "iron cage" and a "polar night of icy darkness." To come to the point, then, in so-called "advanced capitalist societies" (or whatever they should be called), which are mass societies imbricated in the logic and techniques of mass production, mass manipulation, and mass mobilization, "social movements" (or whatever they should be called) exist side by side, they are penetrated by, and they move in

an uneasy dialectical tension with the various orchestrations "from above" of a "system," a ruling class, state administration, a culture industry, ideology in Marx's sense, and the deep underlying imperatives of the law of value, which operates overarchingly as the prime directive (to steal an expression from *Star Trek*). Under these conditions, it seems true enough that class consciousness is often dulled or partly sublimated, even in broad sectors of the working-class majority. Yet the class struggle and freedom struggles "from below" are ongoing, and Marcuse's thesis in *One-Dimensional Man*, for example, seems too one-sided and overdrawn. Nevertheless, with respect to our consideration of Rawls's majoritarianism, the point is that he defaults to the inertial force of a *status quo ante*, whereas historical experience has shown, at least in the United States, that genuine social transformations often originate in the prophetic actions of individuals and small groups who must be identified as outliers on the margins of the then-dominant social and cultural dispositions and trends (for example, abolitionism, suffrage, the labor movement, the civil rights movement, the women's and other liberation movements, antiwar movements and so forth).

69. Rawls, *ATJ*, 364n19; and Zinn, 366n22.

70. Ibid., 368.

71. Ibid., 377; and for Rawls on the permissibility of conscription, see 380–82 ("Imagine, then, a democratic society in which conscription exists," 381: indeed, imagine such a society!). This is also the context in which Rawls upholds the just war theory, 379–81.

72. Zinn, *Declarations of Independence*, 316–17 and 317n21.

73. See Jeffrey Paris, "After Rawls," *Social Theory and Practice* 28 (2002): 679–99.

74. Ibid., 680.

75. Ibid., 680–81. Paris's periodization is as follows: (1) "1951–1958: Years of Formation," 681–84, during the McCarthy period, concerning which he quotes from John McCumber's *Time in the Ditch: American Philosophy and the McCarthy Era* (2001), which "documents the emerging silence regarding the McCarthyite purges and suggests that this silence became an element of the success of analytical philosophy": "analytical philosophy 'canonized a philosophical discourse that remained within rigid disciplinary and professional confines, bleakly isolating philosophy from history, culture, and society'" (682–83, 683n3; the internal quotation is from Giovanni Borradori); (2) "1963–1969: Years of Tumult," 684–89; (3) "1974–1980: Years of Transition," 689–91; (4) "1982–1989: The End of the Liberal State," 691–95; and (5) "1993: The New Strategy, or, Liberalism Exposed," 695–98.

76. Ibid., 693.

77. Ibid.

78. Ibid.

79. Ibid., 698.

80. Ibid.

81. Ibid., 699. Paris's contrast between a "reasonable faith" and an "unreasonable hope" is not "against reason," but it raises the question broached above: reasonable to whom?

82. Ibid., 685.

83. Ibid., 687.

84. Ibid.

85. Ibid., 688.

86. For an assessment of King's "Beyond Vietnam" forty years later, see my talk, "Permanent war and the illusion of democracy," given to the Spokane Humanist Breakfast on February 2, 2008, and available online at http://tinyurl.com/permanent-war (accessed August 15, 2011).

87. See Howard Zinn, *Disobedience and Democracy: Nine Fallacies on Law and Order* (1968; repr., Boston: South End Press, 2002), and Abe Fortas, *Concerning Dissent and Civil Disobedience: "We Have an Alternative to Violence"* (New York: Signet Books, 1968).

88. For a contemporaneous review of Zinn's and Fortas's books side by side, see Donald H. J. Hermann in the *California Law Review* 57 (1969): 1281–88. Fortas concentrates "on a moral duty of obedience to law. Dissent is possible in a democracy, but disobedience of law can go unpunished only where the law is unconstitutional or invalid, and hence no law at all" (1281). "Zinn, on the other hand, views law as synonymous with the imposition of the power of the state . . . . Zinn posits a clear separation of the government from the people; the people should remain distrustful of a state which by its very nature seeks to obtain ever greater power over them. The law, for the most part, is merely one of the weapons used by the state to subdue the individual; and the law, as applied by the courts, cannot be trusted as a shield for his freedom" (1281–82). Hermann continues: "Both Fortas and Zinn begin their arguments from these rigid positions, and for the most part, they merely deduce standards of behavior from their 'ought' premises rather than facing the more difficult, and necessary, task of establishing the validity of those premises. Fortas states his 'ought' premise as obedience to valid law, and he denominates activity violative of this norm as *illegal*. Zinn lays down his 'ought' premise as individual conduct in conformity to conscience, and describes any conduct failing to conform to this premise as *immoral*" (1282). In Hermann's opinion, "Such absolutist and polar stances would be enough to make dialogue difficult. But each author further impedes discourse by adopting his own definitions of critical terms, by restricting the meaning of certain words thereby limiting alternative positions, and by resorting to

clichés and platitudes tending to foreclose discussion" (1282). On the matter
of definitions, which also brings Zinn into collision with Rawls, Hermann
writes: "Fortas defines civil disobedience as the 'peaceful, nonviolent disobedience of laws which are themselves unjust and which the protester challenges
as invalid and unconstitutional.' Zinn rejects this narrow definition in favor of
a more all-encompassing one: 'Civil disobedience is the deliberate, discriminate violation of law for a vital social purpose. It becomes not only justifiable
but necessary when a fundamental human right is at stake, and when legal
channels are inadequate for securing that right. It may take the form of
violating an obnoxious law, protesting an unjust condition, or symbolically
enacting a desirable law or condition. It may or may not eventually be held
legal, because of constitutional law or international law, but its aim is always
to close the gap between law and justice, as an infinite process in the development of democracy'" (1282). Hermann's further meditations on what is at
issue between Fortas and Zinn need not concern us here.

    89. Stokely Carmichael (1941–98) figures into the conversations between
Berrigan and Coles that I will all too briefly consider below. A founder of the
Black Power movement, he is the coauthor with Charles V. Hamilton of *Black
Power: The Politics of Liberation in America* (New York: Vintage Books, 1967).
He was arrested as a Freedom Rider in 1961 and served seven weeks in
Parchman Penitentiary in Mississippi. He became chair of the Student
Nonviolent Coordinating Committee in 1966. In 1967 his passport was
revoked after he traveled to Cuba. He faced indictment for sedition but was
never prosecuted. In 1968 he became the prime minister of the Black Panther
Party. In 1969 he went into self-imposed exile in Guinea. In 1978 he changed
his name to Kwame Turé. To the end of his life, he remained a pan-Africanist,
a socialist, and a relentless critic of US imperialism. Turé's odyssey enters into
the conversation between Berrigan and Coles in an emblematic way. He
started out in the civil rights movement participating in the orthodox
strategies and tactics flowing from the Montgomery bus boycott in the late
1950s and early 1960s, which were still accepted in the early days of SNCC
on the cusp of Black Power. Coles relates the profound transformation or
conversion of horizons that occurred in Turé's life and asks Berrigan to
respond (see *Geography of Faith*, 109–14). Coles records that in 1964, "Stokely
Carmichael and I together gave a seminar on nonviolence to the college
students who went South to Mississippi for the so-called Mississippi Summer
Project. Now in that six year period of time [between 1964 and 1970] I think
it is publicly known how Stokely changed his ideas—in what direction.
Meanwhile I continue to do my work and I say to myself: I haven't become
bitter the way he is; I haven't left the country the way he has done; I haven't
said some of the things that he has said, about violence being as American as

apple pie; I haven't felt myself wanting to denounce my country as vigorously
and sweepingly as he has. And so I say I am somehow not *bitter*, not *depressed*,
not in a *rage*. I tell myself I haven't gone down the road of anger and despair
and unqualified or irrational political estrangement. And, of course, I say to
myself that I haven't done all that, gone in that direction, because I'm a white
middle class doctor, and I haven't been waging the struggle that Stokely
Carmichael has. Yet I wonder whether it cannot be said that in the last five
years he has in fact grown and become increasingly aware and sensitive to
various issues—and it is for *that* reason he has moved away from the joint
position he and I held in 1964, the joint political and social analysis we made
for the 'students' we 'taught' before they went South to Jackson and the
Delta" (109–110). Coles's rigorous honesty with himself is remarkable and
admirable. He continues, "I suppose it could be argued that what I fancy to
be my 'maturity' and 'equanimity' and 'good sense' and 'historical distance'
are really all signs of my death. In other words, because of the life I lead I am
every day protected and sheltered from the concrete realities that affect
(every minute of every day) ninety percent of the people on this planet. It can
also be argued that I am fatally compromised, and that my way of looking
both at Stokely's political position and his psychological development, as well
as at the economic and social realities of the world around me, reflects my
willingness to live as I do, which the critic of people like me would say means
living as the beneficiary of a colonial world power, able to command
resources from wretchedly poor lands and turn them into the style of living a
man like me enjoys . . . In other words the way I look at Stokely in the last
five or six years (as evidence of deterioration, stress, disintegration, violence)
is a measure of my own predicament" (110). Berrigan begins his reply, "Well,
I'm glad such thoughts are at least occurring to you!" (110).

90. In *ATJ*, Rawls writes that a pacifist's "views are not altogether sound"
(370) and that "pacifism" is "a natural departure from the correct doctrine"
(371), i.e. the just war, which he briefly discusses in connection with the
"contingent pacifism" that could properly enter into the justification of
conscientious refusal (378–82).

91. Ibid., 366n22.

92. Zinn, *Declarations of Independence*, 145; quoting Jefferson from Dumas
Malone, *Jefferson and the Rights of Man* (1951); Zinn's full quotation records
Jefferson's well-known view that "The spirit of resistance is so valuable on
certain occasions that I wish it always to be kept alive. It will often be
exercised when wrong, but better so than not to be exercised at all. I like
a little rebellion now and then . . ." But the question swiftly arises how
seriously we should take Jefferson's view, who is easy enough to quote, let
alone Zinn's, who quotes him easily enough. "[A] little rebellion" during

the period in question takes the shape of Watts, Detroit, Newark, the Democratic National Convention in Chicago, which led the Walker Report to coin the term "police riot" and countless similar scenes across the country.

93. For a critique of the putative right to punish in the context of a burgeoning prison-industrial complex, in which the United States has the singular distinction of the highest rate of incarceration in the world, holding nearly two and a half million people prisoner, see, for example, Angela Davis, *Abolition Democracy* (St. Paul, Minn.: Seven Stories Press, 2005).

94. My appeal to Habermas's notion does not imply agreement with his crisis theory in general.

95. Zinn, *Declarations of Independence*, 289.

96. Ibid.

97. Ibid., (emphasis added).

98. Ibid., 290.

99. Ibid..

100. See Malcolm X, "The Ballot or the Bullet," which is available in audio format (among other places) on YouTube, accessed August 15, 2011, http://tinyurl.com/ballot-or-bullet.

101. See Rawls, *ATJ*, 364n19 and 366n22.

102. Ibid., 367.

103. Ibid. Rawls's parenthetic insertion—"or those having effective political power"—on a charitable reading, should probably be read as disjunctive. Still, one wonders how conscious he was of slurring it together with "the sense of justice of the majority," a reading that is reinforced by his use of the plural possessive pronoun immediately afterwards. The emphasis of his sentence clearly falls on the majority's sense of justice, but his claim that the militant does not appeal to it is simply gratuitous: class-conscious militants, for example, undoubtedly appeal to the sense of justice of the majority, but they direct their militant acts precisely to "those having effective political power."

104. Ibid., 367 (emphasis added).

105. Ibid., 368.

106. Ibid.

107. For one account of Nixon's "madman strategy," see Jonathan Schell, *The Time of Illusion* (New York: Knopf, 1975). Writing in *The Boston Globe* during the Bush Administration in 2005, James Carroll recollected Nixon's words to Robert Haldeman, "I call it the madman theory, Bob." Carroll observes that "what has generated insufficient alarm is Nixon's insane flirtation with the actual use of nuclear weapons." Quoting Nixon again: "'I want the North Vietnamese to believe,' he went on, 'that I've reached the point that I might do anything to stop the war. We'll just slip the word to

them that for God's sake, you know Nixon is obsessed about communism. We can't restrain him when he's angry, and he has his hand on the nuclear button, and Ho Chi Minh himself will be in Paris in two days begging for peace'" (James Carroll, *The Boston Globe*, June 14, 2005, accessed August 15, 2011, http://tinyurl.com/madman-strategy).

108. See Zinn, *Declarations of Independence*. Zinn discusses civil disobedience, Martin Luther King Jr., and Daniel Berrigan in chapter 6, "Law and Justice," 106–46; see esp. 118–23.

109. See Martin Luther King Jr., "Letter from Birmingham City Jail," in *A Testament of Hope: the Essential Writings and Speeches of Martin Luther King, Jr.*, ed. James M. Washington (New York: HarperCollins Publishers, 1991), 289–302.

110. Zinn, *Declarations of Independence*, 119.

111. King, "Letter from Birmingham City Jail," 294 (emphasis added).

112. Zinn, *Declarations of Independence*, 119.

113. Rawls, *ATJ*, 366n22.

114. Ibid., 364n19. I will return to Zinn's mistake below.

115. James M. Washington, in *A Testament of Hope*, 289.

116. King, in ibid., 297–98.

117. See Peter Hudis, "Dr. King's Legacy: The Historic Mirror on the Limits of U.S. Presidential Politics," http://marxisthumanismtoday.org/node/21 (site discontinued). Retrieving a remarkable document from 1951, Hudis quotes King. "In 1951, four years before the Montgomery Bus Boycott that catapulted him to national attention, King wrote the following: 'Karl Marx, the German philosopher and economist, stated that capitalism carries the seeds of its own destruction . . . do we find any truth therein? It is my opinion that there is. I am convinced that capitalism has seen its best days in America, and not only in America, but in the entire world. It is a well-known fact that no social institution can survive when it has outlived its usefulness. This, capitalism has done. It has failed to meet the needs of the masses.' King continued, 'We need only look at the underlying developments of our society. There is a definite revolt by what Marx calls 'the proletariat,' against the bourgeoisie. Everywhere we turn we are faced with strikes and a demand for socialized medicine . . . . I am not saying that there is a conscious move toward socialism, not even by labor, the move is certainly unconscious. But there is a definite move away from capitalism, whether we conceive of it as conscious or unconscious'" (quoted from King, "Notes on American Capitalism," in *The Papers of Martin Luther King, Jr. Vol. I: Called to Serve*, ed. Clayborne Carson [Berkeley: University of California Press, 1992], 435–36).

118. Zinn, *Declarations of Independence*, 128.

119. Ibid., 115, 116; the section is entitled, "Obligation to the State," 114–18.

120. Ibid., 119–20 (emphasis added).

121. Ibid., 121–22.

122. Ibid., 122.

123. King, "Letter from Birmingham City Jail," 293.

124. For the relevant quotation from Augustine, see Augustine, *Political Writings*, trans. Michael W. Tkacz and Douglas Kries (Indianapolis, Ind.: Hackett, 1994), 214 (in which a fictionalized "Augustine" replies to "Evodius," "It seems to me that an unjust law is not a law"); and for Aquinas, see *Treatise on Law* (i.e. *ST* I–II, Questions 90–97), translator unnamed (Chicago: Henry Regnery, 1970), 78; from Q. 95, "Of Human Law," a. 2, "Whether Every Human Law is Derived from the Natural Law," where the *sed contra* passage appeals to the authority of Augustine in *De Libero Arbitrio*. However, in the natural law tradition, the distinction between a just and an unjust law is hardly straightforward. The official Catechism of the Catholic Church affirms the primacy of personal conscience, but this doctrinal affirmation presupposes a well-formed conscience, i.e. a conscience shaped by magisterial teaching (see the *Catechism of the Catholic Church* [New York: Doubleday, 1995], 490–95; the key passage quotes Newman: "conscience is the aboriginal Vicar of Christ," 490). In Q. 95, a. 4, "Whether Human Law Binds a Man in Conscience," Aquinas writes, "*I answer that*, Laws framed by men are either just or unjust. If they be just, they have the power of binding in conscience, from the eternal law whence they are derived . . . On the other hand laws may be unjust in two ways: first, by being contrary to human good . . . Secondly, laws may be unjust through being opposed to the Divine good" (96–97). In connection with laws contrary to human good, Aquinas appeals to the authority of Augustine a second time from the same source. As far as "unjust laws" are concerned, Aquinas concludes, "wherefore neither in such matters is man bound to obey the law, provided he avoid giving scandal or inflicting a more grievous hurt" (98). I think it must be granted that this teaching has explosively radical potential. However, the last quoted clause qualifies the unequivocal application to Dr. King. First one must answer the questions scandalous to whom and "a more grievous hurt" to whom.

125. However, Rawls can accommodate King's theological argument on the basis of his doctrine of "overlapping consensus," whereas Zinn does not appear to have this explicitly *liberal* tool of negotiating intractable differences of religious and philosophical opinion at his ready disposal.

126. See note 3 above.

127. See Zinn, *Declarations of Independence*, 114–18 and 122; he writes, "During [the] four months [Berrigan was underground], while helping take

care of [him], I was teaching my course at Boston University. My students were reading the *Crito*, and I asked them to analyze reasons for not escaping punishment and also to consider Daniel Berrigan's reasons for going underground. They did not know, of course, that Berrigan was right there in Boston, living out his ideas."

128. Berrigan and Coles, *Geography of Faith*, 62–63.

129. Ibid., see 64. I will come to the context below.

130. See Herbert Marcuse, *One-Dimensional Man* (cited in note 68 above). Marcuse concludes his book with the following lines: "However, underneath the conservative popular base is the substratum of the outcasts and outsiders, the exploited and persecuted of other races and other colors, the unemployed and the unemployable. They exist outside the democratic process; their life is the most immediate and the most real need for ending intolerable conditions and institutions. Thus their opposition is revolutionary even if their consciousness is not. Their opposition hits the system from without and is therefore not deflected by the system; it is an elementary force which violates the rules of the game and, in doing so, reveals it as a rigged game. When they get together and go out into the streets, without arms, without protection, in order to ask for the most primitive civil rights, they know that they face dogs, stones, and bombs, jail, concentration camps, even death. Their force is behind every political demonstration for the victims of law and order. The fact that they start refusing to play the game may be the fact which marks the beginning of the end of a period. Nothing indicates that it will be a good end. The economic and technical capabilities of the established societies are sufficiently vast to allow for adjustments and concessions to the underdog, and their armed forces sufficiently trained and equipped to take care of emergency situations. However, the spectre is there again, inside and outside the frontiers of the advanced societies. The facile historical parallel with the barbarians threatening the empire of civilization prejudges the issue; the second period of barbarism may well be the continued empire of civilization itself. But the chance is that, in this period, the historical extremes may meet again: the most advanced consciousness of humanity, and its most exploited force. It is nothing but a chance. The critical theory of society possesses no concepts which could bridge the gap between the present and its future; holding no promise and showing no success, it remains negative. Thus it wants to remain loyal to those who, without hope, have given and give their life to the Great Refusal. At the beginning of the fascist era, Walter Benjamin wrote: *Nur um der Hoffnungslosen willen ist uns die Hoffnung gegeben*. It is only for the sake of those without hope that hope is given to us" (256–57).

131. It is open to a Rawlsian to point out that nothing forbids Rawls from acknowledging the former alternative and that he explicitly acknowledges the

latter alternative in his distinctions among civil disobedience, militancy, and conscientious refusal. With respect to the justification of conscientious refusal, however, Rawls's theory is still "disciplinary" in Paris's sense. And with respect to militancy, Rawls seems to recognize it only to give himself permission to ignore it, as he safely ignores the *concrete* question for *nonideal* theory of which *actual* "nearly just" society he has in mind, if it is not already a merely ideal-theoretical utopia.

132. Berrigan and Coles, *The Geography of Faith*, 62. (As I write this note on the sixth anniversary of the US war of aggression on the people of Iraq, I believe I can add that they *act* like bloodthirsty mass murderers as well.)

133. In his introduction to *The Geography of Faith*, Coles writes that he has no "intention of lining up support of the statement read by Mr. William Kunstler outside of Danbury prison—in which he compared the latest action against the Berrigan brothers with the burning of the Reichstag in the early days of the Nazi era. In my opinion," he continues, "such allegations are unfair, thoroughly unfair, and they give an all too easy and gratuitous victory to the likes of those who now run our Department of Justice" (26–27). Yet his respect, admiration, and even affection for Berrigan are plain in his conclusion: "Meanwhile the rest of us (who live further away from the 'edge' Daniel Berrigan keeps mentioning) will hopefully now and then demand of ourselves at least a measure of what he seems unable to spare himself—and I refer not to suffering or sacrifice, but the hard work of loyalty to the God Isaiah and Jeremiah called upon . . . It is . . . not for one living man to decide what another living man's worth will be when it is all over, when all of us alive are gone and the light of that Judgment Day the Bible speaks of begins to fall upon us. But for better or worse, the Reverend Daniel Berrigan, S.J., has never lost his loyalty to his fellowman and God. He may have erred; he may yet err. He may have said unwise things; he may yet do so. Nearing fifty, a prisoner, very much alive, 'in the middle way,' headed for more notoriety and conflict (right now that is surely clear), he will not want to stop being among us, he will not want to let go of us—until one day he is told to do just that, to leave here and to go there, to become part of God's scheme of things in a way no living man can really imagine, let alone talk about. I fear it will only be then (as is so often the case) that many of us will dare acknowledge what we have all along had in such remarkable abundance in one man" (32–33).

134. Ibid., see 23: "As I have read over the text of our remarks to each other I have worried that somehow we emerge as vulnerable, indeed, easy prey for those categorical minds who would want to have one speaker the 'liberal' or 'moderate' who hems and haws, and one speaker the 'radical' who questions everything and has little sense of the price that any society must ask of its various members." Although he does not quite "hem and haw,"

Coles just is a liberal; and although it would be gratuitous to assert that Berrigan "has little sense of the price that any society must ask," the term *radical* is just the shoe that fits. The common ground Coles shares with Berrigan is their mutual commitment to Christianity, but I have deliberately tried in this essay to bracket the Christian and indeed Roman Catholic discourse, also without which, admittedly, Berrigan cannot be fully understood. My purpose instead has been to frame Berrigan underground in the framework of Marx's move from "religious" to "irreligious" criticism in the *Contribution to the Critique of Hegel's Philosophy of Right: Introduction*, at the same time he also affirms that "the criticism of religion is the premise of all criticism," that "Religious suffering is at the same time an expression of real suffering and a protest against real suffering," and that "The immediate task of philosophy, which is in the service of history, is to unmask human self-alienation in its secular form now that it has been unmasked in its sacred form. Thus the criticism of heaven is transformed into the criticism of earth, the criticism of religion into the criticism of law, and the criticism of theology into the criticism of politics" (*The Marx-Engels Reader*, 53–54).

135. As the dominant ideology of bourgeois society, liberalism is subject to various articulations, for example, a conservative, a neoconservative, or a neoliberal articulation. Hence Paris's formulations, "after Rawls" and "after liberalism" (the latter taken from Immanuel Wallerstein) betray a radical and even revolutionary intent with respect to bourgeois society as a whole.

136. Although *The Geography of Faith* lacks an index, as far as I can tell Berrigan mentions King only once and merely in passing (see 81); Coles does not mention him at all.

137. Other thinkers prominently figure in, such as Bonhoeffer, Bernanos, Simmone Weil, Philip Berrigan, and so forth, but granted the emphasis of this essay, they are not relevant here.

138. To give just one example, in the context of a conversation to which he editorially assigns the title, "Professional Life," Coles says, "perhaps I tend to be pessimistic. I worry that the kind of spirit we have seen in the finest of medical students and law students and divinity students in recent years will gradually be subdued—because in the South in the early sixties I saw many young idealists get discouraged and give up. You keep talking about the war; well, we will settle this war, and then I doubt that many of our young will be as aroused as they recently have been. I am not at all sure that this nation is changing as much as some social critics say it is; nor do I believe the majority of our people want any really drastic changes in the way the nation is set up" (ibid., 106).

139. Ibid., 63–64.

140. In *Phenomenology of Spirit*, trans. A.V. Miller (New York: Oxford University Press, 1977), consult the following phenomenological figures: "The law of the heart and the frenzy of self-conceit," 221–28; "Virtue and the way of the world," 228–35; "Conscience. The 'beautiful soul', evil and its forgiveness," 383–409; and finally, "Absolute Freedom and Terror," 355–63. With a slight rearrangement in the order of Hegel's text, terror can be understood as the impotence of the beautiful soul in action. To begin with "conscience," he writes, "Conscience . . . in the majesty of its elevation above specific law and every content of duty, puts whatever content it pleases into its knowing and willing. It is the moral genius which knows the inner voice of what it immediately knows to be a divine voice; and since, in knowing this, it has an equally immediate knowledge of existence, it is the divine creative power which in its Notion possesses the spontaneity of life. Equally, it is in its own self divine worship, for its action is the contemplation of its own divinity" (397). If this sounds splendid, however, the "moral genius" of the individual conscience does not quite live up to "the divine creative power" of the "Notion." Rather, what eventuates from its purity and rectitude is "the beautiful soul": "The 'beautiful soul', lacking an *actual* existence, entangled in the contradiction between its pure self and the necessity of that self to externalize itself and change itself into an actual existence, and dwelling in the *immediacy* of this firmly held antithesis . . . this 'beautiful soul', then, being conscious of this contradiction in its unreconciled immediacy, is disordered to the point of madness, wastes itself in yearning and pines away in consumption" (406–7). By transposition and homology, one can imagine a "beautiful soul . . . disordered to the point of madness"—the purely world-negating idealism of a "moral genius" confronting a world not much to its liking and "conscious of this contradiction"—lapsing into a rage rather than "wasting away in yearning and pining away in consumption," and insisting on the prerogatives of its "absolutely free self": "the sole work and deed of [such a] universal freedom [as this] is therefore *death*, a death too which has no inner significance or filling, for what is negated is the empty point of the absolutely free self. It is thus the coldest and meanest of all deaths, with no more significance than cutting off a head of cabbage or swallowing a mouthful of water" (360). Here Hegel is insinuating the Terror, the counterfeit of true freedom because it is "abstract" rather than "essential being," "but not essential being as an *immediate existence*, not will as revolutionary government or anarchy striving to establish anarchy, nor itself as the centre of this faction or the opposite faction" (363), that is, in the manner of a Robespierre (as Hegel insinuates him). Coles and Hegel are right, of course, to be wary of moral geniuses, beautiful souls, absolutely abstractly free selves, and terrorist violence.

141. Berrigan and Coles, *Geography of Faith*, 64–65.

142. Ibid., 84.

143. In *Geography of Faith*, which Coles edited based on taped transcripts while Berrigan was in prison, the full text of Berrigan's reply as I have quoted it here is unaccountably absent. Coles describes his editorial process in his introduction to the 1971 edition (21–23). He admits that he gave himself a somewhat free hand, but he also reports that when he showed the manuscript to Berrigan at Danbury, Berrigan "had 'no reservations at all' about sending the manuscript to the publisher" (23). Meanwhile, however, the conversations between Berrigan and Coles were serialized in the *New York Review of Books* in 1971 and *Time Magazine* ran an excerpt from that series in its March 22, 1971 edition (see http://tinyurl.com/dialogue-with-berrigan). Here I am quoting verbatim from the *Time* excerpt. For the parallel passage in *Geography of Faith*, see 84–85.

144. Berrigan and Coles, *Geography of Faith*, 43.

145. Ibid., 43–44.

146. Ibid., 77. (The *Time* excerpt places an exclamation point where Coles has a question mark: "Who is we!")

147. See Hegel, *Philosophy of Right*, translated by T.M. Knox (New York: Oxford University Press, 1967). Hegel's work as a whole is structured by the dialectical movement from "Abstract Right" and "Morality" (*Moralität*) to "Ethical Life" (*Sittlichkeit*) in the family, civil society, and the state.

148. For Hegel's treatment of Sophocles's *Antigone*, see *Phenomenology of Spirit*, 284–88.

LONERGAN AND BERRIGAN: TWO RADICAL
AND VISIONARY JESUITS
Patrick D. Brown

1. Daniel Berrigan, *Jeremiah: The World, the Wound of God* (Minneapolis: Fortress Press, 1999), xi–xii. See also Daniel Berrigan, *To Dwell in Peace: An Autobiography* (New York: Harper & Row, 1987): "I was learning . . . to ask again and again, a quite simple question. In the nature of things, the question was destined to occupy me, not for a decade, but for a lifetime. Indeed, it could be adduced that, were I not so slow a learner, the question would have occupied me earlier, from the first years. What is a human being, anyway? Did I have the spiritual equipment (the matter must be deemed spiritual) to approach at least a hint of an answer? Behold our Jesuit, then, among his Jesuit kind, seeking now answers, now something humbler—the right questions." (345). See note 23 below for a further context.

2. "The Ego Alter Dialectic and the Conscience," *Journal of Philosophy* 42 (1945): 359. As is clear from the context, the "other" mentioned here is

"the divine other" mentioned in the preceding sentence of the same article, and "the spirit" is the Holy Spirit mentioned in the sentence before that.

3. Daniel Berrigan, "Catholicism and Intelligence," in *The Bow in the Clouds: Man's Covenant with God* (New York: Coward-McCann, 1961); Bernard Lonergan, *Insight: A Study of Human Understanding* (New York: Longmans Philosophical Library, 1957); *Insight: A Study of Human Understanding*, 5th ed., ed. Frederick Crowe and Robert Doran, *Collected Works of Bernard Lonergan* 3 (Toronto: University of Toronto Press, 1997). References below will be first to the page number of the 1957 edition, and second to the 1997 5th edition, cited as *CWL* 3. Following the first citation to volumes in the *Collected Works of Bernard Lonergan*, short citations will reference *CWL* followed by the volume and page number.

4. Daniel McInerny, *The Difficult Good: A Thomistic Approach to Moral Conflict and Human Happiness* (New York: Fordham University Press, 2006).

5. Josef Pieper, *Fortitude and Temperance*, trans. Daniel Coogan (New York: Pantheon Books, 1954), 11–12, quoted in McInerny, *The Difficult Good*, 5–6.

6. There is an additional connection. Berrigan was interested enough in Lonergan's thought that he planned to participate in the First International Lonergan Conference in Florida in the spring of 1970. But Berrigan had an appointment with prison at that time, and in April of that year he went underground, charged as he was with the audacity of burning draft cards in a symbolic act of resistance against the violence in Vietnam. See *Foundations of Theology: Papers from the First International Lonergan Conference*, ed. Philip McShane (South Bend: University of Notre Dame Press, 1972), xx; Berrigan, *To Dwell in Peace*, 243.

7. *James* 1:22 ("prove yourselves doers of the word, and not merely hearers who delude themselves.") See generally Karl Rahner, *Hearers of the Word*, trans. Joseph Donceel (New York: Continuum, 1994); Mathew Lamb, *Solidarity with Victims: Toward a Theology of Social Transformation* (New York: Crossroad Publishing Co., 1982); James Marsh, *Process, Praxis, and Transcendence* (Albany, N.Y.: SUNY Press, 1999), part 2.

8. Bernard Lonergan, *Topics in Education*, vol 10, *CWL* (Toronto: University of Toronto Press, 1993), 182.

9. Bernard Lonergan, *For a New Political Economy*, ed. Philip McShane, vol. 21, *CWL* (Toronto: University of Toronto Press, 1998), 8.

10. My phrasing here echoes Eric Voegelin's contention that Western philosophy was not some *sui generis* form of abstract theorizing but was instead in its very origins "an act of resistance" on the part of Plato and Aristotle "against the personal and social" corruption of ancient Greece.

Eric Voegelin, *Reason: The Classic Experience*, in *The Collected Works of Eric Voegelin*, ed. Ellis Sandoz (Baton Rouge: University of Louisiana Press, 1990), 12:265. But my suggestion also echoes, of course, the same realities and the same need for actively resisting them in our own times.

Of his struggles regarding the economic order, or disorder, of our times, Lonergan once remarked: "It's something that I've been working on since 1930. I gave up in 1944, picked it up again in 1966 when I discovered I had a beachhead in economics." *Curiosity at the Center of One's Life* (interviews with R. Eric O'Connor and Lonergan), ed. Martin O'Hara, Gerald MacGuigan, and Charlotte Tansey (Montreal: Thomas More Institute: 1987), 430. For his 1942 manuscript, see *For a New Political Economy*, *CWL* 21:3–106. A distinct, fuller, and deeper manuscript followed in 1944. Ibid., 231–318. Lonergan, in turn, later revised that manuscript in the 1970s and early 1980s. For a version of the 1944 manuscript incorporating those later revisions, see *Macrodynamic Analysis: An Essay in Circulation Analysis*, ed. Frederick Lawrence, Patrick Byrne, and Charles Hefling *CWL* 15 (Toronto: University of Toronto Press, 1999).

11. For a sample of Lonergan's objections to this facile categorization, see, for example, Lonergan, "Theories of Inquiry" (1967), *A Second Collection*, ed. William Ryan, S.J., Bernard Tyrrell, S.J. (Philadelphia: The Westminster Press, 1974), 38 ("I just add, however, that my interest in Aquinas came late."); Lonergan, "Questions with Regard to Method: History and Economics," in *Dialogues in Celebration* ed. Cathleen Going, *Thomas More Institute Papers/80* (Montreal: Thomas More Institute, 1980), 307 ("I was interested in economics long before I was interested in theology."); *Caring About Meaning: Patterns in the Life of Bernard Lonergan* (interviews), ed. Pierrot Lambert, Charlotte Tansey, and Cathleen Going (Montreal: Thomas More Institute, 1982), 68 ("'Transcendental Thomism' was a hold-all invented by an Austrian named Muck. He didn't know much about *Insight*—he just quoted it—and he put me in the basket . . . . But my own thinking is generalized empirical method."); "Interview with Bernard J. F. Lonergan," Kendig B. Cully and Iris V. Cully, *The Review of Books and Religion* 4, no. 5 (Mid-February 1975): 2 and 13 ("He chuckled in recalling what a Catholic professor at Yale said to him, 'They call you a transcendental philosopher, but you're not that at all; you're a good Anglo-Saxon empirical one.' How did he feel about that characterization? 'As far as what is meant by 'transcendental philosophy' by most European philosophers, it's perfectly true.'").

12. I do not, by any means, wish to suggest that their politics were the same; Lonergan kept his politics rather close to his vest in a way that Berrigan, quite obviously, does not. I do, however, wish to suggest that

business and politics as usual were utterly anathema to both, as I hope to show in what follows.

13. Frederick Lawrence, "Political Theology and 'The Longer Cycle of Decline,'" *Lonergan Workshop*, vol. 1 (Missoula, Minn.: Scholars Press, 1978), 234. Lawrence is speaking of Lonergan and Metz, but his observation applies to Lonergan and Berrigan as well.

14. Berrigan, *Jeremiah*, 26. For a brilliant, demanding, and technical treatment of this most fundamental reality of human existence, see Lonergan's chapter on *"Imago Dei"* in *Verbum: Word and Idea in Aquinas*, ed. Frederick Crowe and Robert Doran, vol. 2, *CWL* (Toronto: University of Toronto Press, 1997), 191–227.

15. For a more complex context, see Lonergan's *De Deo Trino: Pars Systematica*, translated as *The Triune God: Systematics*, trans. Michael Shields, ed. Robert Doran and H. Daniel Monsour (Toronto: University of Toronto Press, 2007), 133–81. For further accounts of the *imago Dei* that is the human being as related to the Trinitarian relations and processions, in addition to Lonergan's *The Triune God*, see Philip McShane, *Music That Is Soundless*, 3rd ed. (Cape Breton, Nova Scotia: Axial Press, 2005). See also Robert Doran, "Summarizing 'Imitating the Divine Relations: A Theological Contribution to Mimetic Theory,'" in *Contagion: Journal of Violence, Mimesis, and Culture* 14 (2007), 27–38, especially 36–38.

16. Lonergan, "Respect for Human Dignity," in *The Canadian Messenger of the Sacred Heart* (July 1953), in *Bernard Lonergan, Shorter Works*, ed. Robert Croken, Robert Doran, and H. Daniel Monsour, vol 20, *CWL* (Toronto: University of Toronto Press, 2007), 125.

17. Lonergan, "Respect for Human Dignity," *CWL* 20:124. The phrasing faintly echoes both the *Acts of the Apostles* and Karl Marx. *Acts* 2:44–45; *Acts* 4:34–35; Marx, "Critique of the Gotha Program," in *The Marx-Engels Reader* (2nd ed.) ed. Robert Tucker (New York: W.W. Norton, 1978), 531 ("From each according to his ability, to each according to his needs!")

18. Lonergan, "Respect for Human Dignity," *CWL* 20:125. Lonergan's reference to "leveling down" descends of course, from a philosophical lineage that began with Kierkegaard. See Soren Kierkegaard, "The Present Age" (1846), in *A Kierkegaard Anthology*, ed. Robert Bretall (Princeton: Princeton University Press, 1946), 258–69.

19. Lonergan, "The Role of a Catholic University in the Modern World" [1951], in *Collected Works of Bernard Lonergan, Collection*, ed. Frederick Crowe and Robert Doran, vol. 4 , *CWL* (Toronto: University of Toronto Press, 1988), 112; Lonergan, "Self-transcendence: Intellectual, Moral, Religious," *Philosophical and Theological Papers: 1965–1980*, ed. Robert Croken and Robert Doran, vol. 17, *CWL* (Toronto: University of Toronto Press, 2004), at 325

(referring to "the economic and political determinism resulting from competing egoisms").

20. *Insight*, 692; *CWL* 3:714.

21. Lonergan, "Finality, Love, Marriage" [1943], in *CWL* 4:27. Ideology, in Lonergan's usage, "denotes systematic rationalization, that is, a system of thought worked out to defend, justify, legitimate, an iniquitous style of living, of economic arrangements, of political government, of any of the organized forms of human activity." Lonergan, "Self-transcendence: Intellectual, Moral, Religious," *CWL* 17:323. See also *Method in Theology*, 357 ("man is alienated from his true self inasmuch as he refuses self-transcendence, and the basic form of ideology is the self-justification of alienated man.") One might also say that the fundamental form of sin is the refusal of self-transcendence, including the possibilities of self-transcendence offered by grace, and that its extended forms include all the many varieties of alienation, ideology, rationalization, and bias which embody and support that refusal. See note 75 below.

22. Daniel and Philip Berrigan, "A Sermon from Prison" in *America Is Hard to Find*, ed. Daniel Berrigan, (Garden City, N.Y.: Doubleday, 1972), 104.

23. Lonergan's acts of resistance are massively theoretic and remote, which is not to say that they lack immense and immediate implications. See *Phenomenology and Logic: The Boston College Lectures on Mathematical Logic and Existentialism*, ed. Philip McShane, vol. 18, *CWL* (Toronto: University of Toronto Press, 2001), 210–11 (describing the task of "resolute and effective intervention in the dialectic of history"); ibid., 309 ("Man's concept of man determines fundamentally what kind of technical, social, and cultural situation people will produce. The results of that thinking will be cumulative. If there is a horizon limiting the understanding, then unless there is some intervention each successive situation will constantly increase the evils in the situation until finally the civilization vanishes.") Berrigan's acts of resistance, in contrast, are more immediately poignant and pointed, which is not to say that they lack long-term implications.

24. Thomas Merton, "Prologue," *Raids on the Unspeakable* (New York: New Directions, 1966), 6. See, for example, Alasdair MacIntyre, *Against the Self-Images of the Age: Essays on Ideology and Philosophy* (New York: Schocken Books, 1971). The "self-images of the age" have been explored brilliantly by Charles Taylor in *Sources of the Self: The Making of the Modern Identity* (Cambridge: Harvard University Press, 1989) and *A Secular Age* (Cambridge: Belknap Press, 2007). These defective self-images wend and wind their way into institutions in all sorts of subtle and complicated ways, and the institutions in turn perpetuate them relentlessly with generally

disastrous results. I have attempted to critique some of the more dominant self-images operative in legal pedagogy, and by extension in legal practice, in "Ethics as Self-Transcendence: Legal Education, Faith, and an Ethos of Justice" *Seattle University Law Review* 32 (2009): 293–310.

25. Berrigan, *Jeremiah*, xi.

26. See *generally* Glenn Hughes, *Transcendence and History: The Search for Ultimacy from Ancient Societies to Postmodernity* (Columbia: University of Missouri Press, 2003), especially chapters 1–3.

27. See Lonergan, *Method in Theology* (New York: Herder and Herder, 1972), 250.

28. Aquinas, *Summa Theologiae*, I–II, Q. 69, art. 4. The translation quoted in the text may be found in *Summa Theologiae*, vol. 24 (1a2ae 68–70), *The Gifts of the Spirit*, trans. Edward O'Connor C.S.C. (Cambridge: Cambridge University Press, 2006), 61.

29. Daniel and Philip Berrigan, "A Sermon from Prison" in *America Is Hard to Find* (Garden City, N.Y.: Doubleday, 1972), 105.

30. See Lonergan, "Dialectic of Authority," in *A Third Collection*, ed. Frederick Crowe (Mahwah, N.J.: Paulist Press, 1985), 5–12.

31. I find a parallel passage in Lonergan to be a helpful point of comparison. "Bad will is not merely the inconsistency of rational self-consciousness; it is also sin against God. The hopeless tangle of the social surd, of the impotence of common sense, of the endlessly multiplied philosophies, is not merely a *cul-de-sac* for human progress; it is also a reign of sin, a despotism of darkness, and men are its slaves." *Insight*, 692; *CWL* 3:714. Might we not read this as concretely, self-attentively, and self-critically as possible, and with "the agonized conscience of the awakened" of which Niehbur speaks?

32. See, for example, Aquinas's discussion of equity, *Summa Theologiae*, II–II, Q. 120, art. 1 (affirming that in some cases, "to follow the word of law would be an evil, a good to follow what the meaning of justice and the public good demand, letting the letter of the law be set aside."); see also his discussion of the relation between the common good and law in *Summa Theologiae*, I–II, Q. 96, art. 6 ("Every law is ordained for the common well-being, and to that extent gets the force and quality of law; insofar as it falls short here it has no binding force . . . . So that if a case crops up where its observance would be damaging to that common interest, then it is not to be observed."); see also Aquinas' discussion of natural right and legal codes in *Summa Theologiae*, II–II, Q. 60, art. 5 ("Accordingly if it [a legal code] contains something contrary to natural right, it is unjust and has no binding force . . . . And such offending articles are to be classed as corruptions of law, not as laws: this we have already said. Consequently it is not according to them that judgment

should be passed.") See Berrigan, *The Trial of the Catonsville Nine* (New York: Bantam Books, 1970), 102 ("I wish to ask whether or not reverence for the law does not also require a judge to interpret and adjust the law to the needs of the people here and now."); see also *New Hampshire Constitution*, part 1, art. 10 ("Government being instituted for the common benefit, protection, and security, of the whole community, and not for the private interest or emolument of any one man, family, or class of men; therefore, whenever the ends of government are perverted, and public liberty manifestly endangered, and all other means of redress are ineffectual, the people may, and of right ought to reform the old, or establish a new government. The doctrine of nonresistance against arbitrary power, and oppression, is absurd, slavish, and destructive of the good and happiness of mankind.") (quoted in part in *Catonsville*, 105). For similar or nearly identical language, see *Maryland Const.*, Declaration of Rights, Art. 6; *Tenn. Const.* art. 1, § 2; *Va. Const.* art. 1, § 3; *W.Va. Const.* art. 3, § 3; *D.C. Code*, § 4. The last sentence on "nonresistance against arbitrary power" was introduced verbatim as a proposed amendment during the formulation of the Bill of Rights. It was, however, rejected. Herman Ames, *The Proposed Amendments to the Constitution of the United States During the First Century of its History* (New York: Burt Franklin, 1896), 183.

     I am by no means suggesting that there is a simple solution to the antinomies of power and justice, or of civic loyalty and civil disobedience, in Aquinas or elsewhere. But one closed option is well described by Bernanos. "I am therefore free, perfectly free to tell them to their face that they are committing a crime against Christianity by pretending to justify themselves, through a new casuistry of law, justice, and honor . . . . [T]hey have for so long felt themselves incapable of restoring [Christian] order—which means incapable of assenting to the sacrifices necessary for such a restoration—that they have consciously preferred defeat . . . , because such defeat released them from all responsibility." Georges Bernanos, quoted in Hans Urs von Balthasar, *Bernanos: An Ecclesial Existence*, trans. Erasmo Leiva-Merikakis (San Francisco: Ignatius Press, 1996), 252. See also *The Geography of Faith: Conversations between Daniel Berrigan, when Underground, and Robert Coles* (Boston: Beacon Press, 1971), 59 ("We use despair in order not to see things. We become very cynical and critical of any possibility of change in order to protect ourselves from seeing just where we are." [Robert Coles]).

     33. Augustine, *The City of God*, Book 2, trans. Marcus Dods, introduction by Thomas Merton (New York: The Modern Library, 1950), 59–61.

     34. See note 31 above.

     35. *Insight*, 628; *CWL* 3:650–51.

     36. See "The Reign of Sin as False Fact in Society, Economy, Culture, and History" below, on sin as *non ens*. See also Lonergan, "Finality, Love,

Marriage" [1943], in *CWL* 4:27 ("there is a human solidarity in sin with a
dialectical descent deforming knowledge and perverting will").

   37. Individualism, especially expressive individualism, has taken on the
magnitude and character of what Taylor calls "a social imaginary." See
generally, Charles Taylor, *Modern Social Imaginaries* (Durham, N.C.: Duke
University Press, 2006), 23 ("By social imaginary, I mean something much
broader and deeper than the intellectual schemes people may entertain when
they think about social reality in a disengaged mode. I am thinking, rather,
of how people imagine their social existence, how they fit together with
others . . . and the deeper normative notions and images that underlie these
expectations.") For a critique of this now-pervasive social imaginary, and its
distorting effects on our notions of self-love and love of others, see Stephen
Pope, "Expressive Individualism and True Self-Love: A Thomistic
Perspective," *The Journal of Religion* 27 (July 1991): 384 ("in the 'first
language' of expressive individualism, the traditional virtues of altruism,
self-sacrifice, and sympathy for others have been given at best a subordinate
status below the therapeutic values of self-actualization, self-esteem, and
self-acceptance."); ibid., 398 ("To be sure, the effect of sin in the world is
division and strife, egoism and aggression, but these are seen by Thomas as
deviations and corruptions of natural love and as remediable—albeit imper-
fectly and haltingly, in this life—by grace. The prevailing nonteleological
framework of the 'social atomism' that underlies the increasingly dominant
language of expressive individualism, on the other hand, fails to recognize
and appreciate the extent to which we are essentially one of another, bound
together by natural and social ties that form the context, basis, and ally of
self-love.")

   38. John Paul II elevated solidarity to the level of a moral and social
virtue. *Sollicitudo Rei Socialis*, §38, in *Catholic Social Thought: The Documentary
Heritage*, ed. David O'Brian and Thomas Shannon (Maryknoll, N.Y.: Orbis
Books, 1992), 421. But what are the economic or political implications?
Sollicitudo Rei Socialis is not entirely silent on these questions. Very
conspicuously, the encyclical views solidarity as the necessary counterpoise
to the desire for profit and the thirst for power which perennially create
and continuously perpetuate what he called "structures of sin." "When
interdependence is recognized in this way, the correlative response as a moral
and social attitude, as a 'virtue,' is *solidarity*. This then is not a feeling of
vague compassion or shallow distress at the misfortunes of so many people,
both near and far. On the contrary, it is *a firm and persevering determination* to
commit oneself to the *common good*; that is to say to the good of all and
of each individual, because we are *all* really responsible *for all*. This
determination is based on the *solid* conviction that what is hindering full

development is that desire for profit and that thirst for power already mentioned. These attitudes and " 'structures of sin' are only conquered—presupposing the help of divine grace—by a *diametrically opposed attitude . . .*" ibid., 421–22. It is helpful to note that this description of solidarity links solidarity not with easy sentiment but with difficult justice—indeed, with justice as Aquinas defined it. *Summa Theologiae*, II–II, Q. 58, art. 1 ("is justice well defined as the lasting and constant will of rendering to each one his right?"); *Summa Theologiae*, vol. 37, *Justice: 2a-2ae QQ* 57–62, trans. Thomas Gilbey, O.P. (Cambridge: Cambridge University Press, 1975), 19–23.

39. *Summa Theologiae*, II–II, Q. 58, art. 12 ("whether justice is the chief of the moral virtues"); vol. 37, *Justice: 2a–2ae QQ* 57–62, 51 ("The other virtues are commended only for the good they do their possessor, justice, however, for the good it does to another."). For ancients and medievals, *justice* includes that inner justice—a kind of justice within the person—which we call *integrity* and *virtue*, as well as the more conventional sense of giving each person her due through the proper structuring of legal, social, political, and economic institutions and practices. For ancient and medieval thought, distributive justice is only a species, not the genus, of justice. And, of course, without the emergence and development of justice within the person in at least a critical mass of a given population, the chances of socially effective distributive justice are rather slim. Moreover, justice is not merely a matter of putting good will into action. Rather, *practicing justice* depends as much on practicing understanding as it does on practicing good will or action. In Lonergan's poignant words, "good will is never better than the intelligence and reasonableness that it implements. Indeed, when proposals and programmes only putatively are intelligent and reasonable, then the good will that executes them so faithfully and energetically is engaged really in the systematic imposition of ever further evils on the already weary shoulders of mankind." *Insight*, 629; *CWL* 3:652. Significantly, the paragraph from which that sentence is drawn forms an introduction to a section entitled "The Problem of Liberation," and that section in turn is the vestibule to the two chapters on God in *Insight*. See also note 80 below.

40. World Synod of Catholic Bishops (1971), "Justice in the World," in *Catholic Social Thought: The Documentary Heritage*, 292.

41. *Method in Theology*, 40 (noting that neurosis, bias, rationalization, ideology, *ressentiment*, can infect one's horizon. "Nor is that calamity limited to individuals. It can happen to groups, to nations, to blocks of nations, to mankind. It can take different, opposed, belligerent forms to divide mankind and to menace civilization with destruction.") The full sentence is, "Such is the monster that has stood forth in our day." As one can tell from the tone, the sentence was hardly an accidental aside. And, in fact, Lonergan

deliberately added that sentence to an earlier and almost identical draft of the same paragraph that had been completed in March, 1968. Compare *Method*, 40, with "Horizons," *CWL* 17:18, second paragraph.

42. It is obviously difficult to use such terms with precision. Yet at least one might say that "right belief" or "right teaching" does not necessarily mean conservative in the merely inertial sense, and at least one might say that "traditional" is not the same as "traditionalist." It is possible for a traditionalist to betray the tradition, and for a conservative to fail to conserve it. As Jaroslav Pelikan famously quipped, "Tradition is the living faith of the dead; traditionalism is the dead faith of the living." Pelikan, *The Emergence of the Catholic Tradition (100–600)* (Chicago: University of Chicago Press, 1971), 9. By the same token, a liberal may betray the tradition by an incomplete or mediocre appropriation of the tradition. Conserving a living tradition is, after all, an active, not a passive, enterprise. As Lonergan notes, "In teaching and writing history, the historian is mediating the tradition; he is laboring to carry it forward, to conserve it in the active sense of conserving (= creating) by being a living embodiment of it, not only a living but also an articulate, informed, intelligent, wise, devoted embodiment; or he is laboring to destroy it either by a passive conservatism, or by liquidating it, or by endeavoring to put a new tradition in its place . . . he may reduce [the tradition] to triviality . . . he may by his mediocrity bring the tradition to an inauthentic simulacrum of itself; he may bring the tradition to a full consciousness of itself, its achievements, its potentialities, its glaring failures." Lonergan, unpublished notes titled "History," Lonergan Archives, file A622, 10–11 (circa 1962).

43. It goes without saying that *orthodox* does not divide along the lines of the modern Manichean division of *liberal* and *conservative*. What, indeed, is one to make of the simplistic dichotomy of liberal and conservative in a world, and in a church, in which an avowedly conservative pope can pen an encyclical which roundly declares, "Surmounting every type of *imperialism* and determination to preserve their own *hegemony*, the stronger and richer nations must have a sense of moral *responsibility* for the other nations, so that a *real international system* may be established which will rest on the foundation of the equality of all peoples and on the necessary respect for their legitimate differences . . . . Solidarity helps us to see the "other"—whether a person, people, or nation—not just as some kind of instrument, with a work capacity and physical strength, to be exploited at low cost and then discarded when no longer useful, but as our "neighbor," a "helper" (*cf.* Gen. 2:18–20), to be made a sharer, on a par with ourselves, in the banquet of life to which all are equally invited by God." *Sollicitudo Rei Socialis*, §39, in *Catholic Social Thought: The Documentary Heritage*, 422.

44. See, *for example*, World Synod of Catholic Bishops (1971), "Justice in the World," in *Catholic Social Thought: The Documentary Heritage*, 288 (noting "the serious injustices which are building around the world of men a network of domination, oppression, and abuses which stifle freedom and which keep the greater part of humanity from sharing in the building up and enjoyment of a more just and more fraternal world.")

45. The need for such transpositions runs parallel to the ordinary ontogenetic need to grow in one's apprehension of faith. As Lonergan once framed the issue, "in an educated and alert consciousness a childish apprehension of religious truth either must be sublated within an educated apprehension or else it will simply be dropped as outmoded and outworn." *Method*, 139. As Berrigan remarked in prison a year after Lonergan's comment, in poignantly describing an ex-seminarian and fellow prisoner, "One thing is certain—in multitudes of young people, like him, born in the church, nurtured in sacramental experience, schooled and shriven and instructed—the break is a clean one . . . . They remember the church in somewhat the way one remembers an aging grandparent who died in one's youth, whose vigor and best years went by too early to make any difference . . ." *Lights on in the House of the Dead: A Prison Diary* (Garden City, N.Y.: Doubleday, 1974), 30–31. How much of the pathos noticed by Berrigan reflected the wrenching cultural dislocations of the 1960s, and how much reflected the large-scale problem of the dialectic of sacralization and secularization (or indeed, institutional sins of backwardness—see the following footnote for relevant context), are large and important questions. See Lonergan, "Sacralization and Secularization," in *CWL* 17:259–281.

46. Lonergan, "Dialectic of Authority," *A Third Collection*, 8. The need to live on the level of the times is a fairly constant theme in Lonergan's thought. See, *for example*, "Essay in Fundamental Sociology—Philosophy of History," unpublished manuscript fragment [circa 1933–34], 126 (criticizing "Thomists whose last thought is to imitate St Thomas in this matter of thinking in pace with the times."); *Method*, 350 ("the understanding to be reached is to be on the level of one's times. In the medieval period it was static system. In the contemporary world, it has to be at home in modern science, modern scholarship, modern philosophy."); ibid. 351; ibid., 367 ("To operate on the level of our day is to apply the best available knowledge and the most efficient techniques to coordinated group action. But to meet this contemporary exigence will also set the church on a course of continual renewal.") See also Lonergan, "Questionnaire on Philosophy: Response," *CWL* 17:366 ("It has long been my conviction that if Catholics and, in particular, if Jesuits are to live and operate on the level of the times, they must not only know about theories of history but also work out their own.")

47. Thomas Merton, "Prologue," *Raids on the Unspeakable*, 6.

48. "The Role of a Catholic University in the Modern World," *CWL* 4:111. That "movement from real possibility to concrete achievement" itself takes place within the tension of grace and sin, authenticity and unauthenticity. "Note that the two aspects, the practical and the existential, are not separable. However practical any decision is, it reveals and confirms and intensifies the authenticity or unauthenticity of the practical subject. Inversely, however existential any decision is, it attains substance and moment in the measure that it transforms one's conduct and pursuits." Lonergan, "Philosophy and the Religious Phenomenon," *CWL* 17:398.

49. Karl Barth, *The Knowledge of God and the Service of God According to the Teaching of the Reformation*, trans. J. L. M. Haine and Ian Wanderson (London: Hodder and Staughton, 1960), 49–50.

50. Niehbur, "The Ego Alter Dialectic and the Conscience," *Journal of Philosophy* 42 (1945), 359. For a more recent and rather terse contribution to the critique of religious legalism, see Philip McShane, "Humus 2: *Vis Cogitativa*: Contemporary Defective Patterns of Anticipation" (2008), and the 1955 letter from Lonergan quoted there (available at: http://www .philipmcshane.ca).

51. See, in this context, that thundering catalogue of sin and misery in the first part of chapter 22, book 22 of Augustine's *City of God*—not to mention Paul's catalogue in *Romans*, 1:29–32. In the text, I am referring in part to the systematic or culture-wide displacement of the ideal of self-respect by self-esteem, of transcendent hope by optimism, of *caritas* by altruism, of faith in divine providence by an undifferentiated, uncritical, and generic self-approval. (See note 37 above, for further context on the therapeutic strain in our everyday language and culture.) But I am also referring to a diminishing sense of our own finitude and fallibililty as humans and to a correlative superficiality in American culture accompanied by a corresponding increase in what can only be called *hybris*. There is no particular reason to believe that we are not capable of, and indeed actively practicing, greed, envy, malice, lies, self-deceit, self-conceit, sloth, and all the rest, however much our conventionally backed self-esteem assures us otherwise. What is even more destructive, however, is the increasing loss of any socially effective and culturally mediated sense of what Aquinas calls *complacentia boni*, of basic serenity in the desire and presence of the good. For a sustained and nuanced interpretation of Aquinas relating to this topic, see Frederick Crowe, "Complacency and Concern in the Thought of St. Thomas," *Three Thomist Studies*, ed. Michael Vertin (supplemental issue of *Lonergan Workshop* vol. 16, 2000), 71–204. We have, it seems, replaced *complacentia boni*—what Lonergan refers to both poetically and with theological accuracy, as the sense of living

in a "friendly universe" (*Method in Theology*, 117)—with a terrifyingly simplistic and superficial ideology of optimism.

52. "Listening to the cry of those who suffer violence and are oppressed by unjust systems and structures, and hearing the appeal of a world that by its perversity contradicts the plan of the Creator, we have shared our awareness of the Church's vocation to be present in the heart of the world by proclaiming the Good News to the poor, freedom to the oppressed, and joy to the afflicted." World Synod of Catholic Bishops (1971), "Justice in the World," in *Catholic Social Thought: The Documentary Heritage*, ed. David O'Brian and Thomas Shannon (Maryknoll, N.Y.: Orbis Books, 1992), 288; see also ibid., 290 ("This desire, however, will not satisfy the expectations of our time if it ignores the objective obstacles which social structures place in the way of conversion of hearts, or even of the realization of the ideal of charity.")

53. One must include within this not only the cultural structures recurrently productive of sin, but also, so to speak, sins against developing cultures of human authenticity. Consider only one, among many possible instances, the bourgeois reduction of the genuine grounding function of culture to nothing more than amusement. "Modern society has reduced culture to a recreational activity to be indulged in by those who are able to count on the economic service of others." Louis Dupré, *Marx's Social Critique of Culture* (New Haven, Conn.: Yale University Press, 1983), 17. See also Neil Postman, *Amusing Ourselves to Death: Public Discourse in the Age of Television* (New York: Viking, 1984); R. G. Collingwood, *The Principles of Art* (Oxford: Oxford University Press, 1938), 94–104.

54. See Lonergan's definition of the cultural sphere: "there is the cultural level, where human living depends upon man's ideas upon man. Culture in the anthropological sense is the currently effective totality of immanently produced and symbolically communicated contents of imagination, emotion, and sentiment; of inquiry, insight, and conception; of reflection, judgment, and valuation; of decision and implementation. In these fields man presupposes nature but also makes himself by taking thought." *CWL* 18:302; ibid., 303 ("each successive situation provides a concrete and almost visible *objectification* of what man has been feeling, thinking, and deciding about man").

55. "To material, economic, and political distortion there probably will be added cultural distortion as well." Lonergan "The Human Good," *CWL* 17:345.

56. Lonergan refers to this distinct level under the heading of "sin as aberration, as the evil that is opposite to cultural development, to development on the reflective level . . ." *CWL* 1:6263.

57. See Lonergan, *Method*, 32 ("Over and above mere living and operating, men have to find a meaning and value in their living and operating. It is the function of culture to discover, express, validate, criticize, correct, develop, improve such meaning and value.") Perhaps the seven terms he uses in the second sentence are very loosely correlated with the first seven of Lonergan's eight functional specialties.

I cannot in the present context relate "sinful cultural structures" to the stages of meaning or to "the dialectic of community" as it operates within the dynamics of culture. But that much larger context is relevant here. For a penetrating treatment of the topic, see Robert Doran, *What Is Systematic Theology?* (Toronto: University of Toronto Press, 2005), 156–79.

58. John Paul II, *The Gospel of Life* (*Evangelium Vitae*) (New York: Times Books, 1995), 41 (para 23) (describing "a culture of death" in which "the values of *being* are replaced by those of *having*" and the notion of quality of life becomes "interpreted primarily or exclusively as economic efficiency, inordinate consumerism, physical beauty or pleasure, to the neglect of the more profound dimensions—interpersonal, spiritual and religious—of existence").

The Catholic critique of a "culture of death" goes well beyond the specific context of *Evangelium Vitae*. It extends into all the cultural correlatives of what Hopkins named "the death-dance in our blood," and they are legion. Gerard Manley Hopkins, "The Blessed Virgin Compared to the Air We Breathe," in *Gerard Manley Hopkins*, ed. Catherine Phillips (Oxford: Oxford University Press, 1986), 159.

59. Wolfgang Huber, *Violence: The Unrelenting Assault on Human Dignity*, trans. Ruth Gritsch (Minneapolis: Fortress Press, 1996), 23–24.

60. Berrigan, "Forward," to Huber, *Violence: The Unrelenting Assault on Human Dignity*, xii.

61. Lonergan, "Questionnaire," *CWL* 17:367.

62. Berrigan, *To Dwell in Peace*, 137.

63. The term refers to an artistic technique of imprinting involving the transfer of images from a specially prepared paper to another object such as glass, porcelain, etc. *The Compact Edition of the Oxford English Dictionary* (Oxford: Oxford University Press, 1971), vol. I, 659. On the transference of images (more technically, phantasms as pre-motions) between generations as a fundamental element of historical process, see Lonergan's historical manuscripts from the 1930s, some of which remain unpublished. (See note 102 below for a list of the manuscripts that have been published.) On phantasms as historically operative pre-motions, see, for example, "The Philosophy of History," MS, 98 ("Nonetheless, these human elections, though free, are strictly subordinate to a statistical law . . . .

What differentiates one social epoch from another does not lie in the individual wills of the time but in the upper and lower limits set these wills by the previous age. No man can be better than he knows how and no man can be worse than his temptations and opportunities. Thus the heritage of intellectual vacuity and social chaos given by the nineteenth century to the twentieth is the real reason why the twentieth is such a mess.") On the redemptive counterpoising premotion stemming from Christ, see ibid.,121.

64. *Method*, 79.

65. See Martin Heidegger, *The Question Concerning Technology*, trans. William Lovitt (New York: Harper & Row, 1977), 28 ("The threat to man does not come in the first instance from the potentially lethal machines and apparatus of technology. The actual threat has already affected man in his essence."); Robert Doran, *Theology and the Dialectics of History* (Toronto: University of Tortonto Press, 1990), 505 (describing "the mechanomorphic instrumentalization of consciousness that is responsible for the multiple distortions of the dialectical processes of history that constitute the present situation."); ibid., 520 (noting the specific form of repression that is "achieved by the instrumentalization of reason and the concomitant neglect of aesthetic sensitivity that are the immanent if perverted form of mechanomorphic society emergent from the distorted dialectic of community."); Erich Fromm, *"On Disobedience" and Other Essays* (London: Routledge, 1984), 40–41 ("necrophilia . . . is a phenomenon deeply rooted in a culture which is increasingly dominated by the bureaucratic organizations of the big corporations, governments, and armies, and by the central role of man-made things, gadgets, and machines. This bureaucratic industrialism tends to transform human beings into things. It tends to replace nature by technical devices, the organic by the inorganic.").

66. See the somewhat chilling Wikipedia entry on "management cybernetics" at http://en.wikipedia.org/wiki/Management_cybernetics.

67. See Dominic Pettman, *After the Orgy: The Politics of Exhaustion* (Albany: SUNY Press, 2002), 141–67.

68. On the academic world as an institution rife with necrophiliac trends, see Berrigan, *To Dwell in Peace*, 186–214 and 294–307 (on his years at Cornell, Tulane, and Berkeley); see also Philip McShane, "Modernity and the Emergence of Adequate Empiricism," in *Lonergan's Challenge to the University and Economy* (Washington, D.C.: University Press of America [1980]): "But the difficulties, as any academic reading this knows in his or her bones, are an all-pervading presence of politics and power, of paranoia and paper, of committees and non-conversations, and, at its deepest, of intellectual necrophilia. I am not here writing about clear instances of corruption. I am writing about the daily flow of talk and tests and memos and meetings in its

continual contribution to alienation" (83) On the distorting effect on the operative self-image of the human being, see generally Philip McShane, *Lack in the Beingstalk* (Cape Breton, Nova Scotia: Axial Press, 2008).

69. Thomas Merton once wrote: "Love takes one's neighbor as oneself, and loves him with all the immense humility and discretion and reserve and reverence without which no one can presume to enter into the sanctuary of another's subjectivity." Merton, *The Wisdom of the Desert: Some Sayings of the Desert Fathers* (New York: New Directions, 1960), 18. And, I would add, without which no one can enter into the sanctuary of her own subjectivity. See also McShane, *Lack in the Beingstalk*, 193, 197 ("I am suggesting a view of adult growth in meaning distasteful in the contemporary cancer ward of verbal consuming pseudo-growth . . . . You are incessantly invited to settle down. You are invited to call for plain meaning in a necrophiliac obviousness. You are invited to expect to eventually meet yourself of last year, of twenty five years ago, as an obvious equal.")

70. *Method*, 103 ("Man's transcendental subjectivity is mutilated or abolished, unless he is stretching forth towards the intelligible, the unconditioned, the good of value.")

71. Lonergan, "Analytic Concept of History," ed. Frederick Crowe, in *Method: Journal of Lonergan Studies* 11 (1993 [1938]): 22. The context of Lonergan's comment in 1938 is the distortion introduced into a social system by privileged and oppressed classes, but I see no reason why the concrete and expansive nature of the dynamic would not be the same on the level of cultural meanings and values.

72. Lonergan, *Method in Theology*, 99.

73. Berrigan, "Letter to the Jesuits," *America Is Hard to Find* (Garden City, New York: Doubleday, 1972), 35. Berrigan uses the phrase in the specific context of the Vietnam War.

74. Lonergan, "The Role of a Catholic University in the Modern World," *CWL* 4:110–11. As Lonergan emphasizes, one has to think of this quite concretely. And as he notes in another context, almost three hundred years of "doctrines on politics, economics, education, and . . . ever further doctrines . . . have done not a little to make human life unlivable." *CWL* 10, *Topics in Education*, 232.

75. For a compact statement on the relation between sin and grace in this context, see Lonergan, *Method*, 364. ("Sin is alienation from man's authentic being, which is self-transcendence, and sin justifies itself by ideology. As alienation and ideology are destructive of community, so the self-sacrificing love that is Christian charity reconciles man to his true being, and undoes the mischief initiated by alienation and consolidated by ideology.")

76. Eric Voegelin, *Order and History: The Ecumenic Age*, vol. 4 (Baton Rouge: University of Louisiana Press, 1974), 57.

77. Philip McShane, *Quodlibet 19*, "The Solution to the Problem of Feelings in Lonergan Studies," 12, http://www.philipmcshane.ca.

78. It is also a sense of *sin* that resonates with the "masters of suspicion," as Ricouer famously calls Marx, Nietzsche, and Freud. Paul Ricouer, "Psychoanalysis and the Movement of Contemporary Culture," in *The Conflict of Interpretations: Essays in Hermeneutics*, ed. Don Ihde (Evanston: Northwestern University Press, 1974), 148–50. As Lonergan once remarked, "one of the fundamental inspirations of Karl Marx is perhaps his hatred and critique of the sins of the bourgeoisie in the nineteenth century . . . . Again, in Nietzsche there is a hatred and critique of the sins of the masses, of what is all too human, of their resentment against human excellence of any kind." *CWL* 10, *Topics in Education*, 58.

79. *Summa Theologiae*, II–II, QQ 59–78; see also Martin Rhonheimer, "Sins Against Justice," trans. Frederick Lawrence, in *The Ethics of Aquinas*, ed. Stephen Pope (Washington, D.C.: Georgetown University Press, 2002), 287–303.

80. Augustine, *Against Faustus the Manichean*, 22.78, quoted in Donald X. Burt, *Friendship and Society: An Introduction to Augustine's Practical Philosophy* (Cambridge: William Eerdmans Publishing, 1999), 162. This ancient sense of "justice" is related to the modern sense of "justice" but differs from it as well. It refers to justice within the soul, the habitual and proper ordering of its activities and levels in an effective orientation to its transcendent goal. Yet as Plato taught so clearly in the *Republic*, a society is simply the souls of its members "writ large"; humans that are disoriented will produce a society that is disoriented; and an actively or aggressively disoriented society will twist each new generation into its distorted image. In the limit the social and political situation becomes, in Platonic terms, "a city of pigs," *The Republic of Plato*, trans. Allan Bloom (New York: Basic Books, 1968), 49 (372d), or in Nietzsche's terms, a culture of "the last man." "Zarathustra's Prologue," "Thus Spoke Zarathustra," in *The Portable Nietzsche*, trans. Walter Kaufmann (New York: The Viking Press, 1968), 128–31.

81. Berrigan, *Jeremiah*, 43, 51.

82. *Insight*, 477; *CWL* 3:501–2. Although the treatment of the dynamics of "genuineness" in *Insight* is largely in terms of the individual, the paragraph on "the sanction of genuineness" makes clear that the analysis extends well beyond the frame of the individual person. *Insight*, 478; *CWL* 3:503.

83. The naming, of course, can be a function of what Lonergan called "the variable standard of adequate expression." *Insight*, 557; *CWL* 3:580. So one can agree with an underlying insight concerning sin without necessarily

approving of the accuracy or adequacy of its expression in a given author. Some of Berrigan's expressions in the late 1960s and early 1970s may seem to stem from the fever of the time, products of what Berrigan in 1970 called "the outer and inner space which the last six years have both opened and sucked us into, a giant vortex in nature and in us." Daniel Berrigan, *Lights on in the House of the Dead: A Prison Diary* (Garden City, N.Y.: Doubleday, 1974), 29. But even of those expressions, one can and must ask whether they contain a core of retrievable truth. See R. G. Collingwood, *Principles of Art*, 195 ("we must, in fairness . . . ask ourselves whether it is rejected as altogether mistaken, or only as overstating something which, when the overstatement is removed, turns out to be true.")

84. Abraham Heschel, introduction to *The Prophets* (New York: HarperCollins Perennial Classics, 2001), xxix. (For Berrigan's friendship with Heschel, see *To Dwell in Peace*, 178–79.) In the context of the "prophetic" function of history, Lonergan once made this remark: "Prophetic: it expresses a viewpoint on what the direction of the future should be; it interprets or reinterprets the past coherently with its ethical and prophetic views." Unpublished notes titled "History," Lonergan Archives, file A622, 3 (circa 1962).

85. Berrigan, "Forward," in Wolfgang Huber, *Violence: The Unrelenting Assault on Human Dignity*, xii.

86. Heschel, introduction to *The Prophets*, xxix.

87. *Jeremiah*, 8:18.

88. Voegelin, *Israel and Revelation*, 488.

89. Ibid. at 486.

90. Collingwood, *Principles of Art*, 336.

91. Ibid.

92. Ibid.

93. Flannery O'Connor, "The Fiction Writer and his Country" (1957), quoted in *Flannery O'Connor: Spiritual Writings*, ed. Robert Ellsberg (Maryknoll, N.Y.: Orbis Books, 2003), 62–63 (emphasis added).

94. And perhaps also surrounded by Catholics who believe in a consistent life ethic. Berrigan's opposition to war and violence is well-known. For his opposition to abortion, see Berrigan, "Forward," in Wolfgang Huber, *Violence: The Unrelenting Assault on Human Dignity*, trans. Ruth Gritsch (Minneapolis: Fortress Press, 1996), xiii ("Let the just-war theory, along with hoary justifications of slavery, capital punishment, abortion, and other assorted grotesqueries, be granted, at long last, Christian burial."); "The Strange Case of the Man Who Could Not Please Anyone," in Daniel Berrigan, *Testimony: The Word Made Fresh* (Maryknoll, New York: Orbis Books, 2004), 197–98 ("I said at the time, and later, and still say, abortion is

a horror, as capital punishment is a horror. A civilized people has no business disposing of others, no matter who, no matter what stage of life . . . A civilized culture is known for cherishing, rather than obliterating, the lives in its midst, 'midst' understood as a kind of unbroken line, a lifeline. Call it conscience, call it moral understanding. It extends from the womb to death row to Iraq.") On being surrounded, see ibid. 198 ("Such opinions as these, need I say, were also found offensive, this time by the secular left . . . . According to the Catholics, you had to oppose abortion and support war . . . . And according to the seculars, you had to oppose the war and support abortion on demand.")

95. I owe this phrase to Hans-Georg Gadamer, who used it to describe the effects induced in students by the American educational system. He made the remark at a conference on hermeneutics and structuralism at York University in November 1978. The remark is recorded on a video of the final session, which was a panel discussion, moderated by Philip McShane, between Gadamer, Voegelin, Lonergan, Allan Bloom, and Roger Poole.

96. See "The Reign of Sin as False Fact in Society, Economy, Culture, and History" below on sin as "false fact."

97. Berrigan's growing body of commentary on the Old Testament provides eloquent testimony to his commitment 'to add to and perfect the old by means of the new.' Daniel Berrigan, *Daniel: Under the Siege of the Divine* (Farmington, Penn.: Plough Publishing, 1998); *Exodus: Let My People Go* (Eugene, Oreg.: Cascade Books, 2008); *Ezekiel: Vision in the Dust* (Maryknoll, N.Y.: Orbis Books, 1997); *Genesis: Fair Beginnings, then Foul* (Lanham, Md.: Rowman & Littlefield, 2006); *Isaiah: Spirit of Courage, Gift of Tears* (Minneapolis: Fortress Press, 1996); *Jeremiah: The World, the Wound of God* (Minneapolis: Fortress Press, 1999); *Job: And Death No Dominion* (Franklin, Wisc.: Sheed & Ward, 2000); *Lamentations: From New York to Kabul and Beyond* (Lanham, Md: Sheed & Ward, 2002); *Minor Prophets Major Themes* (Marion, S.Dak.: Fortkamp Publishing, 1995); *Wisdom: The Feminine Face of God* (Franklin, Wisc.: Sheed & Ward, 2001). See also his New Testament commentary, *Whereon to Stand: The Acts of the Apostles and Ourselves* (Baltimore, Md.: Fortkamp Publishing Co., 1991).

98. Lonergan, "Moral Theology and the Human Sciences," *CWL* 17:302.

99. Those who study Lonergan will know his stand on this score. But it is most easily illustrated in his repeated comments about the necessity of an adequate economic theory for alleviating or eliminating poverty. See, for example, "Sacralization and Secularization," *CWL* 17:280 ("Cardinal Daniélou speaks of the poor. It is a worthy topic, but I feel that the basic step in aiding them in a notable manner is a matter of spending one's nights and days in a deep and prolonged study of economic analysis.") His stance is also

evident in his critique of Catholic social thought as not technically proficient. "Questionnaire," *CWL* 17:370 ("perhaps the great weakness of Catholic social thought is its apparent lack of awareness of the need for technical knowledge."); "Healing and Creating in History," *A Third Collection*, 109n14 ("Moral precepts that are not technically specific turn out to be quite ineffectual").

Lonergan's observation on the moral precept of the "family wage" in Catholic social thought is revealing. "The obligation to pay a family wage may be concluded from evident moral principles. But the de facto operative economic theory may be that of a market economy, so that any employer that does pay a family wage sooner or later goes bankrupt because his wicked competitors do not pay a family wage. The de facto result is that a family wage is not paid and, indeed, cannot be paid until a modification of the market economy is brought about either by recurrent legislation on minimum wages or by a more radical criticism of the market economy itself." "Moral Theology and the Human Sciences," *CWL* 17:310; see also ibid., 311 ("the human science 'economics' is in need of similar radical criticism").

One last piece of data, not perhaps as insignificant as it may seem. In Lonergan's copy of Joan Robinson's *Aspects of Development and Underdevelopment* (Cambridge: Cambridge University Press, 1979), he marked two passages on page 34: "Economists generally seem to support the capitalists' principle that what is profitable is right. The application of this principle in the Third World leads to a large part of whatever surplus is available being devoted to the kind of production least propitious to all-round economic progress . . . . In fact, the highest level of luxurious living is often found in the poorest countries and, with it, the greatest concentration of power in the hands of the few." See Philip McShane's work on linguistics in light of interiority, *A Brief History of Tongue* (Halifax, Nova Scotia: Axial Press, 1998), the appendix on world hunger and Lonergan's economics ("operation WHALE"), 163. For a more ample contextualization of Lonergan's economics, see generally McShane, *Pastkeynes Pastmodern Economics: A Fresh Pragmatism* (Halifax, Nova Scotia: Axial Press, 2002).

100. The words are from *Ecclesiastes*, 4:1–3, as quoted by Lonergan in five pages of unpublished handwritten notes from the early 1930s titled "General Ethic [Metaphysic of Customs]." If one compares the first page to the third page, the notes seem to be Lonergan's reworking of an outline for a draft of something of his own—perhaps the missing first 94 pages of his *Essay in Fundamental Sociology*, perhaps some other lost work. (There is, for example, an interesting reference to "our outline of a Summa Philosophica" in "Philosophy of History," MS, 123.)

101. Berrigan, *To Dwell in Peace*, 120.

102. Lonergan's early manuscripts on history were not discovered until after his death in 1984. Three of the eight manuscripts have now been published. "Pantôn Anakephalaiôsis [the Restoration of All Things]" (finished in April, 1935) was published in *Method: Journal of Lonergan Studies* 9 (1991): 139–62; "Sketch for a Metaphysic of Human Solidarity" (1935) was published as an appendix to the "Pantôn" article. Ibid., 163–72. In addition, Lonergan's manuscript entitled "Analytic Concept of History," written probably in 1938, has been published in *Method: Journal of Lonergan Studies* 11 (1993): 5–35.

103. See Michael Shute, *The Origins of Lonergan's Notion of the Dialectic of History: A Study of Lonergan's Early Writings on History* (Lanham, Md.: University Press of America, 1993); Patrick Brown, "System and History in Lonergan's Early Historical and Economic Manuscripts," *Journal of Macrodynamic Analysis* 1 (2001): 32–76.

104. "Philosophy of History," unpublished manuscript fragment of a larger lost work titled "Essay in Fundamental Sociology" (circa 1933–34), 126 (criticizing "Thomists whose last thought is to imitate St Thomas in this matter of thinking in pace with the times.").

105. Ibid., 26.

106. Letter of January 22, 1935 to Rev. Henry Keane, quoted in Fred Crowe, *Lonergan* (Collegeville, Minn.: The Liturgical Press, 1992), 22.

107. Evidence for the early Lonergan's commitment to being on the cutting edge rather than the soft center may also be discerned in remarks he made in a letter to a superior in 1938. "As philosophy of history is as yet not recognised as the essential branch of philosophy that it is, I hardly expect to have it assigned me as my subject during the biennium. I wish to ask your approval for maintaining my interest in it, profiting by such opportunities as may crop up . . ." Letter to Rev. Henry Keane, dated August 10, 1938, quoted in Frederick Crowe, "History That Is Written: A Note on Patrick Brown's 'System and History,'" *Journal of Macrodynamic Analysis* 2 (2002), 115–24, 123n27.

108. "Questionnaire on Philosophy: Response," *CWL* 17:366.

109. *Insight* obviously reflects such a concern and conviction, containing, as it does, "a general analysis of the dynamic structure of human history." Lonergan, "Transition from a Classicist World-view to Historical-mindedness," *A Second Collection*, 7. The only published clues to the existence of the manuscripts I am aware of were an aside by Lonergan in "*Insight* Revisited" and a stray remark by Eric O'Connor; the remarks are significant in retrospect but were oblique at the time. "*Insight* Revisited," *A Second Collection*, 271; R. Eric O'Connor, "From a Mathematician," *Spirit as Inquiry: Studies in Honor of Bernard Lonergan, S.J.*, ed. Frederick Crowe, *Continuum* 2,

no. 3 (Autumn 1964): 14 ("My first meeting with Father Lonergan [in 1941] was both disconcerting and surprising. I had recently finished my formal mathematical studies, had heard of him many times but our paths had never crossed, and we were together for about ten minutes. In that time he sketched for me some recent ideas of his for a philosophy of history with concepts that, after the first few minutes, went beyond any questions that I had even glimpsed the possibility of asking.")

110. Plato, *Republic*, Bk. V, 473d, trans. Allan Bloom (New York: Basic Books, 1968), 153–54. See note 164 below.

111. Lonergan, "Gilbert Keith Chesterton," *Loyola College Review* 17 (1931): 7–10, collected in *Shorter Papers*, *CWL* 20:56.

112. See notes 104, 106, and 107 above. See also "Pantôn," *Method: Journal of Lonergan Studies* 9 (1991 [1935]), 162 ("Is then the situation hopeless? Certainly, unless we settle down, face the facts, and think on the abstract level of modern history.")

113. "Philosophy of History," MS, 95 (first page of surviving manuscript). For a passage concerning economics and politics, see ibid., 124–25.

114. Lonergan, "Secondary Patrons of Canada," *The Montreal Beacon* no. 23 (January 3, 1941): 3, in *CWL* 20:66. For Lonergan's references to Trotsky's doctrine of "continuous revolution" in the mid-1930s, see "Outline of an Analytic Concept of History," MS, 14 ("The real truth of the continuous revolution can be found only on a higher level, the level of a self-renunciation that is a new birth into a higher order."); "Analytic Concept of History, in Blurred Outline," MS, 14; "Analytic Concept of History," *Method: Journal of Lonergan Studies* 11 (1993 [1938]): 24.

115. "Pantôn Anakephalaiôsis [The Restoration of All Things]," *Method: Journal of Lonergan Studies* 9 (1991), 156.

116. On the characteristics of the renaissance or "new order," see "Analytic Concept of History, in Blurred Outline," MS, 14–15; "Outline of an Analytic Concept of History," MS, 14–19; "Analytic Concept of History," *Method: Journal of Lonergan Studies* 11 (1993 [1938]): 24–25.

117. "Pantôn," 156.

118. James Joyce, *Ulysses* (corrected text), ed. Hans Gabler (New York: Random House, 1986), 28.

119. "Philosophy of History," MS, 98. See also File A336 in the Lonergan Archives, which contain extracts from a 1933 article titled "Bequests of the Nineteenth Century to the Twentieth."

120. "Philosophy of History," MS, 99. For a later context on the affirmation of the thesis of progress, see *Insight*, 688, *CWL* 3:710 ("The cult of progress has suffered an eclipse, not because man does not develop, nor because development does not imply a revision of what has been, but because

development does imply that perfection belongs not to the present but to the future. Had that implication of present short-comings not been overlooked with such abandon, had the apostles of progress not mistaken their basic views for premature attainments of future perfection, then the disillusionment of the twentieth century could hardly have been at once so unexpected, so bitter, and so complete.") See also *Insight*, 691; *CWL* 3:713 ("So the counter-positions multiply; they occupy a vast territory from high-minded incoherence to simple-minded opportunism and violence").

121. "Outline of an Analytic Concept of History," MS, 10; ibid., 7 ("enlightened self-interest is a contradiction: for the self-seeker sees the world with a subjective bias that excludes enlightenment.")

122. "Philosophy of History," MS, 99.

123. Ibid.

124. Ibid.

125. "Analytic Concept of History," *Method: Journal of Lonergan Studies* 11 (1993 [1938]): 18.

126. The topic of bias as sin in Lonergan's thought deserves a treatment all its own. Here let me simply note that individual and group egoism for Lonergan produce cumulative large-scale "structures of sin," to use John Paul II's designation of a dynamic which makes sin not only economic, social, political and cultural but historical as well. See note 38 above. For unfortunately, the objective falsity or *non ens* of individual and group bias does not somehow magically terminate in discrete individual or group actions. Rather, the objective falsity by the nature of the case becomes relentlessly perpetuated in social, economic, political, and cultural domains. *Method in Theology*, 360 ("To ignorance and incompetence there are added alienation and ideology. Egoists find loopholes in social arrangements, and they exploit them to enlarge their own share and diminish the share of others in current instances of the particular good. Groups exaggerate the magnitude and importance of their contribution to society. They provide a market for the ideological façade that would justify their ways before the bar of public opinion. If they succeed in their deception, the social process is distorted . . . . There emerge the richer classes and the poorer classes, and the rich become ever richer, while the poor sink into misery and squalor."); *Method in Theology*, 54 ("But development, guided by group egoism, is bound to be one-sided. It divides the body social not merely into those that have and those that have not but also makes the former the representatives of the cultural flower of the age to leave the latter the apparent survivals from a forgotten era. Finally, in the measure that the group encouraged and accepted an ideology to rationalize its own behavior, in the same measure it will be blind to the real

situation, and it will be bewildered by the emergence of a contrary ideology that will call to consciousness an opposed group egoism.")

127. Ibid., 21–22.

128. "Analytic Concept of History, in Blurred Outline," MS, 11.

129. *Topics in Education, CWL* 10:60, 62.

130. "Philosophy of History," MS, 106.

131. "Pantôn," *Method: Journal of Lonergan Studies* 9 (1991): 145 ("The unity of man achieved by intellect has to be a unity in truth, if it is to be stable. Peace fundamentally is this unity in truth and only phenomenally is it 'order with tranquility.' Opposed to peace is the atomization of humanity, the *Zersplitterung* that follows from error and sin, and the false substitutes of national self-idolatry or the deification of emperors to secure what reason is powerless to secure.")

132. For this terminology in the early Lonergan, see, for example, *Grace and Freedom, CWL* 1:331–32 ("as objective truth is the object of intelligence and understanding, just as the presence of objective truth is the possibility of understanding and explanation, so also objective falsity is the negation of an object of intelligence and understanding, and the presence of objective falsity is the negation of the possibility of understanding or explanation."); see also A1875, "Philosophy of Morals," 1 (using Hegel's dialectic of master and slave as a paradigm of the "objective falsity of situation") (unpublished notes in the Lonergan Archives).

133. For an account of Augustine's treatment of sin, see Paul Griffiths, *Lying: An Augustinian Theology of Duplicity* (Grand Rapids, Mich.: Brazos Press, 2004), chapter 3.

134. Ibid., 126.

135. "Evil as such is nonbeing." *De Malo*, Q. II, art. 4, *The De Malo of Thomas Aquinas*, trans. Richard Regan, ed. Brian Davies (Oxford: Oxford University Press, 2001), 151; *De Malo*, Q. I, art. 2, 75 (evil as "privation of a due perfection").

136. *CWL* 10: 50. See also the distinctions Lonergan draws in *Insight* between basic sin, moral evil, and physical evils. *Insight*, 666–67; *CWL* 3:689–91. As to basic sin, "all that intelligence can grasp with respect to basic sin is that there is no intelligibility to be grasped. What is basic sin? It is the irrational. Why does it occur? If there were a reason, it would not be sin." *Insight*, 667; *CWL* 3:690.

137. "Pantôn," *Method: Journal of Lonergan Studies* 9 (1991): 146.

138. This notion receives a brief (but in some ways less oblique) treatment in Lonergan's 1943 article, "Finality, Love, Marriage." *CWL* 4:26 (noting that "rationalization may involve any degree of culpability, from the maximum of a sin against the light which rejects known truth, to the

minimum of precluding such futurible advance in knowledge and virtue as without even unconscious rationalization would have been achieved.") There are obvious complexities here relating ultimately to the distinction in *Insight* between genetic or developmental processes on the one hand and dialectical processes on the other. It would seem that sin in the first instance is not the mere absence of a development that would not otherwise be concretely possible, but is rather the operative preclusion of "proximately potential development" through more or less advertent decisions not to follow the lead of intelligence and reasonableness, or decisions not to extend that lead into actions or deeds. For the language of "proximately potential development," see File A491 in the Lonergan Archives (note that the context is not explicitly a discussion of sin).

139. *CWL* 21:6. In *For a New Political Economy*, Lonergan used that phrase to describe the effects of what he called "a scientific generalization" of a field. I believe it is fair to say that Lonergan in the 1930s was attempting something like a scientific generalization for Catholic social thought.

140. The context is fuller in *Insight*, but the basic notion is explicitly operative in the historical manuscripts, and Lonergan explicitly applies it to historical process. "Sin is a surd in the historical process . . . . Hence, sin and its consequents have to be treated as surds in the data of experience . . . it is the truth that lacks plausibility in the face of the accumulated consequents of sin." "A Theory of History," MS, 4. His later terminology shifts some; for example, in 1957 he spoke of "the sociohistorical surd." *Understanding and Being*, vol. 5, *CWL* (Toronto: University of Toronto Press, 1990), 236. But he continued to use the description of the surd as a "false fact." Ibid.

141. *Grace and Freedom, CWL*, 1:331.

142. *Insight*, 667, *CWL* 3:690 ("when a problem contains the irrational, it can be handled correctly only in a highly complex and critical fashion."); *Insight*, 229, *CWL* 3:254 ("The objective social situation possesses the intelligibility put into it by those that brought it about"). Lonergan treats the category of historical objective falsity in *Insight* under a number of different headings, but one of them is his notion of a succession of less comprehensive syntheses culminating in the modern situation. E.g., *Insight*, 690, *CWL* 3:712 ("If this succession of ever less comprehensive syntheses can be deduced from man's failure to understand himself and his situation dialectically . . . still it is far too general a theorem to unravel at a stroke the tangled skein of intelligibility and absurdity in concrete situations. Its generality has to be mediated by a vast accumulation of direct and inverse insights and by a long series of judgments of truth and of value, before any concrete judgments can be made.")

143. "Philosophy of History" MS, 129–30.

144. "Outline of an Analytic Concept of History," MS, 11("To know men empirically is not to know them deeply: *agere sequitur esse* [action follows being] is not true of man as it is of things, because the actions of men are frequently contrary to their nature; so if the realist forms his idea of human nature from human action, his idea is false and its application disastrous—the disaster of *Realpolitik* and liberal economics.") See also *Understanding and Being*, CWL 5:236 ("On the international scale, the actual existence of what should not be is the ground of *Realpolitik*. 'We have to defend the nation; everything would be fine if the other people did what they ought to do, but they don't, and so we can't.'")

145. On this topic, there are many relevant passages throughout the body of Lonergan's work. For three representative samples, see "Finality, Love, Marriage" [1943], *CWL* 4:26–27 ("this deformation takes place not only in the individual but also and much more convincingly in the social conscience. For to the common mind of the community the facts of life are the poor performance of men in open contradiction with the idealism of human aspiration; and this antithesis between brutal fact and spiritual orientation leaves the will a choice in which truth seems burdened with the unreal and unpractical air of falsity."); *Insight*, 689–90; *CWL* 3:711–12 ("The social surd, which should be discounted as mere proof of aberration, is regarded as evidence in favor of error. Man becomes a realist. The dictates of intelligence and reasonableness are found irrelevant to concrete living. The facts have to be faced, and facing them means the adjustment of theory to practice. But every adjustment make the incidental sins of the past into the commonly accepted rule of the present; the social surd expands, and its expansion demands a further adjustment."); "Questionnaire," *CWL* 17:367 ("Further, the more that objective situations are distorted by unintelligent and irrational actions, the less are they capable of giving rise to fresh insights, since all that intelligence can discern in the unintelligible is its lack of intelligibility . . . . Then amoralism . . . sets aside the moralists and appeals to the efficient causes of modern science, for it proposes to be really practical, to be effective, to get things done. But the cult of efficiency in politics and economics easily becomes oppression, revolution, warfare. So we learnt about the liquidation of the opponents of Machiavelli's *Principe*, the liquidation of the feudal remnants blocking the expansion of bourgeois liberalism, the liquidation of the bourgeoisie in the People's Republics.")

146. "The Role of the Catholic University in the Modern World," *CWL* 4:110. Lonergan later related this particular distorting colonization of the life-world to the wave of secular modernity stemming from Machiavelli. "Popular thought easily accepts secularism by its insistence that solutions are sound if they obviously will work. But this, of course, is merely an

unconscious shift back to Machiavelli . . . they look at how men in fact live and not at such stuff as how men ought to live." *Macroeconomic Dynamics: An Essay in Circulation Analysis, CWL* 15:95.

147. "Pantôn," *Method: Journal of Lonergan Studies* 9 (1991): 145.

148. "Philosophy of History," MS, 128–29.

149. Ibid.

150. Ibid, 130. Berrigan has spent a lifetime, of course, committed to the idea that it is no figure.

151. Lonergan, "Quebec's Opportunity," *The Montreal Beacon*, May 2, 1941, review of Moses Coady, *Masters of Their Own Destiny*, collected in *CWL* 20:144.

152. Berrigna, *To Dwell in Peace*, 296.

153. Lonergan, *For a New Political Economy, CWL* 21:8n3. The sentence occurs in an earlier discarded draft of §3 of chapter one; in the draft, the section was titled "The Structure of a New Political Economy."

154. "Questionnaire on Philosophy: Response," *CWL* 17:366.

155. Ibid., 280.

156. Philip McShane, "Editor's Introduction," *CWL* 21:xxxi. For a wide-ranging and extremely helpful context on Lonergan's economics, see Frederick Lawrence, "Editor's Introduction," *CWL* 15:xxv–lxxii.

157. The equations are scattered throughout the analysis, but see *CWL* 21:145 and 210 for a glimpse.

158. *Topics in Education, CWL* 10:52. Marx laboring away in the British Museum was a recurring image for Lonergan of the need for serious theory and of its potential long-term impact. For another example of this motif, see "Towards a Definition of Education," notes from a lecture to the (Student) Education Academy, Regis College, Toronto, Feb. 9, 1949. Boston College Lonergan Center file #49.5.2, 2. ("Marx spent most of his life in the British Museum. Father General said that the most valuable work by the Society is to put out books whose influence may only be apparent fifty years from now.") It is interesting to note that he made this remark in 1949—the year he began work on *Insight*.

159. On the importance and neglect of Lonergan's economics for Lonergan scholarship, see Philip McShane, "Work in Redress: The Value of Lonergan's Economics for Lonergan Students," chapter one of *Redress of Poise: The End of Lonergan's Work* (available at: www.philipmcshane.ca). For an effort to bring Lonergan's economics into critical and dialectical dialogue with the standard contemporary paradigm in economics, see Bruce Anderson and Philip McShane, *Beyond Establishment Economics: No Thank-you Mankiw* (Axial Press, Halifax, Nova Scotia: 2002).

160. *Topics in Education* [1959], *CWL* 10:58.

161. "Pantôn," *Method: Journal of Lonergan Studies* 9 (1991): 145.

162. On multinational corporations, see "Healing and Creating in History," *A Third Collection*, 102–103. On social alienation, "Prolegommena to the Emerging Religious Consciousness of our Times," *A Third Collection*, 60–63. Among the missions of the Church, in Lonergan's view, is the mission to "work systematically to undo the mischief brought about by alienation and ideology." *Method in Theology*, 361. On functional specialization as a systematic or methodical way of screening the results of the human sciences in order to reduce ideology, see A1320, 4 (Public lectures on Method in Theology, 1971, "Communications," available in the Lonergan Archives) ("Theological foundations, which objectify the horizon implicit in the 3 conversions, may now be invoked to decide positions & counter-positions. Thus ideology filtered out.")

163. Most notably, "Analytic Concept of History," *Method: Journal of Lonergan Studies* 11 (1993 [1938]): 21–22, and *Topics in Education, CWL* 10:60–62. For other mentions of the category, see *For a New Political Economy, CWL* 21:30; *CWL* 4:110; *Insight*, 222–228, *CWL* 3:247–253.

164. An early file in the Lonergan Archives, A336, quotes an article by Edward Coyne, SJ, on "National Economic Councils" in *Studies: An Irish Quarterly of Science and Philosophy*, XXII (June 1933): 290 ("Modern democracy, our respublica, is nothing more than an oligarchy licensed for a certain number of years by the unorganized mass of citizens and dependent to a great extent on a reasonably competent and benevolent bureaucracy . . . Simultaneously [citizens] jeopardize the running of this delicate moral mechanism by refusing to part with any of their individual liberty and by ruthlessly or thoughtlessly pursuing their own individual or class interests without any serious care whether those interests run counter to the common good of the whole."). See also "Philosophy of History," MS, 115 ("No modern state, generally speaking, is either economically or politically independent. The world is run by an oligarchy of *Grossmächte* and the justice of their decisions is as much open to question as the existence of their right to make decisions.")

165. *CWL* 21:211.

166. Lonergan's economic theory was at the time, and remains, quite outside the standard economic paradigms. As Lonergan remarked in an interview, "From 1930 to about 1944, I spent a great deal of my free time on economic theory, eventually producing a 120-page manuscript which was, it seemed, either an aberration or, at best, ahead of its time. In the spring of 1976 I began investigating the possibility that times had changed." Thomas More Institute Papers, *The Question as Commitment: A Symposium*, ed. Elaine Cahn and Cathleen Going (Montreal: Perry Printing, 1979), 110; ibid., 32

("I wrote 120 pages but didn't find anyone who could see any sense in it . . . The question is still genuine and authentic . . . Legitimation is not the same as the authentic question, but the authentic question may be delayed from lack of legitimation.")

167. *CWL* 21:111.

168. Ibid., 6–7, 111.

169. Ibid., 36.

170. Ibid.

171. James Marsh, "Self-Appropriation: Lonergan's Pearl of Great Price," in *In Deference to the Other: Lonergan and Contemporary Continental Thought*, ed. Jim Kanaris and Mark Doorley, foreword by John Caputo (Albany: SUNY Press, 2004), 59.

172. *CWL* 21:12.

173. Ibid., 11, 29 ("In some form and to some extent property exists in every exchange process; but this fundamental idea varies from age to age, from country to country, as soon as one begins to inquire into its precise form and the limitations of its application. With such details we are not concerned.")

174. Ibid., 82.

175. *A Third Collection*, 209n14. I do not wish to leave the impression that this list somehow tracks utterly unique features of Lonergan's thought. As Thomas Jeannot has pointed out to me, the features of Lonergan's analysis mentioned here also echo features of Marx's analysis in *Capital* and other texts. Yet I think it is true to say that the profoundly novel nature of Lonergan's circulation analysis is such that his extended treatment of these features is genuinely trans-Marxian, trans-capitalist, and radically innovative.

176. *CWL* 21:25 ("economic theory has to study the three [the capitalist, materialist, and cultural phases] separately, for their laws are distinct . . ."); *CWL* 21:27 ("different economic theories are adapted to different phases of the cycle . . .") This way of naming the phases is modified in the later economic manuscripts. See *generally CWL* 15.

177. Lonergan's opposition to bureaucracy as a technique for mediating the common good began early. The problem with bureaucracy is that it tends rather systematically to suppress new ideas and hence it suppresses or distorts progress. As Lonergan remarked in the mid-1930s: "A bureaucracy cannot integrate the individual differential forces that would make for change and advancement; it suppresses them; it rules by rule of thumb which, however excellent at the beginning of the rule, becomes more and more antiquated, more and more the understanding of a situation that is anything but the existing situation." "Philosophy of History," MS, 103–104.

178. Lonergan, quoted in "Editors' Introduction," *Macrodynamic Analysis: An Essay in Circulation Analysis, CWL* 15:xxxiv.

179. *CWL* 21:70.

180. Ibid., 78.

181. "Bernard Lonergan Responds (3)," *CWL* 20:285.

182. Of course, such analyses must ultimately submit to the kind of detailed, dialectical, and comparative critique suggested by Lonergan's sketch of the method of functional specialization in the human sciences. See, *e.g., Method in Theology*, 250–51.

183. *CWL* 21:99.

184. Ibid., at 99–100. Lonergan's mention of nationalism and armaments in 1942 has an earlier history. The early Lonergan's opposition to nationalism is especially vigorous. See, for example, his characterization of it in "Philosophy of History," MS, 112 ("nationalism—the stupid appeal to a common language and an united geographical position as something of real significance."); ibid.. 116 ("every nation foments nationalism according to its need . . . every country does so, because no country in the present situation can be conducted on an intelligible principle and so it must be conducted on an asinine principle. Again, the action of the sovereign states is necessarily immoral in the matter of armament manufacture: no country dare tell the private firms to close up shop, because no country knows when it will need them.")

185. For a deft and helpful introduction to Lonergan's economics, see Philip McShane, *Economics for Everyone: Das Jus Kapital* (Halifax, Nove Scotia: Axial Press, 1998).

186. *CWL* 21:37.

187. Lonergan, "The Transition from a Classicist World-view to Historical-mindedness," *A Second Collection*, 8.

188. Berrigan, *To Dwell in Peace*, 230.

189. *Insight*, 228, *CWL* 3:253.

190. Ibid.

191. Ibid.

192. *Insight*, 230, *CWL* 3:255.

193. *Insight*, 629, *CWL* 3:652.

194. Ibid.

195. Frederick Lawrence, "Political Theology and 'The Longer Cycle of Decline,'" *Lonergan Workshop*, vol. 1 (Missoula, Minn.: Scholars Press, 1978), 240.

196. H. Richard Niebuhr, "The Ego Alter Dialectic and the Conscience," *Journal of Philosophy* 42 (1945): 352–359, at 359; see note 2 above for the relevant context.

197. *Insight*, 239, *CWL* 3:264.

198. *Insight*, 240, *CWL* 3:265.

199. Ibid.

200. *Ecclesiastes*, 4:1–3, as quoted by Lonergan in the early 1930s. See, note 100 above.

201. Lonergan, "Philosophy of History" MS, 129.

202. Lonergan, "Analytic Concept of History," *Method: Journal of Lonergan Studies* 11 (1993 [1938]): 22.

203. Lonergan, "The Role of a Catholic University in the Modern World," *CWL* 4:10–11.

204. *Insight* 240, *CWL* 3:265.

205. Patrick Kavanagh, *Collected Poems* (New York: W. W. Norton, 1973), 32 ("Beyond the Headlines").

206. Berrigan, *The Nightmare of God* (Portland: Sunburst Press, 1983), 50, quoted in James Marsh, "Self-Appropriation and Liberation: Philosophizing in the Light of Catonsville," MS, 7.

207. "Analytic Concept of History, in Blurred Outline," MS, 15.

208. Lonergan, "Finality, Love, Marriage [1943]," in *CWL* 4:27. For an additional use of the category of "organized lie" by Lonergan, see "Outline of an Analytic Concept of History," MS, 12 (noting that each stage of the successive lower syntheses in modern history calls forth a particular human form of rejecting reason, and produces "the organized lie of a society defending what it was and, for the moment, preventing it from being worse than it will be.") See also *CWL* 20:113 ("Lies are as many as sins. Like sins, they come in all sizes and offer to meet every need—domestic, economic, social, political, cultural, religious. Some last a few days, some a few years, some a few decades, some a few centuries. Only the fittest survive, but the unfit seem always to be replaced.")

209. Lonergan, "Self-transcendence: Intellectual, Moral, Religious," *CWL* 17:323.

210. Berrigan, *Method*, 364.

211. Berrigan, *Jeremiah*, xii.

212. Gerard Manley Hopkins, "As Kingfishers Catch Fire," in *Gerard Manley Hopkins*, ed. Catherine Phillips (Oxford: Oxford University Press, 1986), 129.

GOVERNMENT BY FEAR, AND HOW ACTIVISTS OF
FAITH RESIST FEAR
Gail M. Presbey

1. Daniel Berrigan, *To Dwell in Peace: An Autobiography* (San Francisco: Harper and Row, 1987), 35.

2. Ibid., 57–60, 77–78.

3. Murray Polner and Jim O'Grady, *Disarmed and Dangerous: The Radical Lives and Times of Daniel and Philip Berrigan* (New York: Basic Books, 1997).

4. Berrigan, *To Dwell in Peace*, 99.

5. Ibid., 100.

6. Polner and O'Grady, *Disarmed and Dangerous*, 71.

7. Ibid., 73.

8. Berrigan, *To Dwell in Peace*, 107–8.

9. Ibid., 131.

10. Ibid., 137–38.

11. Ibid., 138.

12. Ibid., 142.

13. Ibid., 144, 151.

14. Ibid., 171.

15. Ibid., 177.

16. Corey Robin, *Fear: The History of a Political Idea* (New York: Oxford University Press, 2004), 28–35.

17. Ibid., 35.

18. Ibid., 37–41.

19. Ibid., 41–47.

20. Ibid., 115–19, 192–93.

21. Ibid., 190, 235–44.

22. Ibid., 163–64, 228, 250.

23. Berrigan, *To Dwell in Peace*, 166.

24. Ibid., 180–82.

25. Ibid., 183–84.

26. Polner and O'Grady, *Disarmed and Dangerous*, 129–36.

27. Ibid., 136–37.

28. Ibid., 167.

29. Berrigan, *To Dwell in Peace*, 187–197; Polner and O'Grady, *Disarmed and Dangerous*, 149.

30. Berrigan, *To Dwell in Peace*, 207.

31. Ibid., 207.

32. Ibid., 208.

33. Polner and O'Grady, *Disarmed and Dangerous*, 177.

34. Berrigan, *To Dwell in Peace*, 213.

35. Ibid., 217.

36. Daniel Berrigan, *The Trial of the Catonsville Nine* (Boston: Beacon Press, 1970).

37. Berrigan, *To Dwell in Peace*, 217.

38. Ibid., 218.

39. Ibid., 220.

40. Ibid., 221; Polner and O'Grady, *Disarmed and Dangerous*, 233–250.

41. Martha C. Nussbaum, "Compassion and Terror," in *Terrorism and International Justice*, ed. James P. Sterba (New York: Oxford University Press, 2003), 234–36.

42. Ibid., 236–38.

43. Berrigan, *To Dwell in Peace*, 231.

44. Ibid., 245.

45. Ibid., 248–53.

46. Polner and O'Grady, *Disarmed and Dangerous*, 190, 193.

47. Ibid., 187–88, 210–11, 244–45, 348.

48. Ibid., 272.

49. Berrigan, *To Dwell in Peace*, 269.

50. Polner and O'Grady, *Disarmed and Dangerous*, 268.

51. Berrigan, *To Dwell in Peace*, 285.

52. Ibid., 284–289.

53. Polner and O'Grady, *Disarmed and Dangerous*, 280–83.

54. Berrigan, *To Dwell in Peace*, 286–89.

55. Polner and O'Grady, *Disarmed and Dangerous*, 295–97.

56. Berrigan, *To Dwell in Peace*, 269.

57. Ibid., 270.

58. Berrigan, *To Dwell in Peace*, 266, 271; Polner and O'Grady, *Disarmed and Dangerous*, 29–97.

59. Robin, *Fear*, 14–15.

60. Ibid., 196.

61. Ibid., 168–71.

62. Ibid., 178–79.

63. Milan Kundera, *The Unbearable Lightness of Being* (New York: Harper Perennial Modern Classics, 1999).

64. John Lennon, *The US vs. John Lennon*, video documentary, directed by David Leaf and John Scheinfeld (Hollywood, Calif.: Lionsgate, 1999).

65. This argument may have been articulated by many, but I would like to thank Sigrid Dale of St. Leo's Pax Christi group for the inspiration for this articulation.

66. Daniel Berrigan, "Swords into Plowshares," in *Swords into Plowshares: Nonviolent Direct Action for Disarmament*, ed. Arthur J. Laffin and Anne Montgomery (San Francisco, Calif.: Harper and Row, 1987), 55.

67. Ibid.

68. Michelle E. Brady, "The Fearlessness of Courage," *Southern Journal of Philosophy* 43 (2005): 203.

69. Ibid., 204.

70. Berrigan, "Swords into Plowshares," 55.

71. Berrigan, *To Dwell in Peace*, 291.

72. Berrigan, "Swords into Plowshares," 64.

73. Ibid., 62.

74. Ibid., 63–64.

75. Aristotle, *Nichomachean Ethics*, trans. D. P. Chase (New York: E. P. Dutton and Co., 1928), 59, III:VI,1115a.

76. Plato, "Apology," in *Great Dialogues of Plato*, ed. and trans. W. H. D. Rouse (New York: New American Library, 1956), 445–46 (38d–41a).

77. Aristotle, *Nichomachean Ethics*, 63–64, III:VIII, 1116b.

78. Brady, "The Fearlessness of Courage," 192.

79. Arthur J. Laffin, "An Introduction to Plowshares Disarmament Actions," (2003), accessed August 15, 2011, http://tinyurl.com/intro-plowshares.

80. Berrigan, *To Dwell in Peace*, 323–29.

81. Daniel Berrigan, *Lamentations: From New York to Kabul and Beyond* (Lanham, Md.: Sheed and Ward, 2002), 92.

82. Ibid., xix.

83. Ibid., xx, 9.

84. Ibid., 123–24, 126.

85. Ibid., 96.

86. Ibid., 115.

87. Ibid., 103.

88. Ibid., 8.

89. Ibid., xviii.

90. Ibid., 102.

91. Ibid., 4, 117.

92. Robin, *Fear*, 169–70, 219.

93. James Guadalupe Carney, *To Be a Revolutionary: An Autobiography* (San Francisco, Calif.: Harper and Row, 1985), 8.

94. Søren Kierkegaard, *Attack upon "Christendom,"* trans. Walter Lowrie (Princeton, N.J.: Princeton University Press, 1968) 7.

95. Ibid., 11.

96. Ibid., 19.

ANNOUNCING THE IMPOSSIBLE
Christopher Harless

1. Daniel Berrigan, "Letter to the Weathermen," in *America Is Hard to Find* (Garden City, N.Y.: Doubleday, 1972), 96.

2. Daniel Berrigan, *Isaiah: Spirit of Courage, Gift of Tears* (Minneapolis: Fortress Press, 1996), 13.

3. Ibid., 13–14.

4. Ibid., 14.

5. Daniel Berrigan, "Gandhi: This Man is Disarmed and Dangerous," *No Bars to Manhood*, 134.

6. Daniel Berrigan, "Exit the King and Crisis of America," *No Bars to Manhood*, 82.

7. Daniel Berrigan, "Conscience, the Law, and Civil Disobedience," *No Bars to Manhood* (Garden City, N.Y.: Doubleday and Co., Inc., 1970), 47.

8. Ibid., 49–50.

9. Daniel Berrigan, "Jeremiah: The Worst is Not Yet," *No Bars to Manhood*, 107.

10. Berrigan later developed a more extended reflection on this theme in *Jeremiah: The World, the Wound of God* (Minneapolis: Fortress Press, 1999).

11. Berrigan, "Letter to the Weathermen," 96.

12. Ibid., 95.

13. Ibid., 97.

14. Mathew 18:20 (New Revised Standard Edition).

15. Daniel Berrigan, "The Book of Revelations," *No Bars to Manhood*, 94–95.

16. Ibid., 95.

17. Ibid., 96.

18. Jean-Paul Sartre and Benny Lévy, *Hope Now: The 1980 Interviews*, trans. Adrian van den Hoven, introduction by Ronald Aronson (Chicago: University of Chicago Press, 1996), 92.

19. In the interview cited above, Sartre said, "I think that the total, truly conceivable experience will exist when the goal that all men have within them—Humanity—is achieved. At that moment it will be possible to say that men are all the products of a common origin, derived not from their father's seed or their mother's womb but from a total series of measures taken over thousands of years that finally result in Humanity. Then there will be true fraternity" (90).

20. Ibid., 92.

21. Daniel Berrigan, "A Camus Glossary," *No Bars to Manhood*, 138.

22. Daniel Berrigan, "How to Make a Difference," *America Is Hard to Find*, 85.

23. Daniel Berrigan, "Lamentations and Losses: From New York to Kabul," in *Destined for Evil? The Twentieth-Century Responses*, ed. Pedrag Cicovacki, Rochester Studies in Philosophy, ed. Wade L. Robison (Rochester, N.Y.: University of Rochester Press, 2005), 223–39.

24. Ibid., 226.

25. Ibid., 238.

26. This is a favorite phrase of Berrigan's. For example, he titled a chapter in a recent book, "Isaiah: Prophet of Hope against Hope." See Daniel Berrigan, *The Kings and Their Gods: The Pathology of Power* (Grand Rapids, Mich.: William B. Eerdmans, 2008).

27. For example, Fred Thompson, the actor, former senator, and candidate for the 2008 Republican nomination for president, voiced such a dismissal of Gandhi in a commentary on the Paul Harvey radio show on March 17, 2007.

28. Chris Hedges, "Daniel Berrigan: Forty Years After Catonsville," *The Nation*, June 2, 2008, accessed August 15, 2011, http://tinyurl.com/40-years-after.

THE "GLOBAL WAR ON TERROR": WHO WINS? WHO LOSES?
G. Simon Harak, SJ

1. Speech in New York Madison Square Garden, October 31, 1936, accessed August 15, 2011, http://tinyurl.com/fdr-speech-1936.

2. *Exodus: Let My People Go* (Eugene, Oreg.: Cascade Books, 2008), 155

3. They were: Brother David Darst; John Hogan; Tom Lewis, an artist; Marjorie Bradford Melville; her husband, Thomas Melville, a former Maryknoll priest; George Mische; and Mary Moylan, a former nun. Father Philip Berrigan and Tom Lewis had previously poured blood on draft records as part of the Baltimore Four, and were out on bail when they burned the records at Catonsville.

4. Daniel Berrigan, *The Trial of the Catonsville Nine* (Boston, Mass.: Beacon Press, 1970). The version performed is usually an adaptation into regular dialogue by Saul Levitt.

5. *The Trial of the Catonsville Nine*, 1972, produced by Gregory Peck, directed by Gordon Davidson. Screenplay by Berrigan and Levitt, http://www.imdb.com/title/tt0069406/.

6. *Investigation of a Flame: A Documentary Portrait of the Catonsville Nine*, directed by Lynne Sachs, 2001.

7. Quoted in Geoffrey R. Stone, *Perilous Times: Free Speech in Wartime from the Sedition Act of 1798 to the War on Terrorism* (New York: W. W. Norton, 2004), 482–83.

8. Ut won a Pulitzer Prize for the photo, "Vietnam Napalm." Phan Thi Kim Phuc went on to publicly forgive her attackers and establish a foundation to help child victims of war.

9. From E. N. Brandt, *Growth Company: Dow Chemical's First Century*, quoted in Jack Doyle, *Trespass against Us: Dow Chemical's Legacy of Profit and Pollution* (Monroe, Maine: Common Courage Press, 2004), 53.

10. As told to Philip Jones Griffiths, *Vietnam, Inc.* (London: Phaidon Press, 2001), 210–11.

11. Doyle points out that "Napalm was never a big business for Dow, and according to one estimate, the company never made more than $5 million worth of napalm in any one year." Ibid., 52.

12. By Dr. Jackie Verrett of the FDA Toxicology Lab in Washington. Ibid., 60.

13. On December 3, 1984, a Union Carbide subsidiary plant in the city of Bhopal, India released about 30 tons of methyl isocyanate (MIC) gas. The International Medical Commission on Bhopal was established in 1993 to respond to the disaster. Amnesty International cites 22,000 total deaths as its conservative estimate.

14. A nerve poison insecticide. Dow has been fined over $700,000 for damages, and court cases are still pending.

15. Almost all of Dow's cases, Bhopal, Agent Orange, the Billie Shoemaker litigation, were settled out of court.

16. Bernard Hibbits, "Federal judge dismisses Agent Orange lawsuit," *The Jurist*, March 10, 2005, http://tinyurl.com/lawsuit-dismissed, accessed August 15, 2011.

17. Christine Kearney "Vietnamese appeal 'agent orange' suit in New York." June 19, 2007, http://tinyurl.com/kearney-vietnam (accessed August 15, 2011).

18. "The mission of the Office of the Under Secretary of Defense for Policy is to consistently provide responsive, forward-thinking, and insightful policy advice and support to the secretary of defense, and the Department of Defense, in alignment with national security objectives." From the official website: http://www.defenselink.mil/policy/, accessed August 15, 2011.

19. See http://tinyurl.com/defense-policy-board, accessed August 15, 2011.

20. See http://www.acq.osd.mil/dsb/charter.htm.

21. Johnston's public political career spanned thirty-two years, including eight years in the Louisiana Legislature and twenty-four years in the US Senate, from which he retired in 1997.

22. Established in 1997, the Project for the New American Century (PNAC) was home to a group of "neoconservatives" who outlined what was required for the United States to dominate the world. See http://www.newamericancentury.org/.

23. Set up in late 2002 by Bruce Jackson, a director of the PNAC and former Lockheed Martin vice president, the CLI consisted mostly of government officials tasked with "selling" the invasion of Iraq to the American public.

24. Undertaken as a solution to Boston's massive traffic congestion, the "Big Dig" (formally known as the Central Artery Tunnel Project) had two dimensions: 1) Replacing the six-lane elevated highway with an eight-to-ten-lane underground expressway directly beneath the existing road, culminating at its northern limit in a fourteen-lane, two-bridge crossing of the Charles River. After the underground highway opened to traffic, the crumbling elevated was demolished and in its place will be open space and modest development. 2) The extension of I-90 (the Massachusetts Turnpike) from its former terminus south of downtown Boston through a tunnel beneath South Boston and Boston Harbor to Logan Airport. The first link in this new connection—the four-lane Ted Williams Tunnel under the harbor—was finished in December 1995. The description of the project is taken directly from the Massachusetts Turnpike Authority's official website: http://www.masspike.com/bigdig/background/index.html.

25. M. R. F. Buckley, "1 Killed In I-90 Tunnel Ceiling Collapse: Panels Crush Car Traveling In Big Dig Tunnel" WCBVTV report, July 11, 2006, accessed August 15, 2011, http://tinyurl.com/bigdigtunnel.

26. See http://tinyurl.com/bechtel-departure. See also the three-volume report by the United Nations Development Program, "Iraq Living Conditions Survey 2004" (http://reliefweb.int/node/412194), and an article on the WHO report on Iraq by Elisabeth Rosenthal, "Iraq's Public Health Services Severely Strained, Group Says," *New York Times*, April 18, 2007, accessed August 15, 2011, http://tinyurl.com/strained-services.

27. See http://tinyurl.com/bechtel-iraq.

28. Norman Solomon, *War Made Easy: How Presidents and Pundits Keep Spinning Us to Death* (Hoboken, N.J.: J. Wiley, 2005), 93 quoting from Orbit International Corp., Form 10-KSB, Securities and Exchange Commission, for fiscal year ending December 31, 2003, 12.

29. White House chief of staff, answering a question about why the administration waited until after Labor Day to try to sell the American people on military action against Iraq. *New York Times*, September 6, 2002.

30. Speaking about his proposed Social Security reforms in upstate New York. Reported in Eugene Robinson, "History according to Rove," *San Francisco Chronicle*, July 13, 2005, accessed August 15, 2011, http://tinyurl.com/history-rove.

31. "Devon Cross is currently Executive Director of The Donors Forum on International Affairs. "She has extensive experience in public policy program development, having held positions with the Gilder Foundation, Donner Canadian Foundation, and The Smith Richardson Foundation. Ms. Cross was senior associate editor of *The Washington Quarterly* and has worked at Foreign Policy Magazine and the International Security Studies

Program, Woodrow Wilson Center. She holds an MA from Paul H. Nitze School of Advanced International Studies (SAIS) at *Johns Hopkins University* and a BA from Bryn Mawr College. She is a member of the Council on Foreign Relations and serves on advisory boards of other civic organizations. Cross resides in Ft. Myers, Florida." http://www.answers.com/topic/lincoln-group.

32. Taken from http://www.answers.com/topic/lincoln-group. The contract was awarded on a competitive basis pursuant to FAR 6.102. The contract number is H92222–05-D-1010. See http://tinyurl.com/dod-contract.

33. Mark and Daragahi Mazzetti, Borzou, *Los Angeles Times*, Novemeber 30, 2005, *U.S. Military Covertly Pays to Run Stories in Iraqi Press. Troops Write Articles Presented as News Reports. Some Officers Object to the Practice.* http://tinyurl.com/run-stories.

34. Mazzetti, *U.S. Military Covertly Pays to Run Stories in Iraqi Press.*

35. Daniel Berrigan, *Testimony: The Word Made Fresh* (Maryknoll, N.Y.: Orbis Books, 2004), 80.

36. Ibid., 93.

37. Frieda Construe-Nag and Myra Ancog Cooke, two maternity nurses in that ward, later said that they had never seen Nayirah there and that the baby-dumping had never happened. Mazzetti, *U.S. Military Covertly Pays to Run Stories in Iraqi Press.*

38. "Nurse Nayirah," http://tinyurl.com/nurse-nayirah.

39. Solomon, *War Made Easy*, 65.

40. Philip Seib, *Beyond the Front Lines: How the News Media Cover a World Shaped by War* (New York: Palgrave Macmillan, 2004), 31.

41. Hans-C von Sponeck, *A Different Kind of War: The UN Sanctions Regime in Iraq*, foreword by Celso Amorim (Oxford and New York: Berghahn Books, 2007), 336.

42. During those years, *Voices in the Wilderness*, led by Kathy Kelly and others, continually tried to bring the country's attention to the murderous effect of the sanctions on the Iraqi people. See http://vitw.org/economic_sanctions/. Kelly and others continue their work for the Iraqi people in *Voices for Creative Nonviolence* (www.vcnv.org).

43. E.g., Marcy Wheeler, *Anatomy of Deceit: How the Bush Administration Used the Media to Sell the Iraq War and Out a Spy*, (Berkeley, Calif.: Vaster Media, 2007), Norman Solomon, *War Made Easy: How Presidents and Pundits Keep Spinning Us to Death* (Hoboken, N.J.: John Wiley & Sons, 2006), Sheldon Rampton and John Stauber, *Weapons of Mass Deception: The Uses of Propaganda in Bush's War on Iraq* (New York: Penguin, 2003).

44. Jeffrey St. Clair, *Grand Theft Pentagon: Tales of Corruption and Profiteering in the War on Terror* (Monroe, Maine: Common Courage Press, 2005), 30.

45. There were 700 reporters embedded. For a fuller discussion of the impact on embeddedness on reporting, see Seib, *Beyond the Front Lines*, 54–67. See especially the quote from Erik Sorenson, President of MSNBC: "Who knows how much the embedded reporters saw. Did we see 8 percent of what happened? Did we see 4 percent of what happened? It's arguable they didn't see a double-digit percentage of what happened" (60).

46. See http://tinyurl.com/execorder13283. The last director was Mary Catherine Andrews.

47. Ibid.

48. Hendrik Hertzberg, "Ups and Downs," November 14, 2005, http://tinyurl.com/hertzberg-ups, accessed August 15, 2011.

49. St. Clair, *Grand Theft Pentagon: Tales of Corruption and Profiteering in the War on Terror*, 31.

50. Nicholas Jackson O'Shaughnessy, *Politics and Propaganda: Weapons of Mass Seduction* (Ann Arbor: University of Michigan Press, 2004), 224.

51. St. Clair, *Grand Theft Pentagon: Tales of Corruption and Profiteering in the War on Terror*, 33.

52. Paul Street, "Occupation Soldiers Agree: We Invaded Iraq 'to Avenge September 11." March 19, 2006, accessed August 15, 2011, http://tinyurl.com/street-invasion. Street is referring to poll results posted on IBOPE ZOGBY, accessed August 15, 2011, http://tinyurl.com/street-poll.

53. G. Simon Harak, "Why Invade Iraq?" *Blueprint for Social Justice* LVI, no. 2 & 3 (November 2002), accessed August 15, 2011, http://tinyurl.com/why-invade.

54. O'Shaughnessy, *Politics and Propaganda*, 214–15.

55. Sean Aday, "The Real War Will Never Get on Television: An Analysis of Casualty Imagery in American Television Coverage of the Iraq War," in *Media and Conflict in the Twenty-First Century*, ed. Philip Seib (New York: Palgrave Macmillan, 2005), 149.

56. Aday, "The Real War Will Never Get on Television," 149.

57. Graham Spencer, *The Media and Peace: From Vietnam to the "War on Terror"* (Houndmills, U.K.: Palgrave MacMillan, 2005), 158–59.

58. George Bush, "Remarks by the President on Homeownership Department of Housing and Urban Development Washington, D.C." June 18, 2002, accessed August 15, 2011, http://tinyurl.com/bush-homes. Such an assertion would have made another "George" give a knowing nod.

59. On September 25, 2005, http://tinyurl.com/firm-helps-pentagon.

60. St. Clair, *Grand Theft Pentagon*, 35.

61. See http://www.doim.army.mil/viweb/combatcam.html (site discontinued).

62. James Bamford, "The Man Who Sold the War: Meet John Rendon, Bush's General in the Propaganda War," *The Village Voice*, no. 988 (17 November 2005).

63. Bamford, "The Man Who Sold the War."

64. R.J. Hillhouse, "Who Runs the CIA? Outsiders for Hire," *The Washington Post*, 8 July 2007, B05, accessed August 15, 2011, http://tinyurl.com/who-runs-cia.

65. See Greg Palast, *The Best Democracy Money Can Buy: An Investigative Reporter Exposes the Truth About Globalization, Corporate Cons, and High-Finance Fraudsters* (New York: Plume, 2004).

66. Jeremy Scahill, *Blackwater: The Rise of the World's Most Powerful Mercenary Army* (New York: Nation Books, 2007), 12–13.

67. I owe the formulation of this insight to Judith Pasternak, my coworker when I was at the War Resisters League.

68. Published in New York by Round Table Press; available online, accessed August 15, 2011, http://tinyurl.com/war-a-racket.

69. Daniel Berrigan, *Whereon We Stand: The Acts of the Apostles and Ourselves* (Baltimore, Md.: Fortkamp Publishing Company, 1991), 193.

70. Ibid, 198.

71. Scahill, *Blackwater*, xvii.

72. St. Clair, *Grand Theft Pentagon*, 64.

73. Tom Turnipseed, "Dick Cheney: War Profiteer," *Common Dreams*, November 17, 2005, http://tinyurl.com/cheney-profiteer.

74. Ibid. See also Lee Drutman and Charlie Cray, "Halliburton, Dick Cheney, and Wartime Spoils," *Common Dreams*, April 3, 2003, using data from the Center for Public Integrity. http://tinyurl.com/cheney-spoils.

75. Antonia Juhasz, *The Bush Agenda: Invading the World, One Economy at a Time* (New York: ReganBooks, 2006), 138–39.

76. "Thousands of Federal Contractors Abuse the Federal Tax System," Statement of Gregory D. Kutz, Managing Director Forensic Audits and Special Investigations, April 19, 2007. Testimony Before the Subcommittee on Government Management, Organization, and Procurement, Committee on Oversight and Government Reform, House of Representatives, accessed August 15, 2011, http://tinyurl.com/tax-abuse.

77. Henry Waxman, *More Dollars, Less Sense: Worsening Contracting Trends Under the Bush Administration* (Washington, D.C.: United States House of Representatives Committee on Oversight and Government Reform Majority Staff, 2007), Executive Summary, accessed August 15, 2011, http://tinyurl.com/more-dollars-less-sense.

78. Juhasz, *The Bush Agenda: Invading the World, One Economy at a Time*, 227.

79. Mary Williams Walsh, "Shriveling of Pensions After Halliburton Deal," *The New York Times*, 2002, 10 September 2002, C1.

80. Frank Lautenberg, "Lautenberg Challenges Cheney," in *Lautenberg Challenges Cheney Statement on Lack of Current "Financial Interest" with Halliburton*, Press Release (2003), accessed August 15, 2011, http://tinyurl.com/lautenberg-cheney.

81. For an excellent examination of Cheney's influence on contracts for Halliburton, see Jane Mayer, "Contract Sport: What Did the Vice-President Do for Halliburton," *The New Yorker*, 2004, 16 February 2004.

82. John Mintz, "President Nominates Cheney's Son-in-Law," *Washington Post*, April 1, 2005, http://tinyurl.com/mintz-president. See also: Art Levine, "Dick Cheney's Dangerous Son-in-Law: Philip Perry and the Politics of Chemical Security," *Washington Monthly*, 2007 March 2007 Available online at http://tinyurl.com/cheney-chemical.

83. Carrie Johnson, and Witte, "Lockheed Puts Faith in Tough Lawyer," *Washington Post*, August 8, 2005.

84. Ibid.

85. Juhasz, *The Bush Agenda*, 194.

86. Ibid., 193–94 Juhasz describes her struggle to find the document, the Draft Statement of which is available on the website of the Center for Public Integrity.

87. Amy Belasco, *The Cost of Iraq, Afghanistan, and Other Global War on Terror Operations Since 9/11* (Washington, D.C., 2007), 2, accessed August 15, 2011, http://tinyurl.com/cost-war-operations.

88. Joseph Stiglitz, Linda Bilmes, *The Three Trillion Dollar War: The True Cost of the Iraq Conflict* (New York: W. W. Norton, 2008). A brief summary of the analysis can be found at: Kevin G. Hall, "Nobel laureate estimates wars' cost at more than $3 trillion," *McClatchy Newspapers*, Wednesday, February 27, 2008, accessed August 15, 2011, http://tinyurl.com/hall-nobel.

89. ATK has an interesting history. It was "spun off" from Honeywell during the Vietnam War, due to intense pressure for protest groups. It is still being protested today, because of its weapons manufacturing—and especially because it makes depleted uranium [DU] rounds for the military.

90. Juhasz, *The Bush Agenda*, 236.

91. Ibid., 238.

92. Pratap Chatterjee, "High-Tech Healthcare in Iraq, Minus the Healthcare" (2007) Online at http://tinyurl.com/high-tech-healthcare. This is, as usual, a well-researched and insightful article by Chatterjee, and bears close reading.

93. See http://tinyurl.com/bechtel-departure.

94. Stuart W. Bowen, *Logistics Civil Augmentation Program Task Order 130: Requirements Validation, Government Oversight, and Contractor Performance (SIGIR-07-001)* (Washington, DC: US Government, 2007), iii–iv, http://tinyurl.com/contractor-misconduct.

95. The contract is available at http://tinyurl.com/award-contract.

96. Charlie Cray, "KBR's Giant New Contract," *The Huffington Post*, 28 June 2007, http://tinyurl.com/kbr-contract.

97. Jeremy Scahill, *Blackwater*, 298. Scahill is citing from U.S. House of Representatives Committee on Government Reform Minority Staff Special Investigations Division, "Halliburton's Questioned and Unsupported Costs in Iraq Exceed $1.4 Billion," Government rept. (2005).

98. St. Clair, *Grand Theft Pentagon: Tales of Corruption and Profiteering in the War on Terror*, 177.

99. Scahill, *Blackwater*, xxii.

100. Jeremy Scahill, "Outsourcing the War," *The Nation*, 11 May 2007, http://tinyurl.com/outsourcing-war.

101. Scahill, *Blackwater*, 161.

102. After the US occupation of Iraq, the UN handed over to the US control of the $8+ billion dollars it had withheld from Iraq in the "oil for food" program. In the last days of Bremer's stay in Iraq, this money was handed out to corporations, with no accounting at all. See William Fisher, "Report: 'Appalling Fraud and Greed' in Iraq Contracts" (2005), accessed August 15, 2011, http://tinyurl.com/fraud-and-greed.

103. Scahill, *Blackwater*, 76–77.

104. St. Clair, *Grand Theft Pentagon* 44.

105. Scahill, *Blackwater*, xxv.

106. Julian Borger, "US Military in Torture Scandal," *The Guardian*, May 15, 2004.

107. Ari Berman, "The Sky's the Limit" *The Nation*, January 13, 2005, accessed August 15, 2011, http://tinyurl.com/berman-limit.

108. Scahill, "Outsourcing the War."

109. Scahill, *Blackwater*, 70.

110. Email from Michael Ratner, president of the Center for Constitutional Rights, to Scahill, quoted in *Scahill, Blackwater*, xxiv.

111. Juhasz, *The Bush Agenda*, 194.

112. Ibid., 195.

113. Ibid., 202.

114. Ibid, 206.

115. 117 Daniel Berrigan, *Minor Prophets, Major Themes* (Freeman, S.D.: Pine Hill Press, 1995), 164.

116. See http://tinyurl.com/exxon-profit.

117. Michael Schwartz, "The Struggle Over Iraqi Oil: Eyes Eternally on the Prize," *Tomgram*, May 6, 2007.

118. Sponsored by US Labor against the War [USLAW], Hasan Jum'a Awwad, Head of the Iraqi Federation of Oil Unions, has written an open letter to Congress, urging them "not to link withdrawal with the oil law." http://tinyurl.com/oil-workers.

119. They are: Betty Williams, Mairead Corrigan Maguire, Rigoberta Menchu Tum, Prof. Jody Williams, Dr. Shirin Ebadi, and Prof. Wangari Maathai. The statement is available online at http://warisacrime.org/node/23813.

120. "We are a leading provider of scientific, engineering, systems integration and technical services and products to all branches of the U.S. military, agencies of the U.S. Department of Defense (DoD), the intelligence community, the U.S. Department of Homeland Security (DHS) and other U.S. Government civil agencies." From the SAIC website: http://www.saic.com/natsec/.

121. See http://tinyurl.com/flake-resolution.

122. "The PMA Group, whose offices were raided by the FBI last year, is one of the leading defense-centered lobbying firms in Washington. It is closing its lobbying operation, and many of its employees have left to join or form other companies. More than 100 members of the House sought and obtained earmarks for PMA clients in the fiscal 2008 Defense appropriations law, according to a CQ study of the Taxpayers for Common Sense database. Those same members received more than $1.8 million in campaign contributions to their political committees from PMA sources from 2001 to 2008, CQ found." http://tinyurl.com/scandal-murtha.

123. See http://tinyurl.com/comgressmen-pma.

124. Jeremy Scahill, "Obama Has 250,000 'Contractors' in Iraq and Afghan Wars, Increases Number of Mercenaries," accessed August 15, 2011, http://tinyurl.com/obama-contractors.

125. P.W. Singer, "Robots at War: The New Battlefield," *The Wilson Quarterly*, accessed August 15, 2011, http://tinyurl.com/robots-at-war. The reader should also consult the series of articles by researcher Eric Stoner for a deeper analysis of this phenomenon.

126. Eric Stoner, "The Dawn of Robot Wars," *Huffington Post*, accessed August 15, 2011, http://tinyurl.com/dawn-of-robots.

127. Berrigan, *Minor Prophets, Major Themes*, 80.

128. For an examination of these "hidden" wounds, see Dave Grossman, *On Killing: The Psychological Cost of Learning to Kill in War and Society* (Boston: Little, Brown, 1995) and Edward Tick, *War and the Soul: Healing Our Nation's*

Veterans from Post-Traumatic Stress Disorder (Wheaton, Ill.: Quest Books, 2005).

129. Gilbert Burnham, et al., *The Human Cost of the War in Iraq: A Mortality Study, 2002–2006* (Baltimore, Md.: Johns Hopkins University, 2006 October), accessed August 15, 2011, http://tinyurl.com/human-cost-war. Though bitterly contested by President George Bush and other supporters of the sanctions policy, independent experts accepted the findings. See "British Ministry of Defense's Chief Scientific Adviser, Sir Roy Anderson, on October 13, stated: "The study design is robust and employs methods that are regarded as close to 'best practice' in this area," Owen Bennett-Jones, *Iraqi deaths survey "was robust,"* BBC World Service, March 26, 2007.

130. See http://tinyurl.com/shadow-of-war.

131. Daniel Berrigan, *The Kings and their Gods: The Pathology of Power* (Grand Rapids, Mich.: William B. Eerdmans Publishing Company, 2008), 87.

132. Kathy Kelly & Brian Terrell, "The Drone War: A Closer Look," CommonDreams.org, April 3, 2009, accessed August 15, 2011, http://tinyurl .com/drone-war.

133. Winslow Wheeler, "Mis-Measuring the Defense Budget," Center for Defense Information, 6 March 2007, accessed August 15, 2011, http://tinyurl .com/mis-measuring.

MICHAEL BAXTER teaches theology at the University of Notre Dame and lives and works at the Catholic Worker in South Bend, Indiana. He is also National Secretary of the Catholic Peace Fellowship.

ANNA J. BROWN teaches political science and directs the social justice program at Saint Peter's College in Jersey City, New Jersey. Brown founded the Dr. Martin Luther King Jr.–Kairos Social Justice House at the college. Most recently, she edited and contributed to the book, *Witness Against Torture: A Campaign to Shut Down Guantánamo* (2008). A long-time member of the Kairos community, which was cofounded by Daniel Berrigan in 1978, she has participated in numerous actions of nonviolent civil disobedience. In January of 2005, she joined the Witness Against Torture community in a seventy-mile walk to visit the detainees held in the Guantanamo and to resist the use of torture. She has also worked for peace and justice in Mexico, El Salvador, Israel, and Palestine.

PATRICK D. BROWN holds a PhD in philosophy from Boston College, where he studied under Bernard Lonergan, SJ, and Hans-Georg Gadamer, and wrote his dissertation on Lonergan's philosophy of history. He also holds a JD from the University of Washington. Following law school, he was law clerk to the Chief Justice of the Washington Supreme Court and practiced law full-time for seven years in both public and private practice. Professor Brown has published articles in various philosophical and legal journals, and has presented papers on topics relating to philosophy, law, methodology, and Catholic social thought at conferences in the United States, Canada, and Korea. He taught for three years in the Seattle University philosophy department before moving to its law school, where he has taught for the last seven years. He is currently Distinguished Scholar in Residence at the Seattle University School of Law, where he teaches, among other courses, land use, property, ethics, law, and Catholic social thought.

WILLIAM DESMOND is professor of philosophy at the Institute of Philosophy, Katholieke Universiteit Leuven, Belgium, and holds the Visiting David Cook Chair in philosophy at Villanova University. His interests are in metaphysics, ethics, aesthetics, and the philosophy of religion. He has taught in Ireland, the United States, and Belgium. He has also been visiting professor at a number of universities, including Boston University, University of Bejing, University of Denver, American University of Cairo, and Boston College. He is past president of the Hegel Society of America, the Metaphysical Society of America, and the American Catholic Philosophical Association. He is the author of many books, including the award-winning *Being and the Between* (1995), *Ethics and the Between* (2001), *Hegel's God: A Counterfeit Double?* (2003), *Art, Origins, Otherness: Between Philosophy and Art* (2003), *Is There a Sabbath for Thought? Between Religion and Philosophy* (2005), *God and the Between* (2008), and *Being Between: Conditions of Irish Thought* (2008).

MARTIN J. DE NYS received his PhD in philosophy from Loyola University-Chicago. He has taught at several colleges and universities in the United States, and is presently associate professor at George Mason University, Fairfax, Virginia. De Nys specializes in nineteenth and twentieth century German philosophy (especially Hegel, Marx, and transcendental phenomenology), philosophy of religion, social and political philosophy, and metaphysics. He has published numerous articles, especially on Hegel and on the philosophy of religion, and is the author of *Considering Transcendence: Elements of a Philosophical Theology* (2008) and *Hegel and Theology* (2009). His work in social and political philosophy focuses on Marx's critical social theory and on the resources that Marx offers for developing on the contemporary scene a social and political theory that allows one to present and justify critical and radical intentions.

ROBERT M. DORAN, SJ, has held the Emmett Doerr Chair in Catholic Systematic Theology at Marquette University since 2006, after having spent twenty-seven years at Regis College in the University of Toronto. While in Toronto, he teamed with Frederick E. Crowe, SJ, to found the Lonergan Research Institute and to launch the publication of Bernard Lonergan's *Collected Works* with University of Toronto Press. He is the author of *Theology and the Dialectics of History* (1999) and five other books along with numerous articles. His notion of "psychic conversion" drew Lonergan's attention and approval over thirty years ago and has supplied him with the major defining characteristic of his own work. Professor Doran is currently working on a volume entitled *The Trinity in History: A Theology of the*

Divine Missions. He brought to Marquette much of the vision that lay behind the founding of the Lonergan Research Institute in Toronto, and this has borne fruit in the establishment of the Marquette Lonergan project, devoted to the digital promotion of Lonergan's work.

G. Simon Harak, SJ, joined the Society of Jesus in 1970. He was a professor of theology at Fairfield University in Connecticut until 1999 when he resigned to work full time with *Voices in the Wilderness*, which he co-founded with Kathy Kelly, Bob Bossie, Mike Bremer and others. In 2003 he became the national anti-militarism coordinator at the War Resisters League, the oldest secular nonviolent group in the United States. In 2007 he accepted the position of Director of the newly formed Marquette University Center for Peacemaking. He has spoken nationally and internationally about war profiteering.

Christopher Harless, philosopher by training, radical by instinct and inclination, and Roman Catholic by faith, received the foundation of his education in his home state of Indiana at Purdue University. Upon completing his master's degree in continental philosophy under the mentorship of William McBride, he moved to New York to continue his training at Fordham University, where he studied under James Marsh. In his doctoral dissertation, he used the writings of Jean-Paul Sartre to argue for a conception of history capable of supporting the kind of radical hope that is required by ethical life and a revolutionary praxis. These themes of ethics, hope, and radical praxis ultimately derive from Christopher's religious and philosophical quest to discover what it means to be a person of faith in a world as often riven by violence as sustained by acts of peace and hope. As an independent philosopher his writing presses the question of how to live with hope in such a world; as a man of faith, he unites his practice of the Catholic tradition to these questions through prayer, study, and life in community. Christopher lives with his family in Denver, where he works as a government performance auditor for the Colorado State Auditor.

Thomas Jeannot is professor of philosophy at Gonzaga University, where he has been teaching ethics and other courses since 1986. He received his PhD from St. Louis University, where he was a student of James L. Marsh. His interests include the history of philosophy, Marxism, critical theory, and the thought of Bernard Lonergan, SJ. The center of gravity of his teaching and writing is the philosophy of liberation.

Robert A. Ludwig has studied the life and work of Daniel Berrigan for more than thirty-five years. He wrote his doctoral dissertation, "Theology and

Politics in America: Daniel Berrigan as a Contemporary Profile," for the Aquinas Institute of Theology in 1972. As part of his research, he did extensive personal interviews with Berrigan. Ludwig is currently undertaking a memoir-biography that details the lifetime evolution of Daniel Berrigan's thought and his public witness, based on over one hundred hours of taped interviews with Berrigan over the past fifteen years. The work is still in progress and expected to be completed by 2012. He is currently Professor of Pastoral Theology and Director of the Institute of Pastoral Studies at Loyola University Chicago. Previously, he served as Director of University Ministry at DePaul University (1989–2004), during which years Daniel Berrigan served as visiting professor on multiple occasions. Ludwig received his BA from Lorcas College (1966) and his MA and PhD from the Aquinas Institute (1972). He studied political theology at Tübingen, Germany (1969–70). From 1972–79 he was Theologian-in-Residence at the University of Colorado in Boulder. He has published numerous articles and several books, including *Reconstructing Catholicism for a New Generation* (1995) and *Jesus and Faith* (ed. with Jeffrey Carlson, 1994).

JAMES L. MARSH is a professor emeritus of Fordham University, was president of the American Catholic Philosophical Association in 2005, and is the author of over sixty articles and of seven books. Two of his most recent books are *Ricoeur as Another* (2002), coedited with Richard Cohen, and *Unjust Legality: A Critique of Habermas's Philosophy of Law* (2002).

WILLIAM L. MCBRIDE was born in New York City and received his AB from Georgetown University. After a Fulbright year in France, he pursued graduate work in philosophy at Yale University, where he received his MA and PhD and then taught for nine years before going to Purdue. He was named Arthur G. Hansen Distinguished Professor of Philosophy in 2001. He held a Fulbright Lectureship at Sofia (Bulgaria) University "St. Kliment Ohridski" in the fall of 1997. He is a Chevalier in the French Ordre des Palmes Acadèmiques. He was a member of the Steering Committee of the International Federation of Philosophical Societies (FISP) from 1998 to 2003, as well as a member of the Program Committee planning the quinquennial World Congress in Istanbul in 2003. There, he was elected Secretary General of FISP for a five-year term, the first American to hold that position. At the 2008 World Congress in Seoul he was elected President of FISP; he is also the first American to occupy that office. The four most recent of Professor McBride's nineteen authored, edited, and coedited books are *Philosophical Reflections on the Changes in Eastern Europe* (1999),

From Yugoslav Praxis to Global Pathos (2001), (with his colleague, Martin Beck Matustik, as coeditor) *Calvin O. Schrag and the Task of Philosophy after Postmodernity* (2002), and *Social and Political Philosophy*, volume 2 of the Istanbul World Congress *Proceedings* (2006). In addition, he has published well over one hundred book chapters, articles and critical reviews.

PATRICK MURRAY is professor of philosophy at Creighton University in Omaha, Nebraska. He is married to coauthor Jeanne Schuler; they have three adult children, John Patrick, David, and Sarita. A native of Chicago, he graduated with a BS degree in physics and mathematics in 1970. He received his PhD in the philosophy of science from St. Louis University in 1979, having completed a dissertation on Marx directed by Professor James Collins. During the 1975–1976 academic years, he studied as a Fulbright (DAAD) Scholar in Frankfurt. He taught at Villanova University for the 1978–1979 academic years, and has been a member of the faculty at Creighton since the fall of 1979. From 1994 to 2005, he served as the chair of the Creighton Philosophy Department. He has been a member of the state board of Nebraskans for Peace for over fifteen years. Patrick Murray is the author of *Marx's Theory of Scientific Knowledge* (1988) and editor of *Reflections on Commercial Life: Classic Texts from Plato to Present* (1997). Currently, Murray is completing work on two books, *The Mismeasure of Wealth: Essays on Marx and Social Form* and (with Jeanne Schuler) *False Moves: Basic problems with Philosophy*.

GAIL M. PRESBEY is a professor of philosophy at University of Detroit Mercy. Her areas of expertise are social and political philosophy as well as philosophy of nonviolence and cross-cultural philosophy. She has done research in Kenya, South Africa, Ghana, and India. Her most recent edited work is *Philosophical Perspectives on the War on Terrorism* (2007). She has coedited a textbook, *The Philosophical Quest: A Cross-Cultural Reader* (2002), and has over forty articles and book chapters published. She also has a longstanding involvement in Peace and Justice Studies. She is currently President of Concerned Philosophers for Peace.

JEANNE SCHULER is an associate professor of philosophy at Creighton University in Omaha, Nebraska. She is married to coauthor Patrick Murray; they have three adult children, John Patrick, David, and Savita. She graduated with a degree in philosophy from St. Louis University in 1973 and received her PhD from Washington University in 1983, with a thesis on "The Logic of Hegel's *Phenomenology*." She has published in the history of philosophy and critical theory, including articles on Hume, Kant,

Hegel, Kierkegaard, and Marx. With Patrick Murray, she has written two recent articles on the dogmas of bourgeois philosophy for *The Modern Schoolman*. She recently published a comparison of Hume and Hegel on the idea of pure immediacy for *The History of Philosophy Quarterly* and is working on a comparison of Hegel and McDowell on perception. With Patrick Murray, she has contributed essays to collections on the films of Stanley Kubrick and neo-noir. She is a regular contributor to *Living Faith* and Creighton's online reflections on the day's scripture readings. With Patrick Murray, she is completing a manuscript entitled *False Moves: Basic Problems with Philosophy*, a set of essays on recovering the world through a critique of the purely subjective and objective. She is a regular participant in the Radical Philosophy Association and has served on the board of the American Catholic Philosophical Association.